# The
# Margaret Mitchell
# Encyclopedia

This is a formal portrait of Margaret Mitchell in later life. It is, however, undated.
Courtesy of the Atlanta-Fulton Public Library System's Special Collections Department.

# The Margaret Mitchell Encyclopedia

ANITA PRICE DAVIS

McFarland & Company, Inc., Publishers
*Jefferson, North Carolina, and London*

ISBN 978-0-7864-6855-3
softcover : acid free paper ∞

LIBRARY OF CONGRESS CATALOGUING DATA ARE AVAILABLE

BRITISH LIBRARY CATALOGUING DATA ARE AVAILABLE

On the cover: Margaret Mitchell, circa early 1930s (Photofest);
background © 2013 Shutterstock

Manufactured in the United States of America

*McFarland & Company, Inc., Publishers
Box 611, Jefferson, North Carolina 28640
www.mcfarlandpub.com*

# Contents

# *Preface*

The idea of writing a comprehensive volume about Margaret Mitchell, author of the Pulitzer Prize–winning novel *Gone with the Wind*, has intrigued me for more than 65 years because of my mother, a beautiful and brilliant woman and an avid reader. In 1947 when I was four years old, Mother told me the plot of the book *Gone with the Wind* and promised we would see the movie when it came to our area. We watched movie posters and the local papers to see where and when the film would show in our area; we would have to go during the day because I could not stay awake late enough to see a night presentation of a four-hour movie.

My father had died in World War II in Europe, December 1944, but my new stepfather eagerly helped us plan our theater visit. On his way to work one morning he planned to take us to Aunt Mamie's home two blocks from the Cliffside Theater. Mother and I would visit during the morning with Aunt Mamie and Cousin Frances, eat a light lunch with them, and the four of us would walk the two blocks to the theater to see the one o'clock show; we would be back at my aunt's in time for my stepdad to pick us up on his way home from work at 5:30 P.M. For months we anticipated the big event! At last we learned of the re-release of the movie *Gone with the Wind* to our area in 1947. Mother and I were thrilled.

My stepfather had taken us to the movies many times. I had watched *The Wizard of Oz* and *Song of the South* without moving. *Gone with the Wind*, however, would be my induction into being a "big girl." I was ready to prove my maturity. It was 1947, I was four, and the re-release of *Gone with the Wind* was here!

I remember my kind stepfather taking Mother and me to Aunt Mamie's as he went to work. I remember trying to keep my clothes clean all morning so I would look nice for the movie. My older cousin Frances and I played board games and did not rush outside to play as we normally did. At last, it came time to walk to the theater!

Alas, the ticket taker took one look at me and said I could not enter the theater. Mother tried to explain that I was not a newcomer to the theater and that I had seen other films there without incident. Mother promised to take me out if I wiggled or spoke. It did no good. The seller denied me admittance.

I cried, and Frances cried. My mother and aunt moved to the sidewalk to discuss their plan of action. Neither of them had seen the movie, and they, too, were disappointed that they would not be able to see the film that they wanted to view. Mother moved again to the sales booth and told the representative that I would summarize the book for her and would promise not to speak or get out of my seat. The woman was not interested!

1

And then fourteen-year-old Frances saved the day. She said that she would walk to her house with me and would keep me while our mothers enjoyed the matinee. Aunt Mamie and Mother agreed — and complimented Frances on her unselfishness. Mother slipped some babysitting money into Frances's pocket; she promised to take both Frances and me to the film when I was older.

Frances and I walked to her home. I was exhausted from crying and lay down to rest on Frances's big bed. When I woke up two hours later, Frances had hatched a plan for us.

Frances would put make-up on me, dress me in one of Aunt Mamie's dresses, and locate a pair of high-heeled shoes for me to wear so I would appear taller. We would then walk to the theater. Frances would use her babysitting money to buy our tickets. Frances assured me that my disguise would hide my identity and would trick the sales girl into believing I was an adult. We would surprise our mothers inside the theater.

Frances reminded me that I had slept over two hours and that my transformation and walk home had taken up additional time. She felt sure the movie was going to be over soon. Perhaps that would be another point in our favor; perhaps the ticket taker would admit us for only a short time.

Alas, the two-block walk to the theater was impossible for a four-year-old in heels that were much too high and much too large in size. We finally gave up our plan about halfway to our destination and returned to Aunt Mamie's home before ever reaching the theater. I shared the story line of *Gone with the Wind* with Frances, and we spent the rest of the afternoon acting out the drama.

Our mothers loved our story when they heard it. They laughed as they shared it with my stepfather, my Uncle Virgil, and countless others through the years. The experience made viewing the film and reading the book even more desirable to me. I did see the movie later, and I eagerly read the novel as soon as I was able to read the heavy volume. Still, the memory of my first attempts to see the film *Gone with the Wind* remains a part of my life after more than 65 years.

In 1949 — two years after my thwarted efforts to view the movie — I remember finding my mother crying in the kitchen. She had heard on the radio that Margaret Mitchell had died in a hospital in Atlanta. Mother told me it was a sad day but a historic one. She told me that as a six-year-old, I should remember where I was when she told me about the tragedy. I have never forgotten hearing in our kitchen the sad news that Margaret Mitchell was dead.

Although *Gone with the Wind* is a classic, Margaret Mitchell's greatest story may actually be her own life. Her passions, her achievements, her romances, her friendships, and her family are even more memorable to those who have the full story.

*The Margaret Mitchell Encyclopedia* provides an updated, comprehensive volume for those who want to consider Margaret Mitchell's life, her writings, her legacy, and her humanitarian works. The verbal portrait of Margaret Mitchell and her legacy is in some ways unlike the images previously projected by her biographers. The emerging picture is that of a talented humanitarian with passion and concern — not the racist Southerner that many writers presented before all the facts were available.

Consider the pages to come, study the provided documentation, and meet the true Margaret Mitchell.

# Introduction

Even though Mitchell died in 1949, new materials about her and about *Gone with the Wind* continue to surface. Archival collections at the Atlanta Historical Center, at the Margaret Mitchell House, at various college and universities, at the National Archives in College Park, at the Library of Congress, and elsewhere frequently receive additional documents, information, and photographs about this writer. These recent acquisitions suggest that previous volumes about Margaret Mitchell's life and her work — no matter how scholarly and complete they might have been at the time of their publication — may no longer be definitive studies. The idea of augmenting the biographies of Margaret Mitchell and of her published books — now two — has long been appealing to me.

The last true biography of Atlanta author Margaret Mitchell bears a copyright date of 1992, before the completion of more than 30 theses and dissertations relating to Mitchell and *Gone with the Wind*, before several lawsuits to determine if recently-published books infringed on Mitchell's copyright, before the discovery and release of many new items relating to Mitchell, before the publication of contested books based on *Gone with the Wind*, and before the publication of countless articles about the author, her best-selling novel, and the film *Gone with the Wind*. Only one book on the book and film has recently appeared.

The year 1992 predates also the release of detailed information about Mitchell's anonymous contributions to Morehouse College and the local library, to the medical education of African American students, and to hospital care, particularly of African Americans. These only recently-accessible receipts, facts and figures, data, files, letters, financial reports, and other items indicate that critics' perception of the Atlanta author as racist was inaccurate; the newly obtained data need to be made available. This biographer used the newly accessible and recently-discovered letters, files, and other materials that the earlier biographers could not consult.

Through the years I have read what I could find on Margaret Mitchell and on *Gone with the Wind*. I read the controversial novels that brought lawsuits, and I continued to read the newly published articles about Margaret Mitchell, her life, and her works.

In 2001 I prepared a grant proposal for funds to visit Atlanta, to study at the Margaret Mitchell House, to research Margaret Mitchell, and to develop a curriculum guide related to the author and the house. I was able to travel to Atlanta, spend several nights in the home of the director of the Margaret Mitchell House, study in the museum at the Margaret Mitchell House (MMH), review the archives and work with the staff there, and prepare a guide for young people who were studying the author and her works. Published by the Atlanta History Center, by my donations, and by a funded grant I had submitted to Barnes and Noble, this activity book has been a part of the education of students, classes, and visitors who order the fun-and-learn booklet or who obtain it while touring the Atlanta area. This guide titled *Margaret Mitchell: A Link to Atlanta and the World* emphasizes the life of Margaret Mitchell, the history of the Atlanta area, the Atlanta sites related to the film, Margaret Mitchell's residences, *Gone with the Wind*, and Mitchell's contributions and involvement in the area, the nation, and the world. The entire curriculum guide and activity book is available online without cost at http://www.atlantahistorycenter.com/Images Live/Users/2/TeachersGuide-MMH-2009_1.pdf.

# Chronology of Margaret Mitchell

**1892** Marriage of Eugene Muse Mitchell (October 13, 1866–June 17, 1944) and Mary Isabel ("Maybelle") Stephens on November 8; these were the parents of Margaret Mitchell.

**1893** John Stephens Mitchell, Maybelle and Eugene's first son, was born and died in 1893. He is buried in Atlanta's Oakland Cemetery.

**1896** Alexander Stephens Mitchell (January 14, 1896–May 12, 1983), Eugene's and Maybelle's second child and Margaret's brother, was born about four years before his sister Margaret.

**1900** Margaret Munnerlyn Mitchell (1900–1949), Eugene and Maybelle's only daughter, was born on November 8. The family was living at 296 Cain Street, their residence when both Stephens and Margaret were born (Walker, page 24).

**1902** The Eugene Mitchell family moved to Jackson Street. (Edwards gives the address as 177 Jackson Street on page 17; Walker and Pyron give the address as 187 Jackson Street on pages 28 and 29, respectively.)

**1903** Margaret's education about Atlanta and the South begins as her family visits relatives, especially on Sunday. She sits on the "bony knees" of Civil War veterans—especially her grandfather Russell Crawford Mitchell—and hears their stories of the Civil War; she sits on the "fat, slick laps" of the women who share their remembrances of life during the Civil War and Reconstruction (Edwards, page 22).

Margaret's early education in the history of the South and Atlanta in particular continues through the years with carriage trips around the area, with visits to the Cyclorama with its painting of *The Battle of Atlanta*, with the remembrances of family and friends, and with horseback rides with Confederate veterans.

Margaret meets Carrie Chapman Catt, the woman suffragette (Pyron, pages 43–44).

Margaret's skirts caught fire from a coal-burning grate (Walker, page 27), an open heating grate (Edwards, page 17), or from the fireplace (Pyron, page 29); her legs were burned. She dressed in pants for play for many years after this.

The family moved to 179 Jackson Street. (On page 17 Edwards cites this residence as having the address of 187 Jackson Street.) The Mitchells remained in this twelve-room, two-story, Victorian style brick house until 1912 (Farr, page 13; Pyron, page 29; Walker, page 28).

**1904** Margaret began dictating stories to her mother before she could write. She began writing before she entered school and began designing cardboard covers for her works.

**1906** Both Margaret and Stephens attended Atlanta public elementary schools. Jane Thomas notes on her website that Margaret first attended Tenth Street Elementary School. Edwards notes Mitchell's school was North Boulevard (page 25). Walker and Pyron give the school as Forrest Avenue. (Walker, page 31; Pyron, page 44).

By age 6, Margaret was taking daily afternoon rides with Confederate veterans (Farr, page 15; Pyron, pages 30–31). She rode her own small roan plains pony that her father had given her when she was five (Edwards, page 24; Walker, page 26). The veterans shared their stories freely with her. Soon, however, her father would sell her horse when it balked on a jump.

The Atlanta Race Riot of 1906 made an indelible impression on Mitchell. This violence may have influenced the mob scene in which Scarlett O'Hara's husband Frank Kennedy loses his life.

**1907** Even before Margaret turned eight, she reportedly could recite all the battles of the Civil War (1861–1865).

**1909** Eugene Muse Mitchell secured a lot on Peachtree for a future home.

**1910** Even as a child, Margaret was already writing plays and stories. Edwards tells a story of how her father criticized her for using in a play she wrote and produced Thomas Dixon's book *The Traitor* without credits. This lesson in plagiarism endured for a lifetime (pages 31–32).

**1911** Margaret suffered another horseback accident during this year. She walked with a limp for some time after this serious accident (Pyron, page 110; Walker, page 28; Farr, page 32).

During this year, she also stayed for a while with family members and picked cotton on their farm. This work would figure later into *Gone with the Wind* (Edwards, page 29).

**1912** The Mitchell family moved into their newly completed house on Peachtree Street (Farr, page 32; Edwards, page 36). (See "Atlanta Addresses Directly Related to Margaret Mitchell" in this document for the house number and a description of the residence.)

**1914** Margaret enrolled in the private finishing school called Washington Seminary. She remained there until her 1918 graduation.

**1917** Atlanta's Great Fire of 1917 directly affected Margaret. It burned the house at 296 Cain Street where Margaret was born, and the house at 179 Jackson Street where Margaret had lived from 1903 until 1912. Margaret volunteered during the catastrophic event and found herself helping to care for the children who had been separated from their families.

**1918** Margaret founded the drama club for Washington Seminary and was the literary editor of its yearbook, *Facts and Fancies.* Before she graduated from Washington Seminary, she had completed a 400-page book titled *The Big Four* (never published) and the shorter work *Lost Laysen,* published years later.

Margaret met Clifford Henry, who was stationed at Camp Gordon in Atlanta. The two became engaged during the summer before he shipped overseas.

In the fall Margaret ("Peggy") entered Smith College in Northampton, Massachusetts.

Margaret learned that Clifford had been killed in October in France.

**January 1919** Maybelle Mitchell (January 13, 1872–January 25, 1919) contracted influenza on January 23 during an epidemic sweeping the nation. Margaret received a telegram to come home on January 24, but her mother had passed before Margaret's train arrived on January 25. Margaret withdrew from Smith to return home to her father at the end of the school year.

**1920** In the spring Margaret had her first date with Berrien "Red" Kinnard Upshaw; Margaret knew Red through her friend Courtenay Ross, whom he had dated.

**1921** On February 21, Margaret was again in a horseback riding accident while she was dating Berrien Kinnard Upshaw (Edwards, page 69). Other sources give different dates for the accident. Pyron gives the fall of 1920; Walker gives the spring of 1920 (Pyron, pages 110–111; Walker, page 65).

On March 13, Margaret and A. S. Weil — a Georgia Tech student — performed an "Apache Dance" at the Micarême Ball that the Debutante Club sponsored. This dance was controversial; the dance plus Margaret's outspoken behavior may have influenced the Junior League when it rejected Mitchell for membership in the fall.

During the winter roommates John Marsh and Berrien Upshaw pursued Margaret ardently; they sometimes dated her on the same night. This triangle was suggestive of the triangle of Rhett, Scarlett, and Ashley Wilkes in *Gone with the Wind.*

**September 2, 1922** Margaret married Berrien ("Red") Kinnard Upshaw, who was from a prominent Raleigh, North Carolina, family. John Marsh, who worked at the *Atlanta Journal,* was Red's best man. Margaret and Red moved into the Mitchell house on Peachtree with her father.

In late fall John Marsh arranged for Margaret to apply for a job with the *Journal.* This was a decade when women usually did not work outside the home, and Marsh knew her chances of securing work as a reporter were slim; still Marsh believed that an interview with City Editor Harlee Branch would be a good experience. The interview went well, but Margaret did not secure that job.

**Mid-December 1922** Angus Perkerson interviewed Margaret for an opening on the *Sunday Magazine* of the *Atlanta Journal*. Margaret's first article appeared on December 31 under her byline "Peggy Upshaw."

**1923** Red Upshaw left the volatile marriage. He returned in July, and Margaret suffered a black eye and two weeks of hospitalization. She filed for divorce on November 14.

**1924** The divorce of Red and Margaret was finalized October 16. John Marsh, who worked for the *Atlanta Journal*, was a source of comfort to Margaret at work and away from work.

**1925** Margaret Mitchell married John Robert Marsh on July 4. They moved into a small apartment at the corner of 10th and Peachtree streets. Peggy affectionately called the house "The Dump." John worked as director of publicity for Georgia Railway and Power Company (later Georgia Power Company). Peggy remained employed with the *Atlanta Journal*.

**1926** On May 3, Margaret left her employment with the *Atlanta Journal* because of health concerns: a sprained ankle and arthritic conditions. During her four years with the *Sunday Magazine*, Mitchell had written 129 articles, worked as a proofreader, served as an advice columnist substitute, reviewed books, and occasionally wrote as a news reporter. Confined to the three rooms of "The Dump," Mitchell began to write a novel, which would take years to complete.

**1932** Margaret and John moved to a larger apartment at 4 East 17th Street. Margaret's novel *Gone with the Wind* was largely complete.

**1935** Harold Latham, an editor for the Macmillan Publishing Company in New York, was touring the South and was looking for new manuscripts. Having heard from Lois Cole, the former office manager of the Atlanta Office, that Margaret might have a manuscript, he approached her about it on April 11 at a luncheon at Rich's Department Store. She took the 70 or so manila envelopes, in random order, to him at his hotel.

Macmillan accepted the manuscript for publication and offered her a contract in July. She would receive a total $500 advance and 10 percent of the royalties up to the first 10,000 copies; she would then earn 15 percent on all copies sold. Macmillan began pushing for a 1936 publication date.

**1936** The official release day for Margaret Mitchell's 1,037-page novel titled *Gone with the Wind* was June 30; its selling price was three dollars. By mid–March the Book-of-the-Month Club had already chosen *Gone with the Wind* as its selection for July. On July 10, Margaret Mitchell sold the contract for the movie *Gone with the Wind* to David O. Selznick for $50,000 (Walker, pages 289–290). Because Selznick had read only a synopsis, he and the book took a cruise together; he immediately began to condense it and consider the casting. Selznick hired Sidney Howard — a Pulitzer Prize scriptwriter — to develop the screenplay.

**1937** In the year following the release of the novel *Gone with the Wind*, Margaret personally answered every letter that she received. She, John Marsh (her husband), and Stephens Mitchell (her brother and lawyer) worked diligently to protect the copyright of *Gone with the Wind*; they were able to alter the ambiguous and inconsistent copyright laws — especially those that varied from country to country. The novel *Gone with the Wind* won a Pulitzer Prize in 1937.

**1938** George Cukor was now the signed director for the film, and Clark Gable was "Rhett Butler." The actress to play Scarlett was still uncertain. Because the scene of the burning of the munitions stores was on schedule for December, Selznick had to use stand-ins for Butler and O'Hara. While David Selznick was on the set, Myron Selznick — his brother and talent agent — brought Vivien Leigh to meet David. Myron said, "I want you to meet Scarlett O'Hara." David said that at once, he knew Myron was right!

**1939** The first day of filming *Gone with the Wind* was January 26. Rewrites, costumes, additional filming, and further additions and changes in casting followed. More than 9,000 people were a part of the production, which was complete by July 31. Margaret Mitchell tried to keep a "hands-off" attitude. The dates for the Atlanta premiere of the film *Gone with the Wind* were December 13, 14, and 15.

**January 13, 1940**  Margaret Mitchell entered the hospital for surgery for the removal of abdominal adhesions. John Marsh was suffering from exhaustion.

**March 1, 1940**  Newspaper headlines announced that the film *Gone with the Wind*, its actors, its actresses, and its makers had won ten Academy Awards. The production itself was the 1939 Best Picture. Hattie McDaniel was the best supporting actress. Victor Fleming won for the best direction, and Sidney Howard had the best screenplay. Awards went to the art technicians, the film editors, and the color photographers. William Cameron Menzies earned a special award for his use of color in the introduction, and Producer David O. Selznick received the Irving Thalberg Memorial Award. The National Association for the Advancement of Colored People presented a special statuette to Hattie McDaniel.

**1941–1945**  The United States was engaged in World War II. Margaret Mitchell worked tirelessly for the American Red Cross and the war effort. She wrapped bandages, enlisted blood donors, wrote letters to service personnel, served as an air raid warden, and sold savings stamps and war bonds throughout the war.

Mitchell christened the USS *Atlanta* on September 6, 1941. After the sinking of the USS *Atlanta*, Margaret christened a new *Atlanta* in Camden, New Jersey, in February 1944. War bonds bought the new *Atlanta*.

Mitchell paid toward the rebuilding of a city in France that the Allies accidentally bombed.

In addition to her contributions to the war effort, Margaret also tended her father throughout his illness and death in 1944.

**1945–1949**  In 1945, John suffered a heart attack, and Margaret tended him. She also found time to help the Florence Crittenton Home for unwed mothers and worked with prisoners in the Atlanta Federal Penitentiary on their writing skills; she offered prizes for the best writings produced. She also donated to help pay for the medical education of numerous African Americans.

**August 11, 1949**  In Atlanta shortly after 8 P.M. on this Thursday, John Marsh and Margaret Mitchell were beginning to cross Atlanta's busy Peachtree Street. The two were going to the Peachtree Arts Theatre, which specialized in foreign films, to see *A Canterbury Tale*. A speeding car driven by Hugh D. Gravitt struck Margaret Mitchell and dragged her seven feet. She entered Grady Memorial Hospital at 9 P.M.

**August 12–16, 1949**  Messages to the injured Margaret Mitchell came from Georgia Governor Eugene Talmadge, President Harry S Truman, and countless other well-wishers. The prisoners in the Atlanta Federal Prison volunteered to donate their blood for her recovery.

**August 16, 1949**  Margaret Mitchell died at 11:59 A.M. Condolences began to flood John Marsh's home.

**August 17, 1949**  Margaret Mitchell Marsh's funeral was the day after her death. Only 300 invited guests could attend the memorial services at Spring Hill Funeral Home in Atlanta; Dean Raimundo de Ovies of St. Philip's Cathedral, Atlanta, officiated. Burial was in the Oakland Cemetery in Atlanta. The city paused at ten o'clock as a tribute to her. Someone was already beginning to collect money for a Margaret Mitchell Memorial Pavilion.

**1994**  The Georgia Women of Achievement inducted Margaret Mitchell into its ranks. Its mission is to honor (1) women who have made extraordinary contributions within their fields of endeavor, (2) Georgia women and Georgia natives who are clearly identified with the state, and (3) women who will inspire future generations to utilize their own talents. Margaret Mitchell clearly fit these criteria.

**2000**  The Georgia Writers Hall of Fame inducted Margaret Mitchell.

# The Encyclopedia

## abuse of Margaret Mitchell

Margaret Mitchell married Berrien Kinnard ("Red") Upshaw on September 2, 1922. Almost immediately she began to suffer both mental and physical abuse. The abuse continued throughout their marriage (September 2, 1922–October 16, 1924).

Almost as soon as the marriage began — even during the honeymoon at the Grove Park Inn in Asheville, North Carolina, and their trip to visit Red's family in Raleigh — the two began to quarrel. Red wanted Margaret to leave the Peachtree Street home and to follow him. He had no job and no residence for them. He was drinking heavily.

Margaret wrote to their friend John Marsh about their problems. John was working in the Washington office of the Associated Press; she asked him to come back to Atlanta. Marsh responded in a manner that he hoped would be conciliatory, but he shared his concerns about the situation with his sister Frances. Margaret corresponded about her problems also with Clifford Henry's parents.

Things reached a head shortly after John Marsh's return to Atlanta. Red and she decided to divorce, and they went together to John's hotel room to share their decision with their mutual friend; Margaret and John had worked together at the *Atlanta Journal*, and Red and John had roomed together in college. After telling John their news, Margaret returned to Peachtree, but Red stayed with Marsh. In exchange for a loan from John, Red agreed not to contest the divorce. He left Atlanta for North Carolina, however, without signing the papers (Edwards, page 88).

After six months, Red returned unexpectedly to Peachtree on July 10, 1923. The two began to quarrel, and Margaret insisted that they go inside so as not to involve the neighbors. They went inside, and Red demanded his conjugal rights. He struck her

on the arm, and her cries brought Bessie Jordan, the faithful family servant who was working at that time (Edwards, pages 102–103). The counsel at the trial added that Red "jerked her against a bed, causing her to be bruised all over her body" (Edwards, page 102). Red turned and struck her viciously in the left eye. Margaret was hospitalized for two weeks as a result of the beating. She was out of work for six weeks to hide the results of Red's abuse (Edwards, pages 102–103).

To prevent further abuse, Margaret Mitchell kept a pistol beside her bed until she learned of the death of Berrien Kinnard ("Red") Upshaw in January — before her own August death — in 1949 (Edwards, page 103; Farr, page 57; Pyron, page 194).

Margaret Baugh, Margaret Mitchell's personal secretary, confirmed the story of the pistol in an October 12, 1964, letter to Lois Cole: "All I know is there was a pistol on her bedside table for years. She explained why. Once when I asked her if she could shoot it, she said of course, her mother had taught her or seen to it that she learned to shoot. In January 1949 Red's stepmother wrote that he had died. I didn't notice at first, but a while afterward I realized that the pistol was no longer there and it never reappeared.... I took the pistol for more than a gesture. I expect she had reason for it. You know Red was an alcoholic and was in and out of mental institutions for years" (Pyron, page 194).

## Academy of Motion Picture Arts and Sciences

In 1927, 36 influential men and women in the motion picture industry formed the honorary membership organization of the Academy of Motion Picture Arts and Sciences. By 2011 more than 6,000 artists and professionals belonged to the group, whose board of governors included representatives from each of the craft branches.

The academy encourages filmmaking excellence through its range of coveted awards; it intends its Oscar statuettes and its plaques, trophies, and certificates to represent the highest achievement level in motion picture arts and sciences. *Gone with the Wind* won ten awards in 1940, the most earned until 1959.

### Academy of Motion Picture Arts and Sciences 1940 awards for *Gone with the Wind*

The 1939 film *Gone with the Wind* runs 222 minutes, an innovative length for the year of its production. As the recipient of both competitive and honorary Academy Awards, the movie became the first to win more than five Academy Awards. The academy's record of ten awards presented on February 19, 1940, to *Gone with the Wind* and its staff and crew stood for about two decades; *Ben-Hur* (1959) won eleven Oscars and became the first film to break the record.

The ten awards earned by *Gone with the Wind* in 1940 were:

1. The Technicolor film received an Honorary Award. William Cameron Menzies accepted the plaque, which acknowledged the outstanding achievement in using color to enhance dramatic mood.

2. Vivien Leigh as "Scarlett O'Hara" won an Oscar for Best Actress in a Leading Role.

3. Hattie McDaniel as "Mammy" earned an Oscar as the Best Actress in a Supporting Role. She became the first African American to receive an Oscar nomination and to win the coveted prize.

4. Lyle R. Wheeler received an Oscar for Best Art Direction.

5. Academy Awards honored Hal C. Kern and James E. Newcom for their editing.

6. Ernest Haller and Ray Rennahan won Oscars for Best Cinematography (Color).

7. Victor Fleming earned an Oscar as Best Director.

8. Selznick International Pictures received the Academy Award for Best Picture.

9. Sidney Howard received the Academy of Motion Picture Arts and Sciences Award for Best Writing/Screenplay.

10. R. D. Musgrave (for Selznick International Pictures) earned the Technical Achievement Award ("Awards for Gone with the Wind"; "Gone with the Wind Awards").

Thomas Mitchell earned an Oscar for Best Supporting Actor in his role in *Stagecoach*. (Mitchell did not win the award for his role as Gerald O'Hara in the film *Gone with the Wind*, as Edwards indicated on page 295).

### Academy of Motion Picture Arts and Sciences nominations (without concomitant awards) for *Gone with the Wind* and its cast

The film *Gone with the Wind* and its staff and cast received several nominations from the Academy of Motion Picture Arts and Sciences in addition to the awards discussed in the previous entry. These went to (1) Clark Gable as Best Actor in the Leading Role of "Rhett Butler"; (2) Olivia de Havilland as Best Actress in the Supporting Role of "Melanie Hamilton"; (3) Jack Cosgrove for photography; (4) Fred Albin and Arthur Johns (sound) for Best/Special Effects; (5) Max Steiner for Best Music, Original Score; and (6) Thomas T. Moulton for Best Sound, Recording. ("Awards for *Gone with the Wind*"; "*Gone with the Wind*/Awards").

### accidents

Throughout her life, Margaret Mitchell was plagued with accidents, the last of which took her life.

*Skirts caught fire.* When Margaret was about three and living with her family at 179 Jackson Street (about the year 1903), she suffered from an accident in which she was burned. Walker describes the accident as occurring from a coal-burning grate. Edwards suggests that Margaret was standing over an open heating grate when the fire happened. Pyron suggests that the fire that came from the fireplace was extinguished by Stephens because Maybelle Mitchell was not home at the time (Walker, page 27; Edwards, page 20; Pyron, page 29).

At any rate, the outcome was the same: Margaret Mitchell's skirts caught fire. The various authors differ in their descriptions of the severity. Walker notes that the resulting burns to Margaret's legs were "not serious." Pyron says that neither Margaret nor Stephens were injured at all.

Edwards presents a different picture of what was probably Margaret Mitchell's first serious accident. She suggests that Margaret was standing over an open heating grate when the fire happened and that Maybelle rushed to the scene. "For weeks the little girl was bedridden, tended by Maybelle and entertained by Grandmother Stephens with stories of her own childhood. When she was allowed up, bandages still swathed her legs, and Maybelle dressed her in Stephens's old clothes to conceal them" (Edwards, page 20).

Maybelle Mitchell's reaction to the accident did not vary in any of the versions of the story. She continued to dress her daughter Margaret in boys' clothing to prevent the little girl's catching fire again. Margaret was comfortable with these clothes, even though the neighbors began calling her "Jimmy" (Edwards, pages 17, 20; Pyron, page 29; Walker, page 27).

*Horseback riding accident, 1911.* When the family sold its ponies and bought a horse named *Bucephalus* before their move to Peachtree Street, Margaret rode the animal with much pleasure for hours each day. She loved racing him and galloping astride him up and down the streets. Stephens and their cousins watched in horror one day as the horse lost its balance and fell with Margaret beneath him. Her leg was badly crushed. After surgery and a long convalescence, Margaret was left with a limp (Edwards, pages 33–35).

*Pony cart accident with Courtenay Ross while they were high school students.* Courtenay Ross and Margaret Mitchell attended Washington Seminary together. Peacock quotes Courtenay Ross's description of their pony cart accident during their high school days. "Peg had one serious affliction, brittle bones. We borrowed a pony and cart. We were driving down Peachtree Street, when something startled the pony ... overturning the cart. We were plunged onto the sidewalk. I was on the bottom, Peg on top, yet she broke a rib. As for me, I had some difficulty sitting down. Peg had to wear laced up shoes to protect her ankles" (pages 14–15).

*Accidents Margaret mentioned to Allen Edee (1919–1921).* Peacock describes the injuries and illnesses that Margaret experienced and shared with her friend Allen Edee: "Reflected in her letters to Allen Edee from 1919–1921 are several bouts with ailments: operations for appendicitis and adhesions, a siege with influenza, a torn ligament, a broken foot and internal injuries from a horseback accident" (page 15).

*Horseback riding accident (1920).* On a trip to Athens in 1920 after Maybelle Mitchell's death and after Margaret's return from college, the young woman again injured her foot and leg; arthritis resulted. Margaret complained also with abdominal adhesions that she claimed came as a result of the fall that ended her horseback riding forever.

Pyron states that this second, severe, horseback-related accident occurred in the fall of 1920. Walker sets the date as in the spring of 1920 while she was on a date with Red Upshaw. Edwards gives a different account; she claims the February 1921 incident occurred on a horseback ride near Stone Mountain (Pyron, pages 110–111; Walker, page 65; Edwards, page 69).

*Automobile accident (1934).* The greatest fears of both John R. Marsh and Margaret Mitchell (according to John's sister Frances Marsh Zane and others) were the fears of cars and automobile accidents (Walker, pages 292–293). Margaret Mitch-

ell's death (August 1949) was the result of a speeding driver. A 1934 accident caused her serious injuries.

On November 22, 1934, John Cohen, owner and publisher of the *Atlanta Journal*, and John Marion Graham, a distant cousin and expert in Georgia legal history, had dinner with John and Margaret. About midnight, Mitchell and Marsh offered to take Cohen home; Graham had already departed.

On West Peachtree, Margaret prepared to turn left on Eighth Avenue. When she noticed in her mirror that there was a car approaching her from the rear, she pulled to the right side of the road and stopped. The intoxicated (according to John and Margaret) driver of the Terraplane Roadster smashed into the rear of the Marshes' vehicle. John R. Marsh described the accident and their resulting injuries in a letter dated April 10, 1955, to Eugene M. Mitchell. "All three of us had our necks snapped very badly and could scarcely move our heads for a day or two on account of our stiff necks. Mr. Cohen and I, however, suffered no injuries except the shock and muscular strains" (Pyron, page 203).

Margaret could not move her head for about ten days and suffered from pain for more than two months; even five months later, her neck was still sore. Nausea was a persistent problem. On April 9–10, 1935, Margaret, John, Stephens Mitchell, and Eugene Mitchell prepared to bring suit against the driver (Walker, pages 194–195).

*Fatal automobile accident of Margaret Mitchell (August 1949).* Margaret Mitchell had her last major accident at shortly after 8:00 P.M. on August 11, 1949. On that night, she was crossing Peachtree Street to see a foreign film at the Peachtree Arts Theatre; Hugh D. Gravitt was driving the speeding car that struck her.

An ambulance took Margaret to Grady Hospital on Butler Street; Grady Hospital was the facility to which she had donated funds to help establish an emergency room that would treat African Americans. After she died five days later, her body went to Spring Hill Funeral Home. Her final resting place was Atlanta's Oakland Cemetery.

Anne Edwards (author of *Road to Tara*) had said, according to the Granberry family, that Margaret had written in a letter to Edwin Granberry "that she was going to die in a car-crash, and felt very certain of it." Edwin Granberry was adamant that she never wrote such to him (Julian Granberry, page xiv).

**See also A Canterbury Tale; de Ovies, Dean Raimundo; Grady Hospital; Granberry, Julian; Gravitt, Hugh Dorsey; Oakland Cemetery; St. Philip's Cathedral; Addresses Directly Related to Margaret Mitchell.**

## Acorn Cottage

Herschel and Norma Brickell owned a cottage near Ridgefield, Connecticut. They called their place *Acorn Cottage*. The Brickells visited with Margaret and John on several occasions. Margaret was at Acorn Cottage when she suffered hemorrhages in the eyes that briefly took her sight (Walker, pages 303–304).

Many rumors circulated about Margaret Mitchell through the years. One falsehood that particularly angered John R. Marsh was one about where Margaret Mitchell was when she wrote *Gone with the Wind*. This gossip indicated that Margaret had written her novel at Acorn Cottage (Walker, page 468).

*See also* Brickell, Herschel; illnesses and health concerns of Margaret Mitchell.

## Adams, J. Donald

J. Donald Adams, editor of the *New York Times Book Review*, devoted the entire front page of the July 5, 1936, *Book Review* to Margaret Mitchell and *Gone with the Wind*, which had a release date of June 30 that year. To thank Adams and to tell him how happy the article had made her, Mitchell wrote him a personal letter on July 9, 1936. She explained that she "ran a temperature after reading your kind review" (Harwell, *Letters,* page 30).

Mitchell noted that she was writing the July 9, 1936, letter after her return from Gainesville, Georgia. She explained to Adams why she had gone to Gainesville only a few days after the release of her book. "Everyone has been so very kind and the town and state papers so grand to me and friends and kin so shamelessly proud and loving that I got frightened for the first time in my life and last week I bolted out of town, minus baggage, reading matter and any remnant of brain. And since then I've been riding about the countryside looking for a place where I didn't know anybody or where I wasn't kin to anybody so I could settle down and read reviews and get some rest and write some letters. I never found the place so I doubled back and came home" (Harwell, *Letters,* pages 30–31).

*See also* Gainesville, Georgia.

## addresses directly related to Margaret Mitchell (arranged chronologically)

Margaret lived her entire life in Atlanta — except for the 1918–1919 school year when she was a freshman at Smith College in Northampton, Massachusetts. Listed chronologically below are both the street addresses where she lived and other Atlanta addresses that figured prominently into her life and death:

*296 Cain Street.* Both Stephens Mitchell and his younger sister Margaret Munnerlyn Mitchell were born in the house at 296 Cain Street to Eugene Muse Mitchell and Mary Isabel ("Maybelle") Stephens Mitchell. (Pyron refers to the wife of Eugene Muse Mitchell as "May Belle," not "Maybelle.") The 1917 "Great Fire" destroyed this house (Pyron, pages 74–76).

*187 Jackson Street.* Located at the southeast corner of Jackson and Highland Avenue was the larger house into which Eugene Mitchell moved his family in 1902. Walker notes that this residence remained the Mitchell family home only until 1903. Edwards gives the 1902 address as 177 Jackson, not 187 (Walker, page 27; Edwards, page 17).

*179 Jackson Street.* In 1903 Eugene and Maybelle Stephens Mitchell again moved their family, this time to 179 Jackson Street. (Edwards gives the address as 187 Jackson Street.) They remained in this twelve-room, two-story, Victorian Style home of brick until 1912, when they moved to Peachtree Street. The Atlanta "Great Fire" of 1917 destroyed this house, as it did the one at 296 Cain Street (Pyron, page 29; Walker, pages 27–28; Edwards, page 17).

*1149, 1401, or 1701 Peachtree Street.* The address of the house in which Eugene Muse Mitchell and his family moved in 1912 varies according to source. Walker notes that the Mitchells' Peachtree mansion is in Classical Colonial style. She gives the address as 1149 Peachtree — later renumbered as 1401 Peachtree; Tommy H. Jones gives the house number as 1701 Peachtree.

Farr gives the style of the Peachtree home as Classical Revival. He describes the ground floor as being 70 feet long and including a parlor, a sitting room, a music room, a dining room, a large kitchen, a pantry, and a large entrance hall; he indicates also that the upstairs bedrooms opened onto porches.

At any rate, Margaret spent her life from age 12 until her marriage to John Marsh at her father's home on Peachtree Street, except for her 1918–1919 year at Smith College.

Eugene Mitchell's Peachtree home was the residence where Margaret and "Red" Upshaw lived during their brief marriage. The location where the house once stood now has the address 1401 Peachtree Street or 1701 Peachtree, but the house no longer stands. Margaret's brother Stephens had the home demolished in 1952 so other families would not live there. A plaque commemorates the site of the home where Mitchell spent her adolescence (Farr, page 32; Walker, pages 27–28; Pyron, pages 28–29; Tommy H. Jones).

*10 Henshaw Street, Northampton, Massachusetts.* For the year (1918–1919) that Margaret attended

Smith College in Northampton, Massachusetts, she lived at 10 Henshaw Street. Walker notes that Margaret affectionately called this residence "Ten Hen" (Edwards, page 52; Walker, page 82).

After her return to Atlanta in 1919, Margaret moved in again with her father at 1149, 1401, or 1701 Peachtree Street. She remained at this residence with her father even after her brief marriage to Berrien "Red" Kinnard Upshaw on September 2, 1922. She moved out after she married John R. Marsh on July 4, 1925, and after their brief honeymoon at in North Georgia (Pyron, pages 199–201; Tommy H. Jones).

*806 Peachtree Street, 17 Crescent Avenue (990 Peachtree Street).* Cornelius Sheehan originally owned the three-story brick home at 806 Peachtree. In 1919 a later owner moved the house a short distance back from the street and began using the Crescent Avenue entrance; the new address became 17 Crescent Avenue. This new owner converted the home into a ten-unit apartment building called Crescent Apartments.

John R. Marsh moved into Apartment 1 in 1924. Margaret Mitchell and John celebrated his 29th birthday by dining in the apartment on October 6, 1924, just before the legal divorce of Berrien Upshaw and Margaret Mitchell on October 16.

In July of 1925 John Marsh and Margaret Mitchell moved into Apartment 1 after their July 4 marriage and honeymoon. The couple lived in this apartment that Margaret affectionately called "The Dump" until 1932. In "The Dump" Margaret Mitchell penned most of *Gone with the Wind.*

Apartment 1 had two rooms—a bedroom and sitting room—plus a kitchen and bath. The location of Margaret Mitchell's typewriter was in front of the windows in the sitting room. The two calling cards that Margaret Mitchell Marsh placed on the

This photograph by Freddie Bennett shows the interior of "The Dump," where Margaret Mitchell typed most of the manuscript for the book *Gone with the Wind.* Her typewriter is in this photograph in front of the window. The typewriter, however, is no longer at the Margaret Mitchell House; it is (2011) on display at the Atlanta–Fulton County Public Library, as her estate specified. (Courtesy of the James G. Kenan Research Center at the Atlanta History Center.)

door of Apartment 1 read "Mr. John R. Mash" and "Miss Margaret Munnerlyn Mitchell" (Edwards, pages 118–119).

The apartment itself is open to the public at the Margaret Mitchell House and Museum in Atlanta, Georgia. The current address of the Margaret Mitchell House and Museum is 990 Peachtree Street.

*4 East 17th Street.* In the fall of 1932 Margaret removed the calling cards from the door of Apartment 1 when John and she moved from "The Dump" to the Russell Apartments at 4 East 17th Street; only one other apartment remained occupied when they moved from the brick building into the larger space. This apartment — their second together — had large windows, which provided light but allowed much of their heat to escape in the winter.

Margaret painted the dining room in her favorite color: watermelon pink. The couple had an apple green living room; all the woodwork was painted white. For the bedroom and bath they used floral wallpaper with pinks, creams, and greens. A unique feature of the apartment was a sun parlor, a glassed-in porch with white wicker furniture that they used as an office space. The couple remained in their Russell Apartment until 1939, when they moved into their third and last apartment together at 1268 Piedmont Avenue.

*West Peachtree Street at Eighth Street.* An intoxicated (according to John Marsh and Margaret Mitchell) driver rear-ended the car that Margaret was driving about midnight on November 22, 1934. The site of this 1934 traffic accident was eerily close to the place a car driven by Hugh D. Gravitt would strike Margaret Mitchell in 1949. Neither John S. Cohen, a passenger in the car, nor John R. Marsh was seriously injured (Walker, page 194).

*659 Peachtree, NE (corner of Peachtree and Ponce de Leon Avenue).* The Georgian Terrace Hotel at 659 Peachtree, NE, figured prominently into the life of Margaret Mitchell and her famous novel. It may have been here in the hotel lobby (April 11, 1935) that she delivered the disorganized envelopes bearing the manuscript of what would be *Gone with the Wind* to Macmillan editor Harold Latham (Edwards, page 3; Brown, page 16).

Other sources disagree as to where Mitchell delivered the envelopes. Lois Cole, associate editor of Macmillan Publishing Company, recalled the lobby of the Biltmore Hotel at 817 West Peachtree Street. Margaret's personal secretary, Margaret Baugh, previously a secretary in the Atlanta Office of Macmillan Publishing Company, remembered the place as the Hotel Ansley on Peachtree Street at Broad in Atlanta (Brown, 16).

It was in the Georgian Terrace Hotel at the corner of Peachtree and Ponce de Leon Avenue that many of the cast and crew of the film *Gone with the Wind* stayed during the Atlanta premiere of the film. The dates of the Atlanta Premiere were December 13–15, 1939.

*1268 Piedmont Avenue.* In 1939 John and Margaret Mitchell Marsh moved to a larger home: Apartment #3 at the Della-Manta Apartments at 1268 Piedmont Avenue. This would be their third and last apartment together.

It was here that Margaret Mitchell Marsh and John R. Marsh hosted a small party for some of the cast and crew of *Gone with the Wind*. This exclusive occasion was on the evening of Wednesday, December 13, 1939 — before the Friday, December 15 premiere showing.

The Della-Manta Apartments were across the street from the Piedmont Driving Club at 1215 Piedmont Avenue. When John Marsh's doctor recommended that the seriously-ill John drink some alcohol each day for his heart and circulatory system, Marsh began asking for help to cross the street for daily visits to the Piedmont Driving Club. There he would have a drink and stay for about forty minutes.

Margaret and John also began engaging in an occasional "extravagance," one of the few pleasures that they could enjoy together. They began sending across the street to the Piedmont Driving Club for cocktails and their dinner; a waiter would serve them in their own living room in the Della-Manta Apartment Building (Farr, pages 218–220).

In her will, Margaret Mitchell had asked that her surviving executor (her husband John Marsh or her brother Stephens Mitchell) destroy the original manuscript of *Gone with the Wind* after her death. For that reason, Margaret's and John's housekeeper Bessie Jordan, under the watchful eye of John Marsh, burned the manuscript — except for some pages that John kept for authentication. Jordan — with the assistance of Eugene Carr — used the furnace in the basement of the Della-Manta Apartments to accomplish this task.

*501 McDonough Boulevard.* This location of the Atlanta Federal Prison was a site that Margaret Mitchell visited frequently as a volunteer. In addition to speaking engagements there to thank the inmates for their contributions to the war effort and for their volunteer work, Margaret sponsored a yearly creative writing contest for the prison's publication *The Atlantan*.

*1137 Peachtree Street, NE.* The Peachtree Arts Theatre (1940s–1970s) was at the northeast corner of Thirteenth and Peachtree streets; this address was three-quarters of a mile from the 1949 residence of John and Margaret Mitchell Marsh. On August 11, 1949, the theater was showing the British film *A Canterbury Tale*.

John Marsh and Margaret Mitchell Marsh were crossing Peachtree near Thirteenth Street shortly after 8:00 P.M. to reach the theater. A speeding car driven by Hugh D. Gravitt struck Margaret.

*36 Butler Street, Southeast.* After the accident, an ambulance took Margaret Mitchell directly to Grady Hospital to which she had made sizeable donations in the past; she died there five days later. The location of Grady Memorial Hospital in 1949 was on Butler Street, where it had opened in 1892; it has since relocated several times. At Grady Memorial Hospital in Room 302, Margaret Mitchell Marsh died at 11:59 A.M. on August 16, 1949.

*1020 Spring Street, NW.* The location of the Atlanta funeral home that John Marsh engaged to care for his wife, Margaret Mitchell, was Spring Hill Funeral Home at 1020 Spring Street, NW. John Marsh scheduled a private funeral service there. The service, which he limited to only 300, was for Thursday, August 18, 1949, at 10:00 A.M. Dean Raimundo de Ovies of St. Philip's Cathedral, Atlanta, officiated.

*248 Oakland Avenue, SE.* Margaret Mitchell Marsh's burial in Oakland Cemetery followed the August 18 service. (The cemetery, established in 1854, currently carries the physical address 248 Oakland Avenue, SE.)

John Robert Marsh reserved a gravesite beside that of his wife in Oakland Cemetery for himself. Margaret Mitchell Marsh has a plot that is near that of Eugene Muse Mitchell (her father), Isabelle "Maybelle" Stephens Mitchell (her mother), and Russell Stephens Mitchell (her infant brother who died in 1894 before her birth). Later, her brother Alexander Stephens Mitchell (1896–1983) was buried in Oakland Cemetery.

*990 Peachtree Street, Northeast.* The Margaret Mitchell House and Museum opened on May 17, 1997, in what had been the Crescent Apartment Building where the Marshes resided. The Margaret Mitchell House because of address changes and entrances used, not relocation, is at the intersection of 10th and Peachtree streets. The House bears the address 990 Peachtree Street, Northeast, not the old 17 Crescent Avenue address.

*Margaret Mitchell Square.* In Downtown Atlanta is an area dedicated to one of Atlanta's most famous authors, the area is Margaret Mitchell Square. One of the features of the square is the Atlanta-Fulton County Central Library at 1 Margaret Mitchell Square. Highlights of the park include a cascading waterfall and a columned sculpture.

*See also* Ansley Hotel; Atlanta Federal Prison/ Penitentiary; Atlanta premiere of the film *Gone with the Wind*; Baugh, Margaret Eugenia; Biltmore Hotel; *A Canterbury Tale*; Carr, Eugene; Cole, Lois; de Ovies, Dean Raimundo; Georgian Terrace Hotel; Grady Hospital; Gravesites of Margaret Mitchell's immediate family; Gravitt, Hugh Dorsey; Jordan, Bessie Berry; Latham, Harold Strong; Margaret Mitchell House and Museum; Margaret Mitchell Square; Oakland Cemetery; Piedmont Driving Club; Rich's Department Store; Spring Hill Chapel; St. Philip's Cathedral.

## agents

Two agents that Margaret Mitchell used were Marion Saunders and Annie Laurie Williams. Williams sought to market *Gone with the Wind* with Hollywood. Saunders attempted to sell *Gone with the Wind* abroad.

*See also* Saunders, Marion; Williams, Annie Laurie.

## alcohol

Margaret Mitchell may not have been the woman with the "drinking problem" that Edwards characterizes her as being, according to Pyron (pages 155–156). Edwards mentions the problem that Margaret's first husband, Berrien Kinnard ("Red") Upshaw, had with alcohol. "Red" assaulted Margaret Mitchell physically before guests when he had been drinking heavily (page 88).

Anne Edwards does note that Mitchell "liked to drink, particularly with good friends, and she liked 'drunken brawls'—meaning such gatherings as the Georgia Press Association where quite a bit of alcohol was consumed." Edwards writes further that it is "probable that Peggy [had] a drinking problem, though she refused to admit it and never seemed to allow it to control her life" (page 265). Edwards describes Margaret Mitchell's appearance after the publication of *Gone with the Wind* as having eyes that were heavily lidded from alcohol consumption. She states further that "years of indulging her taste for 'corn likker' has made her face puffy" (page 302).

Edwards explains further that John and Margaret loved having friends to come to "The Dump" and to bring their own bottle. Margaret often attended the Georgia Press Association meetings with John; Edwards also notes that Margaret "enjoyed playing hostess" and inviting attendees to visit their room. The Marshes dispensed drinks in Dixie cups and shared in "drinking corn." Edwards elaborates that Margaret loved to down "as much corn as the most hardened of newspapermen" (page 159).

Pyron—in contrast to Edwards—writes that

Margaret Mitchell seldom drank and disliked alcohol; he does concede, however, that she developed a reputation "for holding her liquor." Frank Daniel—a co-worker with Margaret on the *Atlanta Journal Sunday Magazine*—related to Dyden Asbury Pyron his recollections of having his first hangover after drinking with Margaret Mitchell. He remembered how she poured it out and tossed it back, and he decided to keep up with her. Daniel suffered! (pages 155–156).

Walker describes twenty-one-year-old Margaret as "the rowdy, fun-loving flapper who took enormous pleasure in shocking Victorian dowagers—the joke-telling, gin-drinker who could hold her 'likker,' dance all night, and still be able to see to it that all the drunks got home safely" (Walker, page 20).

Walker observes that Margaret Mitchell was very much opposed to Prohibition and encouraged her friends to vote against it; she disliked not having the right to choose whether to drink. In a 1926 letter to John's brother Henry, Margaret writes that she had been without alcohol for a year; still, her "gin drinker's liver" showed up in medical reports. Some time afterward, she wrote that she blanked out after three drinks of cheap "corn." The letter indicates that she made a display of singing and shouting before passing out cold (Walker, pages 137–138, 145–146). In a letter to John's sister Frances, Margaret notes in 1926 that neither she nor John would ever again be able to drink for health reasons (Walker, pages 156–157). These comments seem to indicate that Margaret may not have had the problems that Edwards suggests were present in her later years.

*See also* Daniel, Frank.

## Alderman, Grace

Grace Alderman was a stenographer and employee of Georgia Railway and Power Company, which employed John Marsh in the public relations division. Between August 13, 1935, and January 30, 1936, Alderman retyped most of the revised and corrected manuscript of what would be *Gone with the Wind*. She prepared the typewritten document for Margaret Mitchell (and John Marsh) to submit to Macmillan Publishing Company.

On August 13, 1935, Margaret Mitchell had received the envelopes containing the chapters of the manuscript that Macmillan was tentatively calling "A MS of the Old South." It was readily apparent that John Marsh and Margaret Mitchell would have to hire a typist to retype the pages as they corrected and revised them.

Rhoda Williams, John's secretary, was one of the few Atlanta people—Eugene Muse Mitchell,

Stephens Mitchell, P. S. Arkwright (president of Georgia Power), and Margaret's personal secretary (Margaret Baugh)—who knew of the signed contract and the needed revisions. John had to ask someone who could advise him of a proficient typist to engage.

Rhoda suggested an unmarried, prudent young woman who had just come to work as a stenographer for Georgia Power. This new employee—Grace Alderman—consented happily to the extra work. She worked on her own typewriter in her own home in the evenings after work and on the weekends. The work was very tedious not only because Alderman had to type carbon copies but also because Marsh and Mitchell continued to make revisions and corrections to her retyped copies.

On January 7, 1936, Margaret Baugh—Mitchell's full-time, personal secretary—was able to telegraph Macmillan to inform the publisher that three-fourths of the manuscript was being forwarded. On January 26, 1936, Baugh and Alderman had finished all of the typing—except for a few pages in Part 5.

Margaret Baugh telegraphed Lois Cole at Macmillan Publishing Company at 4:00 P.M. on Tuesday, January 29, 1936, to inform Cole that Baugh herself would mail the completed manuscript the next day (Walker, pages 217, 230, 233).

*See also* **Baugh, Margaret Eugenia; Cole, Lois; Williams, Rhoda.**

## Alsberg, Henry

The director of the Federal Writers' Project (FWP) from its 1935 beginning through late 1939 was Henry Alsberg. Alsberg was a former lawyer who became interested in the theater as a writer and as a director of off-Broadway productions. The purpose of the FWP was to stimulate the economy. An associate director with Alsberg in the FWP Agency was Reed Harris. Harris was a correspondent of George Brett, Jr., during the time when Susan Davis brought the lawsuit against Macmillan Publishing Company for the "plagiarism" of *Gone with the Wind*.

*See also* **Davis, Susan Lawrence; Harris, Reed.**

## altruism of Margaret Mitchell

Maybelle Mitchell taught her daughter Margaret generosity and concern for others. Maybelle had been concerned with voting rights for women and with the well-being of others; her example was a model for Margaret Mitchell's many acts of altruism.

The generosity of Margaret Mitchell at the premiere of *Gone with the Wind* on December 15, 1939, was particularly impressive to those about her.

Pyron described Mitchell's words to the crowd assembled in Loew's Grand Theatre in Atlanta on December 15, 1939, as being a perfect example of "classic Mitchell generosity."

Mitchell noted first in her speech that when down on one's luck, one looks for others; Mitchell observed, however, that it was really when one was experiencing good times, as she was that night, when one really needed others. She continued to thank people everywhere for their help and kindness to her.

After focusing on others, Margaret next praised David O. Selznick. She began with some humorous remarks about him. She reminded the crowd how it had laughed at Selznick's slowness in selecting the cast member for the character of Scarlett O'Hara; she told them that they had speculated that he might wait until Shirley Temple had grown up. The crowd laughed in agreement. Her remarks were received with equal generosity.

When World War II began, Mitchell gave generously of her time to help with raising funds for war bonds. She made speeches and rolled bandages. She joined the American Red Cross. She sponsored the fund raising project for the Navy cruiser *Atlanta*. In only two months she and the women of the American Red Cross had raised nearly $65 million (Walker, page 456). After its construction, she christened the vessel. Dressed in her Red Cross uniform, she spoke personally to each member of the crew.

Margaret accepted the responsibility of air raid warden for her for her district. She assumed the major responsibility to raise money after the Japanese sank the *Atlanta* on November 13, 1942. Her fund raising even took her to the Atlanta Federal Penitentiary.

She invited enlisted men to her home, gave them rides, wrote letters, and helped entertain the troops. Her generosity began at home with the care that she gave her father and husband during their illnesses.

As a sponsor of the writing contest of the inmates at the Atlanta Federal Penitentiary, Mitchell shared her talents with others. She visited the penitentiary on many occasions and personally judged the entries of those who contributed to their newspaper, *The Atlantan.*

Mitchell worked with Benjamin Mays to sponsor the medical education of many African Americans. Her generosity helped many young people enter the medical field.

Mitchell remembered others in her will.

*See also* Atlanta Federal Prison/Penitentiary; The *Atlantan*; Kobernaut, G.M.; USS *Atlanta*; will of John Marsh; will of Margaret Mitchell.

## American Booksellers Association Annual Award (1937)

In February 1937, the American Booksellers Association presented its annual award for the best fiction of the preceding year. This National Book Award is not to be confused with the National Book Association Award. The ABA National Book Award is an industry prize for which the members of the American Booksellers Association select the recipient; the award goes to honor the books that they most admire and enjoy selling.

The recipient of the ABA award for the most distinguished 1936 novel was *Gone with the Wind* (Brown, page 149).

## American Red Cross

Margaret Mitchell was an active volunteer for the American Red Cross— especially during World War II; in fact she sold more war bonds and savings stamps than any other person in Georgia. In a letter to Lois Cole, Mitchell wrote of her activities; both Finis Farr and Marianne Walker quote from this undated, unidentified letter. In it she spoke of "galumphing about the countryside making speeches and selling bonds." (This was quite an accomplishment for Mitchell, who had held a fear of public speaking.) She raised $212,000 in four hours selling bonds and stamps in Rich's Department Store in Atlanta at one time.

The American Red Cross in Atlanta asked Mitchell to thank the inmates of the Atlanta Federal Prison for their contributions to the war effort. Many of these prisoners had volunteered for malaria experiments, bought war bonds, and contributed to the Red Cross. Putting aside her fear of public speaking, Mitchell spoke to 2,400 inmates on January 7, 1942.

In October of 1942 in her work as air warden, a practice exercise had her dressed in a helmet, directing traffic, and instructing people where to take shelter. In December of the same year Mitchell joined other women in attaching chevrons to and mending uniforms, serving meals, and otherwise assisting the 2,000 soldiers camped in Piedmont Park.

She operated an electric cutter in the sewing unit at West Peachtree; she cut a dozen surgical dressings at a time at this facility. She also worked at the Red Cross canteen in Atlanta.

*Commissioning of the USS* Atlanta *(CL-51).* Margaret Mitchell was an honored guest at the commissioning of the USS *Atlanta* on December 24, 1941; she wore her Red Cross uniform. The ship's captain, P.S. Jenkins, arranged for her to shake hands with each sailor aboard the ship.

*The Second USS* Atlanta. When Margaret learned that the USS *Atlanta* and the men had been lost off the coast of Guadalcanal on November 12–13, 1942, she immediately called the women of the local Red Cross to her side. Together, they began a fundraising campaign of $35 million to replace the *Atlanta*.

In March of 1943 John L. Connor, chair of the City of Atlanta's war bond selling campaign, presented a check of $63 million to Secretary of the Navy Frank Knox. The check was to cover the cost of replacing the USS *Atlanta* (CL-51), sunk in November 1942. The campaign had greatly exceeded its goal of $35,000,000; the new cruiser was the USS *Atlanta* (CL-104).

**See also Atlanta Federal Prison/Penitentiary; Fears of Margaret Mitchell; Rich's Department Store; USS *Atlanta*.**

## Anderson, Paul

Margaret Mitchell's will stipulated that John R. Marsh, her brother Stephens Mitchell, and the Trust Company of Georgia should serve as her executors. In 2011 Paul Anderson and Thomas Hal Clark were two of the three original trustees authorized by Stephens Mitchell to manage the rights of *Gone with the Wind* (Brown, page 239n).

## Anderson, W. T.

W. T. Anderson was the editor and publisher of the *Macon Telegraph* and later the *Macon News* for more than 30 years. Anderson told Mitchell that one of his writers— Susan ("Sue") Myrick— had mentioned that Margaret had refused to go to Hollywood for the filming of *Gone with the Wind*. Anderson suggested Myrick as a possible consultant to the movie. Not only did Myrick know about the South, but she had studied the stage, knew Southern dialect, understood the characters, and was— except for Margaret herself— perhaps the best person to advise Selznick Pictures (Walker, page 400).

## Angel, Henry Love

Henry Love Angel was a contemporary of Margaret Mitchell; both were born in 1900 and both spent the bulk of the years 1912–1945 in Atlanta. Angel saved the letters from Margaret Mitchell, their photographs, and a notebook with her never-before-published novella *Lost Laysen*.

Hubbard traces the genesis of the materials as being passed down to Love's son and later in 1952 to his step-grandson (Henry Love Angel, Jr.). The younger Henry Love Angel, Jr., was an electronics salesman when he received the materials. Henry

Love Angel had died in 1945 and Margaret Mitchell in 1949.

Henry Love Angel, Jr., remembered he had not read the materials carefully; he had merely put them in a "plastic pouch" and stuffed them into a drawer— until 1994. Angel heard that a museum for Margaret Mitchell had opened. He presented the materials to the museum. The pouch contained *Lost Laysen*, 15 letters, and 57 photos. Some of the photos were of Angel and Mitchell; many of the photographs showed them acting out dramas (Hubbard).

Henry Love Angel was born in Wilmington, North Carolina, in 1900. He moved to Atlanta during the 1912-1913 school year. He, Courtenay Ross, and Margaret Mitchell became good friends. In 1919 after Margaret Mitchell returned home from Smith College, Henry Love Angel was at Camp Benning south of Atlanta. He and Mitchell found time to resume their friendship and their antics; they continued to act out dramas— one of which was always Henry begging for Margaret's hand. When Angel returned to Atlanta after the end of World War I, he found himself in contention with others for Margaret Mitchell's affections (Mitchell, *Lost Laysen*, pages 13–30). *Lost Laysen* was Margaret Mitchell's work when she was only 15. ("Springfield-Greene County Library District" says 16.) It tells the story of a South Sea island missionary— a woman— and the sailor who loves but cannot win her.

Angel kept the letters that Margaret Mitchell wrote him between 1920 and 1922. He was a World War I veteran; he lived on an estate belonging to a friend outside of Atlanta. Henry Love Angel seems more serious about Margaret Mitchell than she was about him. Hubbard quotes one of Mitchell's 1922 letters: "Henry, for God's sake, if I ever say I care about you— or feel just the same toward you except that I can't marry you, please take my word for it…. I do love you, old-timer, and feel you are my boy as long as you want to be my boy" (Hubbard).

Mitchell wrote to Henry about her friendship with Winston "Red" Withers. She attempted to maintain her relationship with Henry and to keep her relationships with others. In June of 1922 Mitchell wrote to Henry about Red Withers. "Do you think that my love for Red has changed me in any degree toward you? … I hate to think of there being a barrier between us" (Hubbard).

Mitchell married Berrien Kinnard ("Red") Upshaw in the fall of that year. Three months later Henry Love Angel married a telephone operator named Grace Rayfield. Red's and Margaret's mar-

This 1903 photograph shows a young Margaret Mitchell with a kitten belonging to the photographer. Stephens remembered that Margaret was reluctant to have her photograph made, but the photographer convinced her that he wanted to photograph his kitten. Margaret, who loved animals, was eager to help. (Courtesy of the Atlanta–Fulton County Public Library System's Special Collections Department.)

riage was over by 1924. Grace's and Henry's endured.

After Henry Love Angel died of lung disease in 1945, Henry Love Angel, Jr., paid a visit to Margaret Mitchell. He described the visit: "I went over there, and we ate some kind of hard crumpet thing and talked. She just kept looking at me — staring — and finally she said, 'You look just like your daddy'" (Hubbard).

Angel's materials have been a mixed blessing to his son. He sold them to Patsy Wiggins, the proprietor of the Road to Tara Museum, for $60,000. He hoped to use the money to build a Florida retirement home. Henry Love Angel, Jr., found, however, that Scribner paid the Road to Tara Museum and the Mitchell estate $1,000,000 for rights of publication. Angel expressed regrets at not auctioning the materials in New York (Wiggins pointed out, however, that he will receive 7 percent of her share) (Hubbard). The public, however, is

This family portrait shows Margaret Munnerlyn Mitchell, her mother Maybelle Stephens Mitchell, and her brother Alexander Stephens Mitchell; the date was about 1903. (Courtesy of the Atlanta-Fulton Public Library System's Special Collections Department.)

now able to read *Lost Laysen*, view the photographs included in the volume, and read the letters duplicated in the book.

*See also Lost Laysen*; Road to Tara Museum; Wiggins, Patsy.

## animals

Margaret Mitchell always loved animals — particularly cats and horses. Through the years, the Mitchell family had two alligators, dogs, ducks, turtles, horses, and several cats. Margaret recalled her mother's patience and tolerance of the menagerie that often occupied their house and yard.

When Margaret was three, Maybelle Mitchell (Margaret's mother), eight-year-old Stephens (Margaret's older brother), and young Margaret sat for a family portrait. After the group photograph, Maybelle Mitchell wanted Margaret to sit for an individual portrait. When Margaret became teary-eyed, the photographer produced a tiny kitten for her to hold. Margaret was ecstatic. Stephens Mitchell remembered that Margaret believed the photographer wanted a portrait of his cat. She was happy to hold the cat and help with "his" project (Pyron, page 31).

Margaret Mitchell and her dance partner, A. Sigmund Weil, horrified the Junior League with their Apache dance performance at the debutante ball. (Courtesy of the Atlanta-Fulton Public Library System's Special Collections Department.)

*Before Scarlett* details that the Mitchell family had numerous pets when they lived on Jackson Street. "They usually had a collie dog and it was always named 'Colonel' after Teddy Roosevelt" (Eskridge, page 2). When the family moved to Peachtree Street, Margaret had the responsibility of getting the cat from Jackson Street to the new house. This involved taking the cat on a streetcar. During the trip, the cat escaped and a policeman had to help in the rescue (Eskridge, pages 2–3).

The animals were more than just objects. They carried names and personalities. The two ducks were Mr. and Mrs. Drake, for instance (Eskridge, page 3).

Animals continued to figure prominently in the life of Margaret Mitchell through the years. She rode horseback from an early age, suffered a fall from Bucephalus and on a date with Berrien "Red" Upshaw, kept cats as pets all her life, and shared her enthusiasm for animals with her readers after she went to work for the *Atlanta Journal*.

*See also* accidents; Bucephalus; cats; elephant; monkey.

## Ansley Hotel (also Hotel Ansley)

Margaret Baugh, Margaret Mitchell's personal secretary and previously a secretary in the Atlanta Office of Macmillan Publishing Company, told the story of Margaret Mitchell delivering the manuscript of *Gone with the Wind*. Baugh noted that Mitchell delivered the work to Macmillan's Editor-in-Chief and Vice-President Harold Latham in the lobby of the Ansley Hotel on Peachtree at Broad. Lois Cole, associate editor of Macmillan Publishing Company, mentioned that Mitchell took the unorganized envelopes holding the chapters to Latham in the lobby of the Biltmore. Brown notes these discrepancies. Anne Edwards writes that Mitchell visited Latham in the lobby of the Georgian Terrace Hotel, 659 Peachtree, NE (corner of Peachtree and Ponce de Leon Avenue), in Atlanta.

Neither Latham, Walker, nor Pyron identify the hotel. No definitive answer is possible (Brown, page 16; Edwards, page 3; Latham, page 49; Walker, page 198; Pyron, page 299).

*See also* **Biltmore Hotel; Georgian Terrace Hotel.**

## Apache dance (as performed by Margaret Mitchell and A. Sigmund Weil)

On March 13, 1921, Polly Peachtree wrote in the social section of the *Atlanta Journal* about the Atlanta debutants and their parties. She stated that the Daughters of the American Revolution (DAR) had sponsored the benefit ball performance of the Georgia Tech student A. Sigmund Weil and the "pretty" Margaret Mitchell. Weil had impersonated a Paris hoodlum. Accompanying him was Margaret in a costume with a black satin skirt slit in the front, black stockings, and a crimson sash; Margaret emitted shrieks of pain, passion, and terror as she danced.

One of the lines from an *Atlanta Constitution* article of March 13, 1921, named Margaret Mitchell. The article observed that Margaret had sacrificed herself to aid the DAR. Some elders were horrified by the shocking dance and the kiss at the end of the dance. After her dance and after an argument with the Junior League about its use of the collected funds, Margaret did not find her name listed on the roster of the Junior League. During the December 1939 premiere of *Gone with the Wind* Margaret did not attend the ball that the Junior League sponsored. Some Atlanta residents suggested Mitchell was snubbing the organization that had once snubbed her.

## Arkwright, Preston Stanley

Preston Stanley (P. S.) Arkwright (1874–1946) was president of Georgia Power and Light Company, where John Marsh worked in public relations. He became president of Georgia Railway and Electric Company about 1902. He remained in this executive position until his 1946 death. With the accession of new power companies, the company had become Georgia Railway and Power Company in everyday usage (Calhoon). The *New York Times* on December 3, 1949, reported 75-year-old Arkwright's death from pneumonia. His death in Emory Hospital came in the same year that Margaret Mitchell had died in Grady Hospital in August.

During the time that John Marsh was helping Margaret with the revisions of *Gone with the Wind* and when John was ill, Arkwright was lenient with Marsh about his punctuality and would not hear of John's resigning. Arkwright even offered John a leave of absence with pay. John at last took the leave—without pay.

Arkwright was one of only a few people who knew of the work that John and Margaret were doing to revise the manuscript. Others who were privy to the information were Stephens Mitchell, Eugene Muse Mitchell, Rhoda Williams, Margaret's typist Grace Alderman, and Margaret's secretary Margaret Baugh.

## Asasno

Asasno was a popular Atlanta photographer who photographed Margaret Mitchell. John R. Marsh, however, refused to allow Edwin Granberry of the *New York Sun* to use Asasno's touched-up photograph of her in the article he was writing after an interview. Marsh noted that the Asasno's work made her appear younger and called the works "photo deceptions" (Walker, page 350).

John R. Marsh would not allow the publication of this Asasno Studio portrait of his wife, Margaret Mitchell; he considered the "touched-up" photograph to be a "photographdeception." (Courtesy of the Atlanta-Fulton Public Library System's Special Collections Department.)

## Astor Theatre

Two New York theaters simultaneously premiered *Gone with the Wind* on December 29, 1939. This was only a few days after the Atlanta premiere of December 13–15, 1939. One of these theaters was the Astor. The other was the Capitol.

The first two lessees of the Astor Theatre were producers/managers Lincoln A. Wagenhals (1869–1931) and Collin Kemper (1870–1955). They opened the Astor at the corner of Broadway and W. 45th Street in 1906. Considered one of Broadway's most elite venues for decades, the Astor was able to seat over 1,500 guests of the screen and stage.

The five-story Astor Theatre was beside the Hotel Astor. George Keister decorated the interior in the "simple-yet-elegant Greek Revival style." The original predominant colors were red, gold, and ivory (Cinema Treasures: Astor Theatre").

From 1912 to 1916 George M. Cohan and his partner Sam Harris assumed responsibility for the Astor Theatre. The Shubert Organization took it over in 1916 and operated it until the beginning of the Great Depression. Movies replaced live presentations in the Astor in 1925. The Astor was the site of the 1939 New York premiere of *Gone with the Wind*. The Capital was simultaneously showing the film the same night.

MGM in the 1940s began premiering its Technicolor musicals on Broadway. The Astor was its site for these big-screen productions.

The Astor underwent a radical modernization. A stark décor replaced the former interior. Orchestra seating, murals on the side walls, and a single balcony characterized its new look. A wall-to-wall screen provided a showing place for the new films. Marble covered the outside façade; this gave the exterior a simplified look.

Maintenance problems brought about the closing of the Astor in 1972. Preservationists sought for a decade to keep the landmark for historical reasons. The razing of the structure came in 1982 and Marriott Marquis New York Hotel occupies the site of the Astor Theatre ("Cinema Treasures: Astor Theatre").

*See also* New York premiere of *Gone with the Wind* (the film).

## Atkinson, Helen

Helen Atkinson was a good friend of Margaret Mitchell at Smith College. Both women lived at Ten Henshaw in Northampton, Massachusetts. Atkinson had plans to be a teacher (Edwards, page 52).

## Atkinson, Paul

A business executive from Madison, Georgia, Paul Atkinson bought *The Battle of Atlanta* from the Miller heirs. His purchase helped place *The Battle of Atlanta* painting in Atlanta and helped kindle Margaret Mitchell's interest in the Civil War and helped improve her knowledge of the battle.

The Miller family, from whom Atkinson purchased the painting, had come into possession of the painting when William Wehner (whose company had hired the painter) faced legal problems. *The Battle of Atlanta* is still (2013) on display in the Atlanta Cyclorama.

Atkinson owned also *Storming of Missionary Ridge and Battle Above the Clouds*, another cycloramic painting by William Wehner's company. The two paintings were on display initially in Chattanooga and later in Atlanta. H.H. Harrison of Florida later bought the painting *The Battle of Atlanta* from Atkinson.

*See also* Battle of Atlanta painting.

## Atlanta

Atlanta is the county seat of Fulton County in Georgia. It is in the foothills of the Blue Ridge Mountains and is on the Chattahoochee River. As the chief railroad junction in the South and with the busiest airport in the country, Atlanta has long been a transportation hub for the nation. In addition, Atlanta has always been the world headquarters of Coca-Cola and has been the nation's headquarters for Delta Air Lines since the 1940s. Since 1998 Atlanta's Hartsfield-Jackson Atlanta International Airport has been the world's busiest airport.

**USS *Atlanta see under* USS**

## Atlanta and Margaret Mitchell

Margaret Mitchell was born in Atlanta in 1900. Except for her 1918-1919 school year as a freshman at Smith College in Northampton, Massachusetts, Margaret Mitchell lived her entire life in Atlanta, the capital city of Georgia. She developed a love of history and of her city by her visits with family to relatives and friends in Atlanta — particularly on Sunday afternoon strolls. She often recalled sitting on the knobby knees of the soldiers and hearing their accounts of the Civil War. Her grandfather Russell Crawford Mitchell would allow her to sit on his lap and feel the groove in his skull where a bullet grazed him during the Civil War. In addition, Margaret's visits to the Atlanta Cyclorama helped her visualize the Civil War and the events of the Battle of Atlanta.

Later after a gift of her own horse and after learning to ride, six-year-old Margaret began riding daily with Confederate War soldiers. She listened to their stories of the Civil War. Her visits on Sunday afternoons in particular with the older women in the Atlanta and Jonesboro areas help her visualize life at home during the Civil War. She learned about how the war affected her area on all fronts.

Also of particular interest to young Margaret Mitchell was the inside of the Georgia State Capitol. She studied the statues, the marble busts, and the flags and banners on display on each floor. The rotunda with its Hall of Fame featuring marble busts of Georgia residents and of the signers of the Declaration of Independence was a favorite of young Margaret.

During the Atlanta Great Fire of 1917, Margaret gained a sense of the fire that occurred in Atlanta when the munitions stores burned. Mitchell helped in caring for those left homeless by the burning buildings. These images and this information helped her when she began writing of the fires of Atlanta during the Civil War.

*See also* Atlanta Cyclorama.

## Atlanta Auditorium Armory

Built in 1907–1909 for performances and as headquarters of the Georgia National Guard, the Atlanta Auditorium Armory gained national prominence during the world premiere of the film *Gone with the Wind.* For those who could not obtain tickets for the film premiere, on Friday, December 15, 1939, the Atlanta Auditorium and Armory housed an alternate event: a dance. The same decorations were in use for the Friday ball event; Kay Kyser played.

Less than a year later (November 11, 1940) a cigarette—carelessly tossed—sparked a fire at Atlanta Auditorium Armory. The blaze gutted the front section of the four-story structure and the roof caved in. A firewall protected the auditorium, and no one was injured or killed, so there was much for which Atlanta could be thankful. Marble and concrete were the primary re-building materials.

## *Atlanta Constitution*

In the early 1920s when Margaret Mitchell was looking for a job, Atlanta had two main newspapers. These papers were *The Atlanta Constitution*, a morning newspaper that was the more liberal of the two publications, and the *Atlanta Journal*, an afternoon paper with a stance that was center-right.

The *Atlanta Constitution* had included some articles about Margaret Mitchell prior to 1922, when she determined to try to find work at an Atlanta paper. Margaret Mitchell's name had appeared in articles in the *Atlanta Constitution* in 1921. When the society editor at the *Constitution* wrote of the 1921 debutants, Margaret's name had been in the article. On March 13, 1921, after Margaret Mitchell had performed her Apache dance, the *Constitution* described Margaret Mitchell as "offering herself and all she was on the altar of charity."

Margaret Mitchell did not apply for a job as a reporter at the *Constitution*. One reason may have been because women did not usually serve as reporters at the paper. Another reason may have been the night hours that she would have to work.

*See also* Apache dance.

## Atlanta Cyclorama

A building in Grant Park building currently houses the cycloramic painting *The Battle of Atlanta*. This is one example of an art form that started in America and was popular at the end of the Nineteenth Century before motion pictures and is one of the few remaining examples of this art form in the world.

Cycloramic paintings ideally featured the painting on the outer wall of a round room. The attendees sat or stood in the center of the facility, where artists had created the pictures "in the round." Frequent subjects for the paintings were scenes that the patrons might never see in person, such as *The Battle of Atlanta*.

Margaret and her family visited this attraction housed in a wooden building often when Margaret was a child; later she visited the modernized Grant Park structure that housed the painting beginning in 1921. An important feature of the building—built after the Great Atlanta Fire—was the fact that it was "fire-proof." Seeing the oil painting and observing the images of the participants in the battle helped to enhance Margaret Mitchell's knowledge of Civil War events.

During the 1930s, the federal government hired some artists through the Works Progress Administration to add a diorama in front of the painting. Clark Gable visited the Atlanta Cyclorama during his trip to Atlanta for the premiere of the film *Gone with the Wind.* A popular story states that Gable remarked to his guide that the only way that the display could be improved would be if it included a likeness of Gable himself. The management added Gable's features to one of the figures in the diorama. These features remain.

With the renovation of the Cyclorama in 1979, the replacement of portions of the diorama was necessary. The red Georgia clay originally used in the diorama had destroyed about 20 percent of the original painting. Workers substituted less destructive plastic and fiberglass with the natural material and help preserve the painting for future generations.

A 1967 thunderstorm damaged the building and the painting. The Cyclorama had to close again for renovation in 1979; it reopened in 1982 with tiered, rotating seating. Visitors see a film narrated by the star James Earl Jones that helps clarify facts about

This postcard shows the Cyclorama Building at Grant Park that replaced the wooden building. Margaret Mitchell visited both structures to view *The Battle of Atlanta*, which is the world's largest oil painting. (R and R News Company in Atlanta and "Colourpicture" Publications, Boston 15, Massachusetts.)

the painting and about the building that housed it (Davis, Stephen).

*See also* Battle of Atlanta; *Battle of Atlanta* painting.

## Atlanta Federal Prison/Penitentiary

Approval for the construction of the Atlanta Federal Prison was final in 1899. The construction was complete by 1902. Originally the prison was a male only, maximum security prison.

The American Red Cross, for which Margaret Mitchell was a volunteer, asked her to thank the inmates of the Atlanta Federal Prison for their contributions to the war efforts for World War II. Many of these prisoners had volunteered for malaria experiments, had bought war bonds, and had contributed to the Red Cross. In the prison auditorium on January 7, 1942, Margaret spoke to 2400 inmates—despite her fear of public speaking. The inmates gave her a standing ovation.

Margaret determined to do something for these inmates. She created a plan to sponsor a yearly creative writing contest for the *Atlantan*, the prison's publication. This program was successful in improving the personality of the participants and exercising their mental capacity, according to the Associate Warden G. M. Kobernaut on November 13, 1950.

After Mitchell was involved in the accident in August of 1949, the inmates offered to donate blood to her. Of the only two flower arrangements that John Marsh personally accepted, one was the massive blanket of white roses grown by the inmates and sent to her funeral (Walker, pages 506–507).

## Atlanta–Fulton County Public Library

Across the street from Margaret Mitchell Square in downtown Atlanta is the Atlanta-Fulton Public Library. Margaret Mitchell's father — Eugene Muse Mitchell — was one of the founders of the Carnegie Public Library in Atlanta. In the years after her father's death, Mitchell made many contributions in his name to the public library system.

In 1980 the current Atlanta-Fulton Public Library building came to fruition and replaced the old Carnegie Library. The architect was Marcel Brouer, a German artist of the German Bauhaus School. Breuer had received his commission in 1969 for the Atlanta-Fulton Public Library after he completed the Whitney Museum. The location of the structure that Breuer designed for the Atlanta-Fulton Public Library is at the same site as the razed Carnegie Library: One Margaret Mitchell Square, Atlanta, Georgia ("Atlanta–Fulton Public Library").

Eugene Muse Mitchell was a founder of the Carnegie Library in Atlanta, Georgia. The library received many of Margaret Mitchell's papers. (Courtesy of the Atlanta-Fulton Public Library System's Special Collections Department.)

## Atlanta–Fulton County Public Library, Margaret Mitchell Permanent Collection/ Exhibition

The Margaret Mitchell Permanent Collection at the Atlanta-Fulton County Public Library includes a variety of items.

*A copy of the will of Margaret Mitchell.* In the permanent collection is a copy of her five-page, handwritten will that carried the date November 21, 1948. In the will Margaret Mitchell Marsh gave (1) all her papers and written materials and (2) all her household furnishings, personal belongings, and effects (among other things) to her husband, John R. Marsh, in fee simple.

*A copy of the will of John R. Marsh.* On July 26, 1951, John R. Marsh signed his will. In this will, he addressed the souvenirs and mementoes of Margaret Mitchell's literary career. Marsh identified these items as including newspaper and magazine clippings, Mitchell's Pulitzer Prize certificate, the bronze paperweight that the American Booksellers Association had presented to her, tokens and

awards that Mitchell had received to honor her, press photographs, original illustrations that the artist Axel Mathiesen had given her, various editions of *Gone with the Wind* and their cases, and mementoes from other authors. Marsh gave and bequeathed these items to the Atlanta Public Library. Many of these items—including a typewriter of hers—are on the fifth floor of the Atlanta-Fulton Central Library, at 1 Margaret Mitchell Square in downtown Atlanta.

*Other items in the Margaret Mitchell Collection/ Exhibit.* These include some photographs related to Margaret Mitchell and her family, her library card, a facsimile of one of the pages of the original manuscript, and Mitchell's personal books—including the books she used to research *Gone with the Wind* (Atlanta–Fulton County Public Library).

*See also* will of Margaret Mitchell; will of John Marsh.

## Atlanta Historical Society

To help preserve the history of the city of Atlanta, fourteen civic-minded citizens of Atlanta, including Eugene Muse Mitchell and Alexander Stephens Mitchell, met in 1926 to charter the Atlanta Historical Society. These founders met in homes, collected photographs and early documents, and published research bulletins to create an interest in the history of Atlanta among friends and citizens of the city. Eugene Muse Mitchell served as a president.

The Atlanta Historical Society honored Margaret Mitchell with a reception on Saturday, June 28, 1936, just before the official date (Monday, June 30, 1936) of the trade release date of *Gone with the Wind*. Margaret asked in her will that $1000 go to the Atlanta Historical Society; John R. Marsh in his will stipulated in item eleven the bequeath to the Atlanta Historical Society of $1000.00 in fee simple.

## Atlanta History Center

The Atlanta Historical Society, organized in 1926, grew in scope and in size until in 1990 it located on 33 acres in Buckhead with the name "The Atlanta History Center." The address of the Atlanta History Center is 730 W. Paces Ferry Road, Atlanta, Georgia.

Included in the Atlanta History Center are the Atlanta History Museum, the Centennial Olympic Games Museum, the Swan House, the Tullie Smith Farm, six historic gardens, the Kenan Research Center, and the Margaret Mitchell House and Museum (located in Midtown). The center, one of the nation's largest museums, today conducts living history programs, festivals, lectures by authors, camps, and other educational events.

## *Atlanta Journal/Sunday Atlanta Magazine*

Atlanta attorney Edward Hodge first published *The Atlanta Journal* in 1883. In 1887, Hodge sold the paper to Clark Howell. Howell and his family were owners of the *Atlanta Journal* until 1950, when they sold the publication.

In December 1922 Margaret Mitchell Upshaw interviewed for a job with the *Atlanta Journal/Atlanta Sunday Magazine*. Women did not usually work outside the home in the 1920s. In particular, women did not often work as newspaper reporters. Angus Perkerson, however, hired Margaret Mitchell Upshaw for the *Atlanta Sunday Magazine*.

Margaret used the byline Peggy Upshaw on her first article on December 31, 1922. After she and her husband Red Upshaw separated, Margaret used the byline Peggy Mitchell. In the days to come readers would know her by the name Margaret Mitchell. During her time (1922–1926) with the *Sunday Magazine/Atlanta Journal*, she sometimes worked a six-day, sixty-hour week. She wrote 85 news sto-

ries and 139 features with her byline, despite sick leaves.

*Margaret Mitchell's Descriptions of the Atlanta Journal Offices.* When Margaret Mitchell (Upshaw) went to work at the *Atlanta Journal* it was in a five-story, brick building beside the railroad tracks. Copy editor Joe Kling described the building as "hopelessly dirty inside and out"; neglect and the smoke from the passing trains brought about much of the dirt. Kling cautioned that the café on the first floor was full of cockroaches (Walker, page 102). Mitchell called the café the "Roachery." She named the third-floor office where she worked "The Black Hole of Calcutta" (Walker, page 103).

Bill Howland, who worked with the *Atlanta Sunday Magazine* with Mitchell, reported that their unabridged dictionary was beside the city desk. Margaret was so small that she had difficulty reaching the large volume; she usually stood on her tiptoes and leaned over to read the print. When she assumed that stance, she often revealed some white flesh above her rolled and gartered stockings. Harlee Branch, the city editor of the *Atlanta Journal*, called Margaret into his office. He asked her not to use the dictionary. He explained that the young men were upset when she used the book (Walker, page 98).

*Atlanta Journal "Margaret Mitchell Memorial Issue."* On December 18, 1949, the *Atlanta Journal* published a special edition: "The Margaret Mitchell Memorial Issue." The thirty-nine pages included some color photos. This tribute came on the tenth anniversary of the Atlanta premiere of the film *Gone with the Wind* and shortly after her death that August. The issue contained details of her death, information on her writing of *Gone with the Wind*, examples of some of the condolences from all over the world, stories from her youth, reminders of the film's premiere, a transcript of radio interview, and some of her articles for the *Atlanta Journal/Atlanta Journal Sunday Magazine*.

## Atlanta Library Club

After the 1936 publication of *Gone with the Wind*, Margaret Mitchell began to receive invitations to speak to many groups; everyone seemed to want to throw her a party. Mitchell, however, did not like to speak publicly. A few weeks earlier she had been the guest speaker at the breakfast meeting of the Macon Writers' Club. That had gone well, but her speech to the Atlanta Library Club did not go as well. She wrote to Harold Latham on June 1, 1936, that she drew a blank. When she "came to," she had been telling "indelicate stories."

One of these "indelicate stories," she wrote to Latham, had recounted when she stopped to ask a farmer when cotton was usually planted; she needed the information for her book. He told her and asked what it was like to be a writer. She said that the hard work made her scratch, sweat, and smell. She shared the old farmer's comment: "Just like spreading manure!" (Edwards, pages 200–201, 354).

## Atlanta premiere of the film *Gone with the Wind* (December 13–15, 1939)

On July 17, 1939, Producer David O. Selznick wrote Atlanta Mayor William B. Hartsfield to tell him that the rumors that the premiere of *Gone with the Wind* would not be held in Atlanta were unfounded. Selznick indicated that neither Selznick International Pictures nor the distributor (Loew's, Incorporated) "had ever given any thought to opening in any place but Atlanta" (Harwell, *Letters,* 285).

*William B. Hartsfield and the Atlanta premiere.* Hartsfield (Atlanta mayor 1937–1941 and 1942–1962) declared a three-day celebration. He encouraged women and girls to wear hoop skirts and men to don tight trousers and grow beards for the festivities.

On Wednesday, December 13, 1939 — the first day of the celebration — the stars begin to arrive in Atlanta. Most came by plane.

Hartsfield planned to present flowers to many of these visitors. Howard Dietz, who managed the public relations for *Gone with the Wind,* and his wife were to arrive at 8:25 A.M. Ann Rutherford, who played Scarlett's youngest sister Carreen, had an arrival time of 10:00; her mother would accompany her.

*Candler Field and Atlanta premiere.* The scheduled arrival time for Vivien Leigh ("Scarlett") and her fiancé Laurence Olivier, Olivia de Havilland ("Melanie"), producer David O. Selznick, Mrs. Irene Selznick, and some others was 3:15 P.M., December 13, 1939, at Candler Field.

*Stone Mountain and the Atlanta premiere.* A popular but difficult-to-document account of the premiere is the heavy tail winds that threatened to make the arrival time of Vivien Leigh, Olivia de Havilland, the Selznicks, and the others on the Eastern Airline plane earlier than expected. When the welcoming committee realized that their arrival was imminent and that the floral arrangements were not at the airport, Mayor Hartsfield dashed to the new control tower of Candler Field and asked to speak to the copilot. (The control tower had been in operation only since March of 1939.) Hartsfield pleaded for the pilot to detour over Stone Mountain to stall for time while Hartsfield obtained the presentation flowers.

This detour would also give Leigh and the other passengers a view of Augustus Lukeman's carving of General Robert E. Lee and President Jefferson Davis. The third carving (Lieutenant General "Stonewall" Jackson) on Stone Mountain was not complete at this time.

*The arrival of the stars.* After the impromptu air tour, Vivien Leigh and Laurence Olivier, Olivia de Havilland, David O. Selznick, Irene Selznick, and the other passengers landed in Atlanta. Their three-day whirlwind was about to begin.

The renowned figures received their gifts of welcome, and a cavalcade of cars took the celebrities and their luggage to their hotels. Vivien Leigh, Clark Gable, Carole Lombard, the Selznicks, and most of the top names from the film would be staying at the Georgian Terrace Hotel, 659 Peachtree, NE (corner of Peachtree and Ponce de Leon Avenue) in downtown Atlanta. The Georgian Terrace Hotel may have been where Margaret Mitchell delivered the original manuscript of *Gone with the Wind* to Harold Latham in its haphazard form. (Edwards, page 3).

Although not publicly announced, the engaged couple Vivien Leigh and Laurence Olivier were special guests at the Nunnally private residence in Atlanta. The room accommodations record for the Georgian Terrace Hotel, however, lists Olivia de Havilland in Rooms 904–905 of the Georgian Terrace Hotel and Laurence Olivier in Room 523 (Herb Bridges, *Gone with the Wind: The Three-Day Premiere,* page 67).

*Premiere gown of Margaret Mitchell.* Readers of the *Atlanta Constitution* on Wednesday, December 13, 1939, received a news scoop: a preview of Margaret Mitchell's premiere gown for the evening of Friday, December 15, 1939.

*Guests at Margaret Mitchell's home.* On the evening of December 13, 1939, Margaret Mitchell and her husband John Marsh invited some visitors to their home, Apartment 3 at the Della-Manta Apartments, 1268 Piedmont Avenue; their home was across the street from the Piedmont Driving Club at 1215 Piedmont Avenue. The Marshes' invitation list included Vivien Leigh, Olivia de Havilland, Laurence Olivier, David O. Selznick, Irene Selznick, Susan ("Sue") Myrick (*Macon Telegraph* reporter and the film's voice coach), Wilbur Kurtz (the film's historical consultant), and Kurtz's wife, Annie Kurtz (Edwards, pages 281–283).

*The second day of the Atlanta premiere.* Additional celebrities arrived in Atlanta on the festival's second day: December 14, 1939. Laura Hope Crews ("Aunt Pittypat" in the movie) arrived at the Union Station on Thursday, December 14, 1939, at 8:20 A.M. Also arriving was the well-known actress

Claudette Colbert, who did not appear in *Gone with the Wind* but who had come "to see the fun." Her escort was Cesar Romero.

*First major event of December 14, 1939.* The first major event of the day of December 14, 1939, was a ceremony at 10:15 A.M. at a historic gas light at Whitehall and Alabama Street. The central feature of the ceremony was a lamp that was first lit on Christmas Day 1855. It burns as a perpetual flame of the Confederacy and serves as a memorial to the traditions of the South.

William Kurtz, the historian for the film, presented a history of the lamp before it was re-lit at the ceremony. In attendance were such dignitaries

First lit in 1855, the Eternal Light of the Confederacy in Atlanta, Georgia, burns with a perpetual flame and commemorates Southern traditions. Visiting the site of the lamp was an important part of the premiere of *Gone with the Wind* in December 1939. (Atlanta News Agency, Chamblee, Georgia, and Colourpicture Publishers, Boston, Massachusetts) (Colourpicture is no longer in operation.)

as Mayor William Hartsfield and Mrs. T. J. Ripley, president of the Atlanta Chapter of the United Daughters of the Confederacy. This eternal light is a site that visitors still seek when touring Atlanta.

*Luncheon on December 14, 1939.* Another important part of the Atlanta events of December 1939 was a luncheon at Rich's Department Store. Brown notes that the honored guests were Macmillan executives and Margaret Mitchell. She makes no mention of the Southern Pulitzer Prize-Winning women: Margaret Mitchell, Marjorie Kinnan Rawlings, and Julia Mood Peterkin or of the Atlanta Women's Press Club (Brown, 205).

Walker observes that the luncheon was for Macmillan Publishing Company executives and for the three Pulitzer Prize winning Southern women. The book buyer at Rich's hosted the event, according to Walker (page 420).

Pyron notes that the Atlanta Women's Press Club hosted the luncheon. He observes that the three Southern women who had won the Pulitzer Prize were in attendance (page 377). Edwards does not give the sponsor, but she does note the three Pulitzer Prize-winning women — among others — who attended (page 376). Farr explains that the book buyer at Rich's Department Store arranged the luncheon as part of the 1939 Atlanta film premiere; the event at Rich's brought together Macmillan executives, Rawlings, Peterkin, and Margaret Mitchell (Farr, page 3).

The luncheon would be the first event Margaret Mitchell had agreed to attend at Rich's since the store had cancelled her book signing during the release week of *Gone with the Wind* in 1936. A calamity occurred at the December of 1939 luncheon. Margaret Mitchell missed her chair and fell to the floor (Walker, page 420).

*The arrival of Clark Gable.* The schedule for the Three-Day Atlanta Celebration listed the stars Clark Gable and his wife Carole Lombard as arriving on Thursday, December 14, 1939, at 3:30 P.M. on a Sky-Sleeper from Hollywood. Their American Airlines plane bore the label *MGM "Gone with the Wind" Special Flight to Atlanta Premiere.* Although their flight from Los Angeles to Candler Field actually took fifteen hours, which was longer than expected, they were still able to participate in some of the events of the day.

*The parade of December 14, 1939.* A parade consisting of thirty convertibles on Thursday, December 14, 1939, took Clark Gable, Carol Lombard, and some of the other stars from Candler Field to the Georgian Terrace. The crowds stood sometimes six deep at the curb for the nine-mile route. Estimates were that 650,000 people — many from out of town — attended; this was an impressive number

Marjorie Kinnan Rawlings (right) and Margaret Mitchell (left) — two Pulitzer Prize winners — meet during the Atlanta premiere of *Gone with the Wind* for a lunch at Rich's Department Store; Julia Peterkin, a third woman Pulitzer Prize winner, also was in attendance. (Courtesy of the Atlanta-Fulton Public Library System's Special Collections Department, Call No. 805, O'Neal photographer.)

because the entire population of the city of Atlanta was 300,000.

Bands, drill teams, and local celebrities welcomed the stars. The crowd sang "The Star-Spangled Banner," and pyrotechnical experts fired tributes. Mayor William B. Hartsfield, the governors of five Southern states, and orchestra leader Kay

Kyser greeted the crowd; Kyser would play for the Junior League Charity Ball that night.

*The Junior League Charity Ball.* The Junior League Charity Ball of December 14, 1939, was a major event of the three-day events.

*Governor Eurith Dickinson Rivers.* Eurith D. ("Ed") Rivers served as Georgia governor from 1936 to

This postcard shows the scene outside Loew's Grand Theatre on December 15, 1939, the night of the Atlanta premiere of *Gone with the Wind*. (Courtesy of the James G. Kenan Research Center at the Atlanta History Center.)

1940. Rivers (1895–1967) had proclaimed the day of the premiere showing of *Gone with the Wind* (Friday, December 15, 1939) as a state holiday.

*The Cyclorama and the Atlanta premiere.* On December 15, 1939, the City of Atlanta scheduled for dignitaries a special showing of Grant Park's 42 x 358 foot cycloramic painting: *Battle of Atlanta*.

About 150 guests received invitations. During the tour Clark Gable jokingly noted to George Simmons, the Atlanta City Parks director, and William B. Hartsfield, mayor, that what was missing was a likeness of Rhett Butler.

The Works Progress Administration in 1934–1936 had funded three artists—Weis Snell, Joseph Llorens, and Wilbur Kurtz—to design a diorama and to create some figures to serve as a foreground to the huge painting. After Gable's comments on his 1939 visit, Mayor Hartsfield asked Weis Snell to paint a face on one of the figures so that it resembled Clark Gable (Davis, Stephen).

*Atlanta Women's Press Club Tea.* The Atlanta Women's Press Club held a tea party on the after-noon of December 15, 1939. Clark Gable and Margaret Mitchell both attended (Edwards, pages 285–286).

*The world premiere.* The public gathered at the decorated Loew's Grand Theatre on Friday, December 15, 1939, to catch a glimpse of the stars and of Margaret Mitchell. When Clark Gable and his champagne-satin clad wife, Carole Lombard, arrived at the theater, they found eighteen thousand people gathered on the streets outside and two thousand more inside the theater. Nine searchlights with 4 million candlepower illuminated the façade of the front of the theater. Two medallions showing the faces of Clark Gable and Vivien Leigh reached a height of three stories outside the Loew's Grand.

Julian Boehm, the master of ceremonies of the event and an insurance agent by profession, called Clark to the microphone setup outside the Loew. Gable declined to speak to the crowd; he said instead that the evening belonged to Margaret Mitchell.

*Four honored guests at the Atlanta premiere.* Four

honored guests who attended the premiere the night of December 15, 1939, were four veterans of the Battle of Atlanta. These men, who were all in their nineties, were residents of the Georgia Confederate Soldiers' Home, which was a ten-minute ride from the Loew's Grand Theatre. Gable had invited the four and had made sure that they would all have seats near the front of the Loew's. The audience greeted the veterans with applause as they walked down the aisle to their seats.

Dressed proudly in their gray Army uniforms of the Confederate States of America, the veterans willingly posed for photographers, participated in newsreels, and spoke unhesitatingly over national radio. When Margaret Mitchell entered the theater a few minutes later dressed in her pink tulle, she paused to shake hands with and speak to each of the four before taking her seat. Mitchell was paying tribute to the evening's real heroes: the survivors of the Battle of Atlanta.

*Tributes made.* The recognition of and tributes to Margaret Mitchell, the Confederate veterans, the film, and the stars continued throughout the evening. The Confederate veterans watched intently and even leaned forward in their seats; to hear better at times, they cupped their ears in their hands.

Julian Boehm master-of-ceremonies, asked blessings on "our little Peggy Marsh." Mayor Hartsfield escorted the stars of the film to the front amidst thunderous applause. After a minute, he asked Margaret Mitchell to come to the microphone. Margaret gave a brief speech during which she appeared to be under tremendous strain.

At the end of the premiere, a reporter asked ninety-two-year-old Confederate veteran J. A. Skelton what he thought of his first movie. Skelton described it as the "gol-darndest thing" he had ever seen (Rosenburg, pages x-xi).

The eldest — and the most talkative — of the four Confederate veterans in attendance was ninety-five-year-old General James R. Jones. He claimed to be the "ladies' man" of the four and volunteered to kiss any woman if he had the opportunity. General Jones was able to boast after the evening that he had kissed the gold lamé–clad Vivien Leigh two times. His comment on the film was that indeed it looked just like the Civil War had looked. At the end of the film, one of the veterans stood up from his seat, raised his cane, and barked that the movie was what he had been trying to tell them all along. Peggy Mitchell had told it for him! (Rosenburg, pages x-xi).

*Conspicuous absences.* Conspicuously absent from the Atlanta Premiere of *Gone with the Wind* were three cast and crew members.

1. Hattie McDaniel ("Mammy"). She did, however, attend the Academy Awards Ceremony in February of 1940.

2. Victor Fleming, who had directed both *Gone with the Wind* (1939) and *Wizard of Oz* (1939).

3. Leslie Howard (who had played "Ashley Wilkes"). England had just entered World War II, and Howard had joined the cause ("The Making of *Gone with the Wind*, Part II").

*Margaret Mitchell's summations.* Margaret Mitchell summed up her impression of "the movie people" who attended the Atlanta premiere; she called them "charming" and noted that the Atlantans "who met them fell in love with them." She remarked in her March 26, 1940, letter to Lillian Harding, in Pasadena, California, that "we will never see the town so excited again."

Margaret described the crowds on the street as being even larger than those who had greeted President Franklin D. Roosevelt or Charles Lindbergh. She noted that everything was orderly. Mitchell described the crowds as "well-bred" people who did not try to mob the dignitaries. She was so proud of Atlanta that she "nearly burst" (Harwell, *Letters,* 298–299).

Other premieres in New York and Los Angeles followed. Margaret Mitchell did not attend these, however.

***See also*** addresses directly related to Margaret Mitchell; Ansley Hotel; Atlanta Cyclorama; *Atlanta Resurgens*; Battle of Atlanta; *Battle of Atlanta* painting; Baugh, Margaret; Biltmore Hotel; Colbert, Claudette; Cole, Lois; Confederate Soldiers' Home; Crews, Laura Hope; de Havilland, Olivia; Fleming, Victor; Gable, (William) Clark; Georgian Terrace Hotel; Hartsfield, William Berry; Howard, Leslie; Junior League Charity Ball; Kyser, Kay; Latham, Harold Strong; Leigh, Vivien; McDaniel, Hattie; Nunnally home; premiere gown for Margaret Mitchell; Rich's Department Store; Selznick, David O.

## Atlanta premiere of *Gone with the Wind,* Second Premiere

When Margaret Mitchell and John R. Marsh returned from their trip to Richmond, Virginia, and their visits with Ellen Glasgow, James Cabell, and the Dowdeys in October of 1940, they found Atlanta in the midst of preparations for the Second Premiere ("a ridiculous contradiction in terms") of *Gone with the Wind* (Edwards, pages 296–297).

Scheduled for December 15, 1937, one year after the original Atlanta premiere, the event would provide some glamour to a regular run of the film. Selznick intended the event for those who had not been able to attend the expensive, reserved-seating event of the previous year. Selznick helped handle the details.

High on his list of instructions was this directive: "*Don't* write publicity stories about Margaret Mitchell." Margaret and John were supportive of the event until Selznick announced the corset-lacing scene would be live on the stage with the film's two Academy Award actresses, Vivien Leigh and Hattie McDaniel. Margaret Mitchell threatened a lawsuit because she saw such a re-creation as impinging on her stage rights. McDaniel, however, declined to attend the event — probably because of the strict segregation laws in Atlanta.

British War Relief was the designated recipient for all profits from the event, which was not a gala affair as the 1939 event had been. When rain and wind delayed the arrival of Vivien Leigh's plane, Margaret Mitchell served as official press hostess. Surprisingly, however, Margaret felt not relief but a letdown that there were not more in attendance and that there was not more fanfare. Edwards suggested that Margaret seemed to believe that her fame and the furor over *Gone with the Wind* would last forever, and that the author was disappointed when they did not continue (Edwards, pages 297–298).

*See also* Leigh, Vivien; McDaniel, Hattie; Selznick, David O.

## Atlanta Race Riot of 1906

A massive civil disturbance September 22–24, 1906, resulted in white mobs killing dozens of African Americans, wounding scores of people, and inflicting extensive property damage. The causes of the riots were many.

A main contributor was the increased population growth of Atlanta; many people were crowded together. In 1900 the population of Atlanta was 89,000; ten years later it had surged to 150,000. The increase in African American residents had been particularly impressive. In 1880 there were 9,000 African Americans living in Atlanta; by 1900 there were 35,000 — almost four times as many.

Atlanta's huge population growth meant increased job competition, increased class distinctions, an amplified need for community services, greater class distinctions, and — in the segregated city — heightened difficulties in enforcing the "Jim Crow" laws separating the races.

During Reconstruction (1867–76) African American men had received the right to vote and had begun to advance economically, educationally, and socially. Many people from both groups resented this progress and blamed African Americans for the unrest.

In 1906 both Hoke Smith, former publisher of the *Atlanta Journal*, and Clark Howell, editor of the *Atlanta Constitution*, were gubernatorial candidates. Smith insisted that disenfranchisement of African Americans was necessary to "keep them in their place"; he used the paper to enforce his opinion. Howell, on the other hand, insisted that disenfranchisement was not necessary because the poll tax and the Democratic white primary were sufficient in controlling the black votes. Howell also insisted that Smith actually cooperated — a bad thing to him — with both African Americans and whites. Both Howell and Smith used their papers to advance their positions. Other newspapers entered the fray, and emotions began to boil.

White men and boys by the thousands gathered in downtown Atlanta. The crowd became a mob. The mob members surged throughout central Atlanta, assaulted hundreds of African Americans, attacked business establishments belonging to African Americans, forcefully entered some trolley cars, and beat African American men and women.

Although the militia responded, the mob did not immediately lessen its activities. In fact, before the attacks subsided, the mob violence had spread to Brownsville, Georgia. Many African Americans died in the riots. Although the exact number of deaths is unknown, estimates range between 25 and 40 (Pyron, page 231).

During the Atlanta Race Riot, a mob of 10,000 white men attacked two African American barbers and killed them. They went on to kill a third man and dragged the bodies to the Henry W. Grady Monument. They left the bodies there for all to see ("Public Art around the World: Henry W. Grady Monument").

The event was a horror to young Margaret. During the three days that the white mob controlled Atlanta, Margaret and Stephens were alone with their father in the house. Maybelle Mitchell was spending a month in a northern sanatorium. Pyron indicated that Eugene Mitchell left a record of the event. A neighbor, John Slaton, went to each house warning each family to prepare its guns and stand ready. Eugene was standing ready with his ax and an iron water key; Margaret reminded him of an antique sword that might serve better (Pyron, page 31).

Margaret's friend Elinor Hillyer remembered that twenty years later, Margaret still recalled her terror at hearing the firing of guns and pistols in the night. Margaret also recalled her happiness when she crawled from beneath the bed to see the militia moving up Jackson Street and camping on their lawn and street (Pyron, pages 31–32).

Although history books often omit this page in Atlanta's past, Margaret Mitchell remembered the violence from her childhood. Some reviewers of Mitchell's book *Gone with the Wind* suggest that the 1906 event was the source of the novel's scene in which Scarlett's second husband Frank Kennedy and their neighbors seek retaliation for Scarlett's harassment on her buggy ride home. Kennedy is shot through the head on this mission, according to the novel.

*See also* **Grady Statue; Jim Crow laws; Kennedy, Frank; Ku Klux Klan.**

### Atlanta Resurgens

The motto *Atlanta Resurgens* appeared on a banner as part of the decorations welcoming guests of the Junior League Charity Ball in the Atlanta Auditorium Armory on the evening of December 14, 1939. Loosely translated, the motto means "Atlanta's Rising Again." It suggests that Atlanta rebuilt itself after the Civil War and hints that the film *Gone with the Wind* depicts the rebirth of Atlanta.

### Atlanta Terminal Station

When Margaret Mitchell left Atlanta to go to Smith College, she most likely took a Southern Railway Pullman car from the Atlanta Terminal Station northward.

The Atlanta Terminal Station had opened in May of 1905 and served several main railways: the Southern Railway, Central of Georgia, and Atlanta and West Point. One of two main stations in Atlanta at the turn of the century, the station closed in June 1970 and was demolished in 1972.

Architect P. Thornton Marye designed the station and train shed to the Atlanta Terminal Company. The cost of the construction was $1.6 million. In 1925 wrecking balls found the train shed. Later, the company altered the towers of the terminal by removing the upper belfry sections of its twin towers. In 2011 the Richard B. Russell Federal Building occupied the site of the original Atlanta Terminal Station ("Atlanta Terminal Station").

### Atlanta Women's Press Club

Margaret Mitchell was not extremely active socially after the publication of *Gone with the Wind* (1936). The Atlanta Women's Press Club was, according to Mitchell (1939), the only organization that she joined after 1936. In a letter to Macmillan publisher George Brett, Jr., she spoke fondly of the club, which she had joined at its organization. "The only organization I have joined in the last three years is the Atlanta Women's Press Club. The members are all active newspaper women. I am the only non-working member, and I am very proud of my membership, for most of the girls are old

friends of mine and I am still happy that they are still willing to accept me as one of them — as Peggy Mitchell, newspaper woman, rather than Margaret Mitchell, author. In addition, I am under great obligations to them, for they have played an important part in making life endurable for me these past three years. Their consideration for me in their newspaper work has eased my burden in a way that would be hard to describe. Instead of making my life more difficult, as some newspaper people might have done, they have done everything possible to shield me from unpleasantness, and I am under obligation to them that I can never repay" (Harwell, *Letters,* pages 258, 276).

Mitchell refused an invitation from Macmillan publisher George Brett, Jr., to participate in an event to honor her during the Atlanta premiere of *Gone with the Wind* (December 13–15, 1939). She stated that the only event she had agreed to attend during the premiere would be the film itself and a tea sponsored by the Atlanta Women's Press Club party. Later, however, Mitchell did agree to attend a luncheon during the December 1939 premiere of *Gone with the Wind* at Rich's Department Store.

*See also* **Atlanta premiere of *Gone with the Wind* (the film).**

### Atlanta Women's Press Club Party and George Brett, Jr.

In a letter to George Brett, Jr., on May 12, 1939, Margaret Mitchell explained that she planned to accept an invitation from the Atlanta Women's Press Club for a party on the afternoon of December 15, 1939; she mentioned the organization as one whose invitation she could not refuse because of her loyalty to it and because of their consideration of her.

### Atlanta Women's Press Club Tea Party

On Friday, December 15, 1939, Margaret Mitchell attended a tea party hosted by the Atlanta Women's Press Club in the lounge of the Piedmont Driving Club. The Driving Club was just across the street from Apartment #3 at 1268 Piedmont Avenue, where Margaret and John lived. To the event, Margaret wore a black dress and a small black hat with two bows.

Clark Gable, one of the guests, took Margaret Mitchell aside. The two talked for a few minutes in an anteroom. Their meeting made the front page of the Saturday, December 16, 1939, edition of *The Atlanta Constitution.* When reporters asked Gable what he thought of Margaret Mitchell, he replied, "She's the most fascinating woman I've ever met."

Clark Gable and Margaret Mitchell meet at the Atlanta Women's Press Club tea party at the Piedmont Driving Club on Friday, December 15, 1939. The photograph made the front page of the Saturday *Atlanta Constitution*. (Courtesy of the Atlanta-Fulton Public Library System's Special Collections Department, Call No. 805, O'Neal photographer.)

### The Atlantan

The publication that the inmates at the Atlanta Federal Prison produced. Margaret Mitchell sponsored a contest for the best article published.

*See also* Atlanta Federal Prison/Penitentiary.

### Authentic History of the Ku Klux Klan, 1865–1877

Susan Lawrence Davis was the author of the volume *Authentic History of the Ku Klux Klan, 1865–* *1877*, published in 1924. Davis gives credit for much of the information to members of the Klan, including her father, Colonel Lawrence Ripley Davis (page 3).

In 1937, Davis sued Macmillan Publishing Company for allegedly plagiarizing her book when it published *Gone with the Wind*. The suit sought $6.5 billion but was dismissed.

In the beginning of the volume Davis recalls that in her childhood the Ku Klux Klan gave her a sense of protection (page 4). Davis admits using her father's experiences with the Klan as a primary basis for the book. Particularly for these reasons, Freemasonry observes that Davis omits critical analysis from her volume (http://freemasonry.bcy.ca/antimasonry/davis_sl.html).

*The Boston Transcript* indicates that she writes with a "prejudiced pen" (April 19, 1924, page 5 in Knight and James, page 156). One southern newspaper, *The Greensboro* (NC) *Daily News*, reports that in "style, content, knowledge, and taste the book is hopelessly bad" (June 29, 1924, page 2, in Knight and James, page 156). *The Literary Review* describes the book as "highly sentimentalized and idealized" and "not especially well written." The article in *The Literary Review* suggests that the book will appeal chiefly to the readers who hold the same views as Davis (April 19, 1924, page 694, in Knight and James, page 156). *Outlook* reports that one might consult the book with caution for information, but that Davis seems to have written the work as an "impartial historian" (136: 653, April 16, 1924, in Knight and James, page 156).

### autographing *Gone with the Wind*

On February 8, 1937, Margaret Mitchell wrote to Herschel Brickell, reporter with the *New York Post*, to inform him of her current policy on autographing books—just in case anyone should ask him. Margaret indicated that she would not be autographing books for others—even her "kin."

Mitchell explained that her book had sold one million copies by January of 1937. Requests for autographed copies had exceeded a hundred thousand requests (Harwell, *Letters*, 226).

Just after Macmillan published her books Mitchell had answered all of her fan letters personally. On slow days she began receiving 50 letters a day; she might receive 200 letters on her busier days. For a while, Mitchell even signed and returned each book—often including those books with no return postage—that had been mailed to her for autographing. She avoided form letters and attempted to respond to all the letters in the mail bags too heavy for her to lift; she followed the rules of what she had learned about Southern "ladyhood" (Pyron, page 344) and courtesy. Finally the pressure became too much, and she left for a holiday.

*See also* Adams, J. Donald; Gainesville, Georgia.

### automobiles

It was several years after their marriage before John R. Marsh and Margaret Mitchell relented and purchased an automobile. Margaret Mitchell had to relearn how to drive after the purchase because it had been ten years since she had driven.

The purchase came after Margaret's Grandmother Stephens died (February 17, 1934) and left her granddaughter Margaret a small inheritance. In April Margaret bought a green Chevrolet. The couple had to conquer their fear of automobiles to venture out in their vehicle (Edwards, page 159).

The green car that the couple purchased was evidently not a new vehicle; as in many other things, they seemed to pursue the most economical approach. On July 3, 1936, in a letter to Lois Cole, Margaret Mitchell remarked that her friends were "wondering why in hell I persist in driving a 1929 model car and wearing four year old cotton dresses and fifty cent stockings and calling me an old Hetty Green to my face" (Pyron, page 354).

### Avon Books

In 1973 Macmillan Publishing Company relinquished its paperback rights to Avon Books. These soft cover editions increased revenue for the estate of Margaret Mitchell.

In 1976, the film *Gone with the Wind* appeared on television for the first time. Over two nights, NBC aired the film in the fall. The largest audience (33,890,000) ever to watch a single television broadcast—until that time—viewed the first installment on November 7, 1976. The following night 33,750,000 turned on the program; this was the second largest audience ever to view a single program in television history. Avon books printed its paperback *Gone with the Wind* three times as a result of the interest generated through the television showings.

### Baldwin, Faith

Margaret Mitchell refused to write her own biographical articles, and yet she did not usually want to submit to the interviews of strangers. She was deluged with writers wanting to interview her for biographical articles; these would-be biographers approached her on the street, phoned their home day and night, and showed up unannounced at her door at all hours. John Marsh began trying to control this intolerable situation; he decided to select his own biographers.

Marsh asked the popular writer Faith Baldwin (1893–1978) to prepare a biographical article on his wife. Baldwin, who eventually would publish between 85 and 100 novels, was a familiar name also for readers of women's magazines; her books were often popular serials in six installments in these periodicals. An article by Baldwin would hopefully attract attention and respect.

Marsh suggested a piece on Mitchell's home life

for the national women's journal *Pictorial Review*. Baldwin and Mabel Search, an editor with *Pictorial Review*, became the first important guests to visit John Marsh and Margaret Mitchell in their newly-decorated home in the Russell Apartment Building.

Baldwin titled her article "The Woman Who Wrote *Gone with the Wind*: An Exclusive and Authentic Interview." Her work appeared in the March 1937 issue of *Pictorial Review* shortly after Mitchell's acceptance of the American Booksellers Association's 1937 National Book Award. Baldwin's readers and the Marshes commented favorably on the article (Edwards, pages 127, 231–32, 238, 262, 280, 336).

## Ball, Lamar Q.

After the 1936 publication of *Gone with the Wind*, Margaret Mitchell and John R. Marsh submitted to the interview that they had requested from Lamar Q. Ball of the *Atlanta Constitution*. The couple had known Ball for years, and they both felt comfortable talking with him. The resulting article appeared as five installments in November 1936 issues of the *Atlanta Constitution* (Walker, pages 331–332).

Ball was not, however, able to locate John R. Marsh and Margaret Mitchell on the night of May 3, 1937, when he learned of the announcement of the 1936 novel *Gone with the Wind* as the new Pulitzer Prize winner. Margaret Mitchell, the Macmillan representative Harold Latham, her brother Stephens and his wife, and John R. Marsh were attending a performance and choir practice of Bessie Jordan at the Friendship Missionary Baptist Church in Atlanta (Edwards, page 268).

Margaret wrote to Herschel Brickell on May 9, 1937, after receiving news that she had won the Pulitzer Prize. She didn't know which impressed her more, winning the Pulitzer Prize or having City Editor Lamar Q. Ball leave his desk (Harwell, *Letters*, page 143).

*See also* Friendship Baptist Church; Pulitzer Prize; Pulitzer Prize novel for 1937 and Margaret Mitchell's response.

## Barois, Denis

Denis Barois was a French Air Force pilot during World War II. One of his stations in mid–1944 was in southwest Georgia, where he met Margaret Mitchell. They continued to exchange letters and trinkets until her death. In 2009 he spoke out about the help she had given to Vimoutiers, France ("Margaret Mitchell Helped French Town after WWII").

*See also* Vimoutiers, France.

## Battle of Atlanta

In what is now northeast Atlanta, one of the bloodiest battles of the Civil War battle transpired on July 22, 1864. The battle line extended for more than four miles. At the end of eight hours of continuous fighting there were more than 12,000 casualties: 8,499 Confederates and 3,641 Union troops. The South lost General W.H.T. Walker. Union forces lost General James McPherson.

Mitchell remembered talking with many veterans of the Battle of Atlanta. She also had visited the Atlanta Cyclorama often and had studied the painting of *The Battle of Atlanta*. All of this personal "research" figured prominently into her novel *Gone with the Wind*.

*See also* Civil War in Margaret Mitchell's education; McPherson, James Birdseye.

## *Battle of Atlanta* painting

This painting from the American Panorama Company is currently housed in the Atlanta Cyclorama.

*Commissioning.* General John "Blackjack" Logan, who fought with the Union Army in the Battle of Atlanta during the Civil War, commissioned the cycloramic painting *The Battle of Atlanta*. The painting — which was originally 60 feet long by 360 feet high — is accurate, but it presents a Union perspective. For instance, the viewer can identify General Sherman, but General Hood cannot be seen.

Logan hoped to use the painting to advance his political standing because he aspired to the office of vice president of the United States. Margaret Mitchell wrote an article about the painting for the *Atlanta Journal*.

*History.* The American Panorama Company in Milwaukee, Wisconsin, received commissions to produce two Civil War cycloramas — *The Battle of Missionary Ridge* (commissioned for the years 1883–84) and *The Battle of Atlanta* (commissioned for the years 1885–1886). The American Panorama Company also took commissions for a series of paintings on biblical themes.

William Wehner had found artists in Europe with the skills necessary to produce these huge paintings. For the battle scenes, he selected German artists who had experience with cycloramas (and preferably with some battle experience) and brought them to Milwaukee.

Supervising the artists were F. W. Heine and August Lohr. A veteran of the Prussian army, Heine took charge of the master work. Lohr supervised the landscape. There were also three main landscape painters, five main figure painters, and two primary animal painters.

Heine, Lohr, and several other artists came to

Atlanta in 1885 to study the location of the Battle of Atlanta. The artists set up a 40-foot wooden tower at the intersection of the Georgia Railroad and Moreland Avenue. They made sketches of many details and correlated existing landmarks with reports and military maps. As they worked atop the tower, the artists had visits from veterans—both Union and Confederate—and from residents who had information to contribute. A translator helped the artists to understand the helpful recollections that these trustworthy sources were sharing; after all, they were present at the time.

The technical advisor to these German artists was Theodore Davis, who had been a staff artist with *Harper's Weekly* during the Civil War and had witnessed and sketched many battles—including the Battle of Atlanta. His experiences and knowledge contributed significantly to *The Battle of Atlanta*, particularly to the authenticity of both the landscape and the military action.

General John A. ("Blackjack") Logan, who had commissioned the work, died in 1886. He probably never saw the completed painting, originally called *Logan's Great Battle*, that he had commissioned.

In 1887 in Detroit, William Wehner exhibited the painting called *Logan's Great Battle*. A tour—ending in 1888 in Indianapolis, Indiana—followed (*The Battle of Atlanta*).

*Features.* The painting depicts some actual events during the Battle of Atlanta. After the death of General James McPherson during the planning of the battle, General John "Blackjack" Logan had received the temporary appointment to command the Army of Tennessee. About 4:30 P.M. General Logan led a charge against Confederate forces. The painting that Logan commissioned includes some significant details, including the depiction of the heated battle near the Troup-Hurt House; a representation of Old Abe, the bald eagle mascot of a Union regiment; and an ambulance carrying Manning Force, who had been wounded in the face, to a field hospital.

*Ownership.* Wehner and his artists initially stored the painting *The Battle of Atlanta* and some of the art equipment in the Fred Koch house on Leggett's Hill, a location that had figured into the battle. The house was owned by the Miller family.

Because of his legal problems, however, Wehner had to surrender *Logan's Great Battle* to the Miller heirs in 1888. In 1890 the Millers sold *The Battle of Atlanta* to Paul Atkinson of Madison, Georgia.

Atkinson owned also the painting *The Storming of Missionary Ridge and Battle Above the Clouds*, the first cycloramic painting produced by the Wechler Company. The *Missionary Ridge* painting was on display in Chattanooga, Tennessee; Atkinson placed it on display in Atlanta for a while. In 1892 he shipped *The Storming of Missionary Ridge and the Battle Above the Clouds* to Nashville; a tornado subsequently destroyed the painting.

In 1892 Atkinson housed *The Battle of Atlanta* in the Edgewood Avenue facility where *The Storming of Missionary Ridge and the Battle Above the Clouds* had been sheltered. Atkinson sold *The Battle of Atlanta* to H. H. Harrison of Florida. Harrison intended to exhibit the work at the World's Columbian exposition in Chicago. He found, however, that the cost of building an appropriate structure in Chicago was prohibitive; he decided he could not show the work. The painting remained in Atlanta.

Eight inches of snow in January 18, 1893, caved in the roof of the wooden structure housing *The Battle of Atlanta*. Ernest Woodruff bought the damaged painting in 1893 and sold it at auction to George Valentine Gress and Charles Northen. The new owners asked the city to provide housing for the painting in one of the city's parks.

*Housing and maintaining the painting.* Atlanta agreed to house *The Battle of Atlanta* in Grant Park.

The City of Atlanta erected a frame building in Grant Park. It was in this wooden building—near the animals that George Valentine Gress had purchased (1889) from a bankrupt circus, that he would give to the city, and that would later form the basis of the Atlanta Zoo—that Margaret Mitchell had her first view of *The Battle of Atlanta*. The exhibit heightened Margaret's interest in and understanding of the Civil War. Margaret visited the Cyclorama in the wooden building many times in her youth. She never tired of locating the eagle-mascot "Old Abe" in the painting, identifying the Troup-Hurt House, or finding Manning Force, who was being carried to a field hospital.

Other Atlantans, too, were interested in the painting. During the first week of its operation, rumors were that the Atlanta Cyclorama took in $1000 in admissions of 10 cents each—and the veterans entered free.

Charles W. Hubner, the exhibition's first lecturer and a Confederate veteran, added a Southern perspective to the pictured battle. He had served as chief of General Joseph E. Johnston's—later General John B. Hood's—telegraph corps during the war. With his unique way of expressing himself, this poet, published author, and historian was an asset in bolstering attendance.

Grant Park was across the street from 1268 Piedmont Avenue and the Della-Manta Apartments, where John R. Marsh and Margaret Mitchell would reside in Apartment #3 (1939–1949). The Piedmont Driving Club, where Margaret Mitchell and

John Marsh later would enjoy many meals, would also locate in the park at a later time.

An October 1, 1921, dedication ceremony marked the opening of the newly constructed Atlanta Cyclorama Building, which still exhibits the oil painting *The Battle of Atlanta*. This new, neoclassical building was several hundred feet northeast of the wooden building site that Mitchell visited in her childhood. Designed by Atlanta architect John Francis Downing, the 1921 granite and marble structure was fireproof—a desirable feature to protect the painting and to ease the fears of those who remembered the Great Fire in Atlanta in 1917.

The addition of a diorama in 1936 funded by the federal government was a significant improvement to the Atlanta Cyclorama. Through the Works Progress Administration (WPA), an added foreground formed a seamless addition to the painting. Figures and environmental features helped make the audience feel even more a part of the cycloramic experience. The three artists—Weis Snell, Joseph Llorens, and Wilbur Kurtz—designed the diorama and created the figures and items to serve as a foreground to the huge painting ("Atlanta Cyclorama and Civil War Museum").

Additions to the Atlanta Cyclorama seemed important after Clark Gable viewed the painting *The Battle of Atlanta* and the diorama on the afternoon of December 14, 1939, during the Atlanta Premiere of *Gone with the Wind*. Gable mentioned that the only thing missing was his likeness. Mayor William B. Hartsfield asked Weis Snell, one of the original WPA artists who constructed the diorama, to paint a face resembling Clark Gable on one of the figures in the three-dimensional foreground (Davis, Stephen; "Atlanta Cyclorama and Civil War Museum").

Crucial repairs at the Atlanta Cyclorama were mandatory in 1967 after a thunderstorm damaged both the building and the painting. The need for serious repairs and extended refurbishments of the 1921 Atlanta Cyclorama Building and its painting became evident in 1979. The Cyclorama shut down until 1982 so workers could update the museum and the theater and restore the painting. Gustav Berger repaired and re-hung *The Battle of Atlanta*. When the Atlanta Cyclorama reopened in 1982, visitors found a dynamic new program, surround sound and theater lighting; their seating was now tiered and rotating. The cost of this repair and renovation was $14 million.

Continued renovation and restoration of the Atlanta Cyclorama and *The Battle of Atlanta* remains critical. The need for constant maintenance of the historic facility and of the cycloramic painting is even more evident when one considers that the painting was once 60 feet high by 360 feet long cur-

rently measures only 42 feet high by 358 feet long. Restoration of the painting is essential to preserve the priceless object—now the largest oil painting in the world ("Atlanta Cyclorama and Civil War Museum").

***See also*** **Atlanta Cyclorama; Atlanta premiere of *Gone with the Wind*; Battle of Atlanta; Davis, Theodore; Grant Park; Kurtz, Wilbur G.; Llorens, Joseph; Logan, John; Snell, Weis C.**

## Baugh, Margaret Eugenia (1899–1967)

On the day after Christmas of 1935, Margaret Baugh began working part-time as a secretary for Margaret Mitchell. Her goal was to help Mitchell in her preparation of a revised manuscript and to facilitate the shipment of the final copy to Macmillan Publishing Company.

John Marsh and Margaret Mitchell had become acquainted with Baugh in 1934 when Macmillan had reopened its offices in Atlanta. About a year later, Baugh was working as Mitchell's full-time personal secretary. Baugh remained with the couple until their deaths.

*Mitchell provides for Baugh in her will.* Margaret Mitchell wrote her will on November 28, 1948 and provided an annuity for Margaret Eugenia Baugh: "The first call on my Estate shall be the payment to Margaret Eugenia Baugh, my secretary, of the sum to pay up the annuity I am buying for her. If she prefers to have the annuity paid up at one I want this done. If she prefers that my Executors pay it up, so much a year, as I am not doing, and as she prefers at present, then pay it up by the year. I want her wishes followed in this matter. In addition to the annuity, I want Margaret Baugh to receive $5000 (five thousand dollars) from my Estate in cash, stocks, bonds, or government Bonds, as she prefers" (Will of Margaret Mitchell, November 21, 1948).

Margaret's brother Stephens Mitchell hired Baugh to help him with the business concerns relating to *Gone with the Wind* after the death of Margaret Mitchell and John R. Marsh. Baugh remained fiercely loyal to Margaret Mitchell and the way that Margaret handled things. Baugh called herself "the nursemaid of the prodigy" (Brown and Wiley, pages 293–294).

Despite developing throat cancer, Baugh remained on the job. She spent the last days of her life still unmarried and serving as business manager of *Gone with the Wind*. She died at the age of sixty-eight (Brown and Wiley, page 294).

## Baxter, Madeleine "Red"

Madeleine Baxter and Margaret Mitchell formed a lengthy friendship beginning with her time at Ten Henshaw. Madeleine was a roommate of Margaret Mitchell for a while. Because of her red hair, Madeleine soon had the nickname of "Red" (Edwards, page 52). "Red" recalled that Margaret like to recite poetry. Clifford Henry had fed this interest in poetry that Margaret had acquired (Edwards, page 55). Madeleine Baxter attended the ceremonies at Smith College in 1939 when Margaret Mitchell received an honorary degree.

*Before Scarlett: Childhood Writings of Margaret Mitchell* (2000). Hillstreet Press published these previously unpublished, for the most part, writings of a young Margaret Mitchell. Discovered by Wailes Thomas and Jane Eskridge and edited by Eskridge, these writings—along with a Preface, Foreword, and Introduction by Mary Rose Taylor—comprise *Before Scarlett: Childhood Writings of Margaret Mitchell* (2000).

The story of how Wailes Thomas came to be in possession of these works involves his family lineage. Other members of the family explain this lineage further.

***See also*** **Eskridge, Jane; Mitchell, Alexander Stephens; Mitchell, Caroline Louise Reynolds; Taylor, Mary Rose; Thomas, Wailes.**

## Belgium, sales of *Gone with the Wind* *see* foreign copyrights/translations and fair trade laws

## Benét, Stephen Vincent (1898–1943)

When Margaret was bedfast in 1926 with an ankle injury, she read voraciously. One of her favorite writers was novelist and Pulitzer Prize winning poet Stephen Vincent Benét. Margaret wrote to Frances Marsh in 1928 and told her about some of her readings. She mentioned having heard *John Brown's Body* read aloud two times and of reading it herself two other times; the long narrative poem won the Pulitzer Prize in 1929. Benét earned a posthumous (1944) Pulitzer for *Western Star*.

Benét was an admirer of *Gone with the Wind*. His book review of the novel in *Saturday Review* gave Margaret Mitchell both excitement and pleasure. She particularly liked the fact that he considered her *Gone with the Wind* to be realistic (Harwell, *Gone with the Wind as Book and Film*, pages 19–21).

## Bengal, sales of *Gone with the Wind* *see* foreign copyrights/translations and fair trade laws

## Berne Convention Agreement for the Protection of Literary and Artistic Works (1886)

The Berne Convention for the Protection of Literary and Artistic Works received its name because the conference convened in Berne, Switzerland, in 1886. The Berne Convention Agreement was originally among forty nations and protected both literary and artistic copyrights ("International Copyright Law").

Margaret Mitchell and John R. Marsh were horrified to find that the United States—a young nation at the time of the agreement—had not deemed it necessary to enter into the pact. The United States could access foreign material without paying a royalty; the works of American writers might be pirated in other countries without compensation because the United States was not a member of the Berne Convention Agreement. Mark Twain and others had attempted to change this fact (Walker, pages 371–372).

Margaret Mitchell's father had taught her to respect the work of others. She had received a stern lecture from her parents on copyright infringement after she acted in and produced a play based on Thomas Dixon's *The Traitor* without giving him credit. Margaret Mitchell and John R. Marsh determined to protect the copyright of *Gone with the Wind*.

## Berry, Bessie *see* Jordan, Bessie Berry

## "Biggest Day in Jonesboro History"

Jonesboro, Georgia, staged its own re-enactment event to precede the three-day Atlanta festivities on December 11, 1939, before the premiere of *Gone with the Wind*. The *Atlanta Constitution* and the Jonesboro Chapter of the United Daughters of the Confederacy staged the flight of Scarlett, Melanie, Wade Hampton, Prissy, and the newborn Beau the night of the burning of the munitions site. The re-enactment of Scarlett's ride would begin with the four performers and a doll at the old Union Station in Atlanta; it would end at the train station in Jonesboro. The characters would make their "escape" in a creaky, horse-drawn wagon, with a cow tied to the back.

Jonesboro Mayor Hugh Dickson and other civic leaders had arranged publicity for the re-enactment. They announced the staged event was a success upon the arrival of the wagon and called it "the biggest day in Jonesboro history" ("City of Jonesboro").

## Biltmore Hotel

The Biltmore Hotel on Peachtree Street at Broad served some important roles in Atlanta history and in the life of Margaret Mitchell.

WSB (for "Welcome South, Brother") was the first radio station in the South. WSB began sending its broadcasts from the Biltmore Hotel in 1929.

Margaret Mitchell sits before the WSB microphone at the Biltmore Hotel in May of 1937. She speaks about winning the Pulitzer Prize for *Gone with the Wind*. (Courtesy of the Atlanta-Fulton Public Library System's Special Collections Department, Photograph #797.)

Margaret Mitchell spoke on WSB Radio many times before her 1949 death.

The address of the Biltmore Hotel is 817 Peachtree Street. Lois Cole, associate editor of Macmillan Publishing Company, stated that Margaret Mitchell took the unorganized envelopes holding the chapters of her novel to Macmillan's Harold Latham in the lobby of the Biltmore Hotel (Brown, page 16). Other accounts name other locations.

*See also* Ansley Hotel; Atlanta addresses related directly to Margaret Mitchell; Baugh, Margaret; Cole, Lois; Georgian Terrace Hotel; Latham, Harold Strong; Rich's Department Store.

## Biographical articles on Margaret Mitchell (selected)

When the lives of John Marsh and Margaret Mitchell seemed overtaken by the media and by the public, John Marsh decided to try to control the situation. He would select the writers who would interview them; these hand-picked writers would prepare the articles that could shape the image of Margaret Mitchell. Margaret herself re-

fused to write autobiographical articles or to submit to interviews from others who were interested in writing about her life.

Marsh asked Medora Field Perkerson to write a story for the *Atlanta Journal Sunday Magazine*; Medora had been a friend and colleague of Margaret. He hoped Perkerson — the wife of Angus Perkerson, the founder and the editor of the *Sunday Magazine* — could squelch some of the vicious rumors. Medora Perkerson, who had worked with Margaret when she was a reporter for the *Atlanta Journal Sunday Magazine*, had worked in newspapers for years and was also a writer of mystery novels.

John Marsh approached Edwin Granberry of the *New York Sun* also to write an article for *Collier's*, a weekly magazine from 1888 to 1957; Granberry had written a review of *Gone with the Wind* that had pleased John. Marsh himself reviewed Granberry's article several times before its publication.

Marsh also approached Faith Baldwin, a well-known novelist of the time. Baldwin complied with Marsh's request to prepare a biographical article on Margaret Mitchell.

Marsh unhesitatingly contacted Lamar Q. Ball, writer of the *Atlanta Constitution*, about writing a biographical article about his wife. Marsh knew that Ball — like Medora Field Perkerson and Faith Baldwin — was always professional and that Margaret Mitchell would not be hesitant about talking with them.

*See also* Baldwin, Faith; Granberry, Edwin; Perkerson, Medora Field.

## Birdwell, Russell

Russell Birdwell was the publicity manager for Selznick Pictures. Although most members of Selznick's staff (especially Sidney Howard and Kay Brown) were accepting of Margaret Mitchell's "hands-off" attitude toward the filming of *Gone with the Wind*, Russell did not seem as obliging. He sent her a press release to review; it stated that Margaret was going to help with selecting Scarlett and that she hoped to find a Southern young woman for the part; Birdwell's release also indicated that Margaret planned to give a huge party for Sidney Howard when he came to discuss the screenplay with her.

Promptly, Margaret sent Birdwell a telegram that John helped her word; she objected strongly to the release and reiterated that she would not be participating in the making of the film. Birdwell went ahead and published the release without changes.

In addition to the telegram, Margaret also sent a letter to Birdwell on November 21, 1936. In it, she stated that she that she would show Stone Mountain to Kay Brown and feed her fried chicken, but she was leaving the details of the film up to Kay and to Selznick Pictures. Margaret Mitchell was angry with Birdwell, as her letters to him and to others indicated (Walker, pages 390–391, 410, 422).

Later, Susan ("Sue") Myrick, too, expressed anger with Russell. He had kept her newspaper column about the filming of *Gone with the Wind* for four days and had "edited the hell out of it" (Harwell, *White Columns in Hollywood,* pages 166–167, as cited by Walker, page 410). Myrick went on to offer her description of Birdwell. "Well, Birdwell is the revolving bastard if there ever was one. (The Revolving Bastard, in case you don't know, is a bastard any way you turn him.)" (Harwell, *White Columns in Hollywood,* pages 166–167, as cited by Walker, page 410). Walker acknowledges, however, Russell Birdwell's effective role in the 1939 Atlanta premiere of the film *Gone with the Wind*: "Howard Dietz and Howard Strickland, publicists from MGM, arrived first to help Selznick's publicity manager Russell Birdwell, convert Atlanta into one huge, live advertisement for *Gone with the Wind*" (Walker, page 422).

*See also* Brown, Katharine; Myrick, Susan.

## Blowing Rock Writers' Conference

On July 8, 1936, Margaret wrote a letter to Edwin Granberry to thank him for his positive assessment of her novel in his review in the *New York Evening Sun.* In the course of the letter, she told him of her problems in dealing with the calls, the letters, and the visits that were consuming her life since the novel's publication. Realizing the stress that Margaret was experiencing, Granberry invited her to a writers' conference in Blowing Rock, North Carolina. Mitchell accepted the invitation.

The week following her trip to Gainesville, Georgia, Margaret took a train from Atlanta to Hickory, North Carolina. From Hickory, she continued to Blowing Rock for the conference. She arrived on July 13, 1936, and stayed at the Green Park Inn (Pyron, pages 355–356).

This was not Margaret's first visit to the mountains of North Carolina. She and her first husband—Berrien Kinnard Upshaw—had honeymooned at the Grove Park Inn in Asheville, North Carolina.

*See also* Granberry, Edwin; Grove Park Inn.

## Boehm, Julian

Boehm was an insurance agent and the master of ceremonies for the evening of December 15, 1939, at the Atlanta premiere of *Gone with the Wind.* In his presentation, he asked blessings on "our little Peggy Marsh."

*See also* Atlanta premiere of *Gone with the Wind.*

**Bohnenberger Medal** *see* **Carl Bohnenberger Memorial Medal.**

## boll weevil

Similar to the Reconstruction era after the Civil War, Atlanta was experiencing "hard times" during the 1920s, but for a different reason: "The boll weevil had played economic havoc in destroying cotton crops all over the South and as a result, hundreds of banks closed. There was little work for a real-estate law firm, and Eugene Mitchell's income was greatly diminished" (Walker, page 57).

## Book-of-the-Month Club

George Brett of Macmillan Company received a letter on April 15, 1936, from the Book-of-the-Month Club; the letter reported that the club would like to adopt *Gone with the Wind* as its selection for July, August, or September of 1936. The club offered to pay $10,000 for exclusive rights for 50,000 copies; Margaret would receive $5,000.

Margaret immediately took the news to her father. Eugene Mitchell did not encourage his daughter. He told her that it seemed strange that the organization would choose her book. When John returned home, he found his wife in despair. He told her point blank that she was wrong to worry. The notice of the acceptance of *Gone with the Wind* by the Book-of-the-Month Club hit the media with much fanfare.

## Borglum, Gutzon (March 25, 1867–March 6, 1941)

John Gutzon de la Mothe Borglum was an American sculptor best known for his carvings on Mount Rushmore (Keystone, South Dakota) and the one he began on Stone Mountain in Atlanta, Georgia. One of his early, best-known carvings was a gargantuan head of President Abraham Lincoln on a six-ton marble block; this likeness is in the Capitol Rotunda.

Helen Plane with the United Daughters of the Confederacy talked with Borglum in 1916 about a carving of Robert E. Lee on the side of Stone Mountain. Funding and World War I, however, delayed the project.

Borglum finally began the face of Robert E. Lee in 1923 and finished it in 1924. He designed also the 1925 United States commemorative half dollar to memorialize the Stone Mountain Project.

The Stone Mountain Confederate Memorial Association was overseeing the Stone Mountain Project that Borglum had begun. This association cancelled its contract with Borglum after a difficult working situation. In 1925 Augustus Lukeman resumed the Stone Mountain project; it was Augustus Lukeman's unfinished carving that the guests to the Atlanta premiere of *Gone with the Wind* saw in December of 1939.

Borglum received a commission (1927) from South Dakota to prepare a 60-foot monument of George Washington, Abraham Lincoln, Thomas Jefferson, and Theodore Roosevelt on the face of Mount Rushmore. In 1929 the federal government began financing the Mount Rushmore Monument as a national project. Borglum unveiled Washington's head in 1930, Jefferson's in 1936, Lincoln's in 1937, and Roosevelt's in 1939.

The year 1941 marked the completion of the Mount Rushmore project and the death of Borglum from surgery complications. Lincoln Borglum — Gutzon Borglum's son — was able to complete the last details of the Mount Rushmore National Monument for his father.

*See also* Altanta premiere of *Gone with the Wind.*

*Borglum's "Swing" and Margaret Mitchell.* The whole of Atlanta seemed intrigued with the Stone Mountain Memorial that Gutzon Borglum was designing. For a "good story," Margaret Mitchell agreed to be strapped into a boatswain's chair designed by Captain J. G. Tucker (Gutzon Borglum's first assistant) and then "shoved" out the window on the top floor of a fifteen-story Atlanta building; in this manner she would be able to simulate what the workers on the side of the mountain would experience as they prepared the carving. The young reporter could then write about the experience for the readers of the *Atlanta Journal.*

Titled "Hanging over Atlanta in Borglum's Swing," Mitchell's article appeared in print on May 5, 1923. She described graphically in the article how she donned a pair of size 40 overalls and felt the "dizzy whirl" as she left the ground. Margaret admitted feeling both terror and nausea during the experience. During the harrowing moments as she dangled between heaven and earth, the photographer kept telling her to smile! Mitchell survived the escapade and passed the muster of her fellow workers (Allen, pages 234–238).

Her resulting article describes the ordeal of being strapped in a swing "about the size of the palm, of your hand" and "being shoved out a window on the top floor of a very high building which had been selected as an imitation Stone Mountain." Peggy Mitchell decided that someone else would have to do the carving on Stone Mountain (Allen, pages 234–235).

*See also* Borglum, Gutzon; Tucker, J. G.

### Boullard, Marie-Christiane

Marie-Christiane Boullard was director of the historical society of Vimoutiers, France. Her sister married Denis Barois, a French Air Force pilot who had met Margaret Mitchell when he trained in the United States. Mitchell made some monetary donations to the town of Vimoutiers and secured the help of some other agencies to the town, which had been demolished accidentally by Allied bombers.

Boullard spoke in a phone interview in 2009 about how grateful the town was. She spoke also about how Vimoutiers, France, made Mitchell an honorary citizen in July 1949.

The historical society has on file a July 27, 1949, letter from Mitchell. In the letter, Mitchell thanks the town, expresses pleasure, and expresses hope to visit. The letter is addressed to Boullard's father, who managed the hospital there ("Margaret Mitchell Helped French Town after World War II"). Boullard said of the aid: "Unless you have lived through something like that you can't really understand how meaningful this humanitarian aid from the Americans was to us" ("Margaret Mitchell Helped French Town after WWII").

*See also* Barois, Denis; Vimoutiers, France.

### Bowden, Katharine Marsh

Born in 1890, Katharine Marsh Bowden was fourteen years old when her father, Millard Fillmore Marsh, died. Katharine was protective of her younger brother John, who became Margaret Mitchell's husband, all of her life. After her father's death, Katharine went to a nearby boarding academy for a while.

After John's wife died, Katharine came from California and spent a whole month with him after their younger sister returned home. After Katharine returned home, their brother Gordon and his wife Francesca came to spend time with John (Walker, page 513). John's will provided for his siblings Katharine, Ben Gordon, Henry, and Frances.

*See also* Marsh, Gordon; will of John R. Marsh.

### Branch, Harlee

John Marsh — who worked at the *Atlanta Journal* — arranged for Margaret Mitchell to interview for a job with the *Journal*'s city editor Harlee Branch in the fall of 1922. The interview went well, but Margaret did not secure the job with the *Atlanta Journal.* Another position — one with the *Atlanta Journal Sunday Magazine* — afforded her the opportunity that she desired.

**Brazil, sales of *Gone with the Wind*** *see* **foreign copyrights/translations and fair trade laws**

## Brett, George, Jr.

Some disagreements arose with George Brett, Jr., and the Marshes during their relationship with Macmillan Publishing Company. Some of these disagreements occurred after the death of Margaret Mitchell.

John Marsh blamed Brett for a television episode of *The Author Meets the Critics* in which Margaret Mitchell's novel came under attack. Marsh remarked that "our side took a beating" (Brown, pages 273–274).

Brett offered John R. Marsh and the estate a 10 percent royalty on a new Book of the Month Club edition of *Gone with the Wind*. John R. Marsh objected to the terms. He asked Brett to provide him with a document that stated he should receive 10 percent, not 15 percent. Brett could not do so, and Brett changed the terms (Brown, pages 274–275). Marsh managed to keep a cordial relationship with Brett, however.

## Brett, George, Sr.

George Brett, Sr., was president of Macmillan Publishing Company when Margaret Mitchell and Macmillan began their negotiations. In July of 1936—after the publication of *Gone with the Wind*—George Brett, Sr., retired as president. His son George Brett, Jr., assumed the position of president.

## Brickell, Herschel

Herschel Brickell was a reviewer for the *New York Post*. A Southerner from Mississippi, Brickell gave a glowing report on *Gone with the Wind*, which he called an emotional experience. In July of 1936 Brickell came South to visit and met Mitchell for the first time.

Mitchell met Brickell and Edwin Granberry for a Writers' Conference at the Green Park Inn in Blowing Rock, North Carolina. Herschel Brickell and his wife, Norma, invited Mitchell to visit them in Connecticut after she and Stephens Mitchell negotiated film copyrights with Macmillan Publishing Company (Walker, pages 272, 290, 301; Pyron, pages 331, 355–358). The Brickells, in turn, visited with the Marshes in the summer of 1937. The Marshes, however, turned down an invitation to vacation with the Brickells in the summer of 1937 (Walker, pages 363, 366).

After the publication of *Gone with the Wind*, Herschel Brickell wrote to Margaret Mitchell about the positive review he had received from a friend, Pulitzer Prize winner Marjorie Kinnan Rawlings. Margaret's correspondence with Brickell continued only for about four more years. He committed suicide in 1952 (Pyron, pages 336–337, 346–347).

*See also* contract for Gone with the Wind (film); Granberry, Edwin; Green Park Inn; Rawlings, Marjorie Kinnan; Rich's Department Store.

## Bridges, Herb

Herb Bridges studied history at the University of Georgia, but for years his first love was collecting memorabilia related to *Gone with the Wind*. He has carried for years the reputation of being the world's foremost collector of *Gone with the Wind* items. His knowledge and love of the book and film and of the history surrounding the two have resulted in seven books on the subject.

Bridges began his collection at age 11 just after reading *Gone with the Wind* for the first time. When he and a friend argued about who had portrayed Belle Watling in the film, Bridges bought his first *Gone with the Wind* souvenir: a copy of the cast list for the motion picture edition of the movie listing to prove his point. (Ona Munson was the actress.)

In 2005, after more than 40 years of collecting, he decided it was time to sell his collection. Christie's has been a leading auction house for the fine arts since the 1700s; Bridges decided to sell his items at auction and to use Christie's. Bridges's collection brought $334,588.

The diverse collection included such things from the movie as a petticoat from Vivien Leigh that sold for $6,573 and a top hat from Clark Gable which brought $2,629. Christie's auctioned signed photos, Franklin Mint dolls, sheet music, four 15 by 16 inch lobby displays, which brought $2,390, an 81 by 41 inch poster that sold for $3,346; Ona Munson's copy of *Gone with the Wind*, signed by some of the cast members, which sold for $11,353; and "Melanie's" wool sweater (worn by Olivia de Havilland) that sold for $16,730 ("Herb Bridges Collection of *Gone with the Wind* Items Goes For $334,588").

## Brown, Ellen F.

One of the most recent publications about Margaret Mitchell, her book, and the resulting film was that by Ellen F. Brown and John Wiley, Jr., in 2011. The title of the book—*Margaret Mitchell's* Gone with the Wind: *A Bestseller's Odyssey from Atlanta to Hollywood*—reflects its content. This book—co-authored by John Wiley, Jr.—was Brown's first book.

Ellen Brown on her Web site calls herself a bibliophile who spent her childhood with "her nose in a book" ("Ellen F. Brown"). She attended law school in hopes she would be able to earn a living searching "dusty old tomes with fancy leather bindings." She practiced environmental law for a decade.

In 2007 she tried a different way to follow her love of books. She opened an antique book shop and began to do freelance writing on topics related to books. Brown now has turned to writing full time. Her first book was the 2011 volume *Gone with the Wind: A Bestseller's Odyssey from Atlanta to Hollywood.*

Ellen, her husband, two sons, and basset hound live in Richmond, Virginia. She is a board member of the Library of Virginia Foundation and of the James River Writers ("Ellen F. Brown").

*See also* Wiley, John Jr.

### Brown, Katharine "Kay"

Katharine "Kay" Brown was a representative of Selznick International Pictures and served as Selznick's assistant; she headed the New York office of Selznick International Pictures. Annie Laurie Williams sent Kay Brown a copy of *Gone with the Wind* at about the same time that Warner Bros. Studio was reading the book.

Kay was excited about the book. She immediately sent a memo to David O. Selznick: "I beg, urge, coax, and plead with you to read this at once. I know that after you read the book you will drop everything and buy it" (Edwards, 205).

David O. Selznick cabled back a week later to Kay Brown: "MOST SORRY TO HAVE TO SAY NO IN THE FACE OF YOUR ENTHUSIASM" (Edwards, 205).

After Irene Selznick read the book, however, David Selznick reconsidered his decision. He postponed making a final offer, but indicated that he did not think the book was worth a final purchase price of more than $40,000 (Edwards, 205).

Kay Brown met with Margaret Mitchell, the lawyers of Cadwalader, Wickersham and Taft, and other studio representatives to discuss a film contract for the book *Gone with the Wind* with Selznick International Pictures.

Margaret felt very comfortable in communicating openly with Kay Brown. Margaret often put her feelings on paper to Kay. "Life has been awful! I am deluged with letters demanding that I do not put Clark Gable in as Rhett. Strangers telephone me or grab me on the street, insisting that Katharine Hepburn will never do. It does me no good to point out sarcastically that it is Mr. Selznick and not I who is producing this picture" (Edwards, page 249).

After Mitchell learned that the film studio was planning a talent search in the South, she wrote to Brown. "Could you wire me when you are coming, where you are staying, whether you are willing for me to break the story of your trip immediately and if Atlanta is your first stop on the way South? ... I hope you will let me give you a brawl of sorts—

probably a cocktail party to meet the press" (Edwards, page 249).

They maintained a friendship throughout the difficult filming process and afterward. Margaret Mitchell wrote Russell Birdwell that she would show Stone Mountain to Kay and feed her fried chicken, but she was leaving the details of the film up to Brown and to Selznick Pictures. Brown complied with Margaret's wishes not to be consulted about the filming of *Gone with the Wind*. The two maintained a friendship.

Margaret, before her death, confided in a letter to Kay Brown that she wanted the manuscript of *Gone with the Wind* destroyed upon her death. These were the same wishes she expressed to her brother, Stephens Mitchell.

On July 29, 1936, Stephens Mitchell, Margaret Mitchell, and John R. Marsh went to the law offices of Cadwalader, Wickersham, and Taft to meet with representatives of Macmillan and Selznick Pictures to discuss a contract for movie rights for *Gone with the Wind*. Kay Brown was one of the Selznick representatives present; she had been one of the employees who had convinced David O. Selznick to film the story. Marianne Walker notes on page 302 that Margaret liked the "Selznickers" immediately. Brown was one of these "Selznickers."

Kay Brown was important in beginning the casting campaign for the roles for *Gone with the Wind*. Brown, in fact, recommended Vivien Leigh as "Scarlett" after seeing her in the film *Fire Over England* (1937). Selznick said at that time he was not interested. On December 10, 1938, however, things changed. Selznick was filming the fire scene representing the burning of the Confederate munitions in the Atlanta train yards when his brother Myron brought Vivien Leigh to the set. Myron introduced Vivien as "Scarlett." The die was cast.

*See also* Cadwalader, Wickersham and Taft law firm; contract for *Gone with the Wind* (film); *Fire Over England*; Leigh, Vivien; will of John Marsh.

### Bucephalus

The Mitchell family named their horse Bucephalus. The name came from history. Bucephalus was the horse that belonged to Alexander the Great. Alexander rode the horse through many battles and for thousands of miles. The horse was instrumental in helping Alexander to create his empire. Plutarch told the story of Bucephalus.

The legend begins when Philip II, Alexander's father, obtains a wild horse. Alexander watches the horse and determines that it is fearful of its own shadow. Alexander — who was twelve at the time — demonstrates that he can tame the horse; he merely leads the horse toward the sun so that it cannot see its shadow. Soon he can ride the horse that he names Bucephalus, a name that suggests the head of the horse is as broad as that of a bull.

Bucephalus died of wounds in Alexander's last battle (326 B.C.) In memory of his brave, beloved horse, Alexander founded Bucephala, a city thought to be the present-day town of Jhelum, Pakistan ("Alexander-the-Great.co.uk").

### Bucephalus (the Mitchells' horse)

The horse that the Mitchell family owned and that Margaret Mitchell rode with much pleasure at their Jackson Street residence — and shortly after the move to Peachtree Street — was a pedigree named Bucephalus. Margaret was on the horse in 1911 when she suffered a fall and serious injury.

*See also* accidents; Bucephalus.

### "buckwheat people"

The term *buckwheat people* was an expression that Margaret Mitchell remembered hearing her grandmother and her great-aunts use. These rural relatives of Margaret's often used *buckwheat* or *wheat* as an analogy for the way that an individual tended to respond to trouble.

Those people who generally bend to the wind and then rise to their full heights again when the storm has passed are *buckwheat people.* Those people who yield to the pressure around them and do not rise up when the storm has passed are *wheat people.*

Shortly after they met, Margaret nicknamed John "*Buckwheat.*" She then explained the source of the nickname. She admired the fact that John seemed to be a "survivor," as did "Scarlett" and some of her favorite characters in *Gone with the Wind.*

A similar descriptive term for the *buckwheat people* that Margaret Mitchell admired were those with *gumption.*

*See also gumption.*

### buckwheat people (*Gone with the Wind*)

When Margaret was writing *Gone with the Wind*, she began to wonder if she could properly refer to some of them as "buckwheat people." She consulted a horticulturalist to find out if there was a basis for these stories or if they were "wives' tales." A reply letter explained that the stem of the buckwheat is still green when the seed of the buckwheat ripens; if the plant is blown over, the plant may rise again because its growth has not ceased. Plants tend to grow toward the light — phototropism.

Wheat straw, on the other hand, dries out as the grain ripens. Because it is not a growing plant when the grain has matured, it is less likely to rise toward the light again.

The agricultural specialist, then, confirmed the claims Margaret Mitchell's family had made about wheat and buckwheat.

### Bulgaria, sales of *Gone with the Wind*  *see* foreign copyrights/translations and fair trade laws

### *A Burning Passion*

On November 7, 1974, Director Larry Peerce released *A Burning Passion: The Margaret Mitchell Story* to television audiences. Robert Hamilton wrote the script and served as an executive producer, along with Renée Valente; Harker Wade served as a producer also of this 95-minute, made-for-television biography-drama.

Like the film *Gone with the Wind* that had as its basis Margaret Mitchell's novel by the same name, the location for much of the filming of *A Burning Passion* was in California. Specifically, the Bradbury Building at 304 South Broadway in Downtown Los Angeles saw many of the members of cast and crew.

Margaret Mitchell, the subject of the film, spent most of her life in Atlanta, except for a year at Smith College in Northampton, Massachusetts. She married John R. Marsh from North Carolina, and she and John sometimes vacationed there. To suggest these aspects of her life, the crew filmed also at Duke University in Durham, North Carolina, and in Wilmington, North Carolina.

Young actress Shannen Doherty (1971– ) played the title role in the film. Even before this film, however, Shannen may have been familiar to viewers because of her role as a member of the cast of the television show *Little House on the Prairie.*

Perhaps the best-known member of the cast was New York stage (1950s) and television actress Rue McClanahan. McClanahan appears as Margaret Mitchell's Grandmother Stephens in *A Burning Passion.* McClanahan had appeared on such television series as *All in the Family* (1968), *Maude* (1972), and *The Golden Girls* (1985).

The made-for-television biographical drama has a PG-13 rating for sexual content with the Motion Picture Association of America. There is also some brief violence during the 75-minute film ("*A Burning Passion*").

*See also* Doherty, Shannen.

### Butler, Rhett

"Rhett Butler" is the leading male character in both the novel *Gone with the Wind* and the film by the same name, along with Donald McCaig's sequel *Rhett Butler's People.* In the film, Clark Gable was the star who represented Rhett Butler. The United States Postal Service issued a stamp with both Clark Gable as Rhett Butler and Vivien Leigh as Scarlett O'Hara on it.

*See also* **Conroy, Pat; Gable, (William) Clark; McCaig, Donald; *Rhett Butler's People.***

## Cabell, James Branch

On October 25, 1940, Margaret Mitchell and John R. Marsh visited James Branch Cabell on a trip to see family in Richmond, Virginia. Cabell was one of Margaret Mitchell's favorite writers. His novel *Jurgen* was declared obscene and banned; it made Cabell a familiar name. Other novels followed. Finally in 1922, Cabell received acquittal on obscenity charges that came from *Jurgen.* By this time the ban had been in effect for two years. Cabell was now an idol to many people, and his book a best-seller.

Between 1927 and 1930, Cabell published a set of books with eighteen volumes. To eliminate confusion as to whether future works were a part of the set or a discrete volume, Cabell began writing under the name *Branch Cabell.* Between 1932 and 1935, Cabell served as editor of the literary newspaper *American Spectator.* Contributing editors included Sherwood Anderson, Theodore Dreiser, Eugene O'Neill, and Louis Untermeyer. Cabell died of a cerebral hemorrhage at his home in Richmond in 1958 ("James Branch Cabell").

## Cadwalader, Wickersham, and Taft Law Firm

Stephens Mitchell, Margaret Mitchell, and John R. Marsh went to the law offices of Cadwalader, Wickersham, and Taft, in New York on July 29, 1936, to meet with representatives of Macmillan Publishing Company and Selznick Pictures and to discuss a contract for movie rights for *Gone with the Wind.* Kay Brown was one of the Selznick representatives present. These Selznick employees made a favorable impression on both Margaret Mitchell and John R. Marsh (Walker, page 203).

Cadwalader, Wickersham and Taft remains one of the oldest law firms in the United States. Founded in downtown New York in 1792, the firm has served many of the world's and nation's institutions; the firm considered the interests of Margaret Mitchell, Selznick International Pictures, and Macmillan Publishing Company as they considered the filming of *Gone with the Wind.*

*See also* **Brown, Katharine "Kay"; Selznick International Pictures.**

## Cain Street

Margaret Munnerlyn Mitchell (1900–1949) and her older brother Stephens Mitchell were born in the house at 296 Cain Street in Atlanta, Georgia. The house is no longer standing. The Great Atlanta Fire of 1917 destroyed this house where Eugene Muse Mitchell and Mary Isabel ("Maybelle") Stephens Mitchell lived with their son and daughter until 1902. (There are many variations in the spelling of Maybelle's nickname and her given name in biographical materials.)

## Cammie

When Margaret Mitchell returned home at the end of her first year at Smith College, she took over the responsibilities for the home. Margaret kept only the servants Bessie Berry (Jordan), Charlie (the yardman with no surname given), the laundress Carrie Holbrook, and the house girl Cammie (no last name given). Cammie was only three years younger than Margaret.

After Margaret had surgery on her leg in 1920, she had to rely heavily on Cammie, especially for errands. Cammie seemed to enjoy the freedom of being able to leave the home and move about town. She soon married and moved to Birmingham, Alabama (Edwards, pages 65, 69, 80).

Mitchell always denied that any character in *Gone with the Wind* had as its basis a real person. Edwards says, however, that there was an exception with Prissy in the novel. Mitchell described Cammie as "skittish" and being "a smallish black girl, her hair tied back with a white kerchief" (page 138). Edwards notes also, "Cammie could be exasperating, but she could be amusing, too, and she was wily and clever, two traits Peggy admired" (page 138).

Even after asserting that Prissy was the only character in Mitchell's novel based on a real person, however, Edwards mentions some other exceptions. Ashley Wilkes had Clifford Henry as his model. Eugene Muse Mitchell (1866–1944)—especially his grief over the loss of his wife—was the basis of some actions of Gerald O'Hara. Edwards also mentioned some characteristics of Scarlett O'Hara that were suggestive of Margaret Mitchell and of Margaret's Aunt Annie Fitzgerald (page 138).

## Camp Gordon

Camp Gordon—later Fort Gordon—was 9 miles southwest of Augusta, Georgia, and about 142 miles east of Atlanta, Georgia. The military camp took its name in honor of Confederate Major General John Brown Gordon, who was also a Georgia Governor, a United States Senator, and a businessman.

*See also* **Gordon, John Brown.**

Service personnel from Camp Gordon often

came to Atlanta for their leaves or passes. The young people in Atlanta and the various service organizations in the area often hosted parties and social gatherings for the military personnel — especially during World War I. Margaret Mitchell often served as a hostess at these events.

Camp Gordon always held special meaning for Margaret Mitchell. It was at one of these gatherings for military personnel that Margaret met Clifford Henry, a bayonet instructor at the camp.

Clifford Henry was a socially prominent New Yorker and a former Harvard student. He and Margaret met during the summer of 1918 at one of the social gatherings in Atlanta. They saw each other every chance they could during the summer; they became engaged to be married just before he shipped out for France at summer's end. He was killed in October of the same year.

*See also* **Clifford Henry.**

## Candler, Asa

Asa Griggs Candler (1851–1929) was a banker, real estate developer, pharmacist, and philanthropist. An Atlanta mayor, Candler was the founder of the Coca-Cola Company in Atlanta, Georgia; he helped ensure the establishment of Camp Gordon and the Candler Air Field.

On September 9, 1924, the city of Atlanta learned from the Army Air Service that to retain the headquarters of the Fourth Corps in the area, an airfield was a requisite. Even later, an airfield would be essential to the arrival of the dignitaries in attendance at the Atlanta premiere of *Gone with the Wind* in December of 1939; the airport would figure prominently into the schedule of December 13–15, 1939, and particularly December 13, 1939.

Atlanta Mayor Walter Sims vetoed a proposal to pay $65,000 for a proposed airport site: Nichols Farm. The proposed Nichols Farm Airfield site would have been on Brown's Mill Road.

Asa Candler, Atlanta citizen and founder of the Coca-Cola Company, made an offer to the City of Atlanta on December 11, 1924. In return for the payment of the taxes on Candler Auto Track, Candler would permit the area to be used as an airfield for five years. His offer received the support of the American Legion, the Woman's Club of Atlanta, the Atlanta Aero Club, the Junior Chamber of Commerce, and others on February 3, 1925. The City of Atlanta did not move ahead with an airfield at that time.

On February 13, 1925, Candler again presented his offer to the City of Atlanta: use of the land for payment of five years of taxes. After U.S. Senator Walter George indicated that an air route to Florida and through Atlanta was under consideration, the city began to look with more interest at Candler's offer. The city accepted Candler's offer of the Candler Race Track on February 15, 1925. On April 20 Atlanta appointed William B. Hartsfield to chair a committee to administer the operations of the Atlanta Airport to be located on the site of the former Candler Race Track ("Candler Field Race Track").

*See also* **Atlanta premiere of** *Gone with the Wind*; **Coca-Cola; Hartsfield-Jackson Airport.**

## Candler Field

Asa Candler issued the City of Atlanta a five-year, rent-free lease (April 16, 1925) to begin Candler Field, where the Candler Auto Track was located at the time. The City of Atlanta was responsible financially only for the taxes on the 287-acre area that had been Candler Auto Track. Mayor Walter Sims committed the city to develop the race track area into an airfield.

The new name for the air field in the old race track area was Candler Field. The first flight into Candler Field was a Florida Airways mail plane (September 15, 1926). In 1928 Pitcairn Aviation (later called Eastern Air Lines) and in 1930 Delta Air Service (later called Delta Air Lines) began to use Atlanta as their chief hubs. By the end of 1930 Candler Field nationally ranked third, just below New York and Chicago, for the number of daily flights.

In March of 1939 Candler Field opened its first control tower — just before the December 1939 Atlanta Premiere of *Gone with the Wind*. This tower would figure prominently in the events of December 13, 1939.

In the 1940s Candler Auto Track would go by the names of Candler Field, Atlanta Army Airfield, and Atlanta Municipal Airport. In the 1950s its name would change again to the Hartsfield-Jackson Airport ("Georgia's Aviation History"; "Sunshine Skies. Special Section: The History of the Hartsfield-Jackson Airport").

*See also* **Atlanta premiere of** *Gone with the Wind*; **Candler, Asa; Hartsfield-Jackson Airport; Sims, Walter.**

## *A Canterbury Tale*

The foreign film that Margaret Mitchell and John R. Marsh were going to see on August 11, 1949, the night that the speeding car hit Margaret Mitchell and caused fatal injuries. This British film at the Peachtree Arts Theatre had a European release date of August 21, 1944. Its release date in the United States, however, was not until January of 1949.

The plot centers around an American GI, a British soldier, and a London girl. The setting is a small town in South England during World War II. On their way to Canterbury, the three encounter "glue-man," a mysterious person who attacks women who are dating soldiers; his method of attack is putting glue in the women's hair. Solving the mystery of "glue-man," exploring the land and Canterbury Cathedral, considering the personal problems of the three, and reviewing the history and literature of the area are important parts of the romantic movie. The black-and-white film ran 95 minutes in the United States. In 2011, the film was still available on DVD (Edwards on page 332 mistakenly calls the film *Canterbury Tales*, as does Pyron on 461).

### Capitol Theatre (New York)

The New York Premiere of *Gone with the Wind* (the film) was on December 19, 1939. The film played simultaneously at the Astor Theatre and the Capitol Theatre, two landmark theaters in the city.

The Capitol Theatre opened in 1919. In 1924 Loew's Incorporated took over the Capitol, which would become MGM's movie palace. The Capitol was the world premiere host of many classic films, especially *Gone with the Wind*. Stage shows were too expensive for production and admission during the Great Depression.

The economic boom brought on by World War II resulted in the revival of stage shows. In 1952, the Capitol, however, saw its last stage show and the installation of a 25 by 60 foot screen. The Paramount Plaza stands on the site of the old Capitol Theatre ("Cinema Treasures: The Capitol Theatre").

### Capp, Al

The cartoonist Al Capp's syndicated comic strip *Li'l Abner* published a three-week comic strip in October of 1942 titled *Gone Wif the Wind*. The spoof of *Gone with the Wind* included Capp's characters of Li'l Abner as Wreck Butler, Daisy Mae as Scallop O'Hara, and Hannibal Hoops as Ashcan Wilkes. Appearing in more than 600 newspapers across the nation, the cartoon incited the anger of both John R. Marsh and Margaret Mitchell; the couple considered it clear copyright infringement. In anger, Marsh called Capp to discuss the copyright infringement. A heated exchange followed.

Marsh contacted United Features, the publisher for Capp's works. Marsh threatened a lawsuit "for one dollar for every copy of every paper in which the spoof had appeared. This amounted to about seventy-five million dollars, a figure that immediately caught the attention of syndicate executives, who flew to Atlanta to apologize in person. The firm agreed to cancel any future installments in the series and run a public apology in Capp's strip" (Brown, 229). Margaret agreed to give up monetary claims after Capp issued a personal apology to her. Capp used two panels of his Sunday comic strip of *Li'l Abner* to apologize for the strip he had previously prepared.

Mammy Yokum, in the first of these panels, stated that "Mistah Capp" owed Margaret Mitchell a public apology for wounding the "feelin's" of the author of *Gone with the Wind*. The second strip was a formal apology from both United Features and from Al Capp; the two admitted that they had misused the characters from Mitchell's *Gone with the Wind* (Brown, page 229).

### Carl Bohnenberger Memorial Medal

The Southeastern Library Association presented the Carl Bohnenberger Memorial Medal for "the most outstanding contribution to Southern literature." Margaret Mitchell earned this medal in October of 1938 for her book *Gone with the Wind*. The medal received its name from Carl Bohnenberger, who had served as president of the Florida Library Association during 1936–1937.

### Carnegie Public Library *see* Atlanta–Fulton County Library

### Carr, Eugene

Eugene Carr was a person whom John R. Marsh regarded in his will as "our friend and helper." Carr served as janitor in the last residence that John and Margaret shared, the apartment at 1268 Piedmont Avenue, N.E. in Atlanta. Marsh bequeathed to Carr "$500.00 in fee simple" ("Last Will and Testament of John R. Marsh," signed July 26, 1952).

John prefaced the codicil to his will by stating that Margaret Mitchell wanted her papers destroyed. "Knowing the uncertainties of life, she placed upon me the duty of destroying her papers if she should die without having done it. She did so die, and I have tried to fulfill the obligation. As a part of the painful job, I have destroyed the original manuscript of her novel 'Gone with the Wind.'"

It was Eugene Carr and Marsh's housekeeper Bessie Jordan who carried Margaret Mitchell's manuscript, excepting a few pages that might be used for proof of authorship, if ever needed, to the basement of the apartment building at 1268 Piedmont Avenue. Jordan and Carr burned the documents in the furnace of the complex; John R. Marsh looked on as the two carried out the task that Margaret Mitchell had mandated before her death. The trio shed many tears as they accomplished the job (Edwards, page 336).

Walker gives a different account of the burning of the papers. She says that Bessie Jordan and John R. Marsh burned the papers in a wire basket behind the Della Manta Apartment where they had lived together (Walker, page 511).

*See also* **Marsh, John; will of John Marsh.**

## Carthay Circle Theatre, Los Angeles

In 1926 the Carthay Circle Theatre opened in Los Angeles. This was the location for the Los Angeles premiere of *Gone with the Wind* on December 28, 1939, and the world premiere of *Snow White and the Seven Dwarfs* on December 21, 1937.

*The Shoes of the Fisherman* was the last film to play (1969) at the Carthay Circle. An office block now occupies the prior location of Carthay Circle Theatre ("Cinema Treasures: Loew's Grand Theatre, Atlanta, Georgia").

## Catholicism

Yolande Gwin indicated that Margaret Mitchell observed the Christmas season reverently. Yolande wrote: "Peggy used to send out cards at Christmas, the inside was nothing but this: 'To announce the birth of Jesus Christ'" (Gwin, page 27).

Walker notes that Margaret Mitchell deliberately showed her separation from Catholicism at her wedding to John R. Marsh. She had the ceremony performed by a member of the clergy from a church other than the Catholic Church. The Reverend Hiram K. Douglass, assistant rector of St. Luke's Episcopal Church, performed their ceremony (page 87). Farr and Pyron, too, acknowledge that the use of the Reverend Douglass for the ceremony was a clear break with the Catholic Church (Farr, page 57; Pyron, page 137).

Walker and Pyron also see Margaret's use of red roses for the bride's bouquet on September 2, 1922, as symbolizing a break with religion (Walker, page 87; Pyron, page 137). Edwards, however, notes that Margaret Mitchell used a white bouquet — not a red one (page 87).

Although Mitchell was not a regular "church goer" during her lifetime, she did receive a religious burial. Biographer Anne Edwards suggests that Mitchell's religious beliefs might have been influenced by her cook and friend Bessie Jordan. Jordan was "a wise, religious person" who seemed to

Teenage Margaret Mitchell holds a cat while she stands before the front door of her 1149 Peachtree Street home. Thurston Hatcher was the photographer. (Courtesy of the Atlanta-Fulton Public Library System's Special Collections Department.)

have "brought Peggy closer to the church than any member of her family had succeeded in doing" (Edwards, page 149).

*See also* **de Ovies, Dean Raimundo; Jordan, Bessie Berry; St. Philip's Cathedral, Spring Hill Chapel.**

## cats

Cats were an important part of Margaret Mitchell's life. After their marriage, Margaret and John Marsh kept cats as pets.

To young Margaret Mitchell, cats were an important part of her family and childhood. She played house with the animals— particularly a cat named Piedy. Margaret rigged up a basket as an elevator to carry Piedy to the tree house that she and Stephens built. After Piedy's death, Hypatia and Lowpatia became a part of the Mitchell family. Margaret taught Lowpatia a special trick. He was able — on command — to stand up and put his right paw beside his ear in salute. His reward was cantaloupe (Pyron, page 31).

Margaret continued to enjoy cats as pets while she was a teenager on Peachtree Street. In a photograph of her at the front door of their home, she tenderly holds a cat, which appears to be stretching languorously in her arms.

When she became famous, she found that Western Union workers were sharing the messages she sent with other people and discussing the telegrams that came to her before she herself had even received them. She and her friends began to use the names of cats to substitute for the names of real people in their communications.

Mabel Search, an editor from *Pictorial Review,* often used her cats' names: Wish-Wish and Napoleon. Margaret sometimes employed the name "Old Timer" in her messages (Walker, page 355). Margaret and John's other cats included Maud and Count Dracula.

*See also* **Count Dracula; Maud; Old Timer.**

## Catt, Carrie Chapman (1859–1947)

Carrie Catt was a social activist, a reporter, and a teacher. As a woman suffrage movement leader, she founded the League of Women Voters and worked to advance the cause of women. She was an influence on young Margaret Mitchell.

Carrie Clinton Lane was born on January 9, 1859, in Ripon, Wisconsin. She grew up in Iowa. After her graduation from Iowa State College where she studied law (briefly) and trained as a teacher, she received (1881) an appointment as a principal. Carrie began serving as Mason City Superintendent of Schools in 1883. Her husband Leo Chapman — a publisher and newspaper editor — died in 1885. Twenty-six-year-old Carrie Chapman went to work as a newspaper reporter.

Carrie began to lecture for the woman suffrage movement, joined the Iowa Woman Suffrage Association, and served as a delegate to the National American Woman Suffrage Association. In 1890 she married again; this time to George W. Catt, a wealthy engineer. They signed a prenuptial agreement that provided Carrie two months in the fall and two in the spring to devote to her social reformation activities. George's role was to earn their living, and hers was to improve American society.

In 1900, Carrie succeeded Susan B. Anthony as the president of the National American Woman Suffrage Association; she resigned after four years when her husband became ill. She remained president (1904–1923) of the International Woman Suffrage Association, however.

In 1905, George W. Catt died, and Carrie turned her full attention on the woman's suffrage movement. Shortly after she began to work full time for suffrage for women, Carrie Catt came to Atlanta, and Margaret Mitchell met her personally. In 1915 Carrie again accepted the elected position of president of the National American Woman Suffrage Association. In 1920 she was instrumental in the passage of the 19th Amendment.

Her work included helping to found the Women's Peace Party, serving the League of Women Voters until her death, supporting the founding of the United Nations and child labor protection, and working — until her 1947 death — for Jewish relief ("Carrie Chapman Catt").

*Carrie Chapman Catt and Margaret Mitchell.* Three-year-old Margaret Mitchell first became acquainted with Carrie Chapman Catt when Maybelle Mitchell — Margaret Mitchell's mother and a supporter of women's suffrage — took the child with her to a suffragette rally. This occasion was a topic in many of the books about Margaret Mitchell and in a letter from Margaret Mitchell to Gretchen Finletter, author of "Parents and Parades" in the *Atlantic Monthly,* 176 (1945) (Edwards, page 18; Farr, page 23; Finletter, pages 80–84; and Pyron, pages 43–44). "The first time I was ever permitted to stay up later than six o'clock was on the tremendous occasion of a suffragette rally which was presided over, I believe, by Carrie Chapman Catt. The cook went home sick, all the relatives had gone to the meeting, and there was no one to look after me. Mother tied a Votes-for-Women banner around my fat stomach, put me under her arm, took me to the meeting, hissing blood-curdling threats if I did not behave, set me on the platform between the silver pitcher and the water glasses while she made an impassioned speech. I was so enchanted at my eminence that I behaved perfectly, even blowing kisses to gentlemen in the front row. I was kissed by Mrs. Catt, if it was she, and called the youngest suffragette in Georgia and the future of our cause. I was intolerable for days afterwards and only after being spanked, was permitted to witness a parade" [Pyron, pages 43–44].

**Chile, sales of *Gone with the Wind*** *see* **foreign copyrights/translations and fair trade laws**

**China, sales of *Gone with the Wind*** *see* **foreign copyrights/translations and fair trade laws**

## Civil War

The American Civil War dates from 1861 to 1865. Eleven Southern slave states— the Confederate states led by Jefferson Davis— seceded from the Union. Twenty (mostly Northern) free states and five border states waged warfare with the Confederacy until the Confederate states surrendered after four bloody years. Reconstruction followed.

## Civil War in Margaret Mitchell's education

Margaret claimed that as a child she heard everything in the world except that the Confederates lost the war. Mitchell spoke fondly of her Sunday afternoon visits with friends and family members when she was a child. "I was usually scooped up onto a lap…. I sat on bony knees—fat slick taffeta laps— and soft, flowered muslin laps. I did not even dare to wriggle for fear of getting the flat side of a hair brush where it would do the most good. I should add, while I'm talking about laps and knees, that cavalry knees were the worst knees of all. Cavalry knees had the tendency to trot and bounce and jog in the midst of reminiscences and this kept me from going to sleep, fortunately for 'Gone with the Wind.' I heard about the fighting and the wounds and the primitive way they were treated — how ladies nursed in hospitals— how gangrene smelled — what substitutes were used for food and clothing when the blockade got too tight for these necessities to be brought in from abroad. I heard about the burning and looting of Atlanta and the way the refugees crowded the roads and trains to Macon. I heard about everything … except that the Confederates lost the war" (Radio script prepared for Medora Field Perkerson by Margaret Mitchell, and quoted in Farr, page 17).

Other sources of Mitchell's knowledge of history were her riding companions. In her radio script prepared for Medora Field Perkerson, Mitchell told of riding her pony every afternoon with a "fine old Confederate veteran" who had "a habit of gallantly kidding ladies' hands— even my own grubby six-year-old hand" (Radio script prepared by Margaret Mitchell for Medora Field Perkerson, and quoted by Farr, page 15). Margaret said that other veterans regularly joined them on their horseback rides. Daily, Margaret's riding companions "refought the old campaigns, and argued about the tangled, bewildering muddle of politics in the Reconstruction days. So how could I help knowing about the Civil War and the hard times that came after it? I was raised on it. I thought it all happened just a few years before I was born" (Radio script prepared for Medora Field Perkerson by Margaret Mitchell, Farr, 15).

Margaret Mitchell's knowledge about the Civil War increased also as she studied in the Atlanta public schools. Her high school education was at Washington Seminary, a private school in Atlanta. Her one year of college was at Smith College in Northampton, Massachusetts. Margaret's courses at all these institutions provided her with additional background on the Civil War and Reconstruction.

In addition, Mitchell and her family learned about the Battle of Atlanta by visiting the Atlanta Cyclorama and studying the painting *The Battle of Atlanta*. This painting had been in Atlanta since 1892, eight years before Mitchell was born. She loved the painting and never tired of hearing about and seeing the story that it told. Farr wrote, "It is easy to understand the effect this combination of theater and history must have had on Margaret as a child: to the diligent and attentive little girl, her hand clutching her brother's, the Cyclorama must have come with the impact of enormous wonder" (page 30).

*See also* the Atlanta Cyclorama; *The Battle of Atlanta* painting; Mitchell, Russell Crawford.

## Clayton County, Georgia

In *Gone with the Wind* (the book), Jonesboro is the setting for the Tara Plantation. Jonesboro in Clayton County is just 15 miles south of midtown Atlanta. The Mitchell family designated Clayton County as the "Official Home of *Gone with the Wind*" ("Clayton County Georgia").

## Cloister Hotel

In 1928 the 46-room Cloister Hotel opened on Sea Island as a result of the vision of Howard E. Coffin; Coffin was also the founder of Hudson Motor Company. In the beginning Coffin hoped that a stay at the resort would encourage people to purchase land and build a home on Sea Island. His plan succeeded.

Rooms were originally available only to descendents of the original approved members. Manager Alfred W. Jones helped ensure the appropriateness of the guests. Over the years the Cloister grew to 262 rooms; reservations were still difficult to obtain in 1945 when Margaret Mitchell and John R. Marsh checked into the operation. Room reservations are difficult to obtain today.

In 2004 the Cloister Hotel was still under the management of the family of Alfred W. Jones. In that year the 30th annual G8 Summit, June 8–10, 2004, was at the Cloister. The site was the preference of President George W. Bush.

*See also* Marsh, John; Sea Island.

## Coca-Cola

Although Margaret Mitchell was not directly connected with the Coca-Cola Company, she—like all Atlanta residents—profited from the success of the product and the altruism of Asa Candler and, later, Robert Woodruff. Because of his profits from Coca-Cola, which had its base in Atlanta, Asa Candler was able to help with the funding of Emory University in Atlanta and the Atlanta airport Candler Field; it was at Candler Field, with its Candler Control Tower, that many of the planes carrying the Hollywood celebrities landed when they came to the Atlanta premiere of the film *Gone with the Wind*.

Robert Woodruff (December 6, 1889–March 7, 1985) became the president of Coca-Cola in Atlanta in 1923. He continued the philanthropy that Candler had begun. Three sponsored programs, each educational in nature, continued the legacy of Candler and Woodruff after their deaths.

Mitchell enjoyed Coca-Cola. In a letter to a member of the military and former employee of the Piedmont Driving Club, Mitchell mentions the hospitality of the staff of the Driving Club. She speaks of occasionally meeting with Mary Nelson Ream and discussing Civilian Defense work over a Coca-Cola at the Piedmont Driving Club (Gwin, page 114).

Southerners in the 1930s frequently referred to a Coca-Cola or other soft drink as a *dope*. In a letter to Yolande Gwin on June 28, 1936, Margaret Mitchell thanked her for the "swell story" about *Gone with the Wind* and its author. Margaret said that she would call at Gwin's office and "buy you a dope" (Gwin, page 40).

*See also* Candler, Asa; Candler Field; Coca-Cola; Gwin, Yolande; Hartsfield-Jackson Airport.

## Coffin, Howard Earle (1873–1937)

This automotive engineer and industrialist helped develop the Cloister Hotel, where John Marsh suffered a severe heart attack. Born on a farm near West Milton, Ohio, he was the only child of Julius Vestal and Sarah Elma (Jones) Coffin.

Coffin worked in the auto industry, first with Ransom Olds and then as a founder of the Hudson Motor Car Company with Edison and others on the Naval Consulting Board (1915) during World War I. President Woodrow Wilson appointed him in 1916 to the advisory committee of the Council of National Defense; in 1917-18 he headed the Council's Aircraft Board. Even after the war, he advised the government on aeronautical concerns. In 1925 he served to help establish a long-range aviation policy. In 1923 he founded the National Aeronautic Association and served as its president even while he retained the position of vice-president of Hudson Company until 1930. He even found time to help cross-license patents and to continue to promote technical standardization.

He helped found a pioneering company for commercial air transportation: National Air Transport, Inc. (later United Air Lines). He served as its president (1925–1928) and Board Chair (1928–30).

After his 1930 retirement, Coffin moved to his home on Sapelo Island, near Sea Island, Georgia. He chaired the board of Southeastern Cottons, chaired the Sea Island Company; and continued to develop real estate in the Sea Island area—including the Cloister he had helped found. He also found time to advise President Hoover in 1931 on the utilization of the emergency powers of the National Defense Act of 1916.

*See also* the Cloister Hotel; Marsh, John; Sea Island.

## Coffin Award of 1927

The Coffin Award was given to the power company judged to have made the most outstanding contribution to the electrical art and science of the time. John Marsh and the Georgia Power and Light Company won the award in 1927, largely through John Marsh's efforts during 1926–1927 and his *Journal* that Georgia Power and Light submitted as winning entry.

## Colbert, Claudette

Claudette Colbert was a high profile name in the film industry in the 1930s. Although Colbert herself did not appear in the film *Gone with the Wind*, she came to Atlanta "to see the fun." She arrived in Atlanta on December 14, 1939 (Farr, p. 7).

Colbert and Edward G. Robinson had made their film debuts in talking films in *The Hole in the Wall* (1929). Her success in the film and the success of the "talkie" resulted in her forsaking the stage for Hollywood (Beck, page 80). In 1935 Colbert had won the Best Actress Oscar. The Atlanta crowds were in awe of her.

Her film roles continued through the years. Her last role was in the 1987 TV movie *The Two Mrs. Grenvilles*. Claudette Colbert died in Barbados in 1996; she was 92 (Erickson, "Claudette Colbert").

## Cole, Lois

Lois Cole was associate editor of Macmillan Publishing Company in the Atlanta Office. She was instrumental in encouraging Margaret Mitchell to submit her manuscript to Harold Latham, editor-in-chief and vice-president at Macmillan Publishing Company, when he visited Atlanta in April of 1935.

Cole mentioned that Mitchell took the unorganized envelopes holding the chapters to Latham in the lobby of the Biltmore. Margaret Baugh, Anne Edwards, and Marianne Walker, however, tell different versions (Brown, page 16; Edwards, page 3; Walker, page 198).

No definitive location for the manuscript delivery is, therefore, available.

*Lois Cole and Margaret Mitchell.* Lois Cole and Margaret Mitchell became friends after Lois moved to Georgia to run the Atlanta branch of the trade department of Macmillan Publishing Company. The two met over a Saturday bridge game, and Margaret invited Lois for dinner with John and her the following Wednesday; Bessie served her fried chicken, collard greens, and biscuits. After Cole married Allan Taylor, a newspaper man, the couple became even more attached to the Marshes.

*See also* addresses related to Margaret Mitchell; Ansley Hotel; Baugh, Margaret Eugenia; Biltmore Hotel; Georgian Terrace Hotel; Latham, Harold Strong; Rich's Department Store.

## Confederate Soldiers' Home (Atlanta)

Some of the Civil War veterans that Margaret Mitchell remembered from her childhood spent their last years at the Atlanta Confederate Soldiers' Home. R. B. Rosenburg in his *Living Monuments* describes the homes as more than a mere rest facility; Richard K. Kolb comments on these homes also: "Confederate soldiers' homes served simultaneously as a place of refuge, a museum, a military camp, an artificial city and a shrine…. In the public's mind, they served as living monuments from a mythic past to be admired, indeed some would say revered" (Kolb, "Thin Gray Line").

Sixteen Confederate Veterans' Homes opened across the nation; the last opened in 1929 in California. Characterized by stringent entry requirements, these homes made sure that each resident had an honorable discharge and had proof of indigence or disability caused by the war. About one-third of the veterans had been wounded in battle; most did not draw a pension (Kolb, "Thin Gray Line").

Four of the residents of the facility in Atlanta were able to attend the December 15, 1939, premiere of *Gone with the Wind.* As honored guests, they had seats at the front of the Loew's Grand Theatre.

*See also* Atlanta premiere of *Gone with the Wind.*

## Conroy, Pat

Born on October 26, 1945, in Atlanta, the eldest of seven children, Pat Conroy became a writer. His abusive, military father moved the family frequently. Conroy credits his love of language to his mother.

Though the family did not have a lot of books, his mother proudly displayed the Bible and *Gone with the Wind*, the book that Conroy credits with shaping the South. While he was a student at the Citadel, Conroy published his first book — *The Boo.* Another soon followed.

Pat, his wife, and their children moved to Atlanta. Later — alone again — he moved to Rome. He and his new wife moved back to the South. This Southern writer has (as of 2011) five novels and a total of nine books to his credit. His most recent undertaking was preparing a Preface to a 2007 edition of Margaret Mitchell's *Gone with the Wind* (Conroy, "About Pat Conroy").

He remembers *Gone with the Wind* as being the most important book in his mother's life. She made Mitchell's book the most important one to her family also.

He draws an analogy between his life and *Gone with the Wind.* He says that Scarlett O'Hara "raised" him. When he spoke at the Margaret Mitchell House, his audience enjoyed the assertion and seemed to understand as he explained that his mother transformed herself into Scarlett O'Hara. It was, therefore, Scarlett — not his actual mother — who guided and reared the young Pat Conroy. Conroy, therefore, had an obligation to his mother and to the South to prepare the preface to the 60th Anniversary Edition of *Gone with the Wind* with its 1996 re-release.

The Margaret Mitchell Estate selected Conroy to write a sequel to *Gone with the Wind.* Conroy, however, could not reach an agreement with the estate about editorial control; he finally declined the venture — and the $4,500,000 after months of talk. Conroy had wanted to write the book from the perspective of Rhett Butler; Rhett would kill Scarlett while she was still young and beautiful. The first line would have read: "In Atlanta, most people remember me because of my wife."

Pat Conroy's response to the question of whether he would have written a better novel than Margaret Mitchell was emphatic: "Hell, no!" (Conroy, "I Was Raised by Scarlett O'Hara").

Meanwhile the reprints, of *Gone with the Wind* with Pat Conroy's preface continue: the 1996 hardback edition of the 60th Anniversary Edition; the 2007 Kindle edition; the 2007 library bound edition; the 2008 mass market paperback; the 2009 edition (library bound); the 2009 mass market paperback; and now a 2011, 75th Edition (paperback) ("*Gone with the Wind* by Margaret Mitchell with a Preface by Pat Conroy").

## contract for *Gone with the Wind* (the book)

On July 17, 1935, Harold Latham sent a telegram to Margaret Mitchell Marsh. He informed her that Macmillan Publishing Company had reached a unanimous decision to offer her a contract, which would reach her shortly. Latham encouraged Margaret to sign it promptly.

The author's royalties on the book would be 10 percent on the first 10,000 copies and 15 percent thereafter. Macmillan offered her a $500 cash advance against royalties. The publishing company would pay her half upon her signing the contract and would pay her the rest when she had delivered the remaining amount to the firm (Farr, pages 95–96).

Margaret would not sign the contract when it arrived until her brother and father looked over the document. Margaret, however, did not ask for their advice without compensating them. She made them agree to accept 10 percent of the earnings—which she hoped might amount to $5,000. Her two lawyers made only some minor changes. Later they said with hindsight they would have made more alterations (Farr, page 102).

Macmillan Publishing Company wrote to Margaret Mitchell again on February 6, 1936. This time the company asked her for permission to change the provisions of the contract. The publisher pointed out that the length of the book would make printing costly; Macmillan suggested that Mitchell receive a flat 10 percent on copies sold — with no increase after the sale of ten thousand copies. Furthermore, under the new suggested terms, if sales dropped below 5,000 copies in any given year, the percentage for each book sold would be only 10 percent. The suggested changes in contract terms brought about a strain (Farr, pages 112–113).

John R. Marsh reminded Macmillan that Margaret had told them the novel might be too long and that she had sent them a shorter manuscript in the final version. Macmillan, however, had persisted in publishing the longer version of the novel. Macmillan restored the terms of the original contract in late May. After the sale of 25,000 copies, the royalty would increase to 15 percent as the original contract that Margaret Mitchell signed stipulated (Farr, pages 112–113).

## contract for *Gone with the Wind* (film)

On July 10, 1937, Margaret Mitchell learned from former Macmillan employee Lois Cole that Annie Laurie Williams had told her on July 9, 1937, she had closed a contract with David O. Selznick. Williams had received for Margaret Mitchell the promise of the highest contract price for filming a first novel. Williams had revealed to Cole that the closing amount was $50,000 for rights to film Mitchell's *Gone with the Wind*.

Margaret Mitchell and John R. Marsh were concerned about Williams's negotiations. The couple had believed that Macmillan Publishing Company — not Annie Laurie Williams — would be the agent for negotiating the filming contracts with David O. Selznick Productions — or the company/ companies considering the filming of *Gone with the Wind* (Walker, page 289).

According to Mitchell's 1935 contract for *Gone with the Wind*, the author was to retain all "dramatic rights" to the book. She trusted Harold Latham, the editor from Macmillan Publishing Company who had accepted her manuscript in Atlanta that day. Some behind the scenes "hornswoggling" (according to Pyron) went on, however, that John R. Marsh and Margaret Mitchell were not privy to know.

Annie Laurie Williams had received brokering rights between Macmillan and movie studios. Macmillan — without the Marshes' knowledge — relinquished its rights less than a week after Margaret Mitchell assigned the sale to Macmillan. Williams agreed to only 5 percent of the fee for her serving as agent; in return, she assigned the other 5 percent to Macmillan (Pyron, pages 352–353).

In actuality, Williams was already deep in the movie negotiations when, on May 27, she consented to assist Macmillan in selling the film rights. Williams's letter on May, 27, 1936, to Harold Latham indicated that at the time she signed the contract, Williams already had the interest of three companies from a field of buyers: "Warner Brothers wanted the film for Bette Davis, R.K.O. for Katharine Hepburn, and warmest of all, David O. Selznick wanted it for himself" (Pyron, page 353).

In June of 1936 Latham suggested a selling price for the movie rights to *Gone with the Wind*. He told Annie Laurie Williams that $50,000 seemed reasonable for the film rights. No one had ever received such a sum for movie rights in the past (Pyron, pages 352–354).

Margaret Mitchell and John R. Marsh were concerned about how to release the news about a contract for movie rights so that all the newspapers would receive the information at the same time. The story came from the movie company, and they had no control over the matter (Walker, pages 300–301). Pyron indicates that Annie Laurie Williams "leaked it to the press" (Pyron, page 354).

Mitchell was out of town attending a Writers' Conference in Blowing Rock, North Carolina, and staying at the Green Park Inn when the contract arrived. She and John stayed in contact by daily letters and an occasional phone call.

*Contract details.* Walker notes that the film contract arrived in the mail on July 13; Pyron dates its arrival as July 14 (Walker, page 292; Pyron, page 356). A note accompanied the agreement asking Margaret to sign the document and to return it immediately. Margaret was still out of town at the Green Park Inn in Blowing Rock, North Carolina.

John found the ten-page legal agreement was full of technical language. He contacted his wife and told her not to rush home. He advised her that they would have to seek the legal counsel of Stephens Mitchell (her brother) and Eugene Mitchell (her father) and that there was no rush. He also wrote to Lois Cole on the same day: "Please tell Annie Laurie and anyone else who is interested that they should not expect the contract to be signed and delivered back to New York within five minutes or thereabouts after it reaches Atlanta. The Mitchell family just doesn't work that way, as you may have discovered last summer. With their legal training and legal habits, they wouldn't sign any contract without careful consideration and due deliberation. So, in any plans you are making, please allow for at least a reasonable period of time for investigation and study of the contracts at this end of the line" (Walker, page 292).

Despite John's letter, he received a telegram from John Putnam at Macmillan on July 23. (Walker suggests that Lois Cole may have initiated this telegram from Putnam.) Putnam's telegram inquired: "Is there any difficulty regarding movie contract? Have been expecting signed copies daily" (Walker, page 300).

Margaret had some major concerns from the beginning. First, she wanted to approve the final scene of the movie. Second, she wanted a voice in what the studio did with her book. Margaret had voiced these concerns to Harold Latham. He had little interest in her concerns, however, and Annie Laurie Williams appeared to have even less (Pyron, pages 356–357).

John told Annie Laurie Williams that his wife wanted a guarantee that the ending would not be changed, that the novel and its characters would remain the same, that the dialects would remain intact, and that the personalities would be true to the book. He told Williams not to expect the contract returned immediately; he reminded her that they would be securing legal counsel and that Margaret was out of town at the time.

John wrote daily to Margaret and asked her not to waste her vacation time worrying with contract details. He assured her that they would consider the contract when she returned. In the meantime, he would be in contact with Stephens and Eugene and the matter; in fact the three spent many hours debating and considering each line of the agreement.

The major problem that the three saw with the document was that Margaret had no veto clause in the contract. John assured her that her father and brother were protecting her business details and she need not be concerned.

A major concern to John was a provision in the document that gave Selznick International Pictures the option to film Mitchell's next book. John believed that his wife should change the statement to read that *she* would have option to select the film company for her next work; this might ensure that Selznick Productions would produce a creditable film this time (Walker, pages 289, 291–295).

In his letter to his wife, John teased: "Of course, the joke is that you don't intend to write any more books, but the fact that Selznick is sufficiently interested in you to *want* an option on your future production might prove to be a lever through which you can retain some control over what is done in making a movie out of this book" (Walker, page 295; letter to Margaret Mitchell from John R. Marsh on July 16, 1936, and quoted by Walker on page 295).

*July 27, 1936, response from John R. Marsh.* Marsh sent an eleven-page, single-spaced letter to Macmillan Publishing Company expressing their major concerns. He found two major faults with the contract; he called the articles raising concerns "the God Almighty clauses."

1. One clause that John specified that was unacceptable and had to be eliminated gave Selznick International Pictures the right to change the book as it saw fit in converting *Gone with the Wind* to movie form; at the same time, Margaret was responsible for any problem that the Selznick studio had as a result.

2. The second article concerned foreign copyrights. The contract specified that the foreign copyrights were Macmillan's property — not Margaret Mitchell's (Walker, pages 300–301).

*Negotiating the film contract.* Margaret Mitchell came "screaming back down the mountain to Atlanta" on July 23 (Pyron, page 357). Her brother John, as her legal counsel, and she boarded a train for New York on Tuesday evening, July 28. They went immediately from Penn Station to the offices of Macmillan Publishing Company the next day, July 29 (Pyron, page 357).

Pyron, however, indicates that Margaret and her brother Stephens Mitchell checked into the Grosvenor Hotel at 35 Fifth Avenue and Tenth Street. That afternoon the two reported to the offices of Macmillan Publishers (Walker, page 302).

The next day the discussions continued. Margaret realized that she would get nothing else from Macmillan so at last she signed the contract on July 30. She indicated that her signature had come because of her worries; the signature had come because of one of these concerns. Stephens wrote in his memoir that she had eliminated the worries that Hollywood could bring; they "did not want her and she was certain she did not want the worries which Hollywood could bring to her" (Walker, page 302–303).

Stephens boarded a train to Atlanta, but Margaret Mitchell went to the secluded Connecticut cottage of Herschel Brickell and his wife. Margaret arrived just at dusk; the next morning just before breakfast Margaret went completely blind for a brief period. The Brickells' doctor recommended rest for Margaret. Margaret, however, insisted upon returning to Atlanta by train. The contract negotiations for *Gone with the Wind* were complete (Walker, pages 302–307).

Margaret Mitchell wrote a seething letter to Macmillan Publishing Company about the movie contract when she had recovered enough to write again. Her September letter was answered by Harold Latham, who reminded them that her own attorney was present when she signed in July (Walker, pages 302–309).

Walker indicates that Margaret was in charge of her own foreign copyrights. She would have to renew these copyrights regularly. John believed that it would be a huge responsibility to keep up with these details and asked Macmillan to relieve them of these responsibilities. A housewife in Atlanta would not have the means to keep up with the details that Macmillan and its legal staff would have. Jim Putnam, who had tried to hasten the return of the book contract, informed them that Macmillan could not help them. The Marshes would have to do this by themselves; Macmillan had transferred all foreign translation rights to Margaret (Pyron, pages 309–310).

Marion Saunders was an agent in handling foreign copyrights. As a favor, Putnam put John Marsh and Stephens Mitchell in touch with this agent. Stephens, at the request of his sister and her husband, went to New York to work on an agreement with Saunders about the foreign copyrights (Walker, page 310).

John wrote to Jim Putnam at Macmillan on October 9, 1936: "You and the Macmillan Company are certainly taking a very generous attitude in your offer to give back to Mrs. Marsh the rights for all foreign translations of her book. Just what we will do with them when we get them, I don't know" (Walker, page 310). The foreign copyright business operated from a small apartment. John

R. Marsh, Stephens Mitchell, and Margaret Baugh handled their worldwide business to protect their own interests. The four became self-taught experts in foreign copyrights (Walker, page 310).

*See also* **Blowing Rock Writers' Conference; Green Park Inn.**

**copyright, foreign** *see* **Berne Convention; foreign copyrights/translations and fair trade laws**

## Count Dracula

Margaret Mitchell's strong attachment to animals continued all through her life. John R. Marsh shared her fondness for pets.

After John R. Marsh and Margaret Mitchell married, they adopted a stray cat that they called *Old Timer.* When Old Timer disappeared, they adopted a kitten. Margaret suggested one of its parents might have been a flying squirrel. Because of the kitten's ability to seemingly fly through the air, because of its appearance, because of its ability to climb up perpendicular walls, and because of John R. Marsh's reading material at the time, they decided to call the kitten Count Dracula.

John had been hospitalized in May of 1927. Margaret Mitchell had brought him a copy of *Dracula* by Bram Stoker to read. John wrote to his sister Frances Marsh Zane that "the book took a holt" of him and frightened "the liver and the lights out of him"; he bragged that the shock of the story had helped him to get better. The nurses suggested that he get garlic to ward off vampires. John never lost his sense of humor (Edwards, page 143).

John wrote to his mother on May 30, 1947, that he found Count Dracula "a healthy extrovert." John found he was becoming "very fond" of Count Dracula, whose chief interests were "a romp, a fight, things to eat and not being bothered when he is asleep." John described the pet as "a rowdy element in our sedate household." John even expressed the hope that the newcomer would help them to break some of their chains (Walker, page 495).

Margaret was not as tolerant of the new addition to their household. When confronted with John's fond description of the animal, however, she accepted another kitten that they named *Maud* (Walker, page 495).

*See also* **animals; Maud.**

## Crews, Laura Hope

Laura Hope Crews (1879–1942), who played "Aunt Pittypat" in the film *Gone with the Wind*, attended the Atlanta premiere of the movie in 1939. She arrived at the Union Station in Atlanta on Thursday morning, December 14, 1939, at 8:20 A.M.

Crews had first appeared on the stage when she was only four years old. After starring in a play and touring the cities west of Chicago, her parents removed her from the stage and enrolled her in the state normal school in San Jose, California. She returned to the theater after graduation and moved to New York for more work. There she worked with Henry Miller and H. B. Warner. She was on the first call for actresses for the role of Aunt Pittypat in the film *Gone with the Wind* and has a star on the Hollywood Walk of Fame. Crews died in New York, but her burial was in Colma, California ("Laura Hope Crews").

### Cuba, sales of *Gone with the Wind* *see* foreign copyrights/translations and fair trade laws

### Cyclorama

A cyclorama is a 360 degree painting. Developed in Europe, these depictions were particularly popular during a time before motion pictures and televisions; the largest of the oil cycloramas is the one in Atlanta, *The Battle of Atlanta*. The American Panorama Company was responsible for the 1885–1886 painting, commissioned by General John "Blackjack" Logan.

*The Battle of Atlanta* was originally on display in a wooden building, where Margaret Mitchell and her family viewed the painting on various occasions. Young Margaret loved the painting and the history she learned from it. She also viewed the painting in the more modern building into which it moved in 1921.

*See also* Atlanta Cyclorama; *The Battle of Atlanta* painting.

### Czechoslovakia, sales of *Gone with the Wind* *see* foreign copyrights/translations and fair trade laws

### Daniel, Frank

Frank Daniel worked at the *Atlanta Journal Sunday Magazine* at the same time that Margaret Mitchell was on staff there, and afterward. He and Margaret Mitchell associated socially.

Daniel was working on a review of Stephen Vincent Benét's *John Brown's Body* when he visited with Margaret Mitchell in her home; she was working on the manuscript of what would eventually become the novel *Gone with the Wind*. Daniel began reading to Margaret from Stephen Vincent Benét's book; she began to beg him not to read the magnificent verse further to her. She did not reveal

to Daniel that the work was giving her writer's block.

Margaret wrote about this event to Stephen Vincent Benét himself. She recalled how she flung herself on the sofa and stuck her fingers in her ears and screamed protests. "I had to read it all then. The result was that I wondered how anybody could have the courage to write about the war after Mr. Benét had done it so beautifully" (Edwards, page 146).

It was Frank Daniel who broke the news of the death of Margaret Mitchell Marsh to Margaret's brother Stephens Mitchell (Farr, page 228).

*See also* alcohol; Benét, Stephen Vincent; death of Margaret Mitchell.

### Davis, Susan Lawrence

Susan Lawrence Davis (1861–1939) was the daughter of one of the Ku Klux Klan's founding members, Lawrence Ripley Davis. Born in Limestone County, Alabama, Davis claimed to have seen, heard, and accumulated much first-hand documentation from her father and from other founding members of the Ku Klux Klan. She supposedly assembled this information in *Authentic History of the Ku Klux Klan, 1865–1877*, published in 1924.

Davis claimed that *Gone with the Wind* included "whole pages" from her book. She brought a $6.5 billion lawsuit against Macmillan Publishing Company on February 26, 1937, for plagiarizing her book on the Klan's history in the publishing of *Gone with the Wind* (1936). The 261-page brief stated that Mitchell had used some of Davis's "historical facts." Davis noted that Margaret Mitchell had stolen such terms as *scalawag* and *carpetbagger* (Walker, 367). Edwards called the suit "insubstantial" and "ludicrous" (Edwards, 263).

The suit asked the question whether the damages applied to each copy of *Gone with the Wind* published, which would run somewhere around $6,000,000, or whether the damages were limited to the edition in which cases the total claimed would have run to $175,000 (Stout, page 1). Judge Henry W. Goddard dismissed the suit.

Margaret Mitchell expressed her reaction to the lawsuit brought by Davis against Macmillan in February of 1937 in a March 2, 1937, letter to George Brett, Jr. "You could have knocked me over with a fern frond when the old lady made her claim, for I had never heard of her or her book either until the lawyers wrote" (Walker, page 366).

The *Atlanta Constitution* asked Mitchell for her reaction to the dismissal of the suit against Macmillan Publishing Company. She said, "Naturally I am very happy. Although the suit has naturally been quite annoying, I never really worried and was confident all the way through" (Stout, pages 1–2).

Judge Goddard noted that "historical events, including those which relate to the KKK, are in themselves within the public domain, no one being entitled to the exclusive right to use them in literature" (Stout, pages 1–2).

Macmillan Publishing Company seemed to view the suit as generating extensive publicity for *Gone with the Wind*, not a bad thing (Brown, page 155).

*See also* **Authentic History of the Ku Klux Klan, 1865–1877; Goddard, Judge Henry W.**

## Davis, Theodore

Theodore Davis served as technical advisor to the group that was painting *The Battle of Atlanta*. Davis had been a *Harper's Weekly* staff artist during the war; as such, he had witnessed and sketched the battles of several campaigns, including the one in Atlanta. The firsthand knowledge he conveyed to the German artists contributed significantly to the authenticity of the landscape and the military action depicted in the *Battle of Atlanta* painting ("Atlanta Cyclorama: The Story of the Painting").

## Davison-Paxon Department Store

The Atlanta department store Davison-Paxon — the chief competitor of Rich's Department Store — dated, like Rich's Department Store, to just after the Civil War. Davison-Paxon-Stokes sold out to R.H. Macy and Company in 1925 and in 1927 constructed a new building at 180 Peachtree Street. It was at the 180 Peachtree Street location that Margaret Mitchell attended her first book signing during the 1936 release week of *Gone with the Wind*. When Rich's found out that the signing at Davison-Paxon would come before their signing, Rich's cancelled its event. Margaret Mitchell declined the invitation for a later signing at Rich's. It would be some time before they mended the rift.

The first event that Margaret Mitchell agreed to attend at Rich's after the store cancelled her book signing was a luncheon during the Atlanta premiere of *Gone with the Wind* in December of 1939. A calamity occurred at the event honoring Julia Peterkin, Marjorie Kinnan Rawlings, and Margaret Mitchell — three women Pulitzer Prize winners. When she missed her chair and landed on the floor, Margaret wrenched her back. Margaret managed to attend some of the December 14, 1939, events, however (Pyron, pages 119–121).

*See also* **Atlanta premiere of *Gone with the Wind*; Rich's Department Store.**

When Margaret Mitchell was working on *Gone with the Wind*, she sometimes became very agitated with visitors. She wrote to John R. Marsh's sister that she had even quarreled with "Aggie" Dearborn; she described this as an "unheard of" happening. She even grew angry with Courtenay Ross McFedyen (Pyron, page 222–223). By the time that she wrote her will, however, the fight was over.

*See also* **wedding of Berrien Kinnard "Red" Upshaw and Margaret Mitchell; will of Margaret Mitchell.**

## death of Margaret Mitchell

Shortly after 8:00 P.M. on August 11, 1949, in Atlanta, Georgia, Margaret Mitchell and John R. Marsh were crossing Peachtree Street to the Peachtree Arts Theatre to see the foreign film *A Canterbury Tale*.

When a car came speeding down the street, Marsh moved to the curb near the theater. Mitchell moved back toward their car. The driver — Hugh D. Gravitt — lost control of his car, which struck Margaret, knocked her to the pavement, and dragged her 15 feet. Her husband rushed to her side.

Mitchell's fame had not protected her from a drunken driver speeding down the street in an out-of-control automobile. She now lay in the street. A stream of blood ran from her ear.

Both the temperature and the humidity were in the 90s on Peachtree Street. Someone called an ambulance for "a woman lying in the street." In the haste to secure help, the caller had not sought her identity. It was 12 minutes before the emergency vehicle arrived.

John Marsh asked the ambulance driver to take them to Grady Memorial Hospital. This downtown hospital regularly treated accident victims and emergency cases. Margaret herself had made donations to the emergency facilities at Grady Hospital.

By chance, the intern in the ambulance was the son of one of the woman's high school classmates from Washington Seminary. Dr. Edward Pain Lochridge immediately recognized Margaret Mitchell, author of *Gone with the Wind*, and knew she was gravely hurt.

Margaret entered Grady Hospital before 9:00 P.M. Her doctors placed her in Room 302 and ordered oxygen and blood. Her wounds included a skull fracture, injury to her internal organs, and a damaged left leg. She was running a high temperature, a very bad sign. Atlanta brain Surgeon Dr. George Bowman attended Peggy along with Doctors W. C. Waters, Charles Dowman, and Exum Walker. The physicians even took meals in her room.

Visitors began to arrive at the hospital. They tried to be hopeful and helpful. Some recalled how the first streetcar in Atlanta had struck Margaret's grandfather, veteran First Sergeant Russell Crawford Mitchell. He, too, had been unconscious at first, and he had recovered. Their hope was that she would recover also.

More than twenty-four hours later, Margaret's husband, John Marsh, visited her room again before leaving to rest a while. She still had not regained consciousness.

Calls came from Clark Gable, Vivien Leigh, and movie stars around the world. The switchboard at Grady Hospital had to install additional lines to receive the flurry of calls. Telegrams poured into the hospital. Even President Harry S Truman sent a wire.

Grady Hospital set up a special room to receive all the presents for the author. Margaret's friends attempted to respond to the many messages and to keep a complete record of every call, letter, card, and wire. They hoped to be able to show her upon her recovery a complete record of her well-wishers. One of the most touching messages came from the federal prison in Atlanta. The inmates had volunteered to donate their blood to this woman who had taken such an interest in them, spoken to them on several occasions, and sponsored a writing contest for them.

The doctors decided on the morning of August 16 — five days after the accident — that if Peggy were not better in the next few hours, they would perform brain surgery in the early afternoon. John left to eat lunch and rest for a short while before the decision.

Change came rapidly. Radio announcers across the nation carried the news. "Margaret Mitchell is dead. The time of death was 11:59 A.M. Margaret Mitchell is dead. Repeating time of death: 11:59 A.M." It was an event of international importance.

John requested that in lieu of flowers those who wanted to pay their respects should do so by making contributions to Grady Hospital. Someone was already collecting money for a Margaret Mitchell Memorial Pavilion. Still, flowers arrived in abundance. John personally accepted only two arrangements: a massive blanket of white roses the prisoners at Atlanta Federal Prison had grown and personally harvested for their friend and a blanket of red roses and white carnations from the organized florists in the city.

Governor Eugene Talmadge of Georgia proclaimed that at ten o'clock on the day of the funeral all state employees should pause for three minutes to show respect to this Georgian. Mayor Hartsfield of Atlanta asked that all activity in the city pause at ten o'clock as a tribute to her. (Pyron, pages 461–462; Edwards, pages 331–336; Walker, pages 504–507; Farr, pages 228–235).

*See also* de Ovies, Dean Raimundo; Grady Hospital; Gravitt, Hugh Dorsey; Hartsfield, William Berry; will of John Marsh; will of Margaret Mitchell.

## de Havilland, Olivia

Olivia de Havilland ("Melanie Wilkes") attended the Atlanta premiere of *Gone with the Wind*. She did not, however, arrive promptly for the December 14 Junior League Ball. No escort had come to take her to the ball.

De Havilland called the office of the Georgian Terrace Hotel and explained the problem to night auditor Edmund Miller, "a quiet, middle-aged man who lived at the hotel" (Farr, pages 6–7). Miller immediately secured a hotel car for her. He got into the car with her as if he were accustomed to escorting a star every night of his life. "They entered the hall just as Major Howell [editor and publisher of the *Atlanta Constitution*] was about to pass over Miss de Havilland's introduction. Instead of taking time to go around to the box entrances, they hurried directly to the floor, where Mr. Miller delivered Miss de Havilland to Captain Jack Malcolm of the traffic squad, who lifted her up to Laurence Olivier, who in turn lifted her over the railing and into the box with effortless ease. This swift passage from floor to box delighted the crowd" (Farr, 6–7).

Olivia de Havilland would receive a nomination from the Academy of Motion Picture Arts and Sciences for Best Supporting Actress for her performance as "Melanie Wilkes." Her nomination, however, was not accompanied by a concomitant award.

## Della-Manta Apartments

In 1939 John and Margaret Mitchell Marsh moved to a larger apartment. Apartment #3 in the Della-Manta Building at 1268 Piedmont Avenue would be their third and last apartment together. After the conversion in 2005 of the apartment building to condominiums, the new entrance gave the 1258 Piedmont Avenue construction a new address: One South Prado, NE (Jones, Tommy H. "Razing *Gone with the Wind*").

On Wednesday, December 13, 1939, Margaret Mitchell and John R. Marsh hosted a small party for some of the cast and crew of the film *Gone with the Wind* at their Della-Manta Apartment, which had been constructed in 1917. The Della-Manta Apartments were across the street from the Piedmont Driving Club (1215 Piedmont Avenue), where the Atlanta Women's Press Club held its tea party on Friday, December 15, 1939; Clark Gable and Margaret Mitchell were among the honored guests.

Margaret Mitchell lived the last ten years of her

This current photograph shows the Della-Manta Apartment Building (now 1 South Prado) where Margaret Mitchell and John R. Marsh lived for her last ten years. (Courtesy of James L. Rhoden, III, www.Macallangroup.com)

life in the Della-Manta Apartments. After Mitchell's death, John R. Marsh, with the help of Eugene Carr and Bessie Jordan, burned the original manuscript of *Gone with the Wind* in the furnace of the Della-Manta Apartments. Marsh saved only a few pages for proof of authorship (Edwards, page 336). Walker states that Margaret Baugh also helped with the destruction of the papers (Walker, page 511).

*See also* addresses directly related to Margaret Mitchell; Atlanta premiere of *Gone with the Wind*; Atlanta Women's Press Club; Jordan, Bessie Berry; Piedmont Driving Club; will of John Marsh; will of Margaret Mitchell.

**Denmark, sales of *Gone with the Wind*** *see* foreign copyrights/translations and fair trade laws

### de Ovies, Dean Raimundo

Dean Raimundo de Ovies was born in Liverpool, England, in 1877. He was educated in the United States and had a long and illustrious career in the church and in his writing. He was dean of the Cathedral of St. Philip's in Atlanta from 1928 until his 1947 retirement. De Ovies had served as talk-show host on WSB Radio at the Biltmore Hotel in Atlanta and wrote as a columnist (1932–1949) for the *Atlanta Constitution*. De Ovies was the author of four books. He officiated at the funeral of Margaret Mitchell at Spring Hill Funeral Home at 1020 Spring Street, NW, Atlanta. De Ovies had previously pastored at St. Philip's Cathedral until his retirement.

*See also* addresses directly related to Margaret Mitchell; death of Margaret Mitchell; St. Philip's Cathedral; Spring Street Chapel.

### dialect in *Gone with the Wind* (the book)

Capturing the dialects of the characters in her manuscript for what would be *Gone with the Wind* was extremely important to Margaret Mitchell and her husband John R. Marsh. On their road trip across Georgia in 1934, the couple took sections of the manuscript with them. Their trip was to culminate at the Press Association Conference in Savannah, an excellent site for studying the dialect that Margaret wanted to reproduce correctly in her book.

A dialect frequently heard in the Savannah area was Geechee. The word *Geechee* is a name that comes from the Ogeechee River. The dialect went back to the time when shiploads of slaves came to the plantations around Savannah and the Golden Islands. These slaves kept their native language — especially those cut off from the mainland. John R. Marsh and Margaret Mitchell noted that the original dialect was still apparent. The Geechee dialect was difficult for many people to understand.

The African Americans around Charleston, on the other hand, spoke Gullah. When the Marshes traveled in that area, they noted that African Americans often combined Gullah with English. This gave words like *effen* for *if* and *race* for *rice*.

The Marshes took meticulous notes on all their travels. They noted different dialects in the Macon area than in North Georgia and various other regional differences. The various dialects in *Gone with the Wind* are the results of much research; without these records, some history of the state and region might have passed unnoticed.

The character "Mammy" in *Gone with the Wind* is from the Savannah area. She lived in North Georgia for many years, however. Her speech, therefore, varies from the other African American characters in the novel.

The Marshes were particularly familiar with the area around Tallulah Falls and with the people there. Georgia Power Company owned a cabin there. The company allowed the Marshes to use the cabin for retreats; this was a good place to work undisturbed on the manuscript (Walker, pages 193–194).

This phonetic spelling of the words of the characters and meticulously recording the speech of the various areas was a painstaking endeavor. When the couple found that the copyeditor had revised the dialect in many parts of the manuscript, John was furious. He wrote to Lois Cole (February 13, 1936) that the editor had changed some of the words incorrectly. For instance, *mahse'f* now read as *yo'se'f*; Margaret had deliberately avoided the use of more than one apostrophe in the words. They did not want to use the dialect like that in Joel Chandler Harris's works; they had found that those works were difficult to read and that they did not reflect the various regions.

John notes in a letter to Lois Cole that Macmil-

lan must be certain not to change the dialect. All the African Americans in the book do not speak the same way because some were house servants and some assumed other tasks; the backgrounds of the characters also affected their speech. He summed up by saying that they could catch errors in dialect in their proofreading; to emphasize further this request, he noted that it would "break her heart" if someone changed the speech of Margaret's characters. No one was better qualified than Margaret to edit those parts of her work.

When the first edited pages appeared on February 13, 1936, John and Margaret were horrified to find that the editor had changed the speech of "Scarlett" herself. John explained in the letter he wrote that speech in a novel creates more interest in the volume than novels which appear to be "solid and heavy." He went through and mentioned some items that definitely needed to be changed to the way that Margaret had written them.

Lois Cole responded that the manuscript had already gone to press when she received John's letter. Macmillan had stopped the presses, Lois reassured him in her February 15, 1936, letter.

In another letter on February 20, 1936, Lois cautioned the Marshes about making unnecessary changes. There would be a charge for each change after this. Margaret, in a follow-up letter, asked for $10 for a photograph she had sent to Mrs. Hutchinson, a bookkeeper for Macmillan. The Marshes completed their work on March 14, 1936, and the package was returned to New York the next morning. (Walker, pages 221–222; 235–236; 240–242; 244). As a result of the efforts of the Marshes, copyeditor Susan Prink, typesetters, and the proofreaders, the finished book had "fewer than a half dozen errors, no typographical errors, no inconsistencies in dialect, and only a minor error in a character's name" when Margaret calls "Frank Kennedy" "Frank," instead of "Mr. Kennedy" (Walker, page 244).

When Marion Saunders contacted Margaret Mitchell about foreign translations, Walker quotes Margaret as asking John how dialects could be translated (Walker, page 253).

*See also* contract for *Gone with the Wind* (film); Geechee; Gullah.

### Dickson, David Hugh

David Hugh Dickson served Jonesboro, Georgia, for many years. He served as a member of the Jonesboro City Council from 1935 through 1938 and as Jonesboro Mayor (1939–1948; 1953–1984).

It was during Hugh Dickson's first year as Jonesboro mayor (1939) that the town learned that the premiere of *Gone with the Wind* would definitely be occurring in Atlanta. He and other civic leaders arranged publicity for a re-enactment that would become "the biggest day in Jonesboro history," according to Mayor Dickson.

On December 11, 1939, Jonesboro re-enacted the flight of Scarlett, Melanie, Wade Hampton, Prissy, and the newborn Beau from Atlanta the night the munitions site burned. Four performers and a doll began the wild ride at the old Union Station in Atlanta; the ride ended at the train station in Jonesboro. The characters made their "escape" in a creaky, horse-drawn wagon with a cow tied to the back. The *Atlanta Constitution*, the Jonesboro Chapter of the United Daughters of the Confederacy, and town planners staged this event that paved the way for the three-day premiere celebration. Upon the arrival of the wagon in Jonesboro, Atlanta and Jonesboro learned the event was a success ("City of Jonesboro").

Hugh Dickson's name "was synonymous with Jonesboro and banking. He retired from his position as vice president of First National Bank of Atlanta in 1969. Having financial acumen from his long banking career, he made many wise decisions for the city" ("City of Jonesboro"). Dickson continues to receive credit for "many progressive accomplishments which have helped lead us to our present sound financial condition as a city" ("City of Jonesboro").

## Dietz, Howard

Howard Dietz served as manager of public relations for the film *Gone with the Wind*.

## divorce of Berrien Kinnard Upshaw and Margaret Mitchell Upshaw

Margaret filed for divorce from Berrien Kinnard ("Red") Upshaw on June 17, 1924.

Mitchell's marriage to Upshaw had caused division in the Mitchell household. Margaret's father opposed the divorce and yet he had never reconciled himself to the marriage. He believed Margaret had demeaned the family. As a Catholic, he thought it was a mortal sin. There had never been a divorce in the Fitzgerald or the Mitchell family; he was concerned about what others would say (Edwards, page 109).

Neither Eugene Muse Mitchell (Margaret's attorney-father) nor Stephens Mitchell (her brother and a lawyer) were present. Howard Branch — an attorney and family friend — presented the deposition sworn to by Margaret Mitchell to the court. The jury granted her a divorce, but it did not let her resume her maiden name. Neither would it allow an annulment of the union.

Margaret Mitchell returned to court on October 16. She appealed the earlier decision. When she left the court, she left as Margaret Mitchell — not Margaret Upshaw (Edwards, pages 109–110). Walker wrote: "Red had become so unstable that he could not control his anger and began to abuse Peggy physically. After each of these encounters, he would run away for a while, and then return, begging her to forgive him. At that time, she weighed less than ninety pounds and was defenseless against such a muscular man, well over six feet tall. The first time John saw Peggy's arm and face swollen and bruised from a beating Red had given her, he was devastated" (Walker, page 106).

Margaret testified against Red on July 17, 1924, and on October 16, 1924. She testified that on July 10, 1923, after their marriage on September 2, 1922, Red had attacked her so brutally with his fist that she had had to obtain medical care. On another occasion he hit her in the eye; her eye remained swollen shut for several days. He had struck her another time and her arm had become swollen and discolored; she suffered pain from these attacks. Margaret filed for divorce on November 14, 1923 (Walker, pages 106–107).

Edwards, too, details the beating of July 10, 1923, that Margaret Mitchell testified to in court. Edwards added that the counsel noted also that Red Upshaw "jerked her against a bed, causing her to be bruised all over her body." Margaret required hospitalization for two weeks; she kept the beating secret because of her humiliation. Margaret even asked her brother Stephens Mitchell to tell Medora Field Perkerson at the *Atlanta Journal* that his sister was tending a sick relative out of town and would not return for six weeks so others would not see the results of Upshaw's violence (Edwards, page 101–103).

Even though the divorce became legal, Margaret continued to fear Berrien Kinnard ("Red") Upshaw. From July 10, 1923, until she learned of the death of Upshaw on January 12, 1949, Margaret kept a pistol by her bed.

***See also*** **Howard, Branch; pistol.**

## Dixon, Thomas F., Jr.

Thomas F. Dixon, Jr., was born on January 11, 1864, in Shelby, North Carolina. Dixon died on April 3, 1946, in Raleigh, North Carolina. His burial was in Sunset Cemetery in Shelby.

Best known as an author and minister, Dixon also had the reputation as being "one of the most hateful racists of the 20th Century" ("Thomas Dixon"). Dixon's earliest memory was perhaps the lynching of a black man by the Ku Klux Klan; the man had been accused of raping a white woman who was a Confederate soldier's widow. Thomas never questioned the action because his mother, Amanda Elvira McAfee Dixon, told him it was the right thing to do. Throughout his life, Dixon supported the Ku Klux Klan.

Dixon left college to be an actor. When he failed at that, he became a lawyer. After failing in that profession, he became a Baptist minister like his father, Thomas Dixon, Sr. Thomas Dixon, Jr., was a popular fire-and-brimstone preacher in Raleigh, Boston, and New York City; his sermons became equally popular in a book collection.

Dixon left the pulpit and began a new career: traveling lecturer. Sometimes the crowds to whom he spoke numbered in the thousands. Dixon, however, soon left the lectern and became an author.

Dixon's novels condemned African Americans. He especially presented situations where white women received the violence of the antagonists; vigilante justice was the remedy that Dixon advocated in *The Traitor* and *The Clansman* in particular.

Dixon, however, denied hating African Americans. That author even described his feelings toward them as being those of affection—for those who practiced good behavior and responsibility. Because white supremacy was a common mindset at the time, many of his readers noticed nothing strange. Vigilante justice was a regular activity of the Ku Klux Klan.

The bases of D. W. Griffith's controversial film *Birth of a Nation* were *The Clansman, The Leopard's Spots,* and *The Traitor.* The latter figured prominently in the life of young Margaret Mitchell ("Thomas Dixon"). It was when she presented a program based on Thomas Dixon's works that her father said she had plagiarized; she had not acknowledged Dixon in any way. She herself had played Dixon's character Steve Hoyle.

*Thomas Dixon and Margaret Mitchell.* Margaret Mitchell carried the lesson of plagiarism, her guilt at having "stolen" from Dixon when she was a young girl, and even some repercussions for her actions with her for some time after her father's anger. After the publication of *Gone with the Wind* in June of 1936, Margaret Mitchell received a letter from Thomas Dixon, who was then residing in Raleigh, North Carolina. He had praised Mitchell's novel.

With her typical courtesy, Margaret responded to Dixon on August 15, 1936. First, she praised his works: "I was practically raised on your books, and love them very much" (Harwell, *Letters,* page 52). Margaret next cleared her conscience by acknowledging in the letter to Dixon her inappropriate actions of some twenty years before, when she was eleven. She also revealed her fear of the possible consequences.

For many years I have had you on my conscience, and I suppose I might as well confess it now. When I was eleven years old[,] I decided that I could dramatize your book *The Traitor*—and dramatize it I did in six acts. I played the part of Steve.... My mother was out of town at the time. On her return, she and my father, a lawyer, gave me a long lecture on infringement of copy-rights. They gave me such a lecture that for years afterward I expected Mr. Thomas Dixon to sue me for a million dollars, and I have had a great respect for copy-rights ever since then [Harwell, *Letters,* pages 52–53].

*See also* Hoyle, Steve; plagiarism; *The Traitor* and Young Margaret Mitchell.

## Doherty, Shannen

Born on April 12, 1971, this actress was only about twenty-three years old when *A Burning Passion,* the drama-biography of Margaret Mitchell, aired on television. Although she was in her early twenties, Shannen was not new to television and acting. Shannen started her career in acting when she was only ten. Michael Landon—of the *Little House on the Prairie* series—cast her in the 1982 season of his show. Her childhood roles continued to cast her as a brat, as in the television drama *Our House* and in *Girls Just Want to Have Fun,* a movie for teens; Sarah Jessica Parker also appeared in the film. She continued with the brat roles in the film *Heathers* (1988) with Winona Ryder. Her most popular role—before *A Burning Passion*—was in the 1990s television series *90210.*

The "Shannen Doherty Biography" indicates that she "remained in public view due to her frequent arrests, cameo appearances, turbulent romantic life, and tendency to get into fights with celebrities" ("Shannen Doherty Biography").

Excluding *A Burning Passion,* Doherty appeared in "forgettable films and horrible made-for-TV movies" in the 1990s. In 1998 she became a regular on the television series *Charmed.* Other television movies and reality shows became a part of her career ("Shannen Doherty Biography").

## Douglass, Hiram K.

The Reverend Hiram K. Douglass was the assistant rector at St. Luke's Episcopal Church in Atlanta in 1922. On September 2, 1922, he married Berrien Kinnard ("Red") Upshaw and Margaret Mitchell in her father's home. Many saw her use of a member of the Episcopal clergy as a clear break with the Catholic Church.

## Dowdey, Clifford Shirley, Jr. (1904–1979)

Born in Richmond, Virginia, on January 23, 1904, Clifford Dowdey spent his early years in the South and the state of Virginia. In his eulogy after his May 30, 1979, death, the *Times Dispatch and News Leader* called him "The Last Confederate."

Dowdey spoke fondly of his grandmother's living with his parents and him. She had four brothers in the Civil War, and she told him about her memories and their memories of the event. These stories sparked his interest in the Confederacy and the history of his state of Virginia ("Clifford Dowdey").

A graduate of Columbia University (1925), Dowdey worked for a year with the *Richmond News Leader* before returning to New York City to serve as editor (1926–1935) of *Munsey's, Argosy,* and *Dell.* He began his first novel about 1933; it would bear the title *Bugles Blow No More.*

Leaving the journals, he and his wife, Helen, moved to Florida for a season and then back to Richmond, Virginia, where he finished the novel. He continued to write and publish. For the rest of his life, he lived in Richmond and worked as a writer of historical fiction and history.

When Margaret and John went to New York for Margaret to christen the USS *Atlanta* in 1944, they learned of the problems the Dowdeys were experiencing. Helen came to the Waldorf-Astoria to dine with them in their suite on February 8. They learned that there had been another woman involved and that Helen was planning to go to Reno for a divorce. Margaret observed that there might be legal questions about such a divorce, but she could not dissuade Helen (Edwards, pages 312–314). Margaret stayed in contact with Helen Dowdey even after the separation and divorce.

On July 13, 1944, Clifford Dowdey married a clinical psychologist: Frances Wilson. She died July 1970. After the death of Frances Wilson, he married Carolyn DeCamps, a librarian, on September 9, 1971. ("Clifford [Shirley] Dowdey, [Jr.]," *Contemporary Authors Online*).

Clifford, the father of two daughters (Frances and Sarah), is buried beside Frances Wilson Dowdey (1920–1970) in the Hollywood Cemetery in Richmond Virginia ("Clifford Dowdey").

Dowdey's nine novels and ten historical works brought him much recognition. ("Clifford [Shirley] Dowdey, [Jr.]," *Contemporary Authors Online*).

## Dowdey, Helen *see* Dowdey, Clifford Shirley, Jr.

## Downing, John Francis

After the Fire of 1917 that destroyed much of Atlanta, there was a fear of losing lives, the museum, artifacts, and the *Battle of Atlanta* cycloramic painting to fire. In 1921 the City built a neo-classical building that Atlanta architect John Francis Downing had designed for Grant Park, with the impor-

tant feature of being fireproof ("Atlanta Cyclorama and Civil War Museum"). The Atlanta Cyclorama figured prominently in the education of Margaret Mitchell and in the festivities of the Atlanta premiere of the film *Gone with the Wind.*

***See also*** **Atlanta Cyclorama; Atlanta premiere of the film *Gone with the Wind*; Battle of Atlanta painting.**

## Doyle, Alexander

Alexander Doyle was an artist and sculptor born in 1858 in Steubenville. Doyle was important to Atlanta and to the life of Margaret Mitchell because he sculpted the statue of Atlanta editor Henry W. Grady.

Alexander's father had a marble business in St. Louis. This and a family visit for several years to Italy may have affected his decision to pursue sculpture as a profession. By the time he settled in New York, young Alexander showed talent in the art of sculpture.

Alexander did return to Italy in the seventies and oversaw his father's marble business at the Ferara marble quarries, but his main profession was his sculpture. By the time he returned to the United States, he had commissions for many statues: the bronze *Liberty* for Peabody, Massachusetts; the fourteen foot granite statue of *Education* for the Pilgrims' monument in Washington, D.C.; a granite statue of *Margaret* for New Orleans; and many private commissions. These were all complete before he reached the age of twenty-six.

His commissions continued: a 16½ foot, 7000-pound statue of General Robert E. Lee; a 114-foot-high statue *Peace*; thirteen figures— one of which was Senator Ben Hill of Atlanta — that represented the original thirteen colonies; and enough other works to "fill a volume" ("The USGenWeb Project: Alexander Doyle"). His *Henry W. Grady* statue would represent the 1890s.

## Dracula

Animal lovers Margaret Mitchell and John R. Marsh adopted a new kitten after Old Timer's disappearance. Because of the new kitten's behaviors and because of John R. Marsh's reading material at the time of the new kitten's arrival, Margaret and John named the new household member "Count Dracula." The shortened form of the kitten's name was merely "Dracula."

***See also*** **animals; Count Dracula.**

## "The Dump"

Margaret Mitchell Marsh's affectionate nickname for the dark, dank apartment that she and John Marsh occupied at the Corner of 10th and

Peachtree (with its 17 Crescent Avenue address) was "The Dump." The apartment was only about 550 square feet. It was in this apartment — now a part of the Margaret Mitchell House — that Margaret Mitchell wrote the bulk of the manuscript that became *Gone with the Wind*.

*See also* addresses directly related to Margaret Mitchell.

### *A Dynamo Going to Waste*

The book *A Dynamo Going to Waste* is a compilation of the letters that Margaret Mitchell wrote to a young Amherst graduate between 1919 and 1921. The results are published by Jane Bonner Peacock with the permissions of Eugene and Joseph Mitchell and of the Trust Company Bank, as executor of Stephens Mitchell's estate.

### Easters, Melita

Melita Easters wrote a play in which she attempted to portray Margaret Mitchell, her personality, and her times. Easters' play *Mrs. John Marsh … The World Knew Her as Margaret Mitchell* opened on June 2, 2011, with Kandace Christian as Margaret Mitchell. Mary Rose Taylor noted that the play reflected "the author's complexity, humor, and above all *Southerness*" and is "extensively researched and skillfully crafted" ("Don't Miss This Event"). The premiere on June 2, 2011, was an event to coincide with the 75th Anniversary of the publication of *Gone with the Wind*.

In 1991 Easters had a staged reading her dramatization of Margaret Mitchell's life at the Alliance Theater at 1280 Peachtree St. NE. The following year there was a two-week production at the 14th Street Playhouse.

Easters continued to add details to her work. She added also an audio-visual component of newsreels from the 1939 Atlanta premiere of *Gone with the Wind* and historic photographs. Easters herself describes the revised script as "a richer, more complete portrayal of Margaret Mitchell, and it probably has more humor than my original version…. The more you research a person, the greater your understanding. I found I was able to put one or two specific episodes into better perspective. And I allowed myself to be a little looser…. [A]ll the threads of my research now combine to bring to life the rich fabric of Margaret Mitchell's life. My additional research, along with revisiting her work as a reporter have now filled in some of the gaps in that tapestry" (Bookman).

### Ebenezer Baptist Church

Young Martin Luther King, Jr., and the choir of Ebenezer Baptist Church performed for the crowds at the premiere of the film *Gone with the Wind* during December 13–15, 1939. Founded in 1886 by former slave John A. Parker, the original church was on Airline Street, Northeast. Parker's successor on March 14, 1894, was the Reverend Adam Daniel Williams. He and his members built a church on McGruder Street: Mt. Pleasant Baptist Church, which later changed its location.

Adam Daniel Williams married Jennie Parks. Their daughter Alberta Christine Williams married Martin Luther King, Sr.; one of the children of this union was Martin Luther King, Jr.

Williams helped bring about the first Washington High School, the first high school in Atlanta for African Americans (1924).

The Rev. Martin Luther King, Sr. helped secure both equality in teachers' salaries in Atlanta and the voting registration of African Americans even before the Civil Rights Movement. Later the Rev. Martin Luther King, Jr. joined his father as co-pastor of Ebenezer Baptist Church. It was through his worldwide prophetic ministry that Ebenezer developed a new ecumenical and international posture.

Martin Luther King's co-pastor — the Rev. Alfred Daniels Williams King — founded Ebenezer's Children's Chapel in 1969. This educational institution had several different purposes. The Chapel was concerned with young people's education, spiritual enrichment, and oratorical training ("Ebenezer Baptist Church: Church History").

*See also* Ebenezer Baptist Church Choir; King, Martin Luther, Jr.

### Ebenezer Baptist Church Choir

The choir from Ebenezer Baptist Church on Auburn Avenue had a role during the Atlanta premiere of the film *Gone with the Wind*. The choir performed at the Junior League Ball on Thursday, December 14, 1939, at the Atlanta Auditorium.

In 1939 the pastor of the Ebenezer Church was Dr. Martin Luther King, Sr. The pastor accompanied the choir in their performance; he played the guitar. Ten-year-old Martin Luther King, Jr., sang; he wore a white hat in the choir, which was dressed as plantation slaves.

Caldwell observed that the black community was concerned about this guest appearance in the Atlanta Auditorium and that there was "a big backlash." However, Martin Luther King, Sr., cautioned that "not everything we do is political" (Richardson).

The community might have felt different about the appearance had it known more about Margaret Mitchell and her altruism — the means for which came from the sale of her book *Gone with the Wind*

AUDITORIUM, ATLANTA, GA.

Completed in 1909, the Atlanta Auditorium was in part a reaction to the need for a place to assemble during the Atlanta Race Riots of 1906. It was the scene for the Junior League Ball of December 14, 1939, and an alternate ball on December 15, 1939. The auditorium burned in the 1940s. (C. T. American Art.)

and from the movie rights that she sold to Hollywood. Caldwell recognized that Margaret Mitchell "gave a lot of money and time to the black community, which was highly irregular at the time, her being a prominent white woman. She gave money anonymously to set up a clinic and 50 scholarships to Morehouse College [which Dr. King attended]. It was all done under the radar" (Richardson).

"The Dump" on Crescent Avenue — where Margaret Mitchell wrote most of *Gone with the Wind* — is now the Margaret Mitchell House and is open to the public. Prominently displayed is a photograph of the Ebenezer Baptist Church Choir on December 14, 1939, at the Atlanta Auditorium. Dr. Martin Luther King, Sr., pastor, holds a guitar in the photograph. Ten-year-old Martin Luther King, Jr. (January 15, 1929–April 4, 1968), is wearing a white hat in the photograph and is a member of the choir.

### Edee, Allen Barnett, Jr.

Allen Edee was, according to Jane Bonner Peacock, "a handsome young [Pawnee City] Nebraskan whom Margaret met at Amherst when she was at Smith College in 1918–1919" (Mitchell, Edee, and Peacock, page 1). Edee's father had been a landowner and the proprietor of a ready-to-wear store. This "Eastern sophisticate" was on his class track team and sang in the college choir; his nickname was "Gentleman's Cs."

Edee went to New York after his 1919 graduation, and Margaret returned to Atlanta after her first year at Smith College. They continued to correspond from the summer of 1919 until December 1921.

Some thirty years later, Allen Edee's grandson James Philip Edee was given the letters when his father died. Stephens Mitchell — Margaret's eighty-one-year-old brother, would not grant permission for James Philip to publish the letters.

After the death of Stephens, his two sons — Eugene and Joseph — and the Trust Company Bank granted permission for Peacock to publish the correspondence. The result was *A Dynamo Going to Waste* (1985).

### Edwards, Anne

Born on August 20, 1927, in Port Chester, New York, Anne Edwards is known best for her biographies of some important personalities. These celebrities include Margaret Mitchell (1983), the Grimaldis of Monaco (1992), the Reagans (1987, 2003), Vivien Leigh (1977), Katharine Hepburn (1985), Shirley Temple (1988), Queen Mary and the House of Windsor (1984), Queen Elizabeth II and Princess Margaret (1990), Barbra Streisand (1997), Maria Callas (2001), Princess Diana (1999, 2000), Judy Garland (1996), the Great Houdini (1977), P.T. Barnum (1977), the Aga Khans (1995), the DeMilles (1988), Maria Callas (2001), and others.

Edwards's education included the University of California, Los Angeles (1943–46) and Southern Methodist University (1947–48). As a child performer on stage and radio, Anne Edwards began her career in writing by serving as a junior writer at MGM Studios (1944). By the late 1940s and the early 1950s, Edwards was a writer for screen and television. Between the mid–1950s until about 1972, Edwards resided in Europe and the United Kingdom.

Edwards has credit as being the co-writer of the first script of the *Funny Girl* screenplay (1968). She has written more than fifteen biographies, three books for children, seven novels, and co-authored an autobiography. Edwards currently resides in Beverly Hills, California. She has taught writing at the University of California at Los Angeles, has served as past president of the Authors Guild and on its board of directors, and has contributed materials and manuscripts to the Special Collections Department at UCLA ("Facebook: Anne Edwards").

*Edwards, Anne, and Margaret Mitchell.* Anne Edwards is the author of *Road to Tara*, a biography of Margaret Mitchell. Edwards's work dates from 1983.

Joseph Millichap assessed online the biographies of Margaret Mitchell written prior to 1991. His assessments included a review of biographies by Edwards (1983), Farr (1965), and others before 1983. Millichap's review of Edwards's work concludes that the book is very readable and provides fuller documentation than Farr's earlier work. He notes that Edwards was able to make use of recent critics of *Gone with the Wind*. He criticizes Edwards's "lapses into a popular journalistic style" and her use of "elliptical fragments [that] fail to cohere in a conclusive portrait of the woman as writer or the writer as woman." He praises the fact that she includes information on Mitchell's novel "as a cultural and literary text [with] regional and historical background ... and information on the life and loves of the author."

Pyron assesses negatively some passages of the biography by Anne Edwards. Pyron mentions specifically the main topic of Mitchell's novella '*Ropa Carmagin* as described by Edwards. Pyron refers to Edwards's information on the novella as being "ill-founded" (page 216).

Pyron also mentions specifically Edwards's description of the fire that injured Margaret as a child. He calls Edwards's account "a bizarrely fanciful version that violates common sense.... [F]or example, she has the fire coming through forced air grills rather than the open fireplace of fact. She also completely fictionalizes the child's injuries ... and the consequences of the affair.... The distortions in the element of the fire represent the general errors of fact and the still more general distortions in interpretation of this entire biography" (Pyron, page 469n3).

Marianne Walker, another of Margaret Mitchell's later biographers, also has some questions about Edwards's work. On page 537 and 544 of her book *Margaret Mitchell and John Marsh: The Love Story Behind* Gone with the Wind, she questions the accuracy of two sources in Edwards's *Road to Tara* (Walker, pages 537, 544).

*See also* accidents.

### Edwards, Augusta Dearborn

Augusta Dearborn, a friend of Margaret Mitchell for many years, served as the maid of honor in the wedding of Berrien Kinnard ("Red") Upshaw and Margaret Mitchell. Augusta Dearborn married Joseph Lee Edwards. At the time that Margaret Mitchell wrote her will (November 21, 1948), Augusta Dearborn Edwards and Joseph Lee had one son, Lee Edwards. Margaret Mitchell bequeathed him a sum of $100 (Will of Margaret Mitchell Marsh).

### elephant

Margaret Mitchell went through a trial period on her job at the *Atlanta Journal*. The other employees, especially the photographers, wanted to make sure that she was serious about her job there and tried her sincerity. Although they seemed to like Margaret, they also enjoyed seeing just how far she would go to prove herself. This was true with her feat of dangling over the streets of Atlanta in a contraption that the workers on the side of Stone Mountain were going to use as they carved Confederate soldiers on the mountainside.

Besides duplicating the workers' plight on the side of Stone Mountain for a news story, she went backstage with the animals at the circus. With her love of animals, consorting with the animals might have been easier for her than the photographers who accompanied her might have guessed. She even held the monkey for a photograph; her face shows tenderness toward — not fear of — the creature.

Peggy Upshaw (Margaret Mitchell) soon won over the hardened crew, but she was the first to admit that she sometimes risked her neck rather than have someone think she was afraid (Farr, 62).

Minutes after this photograph on September 13, 1924, this elephant picked up an unsuspecting Margaret Mitchell, carried her through the air, and placed her on its head — at a secret signal from the trainer and the photographer. Margaret did not express undue fear, but she held on with both hands. (Courtesy of the Atlanta-Fulton Public Library System's Special Collections Department.)

This was true on September 13, 1924, when she was backstage with the animals.

A few minutes later, the trainer of the elephant — at the secret request of the photographer — would give the elephant the signal to lift Peggy with his trunk and place her on his head. She managed to hide her surprise when the huge animal lifted her high above the ground before depositing her on his head. Later, however, she "admitted she held on with both hands to his ear" (Farr, page 62).

*See also* monkey.

### Eskridge, Jane

Jane Eskridge and Wailes Thomas were teachers who were instrumental in locating and disseminating early writings of Margaret Mitchell. One hot, humid day in August, they were organizing "a sixty-year accumulation of things in the old house" in Atlanta. In their sorting they came upon a collection of early writings and correspondence that had once belonged to Margaret Mitchell. Jane edited the writings, which became the book *Before Scarlett: Childhood Writings of Margaret Mitchell* (2000) and which included some sections by Mary Rose Taylor (From "Introduction" by Mary Rose Taylor, in Jane Eskridge's *Before Scarlett: Childhood Writings of Margaret Mitchell*, ix–xii).

The story of how Margaret Mitchell's papers found their way to the old house is complicated. On May 3, 1927, Stephens Mitchell — Margaret's older brother — married Caroline Louise ("Carrie Lou") Reynolds. Carrie (1902–1950) had an older brother Glascock Reynolds (1903–1967), a noted artist. Glascock did a portrait of Margaret Mitchell. The connection, however, does not stop there. The section on Wailes Thomas details the reason that he and Jane came in contact with the papers.

*See also* Thomas, Wailes.

### Estonia, sales of *Gone with the Wind*  see foreign copyrights/translations and fair trade laws

### Eternal Flame of the Confederacy

The lamp post of "The Eternal Flame of the Confederacy" is one of the original 50 street lights that were first lighted for Christmas in Atlanta in 1855. During a federal bombardment of the city in 1864, a shell fragment ricocheted off the lamp post and struck and killed Solomon Luckie, an African American barber. The lamp post is, therefore, a "memento" of the war.

The post was displayed in City Hall from 1864 until 1880. In 1880 United Daughters of the Confederacy returned the post to its original location at Whitehall and Alabama Street. They added a plaque to honor General A.J. West.

During the Atlanta premiere of the film *Gone with the Wind*, the first major event of the day of December 14, 1939, was a ceremony at 10:15 A.M. The historic gas light was re-lighted and designated the "Eternal Flame of the Confederacy."

Today the Eternal Flame of the Confederacy is within Underground Atlanta at the entrance to the Five Points MARTA station ("The Eternal Flame of the Confederacy").

*See also* Atlanta premiere of *Gone with the Wind* (the film).

### Everett, C. W.

Harold Latham, editor-in-chief and vice-president at Macmillan Publishing Company, informed Margaret Mitchell in 1935 that C. W. Everett, a professor at Columbia University, was reading her manuscript and making suggestions. Margaret asked if his suggestions would be used without her knowledge or permission. In response, Latham sent her a communication that he had received from Everett on July 2 (Edwards, page 165): "The book is really magnificent.... By all means take the book. It can't possibly turn out badly. With a clean copy made of what we have, a dozen lines could bridge the existing gaps.... I am sure that it is not only a good book, but a best seller.... Take the book at once. Tell the author not to do anything to it but bridge the gaps and strengthen the last page" (Edwards, page 167).

Everett had suggested to Latham on July 2, 1935, that Mitchell might want to remove the "venom, bias, and bitterness" that appeared in places; Margaret agreed to this in her July 27, 1935, response to Latham. In response to Everett's comments to Latham about the finality of Rhett's leaving at the end of the book, Mitchell told Latham that she thought Scarlett would eventually get Rhett again (Edwards, page 168).

Everett had also made a suggestion about the title of the book. He suggested the title *Another Day*. Both Macmillan and Margaret Mitchell rejected this title (Edwards, page 180).

### *Facts and Fancies*

During Margaret Mitchell's junior and senior year at Washington Seminary, the name of the yearbook was *Facts and Fancies*. Mitchell had a short story, "Little Sister," published in that yearbook during her junior year and a story titled "Sergeant Terry" published during her senior year. (From "Foreword" by Mary Rose Taylor, in Jane Eskridge's *Before Scarlett: Childhood Writings of Margaret Mitchell*, ix–xii).

See also Before Scarlett: Childhood Writings of Margaret Mitchell; Eskridge, Jane; "Little Sister"; Paisley, Eva; "Sergeant Terry"; Taylor, Mary Rose.

## fair trade laws and other laws and legislation brought about by Margaret Mitchell and Gone with the Wind (book)

Gone with the Wind influenced public policies and regulations about books.

One of the most significant results related to laws about price maintenance. In New York City, for example, stores began to cut the price on the book to draw customers into the store; some stores were even selling the book for less than they had paid for it. This meant that the stores were ignoring price maintenance laws; Macmillan had fixed the price of Gone with the Wind at $3.00. Some stores began to buy the book in quantity from stores that were cutting the price rather than buying the book from Macmillan.

The New York Herald Tribune ran a lead article on March 29, 1937, in the Business Section on the newly legalized fair trade laws. The article "Macy's Resells 35,940 Copies of Best Seller to Macmillan Company" details the deed. This was the first action taken by a retail merchant (Macy's) selling some goods (copies of Gone with the Wind) that Macy's had already purchased from the distributor-publisher (Macmillan); other stores had purchased the books more cheaply from Macy's than from Macmillan and had attempted to return the more expensive books to Macmillan.

Macy's had sold 170,000 copies of Gone with the Wind since its publication. Macy's had been selling the book for $1.51 a copy. George Brett, the president of Macmillan Publishing Company, explained that it had to act to stop the price wars. No other publisher had ever had to take such action. Other companies besides just book publishers were in favor of maintaining resale prices; these companies also supported Macmillan's efforts.

Finally, in August 1937, President Franklin Delano Roosevelt signed into law the Tydings-Miller Bill, known as the Fair Trade Act or the Price Protection Act; it was welcomed by many companies. The single product to bring about this act was the book Gone with the Wind (Walker, pages 353–354).

Gone with the Wind had a second major influence on federal legislation. Because of the enormous taxes that Margaret Mitchell was scheduled to pay in 1936 and 1937 with the phenomenal sales of Gone with the Wind, a change came about in the revenue law. Commonly known as the Margaret Mitchell Law, Code Section 107-C came about because of her, but was not passed until after her death in 1949. The 1952 legislation called attention to the fact that some taxpayers had to pay large taxes on a lump sum of money (income) received in one year for work performed over several unpaid years. These wage earners were often self-employed taxpayers; they asked not that they be free from tax but that the total amount be averaged over the years of work that they earned them (Walker, page 354; Farr, pages 232–233). Margaret Mitchell's personified request called attention to the problem of some self-employed persons, in particular.

The Self-Employed Individuals Retirement Tax Bill of 1962 provided self-employed people a tax deduction for retirement plans that they had to finance from the earned income. For this bill, Margaret Mitchell received attention — even though she had died in 1949 (Farr, page 233).

A law which Margaret Mitchell helped to establish made the United States a member of the Copyright Convention. Margaret had been advocating this membership for some time before the United States actually joined; Mitchell shared with others the foreign copyright problems she had been facing with her book Gone with the Wind; some of the problems she encountered were with specific foreign countries. The United States finally entered into the international copyright agreement in 1955 — six years after her death (Farr, pages 233–234).

See also Berne Convention; foreign copyrights/ translations and fair trade laws.

## Fairbanks, Douglas, Sr.

Conspicuously absent from the Atlanta Premiere of Gone with the Wind (film) in December 1939 was Victor Fleming. Fleming had served as director of two important 1939 films: Gone with the Wind and Wizard of Oz. There was much speculation as to why Fleming did not attend the Atlanta events. Some suggested that Fleming did not attend because of a personality conflict with a member of the cast or crew; others noted that Fleming was angry at Producer David O. Selznick because Selznick had said in a press release that five directors had actually worked on the film Gone with the Wind. Still another possible reason was that he had recently lost a close personal friend in death: Douglas Fairbanks, Sr.

Douglas Fairbanks, Sr. (born Douglas Elton Ulman, Sr. on May 23, 1883, in Denver, Colorado) had died on December 12 in Santa Monica, California; his death had come only the day before the premiere events of December 13, 1939.

Fairbanks was both a film producer and an American motion picture actor who was famous as a swashbuckling screen hero. His athleticism, his romantic roles, and his sincerity had earned him the 1920s title "King of Hollywood."

By 1917 Fairbanks was head of his own film producing company. Some of the pictures he had produced included *The Mark of Zorro* (1920), *The Three Musketeers* (1921), *Robin Hood* (1922), *The Thief of Bagdad* (1924), *The Black Pirate* (1926), *The Iron Mask* (1929), and *The Taming of the Shrew* (1929); Fairbanks, the husband (1920–1935) of leading lady Mary Pickford, costarred in the latter with Mary Pickford.

With Pickford, Charlie Chaplin, and D. W. Griffith, he founded the United Artists Corporation in 1919. United Artists distributed many independently produced films. Although Fairbanks had announced his retirement from acting (1936), he continued working as a producer until his 1939 death ("Douglas Fairbanks, Sr.").

*See also* **Atlanta premiere of *Gone with the Wind*.**

## Farr, Finis

Finis Farr published the first biography of Margaret Mitchell in 1965. With biographies being a favorite genre for the author, he produced many others. The persons about whom he wrote included Frank Lloyd Wright (1962), the boxer Jack Johnson (1964), Franklin Delano Roosevelt (1972), and Eddie Rickenbacker (1979).

Joseph Millichap assessed online the biographies of Margaret Mitchell. His assessments included those by Edwards (1983), Farr (1965), Hanson (1991), Harwell (1983), and Pyron (1991). Millichap did not assess biographies by Walker (1993) and by later biographers.

Millichap recognizes Farr's work (1965) as being the first full-length biography of the author of *Gone with the Wind*. Although it bears the earliest copyright, he considers it useful for those studying Mitchell and her work. Millichap considers the writing readable and accurate; he notes Farr's extensive use of papers. Farr does not include cultural analysis or psychological analysis of *Gone with the Wind* or its author. He calls the work "competent."

Walker recognizes Finis Farr's biography as being an authorized biography. Stephens Mitchell, Margaret Mitchell's older brother, in the early 1960s shared some personal biographical materials with Finis Farr and discussed Farr's preparing the work. Walker notes that henceforth most writings refer to Mitchell's personal materials as his *Memoirs*. Walker does not criticize Farr's work (Walker, pages 76, 168, 221, 228, 276, 524).

## Fayette County Public Library

The Woman's Club of Fayette County, Georgia, organized and opened the first library in Fayette County in the 1920s. Two decades later, the women were again raising funds for new library facilities and for additional books and materials.

When Margaret Mitchell learned of the determination and hard work that these women were exerting, she was impressed. Mitchell eagerly became a contributor to the library fund and a donor

After **Margaret Mitchell's** 1940s donations of money and books to the new **Fayette County Public Library**, the structure took the name **Fayette County Margaret Mitchell Public Library**. Located at 152 Lee Street, Fayetteville, Georgia, the building now houses the Fayette County Historical Society. (Courtesy of Photograph Collection of Fayette County Historical Society.)

of books for the library. The women organizers decided on an appropriate name for the new 195 Lee Street structure: The Fayette County Margaret Mitchell Library; the new name would recognize their benefactress. On September 27, 1948, the new building was complete.

A new brick building followed the 1948 structure. Good use was found, however, for the older facility. The Fayette County Historical Society now occupies it. The facility houses both Civil War and genealogical records. The building accommodates also a collection of photographs, particularly local images ("History of the Fayette County Library").

## fears of Margaret Mitchell

Margaret Mitchell had two main fears: car accidents and public speaking. She was not embarrassed to admit these two fears to others.

*Fear of car accidents.* It seems almost like a premonition that Margaret Mitchell Marsh had a fear of cars, and it would be a car that would take her life in 1949. Margaret's sister-in-law Frances Marsh Zane remarked that she had never seen anyone as fearful of driving and auto accidents as her brother and Margaret. John finally reached the point where he gave up driving, and Margaret had a special routine to which she adhered before starting the engine. Margaret, she observed, seemed obsessed with wrecks and traffic accidents. In 1933 (Edwards says 1934 on page 149) the two finally bought a car; at that point, Margaret had not driven a car in ten years (Walker, page 292).

Pyron indicates that Harvey Smith, a friend of both Marsh and Mitchell, and others were amused at her ceremony before starting the car. "She had this whole ritual that she went through that just drove us all to distraction. She'd get in the car and then spend hours it seemed adjusting the pillows and cushions behind her back. Then out came her glasses which she adjusted. Then she put on an eyeshade, one of those old green ones that newspaper people wore. Next came this routine of checking all the gauges and peering into every mirror. When she finally pulled away from the curb and drove down the street, she never went over 2 miles an hour. And she took every corner like she was driving a big moving van or bus or some such vehicle. If she were turning left, she would swerve way out into the opposite lane, scaring all of us out of our wits. You just wouldn't believe it" (Pyron, pages 292–293).

The purchase came after Margaret's Grandmother Stephens died (February 17, 1934) and left her granddaughter Margaret a small inheritance. In April, Margaret purchased a 1929 green Chevrolet and she and John conquered their fear of automobiles so they could venture out in their vehicle (Edwards, page 159). The car was a used vehicle. In this purchase, as in many other things, Margaret seemed to pursue the most economical approach.

*Fear and dislike of public speaking.* Margaret Mitchell disliked, even feared, speaking in public and addressing groups of people.

1. Mitchell spoke to a writer's group in Macon at the request of Lois Cole. It was her first presentation as a full-fledged writer. She was not pleased with the experience and reported to Cole that she had made her last public speaking appearance. She called the Macon experience as being second only to when she dropped her drawers in the aisle at her church when she was only six or seven.

2. Harold Latham contacted Leigh Bureau of Lectures and Entertainments to inform the agency that Mitchell would be an excellent candidate for a tour. Latham talked directly with the founder of the bureau, W. Carlton Leigh. Leigh had booked such celebrities as First Lady Eleanor Roosevelt. Without reading *Gone with the Wind*, Leigh offered Mitchell a paid tour — with the possibility of an international tour the next year. A paid tour was unusual for an author, who usually profited only from the books sold. Mitchell, of course, declined by telling Leigh she was not a speaker — and not yet a published writer.

Leigh would not give up. He persisted in contacting her for over a month. Mitchell did not relent, and Macmillan seemed to accept her decision.

3. Mitchell slowly began to attend book signings and would occasionally make brief speeches at these events. She never enjoyed these, however.

4. Mitchell finally consented to a speech at the Studio Club and at the Atlanta Library Club. She did not comment on her speech at the Studio Club, but she informed Latham that the speech at the library had gone as poorly as the one that she had given in Macon.

5. She also agreed to an interview at WSB with Medora Field Perkerson. Mitchell suffered a severe case of "nerves" before the broadcast. She did go through with the interview, however.

6. Mitchell was not easily persuaded to do something she did not want to do. She knew how to say "No." She said it frequently; she even tried to say it to the Sears Lending Library who had advertised a speech with a book signing. The author almost cancelled out on the signing. She preferred not to speak.

7. Mitchell was a firm believer in the fact that readers should judge an author on the published works— not the drafts, notes, speech-making, and working copies. She was quick to share her opinions on personal appearances with Macmillan and

to turn down their requests for personal appearances, usually to be unpaid.

8. She refused to promote herself for the sake of the book. She did, however, make personal appearances to aid the war effort, for the American Red Cross, to assist prison inmates, and to christen the light cruiser the USS *Atlanta* and its replacement, and to speak in Atlanta schools (Brown, pages 55–56, 66, 87–89, 112, 121, 125, 225).

9. In a December 26, 1941, letter to Harold Latham, editor with Macmillan Publishing Company, Mitchell noted that no one had broken into "uproarious" laughter at her presentations. She also observed in the letter that the Lord often makes us do the things we least like to do (quoted in Brown, page 226).

*Fear and dislike of photography.* Margaret Mitchell usually disliked posing for photographs.

1. Stephens Mitchell told the story of going to a photography studio for a picture of their mother, his sister Margaret, and him together and separately. When Margaret did not want to pose alone, the photographer convinced three-year-old Margaret that he wanted to capture his kitten on camera. She willingly held the animal for "its" photograph (Pyron, page 37).

2. Margaret's composure shines through in her early photographs. Stephens Mitchell — Margaret's older brother — talked about how their mother wanted to teach Margaret to be independent. This independence shows through in some photographs which show her with feet firmly planted and facing defiantly into the camera (Pyron, page 47).

3. Later in life Mitchell became more reluctant to appear before a camera. According to a letter on October 31, 1935, to Harold Latham, she had told Lois Cole, who worked at one time for Macmillan, that she had had no pictures taken in ten years, "not since the *Journal* used me so frequently to pose by dead bodies, two-headed calves, the first cotton

A confident, teenage Margaret Mitchell in jaunty beret and trousers looks squarely at the camera as she appears clad in hiking attire. (Courtesy of the Atlanta-Fulton Public Library System's Special Collections Department.)

Clad in a feminine dress, Margaret Mitchell appears before the door of the family home in Atlanta; the position of her arms indicates the self-assurance that Stephens says was typical of her in most early photographs. (Courtesy of the Atlanta–Fulton Public Library System's Special Collections Department.)

Margaret Mitchell and her friend Henry Love Angel re-enact a scene from the serial *The Perils of Pauline*. A similar photograph is in Margaret Mitchell's *Lost Laysen*. (Courtesy of the Atlanta-Fulton Public Library System's Special Collections Department.)

bales of the season and the largest watermelon at the county fair" (Pyron, 317).

Margaret expresses concern about her appearance in the letter. She indicates that she is "seventeen pounds underweight." In addition, she had had a recent epidemic of boils on her head; the doctor had shaved places on her head from "the size of a silver dollar to a penny." In jest, however, Margaret did agree to be photographed in postage-sized hats to cover the bald spots or in a turban like T. E. Lawrence might wear — if Latham would find the apparel for her (October 31, 1935, letter to Harold Latham from Margaret Mitchell, as cited by Pyron, page 317).

Margaret sent Lois a photo on April 27, 1936. Her letter said she wanted the photograph back because "I have to pay three books every time I get a slick print for an out of town paper…. Yes, I know this picture looks fifteen years younger than I am … but at least I don't look squinched and mean" (Walker, page 237).

4. Pyron reported an incident in which Margaret Mitchell "hid herself in one of the dining rooms … behind locked doors to avoid the flashbulbs" (page 410).

Margaret's account of the incident in a letter to Harold Latham on April 18, 1938, is somewhat different. "For nearly a year I have had no photographs taken by the newspapers, nor have I given my interviews unless on matters of 'news.' … I see no reason why my face should appear in the papers three times a week for no good reason…. I notified all three papers [*The Journal, The Georgian, The Constitution*] of Mr. Christensen's arrival. *The Journal* and *The Georgian* photographed and interviewed him…. *The Constitution*, however, was hellbent on getting a picture of both of us together, and for twenty-four hours I told them that it could not be done. Just when our dinner was beginning a reporter and photographer showed up and forced their way into our private dining room. John took them and Mr. Christensen out and told them that I had already discussed the matter with the city editor. They phoned [him] and he arrived at the club. He said he would have a picture of us both or else we would be 'pretty damned sorry.' Our reply was that we did not jump through hoops for anybody" (Letter from Margaret Mitchell to Harold Latham, April 14, 1938, Harwell, *Letters,* pages 194–195).

5. Pyron describes Margaret Mitchell's reactions to photographers — even at the Atlanta premiere of *Gone with the Wind* in December of 1939. The event that Margaret attended at the Piedmont Driving Club was begun "in error" and "continued in terror" (Pyron, page 378).

Margaret arrived late to the party and found photographers demanding shots, "and she had to pose with all the stars. She feared and loathed such situations. [Still] she betrayed no turmoil" (page 378).

As the author of *Gone with the Wind*, Mitchell would remain a desired subject of photographers and fans for the rest of her life, whether or not she desired the attention.

*See also* animals; Atlanta premiere of *Gone with the Wind*; Cole, Lois; Latham, Harold Strong; Rich's Department Store.

**Finland, sales of *Gone with the Wind*** *see* **foreign copyrights/translations and fair trade laws**

### *Fire Over England*

The actress Vivien Leigh, who was the final selection for the role of "Scarlett" in *Gone with the Wind*, had appeared in the film *Fire Over England* in 1937. She played "Cynthia," a lady-in-waiting; this was by no means a major role in this movie from London Film Productions (*Fire Over England*).

### fire scene filming for *Gone with the Wind*

The filming of the fire scene for the movie *Gone with the Wind* became a significant occasion. Producer David O. Selznick was filming the scene on December 10, 1938, long before he had approved all the cast. The site of the flaming warehouses was not in Atlanta or Hollywood but on a set in Culver City. Because Clark Gable was not able to attend the filming due to his contract with MGM and because the selection for the role of "Scarlett" was not certain, stunt actors in silhouette appeared on the wagon, which was supposed to be carrying "Scarlett," "Rhett," "Melanie," "Prissy," and the baby. The burning buildings were the gas-soaked remainders of scenes from *King Kong, The Last of the Mohicans*, and *The Garden of Allah*.

As David O. Selznick was watching the ruins, his brother Myron Selznick — a talent agent — appeared on the scene. With him was a British actress named Vivien Leigh, whom David Selznick did not know. Myron introduced her by saying, "I want you to meet your 'Scarlett O'Hara'" (Shavin and Shartar, page 20). Myron's words proved true. Leigh became the leading actress in the movie. In her role as "Scarlett O'Hara," she would win an Oscar for Best Actress in a Leading Role at the 1940 ceremonies.

*See also* Academy of Motion Picture Arts and Sciences; Leigh, Vivien; Selznick, David O.; Selznick, Myron.

### Fitzgerald, Aline

Aline Fitzgerald was the unmarried sister of Margaret Mitchell's grandmother Annie Fitzgerald Stephens. Great-Aunt Aline moved into the Mitchell household just after Maybelle Mitchell died in 1919 and after Margaret had left Smith College to manage the Mitchell house. Grandmother Stephens and Aunt Aline, however, would become angry and move out of the house in the middle of the night (Edwards, pages 67–68).

### Fitzgerald, Philip

Margaret Mitchell's maternal great-grandfather was born in Ireland. He came to America and had a house and land in Clayton County, Georgia. He died in 1798 before Margaret was born.

### Fleming, Victor

Movie director Victor Fleming was born on February 23, 1883, in Pasadena, California. Fleming worked with Producer David O. Selznick on *Gone with the Wind* (1939). He earned an Oscar as Best Director for the film; he did not, however, attend the Atlanta premiere.

Fleming began his career in motion pictures in 1910 as a stunt car driver. He later began filming work for D. W. Griffith. During World War I, Fleming served in the photographic section. He was also the Chief Photographer for President Woodrow Wilson at Versailles, France. Fleming worked with Clark Gable and Spencer Tracy at both Metro-Goldwyn-Mayer and 20th Century–Fox Studios.

Fleming first served as director on the feature film *When the Clouds Roll By* (1919). His early popular sound films included *Red Dust* (1932) and *Treasure Island* (1934). The same year as *Gone with the Wind* (1939), Fleming also directed *The Wizard of Oz* (1939), which propelled Judy Garland to fame; both films received Academy Award nominations. His direction continued with such films as *Dr. Jekyll and Mr. Hyde* (1941) and *Joan of Arc* (1948). His death from a heart attack came on January 6, 1949, near Cottonwood, Arizona ("Victor Fleming Biography").

Fleming remains the only director to have two movies listed in the top 10 of the 1998 American Film Institute's list of the 100 greatest American films. These are *Gone with the Wind* and *The Wizard of Oz*. Victor Fleming's interment is in Hollywood Memorial Cemetery in Hollywood, California ("Biography for Victor Fleming").

*See also* American Academy of Motion Picture Arts and Sciences; Atlanta premiere of *Gone with the Wind*; Selznick, David O.

### Florence Crittenton Home

The Florence Crittenton Home for unwed mothers opened in Atlanta in 1893. Kate Harwood Waller Barrett was a main organizer of the establishment

(Zerfas, Bridgette). Walker reports that Margaret Mitchell "did many generous and thoughtful things for young women in the Florence Crittendon [note spelling disparity] Home for unmarried mothers." Mitchell encouraged the young mothers to continue with their lives. She helped them as they applied for jobs by paying for their manicures, permanents, clothes, and shoes for the interviews (page 465).

## Force, Manning

As a child, Margaret Mitchell never tired of viewing *The Battle of Atlanta* painting at the Atlanta Cyclorama. She especially enjoyed locating "Old Abe" (the eagle-mascot), the Troup-Hurt House, and finding Colonel Manning Force after he is shot in the face and is being carried from the battlefield in the painting ("Atlanta Cyclorama and Civil War Museum").

Manning Ferguson Force was born in 1824 in Washington, D.C. He graduated from Harvard Law School in 1849. In 1850, Force moved to Cincinnati, Ohio, to begin his law practice. In 1861, however, he left his practice to enlist as a major in the 20th Ohio Volunteer Infantry; later he would serve with General James B. McPherson's 17th Corps, which "bore the brunt of the Battle of Raymond" (Drake).

Only half of the men survived, and nearly all of them showed evidence of the battle. When Sergeant Osborn Oldroyd reported to Colonel Force and told Force about the fate of the men, Colonel Force cried.

After the Siege of Vicksburg, Force went to Georgia and participated in the Atlanta Campaign. Colonel Force received wounds to the face during the Battle of Atlanta. In March of 1865, Force received promotion to Major General of Volunteers for his bravery during the battle; in 1892 he earned the Union Medal of Honor. Part of the citation states: "Charged upon the enemy's works, and after their capture defended his position against assaults of the enemy until he was severely wounded" (Drake).

When Force returned to Cincinnati, Ohio, after the end of the Civil War, he served as a Supreme Court judge. He became a prominent writer and lecturer and authored several law books (Drake).

## foreign copyrights/translations and fair trade laws

From an early age, Margaret Mitchell had learned about plagiarism and copyright law from her parents (Edwards, pages 31–32).

She helped to ensure that the United States would become a member of a universal copyright convention, or the Berne Convention, albeit the six years after her 1949 death (Farr, pages 233–234).

Walker indicates that Margaret was in charge of her own foreign copyrights for the book *Gone with the Wind*. Macmillan specified that Mitchell would have to assume responsibility for renewing foreign copyrights regularly. Even though John argued that a housewife should not have the responsibility of legal details, Macmillan would not or could not help them. Macmillan had transferred all foreign copyright and translation rights to Margaret. The Marshes—with Stephens Mitchell to help—worked out an agreement with Marion Saunders, an agent in handling foreign copyrights that Macmillan helped them contact (Pyron, pages 309–310; Walker, page 310). The Marshes and Margaret Baugh, with the guidance of Saunders, operated their business matters from an apartment they rented. Walker declares that the group became experts in foreign copyright (page 310). Mitchell encountered some successes—and some problems—with specific foreign countries, with Macmillan, and with Saunders.

*Gone with the Wind* has become immensely popular throughout the world. Translations have appeared in 40 languages in 50 countries. Wiley indicates that the languages include French, German, Japanese, Spanish, Amharic (Ethiopia), Arabic (Egypt and Lebanon), Farsi (Iran), Burmese (Myanmar), Catalan (Spain), and even in the Kannada language for India.

On September 6, 1945, Mitchell wrote to author Malcolm Cowley who was anticipating the preparation of a literary history of the United States: "It never occurred to me *Gone with the Wind* would be translated into any foreign language. When it appeared in so many languages and had such astoundingly good reviews, I was breathless, and still am" (Wiley, "Seventy Years Later").

*Canada.* On June 30, 1936, the first "foreign" edition of *Gone with the Wind* appeared—in Toronto. The Macmillan Company of Canada Limited was the publisher. Because the United States was not a member of the Berne Convention for the Protection of Literary and Artistic Works, only by publishing a book simultaneously in a member country, such as Canada, could American publishers ensure their copyright protection elsewhere. Wiley noted: "By the time World War II began in September 1939, *Gone with the Wind* also had been published in France (*Autant en Emporte le Vent*), Hungary (*Elfujta a Szel*), Latvia (*Vejiem Lidzi*), Poland (*Przeminelo z Wiatrem*), and Romania (*Pe Aripile Vantului*)."

During World War II, Mitchell and some of her foreign publishers lost contact with each other. When the war was over, several attempted to pay her the royalties that they owed to her. Things soon changed, however, with the installation of the Iron Curtain over Eastern Europe in the middle to late 1940s.

Margaret Mitchell realized that the publishing rights to *Gone with the Wind* were even more valuable after World War II began than before the advent of war. She shared this opinion with Wallace McClure, a U.S. State Department official, on March 31, 1947: "Every country has had its recent experience with war and occupation and defeat, and people in each country apply the experiences of the characters of *Gone with the Wind* to themselves" (Wiley).

Meanwhile, Mitchell continued to struggle with her own wars: piracy cases in China, Greece and Japan.

*Belgium.* Through December of 1947, Belgium had sold 20,000 copies in the French language, and 7,000 were sold in Flemish by 1945. Margaret reacted to the numbers in Belgium and some other foreign countries by saying that they "take my breath away" (Pyron, page 431).

*Bengal.* A request for foreign editions and translations gradually failed to faze Margaret and her staff. Pyron reports that the Bengali request hardly merited from her a second thought (Pyron, page 429).

*Brazil.* Saunders's performance, in the beginning, was acceptable to the Marshes. Mitchell secured a contract in the fall of 1938 for a Portuguese translation that would be sold in Brazil. By June of 1948, Brazil had sold 25,785 copies of *Gone with the Wind.*

*Bulgaria.* Margaret seemed surprised to learn that Bulgaria was interested in her book. She was even more surprised to learn that *Gone with the Wind* had been translated into Bulgarian from the French. She expressed wonder about the final results of such translations (Pyron, page 423).

*Chile.* In 1936, the Marshes were already finding pirated copies of *Gone with the Wind* in foreign nations. Chile was one of the first countries that Margaret Mitchell took to task. Empressa Ercilla, a Chilean publisher, was still writing letters to her about Spanish translations to be printed in Chile. The Marshes thought that they had solved the copyright and translation problems; they found other problems rearing their heads.

Marion Saunders was an aggressive promoter of translations and foreign editions. She began to pester Brett about allowing a publisher in Chile to sell Macmillan's Spanish translation; he firmly disagreed. Brett reminded Saunders that the translation rights for the Spanish edition rested with Macmillan; he shared the information with the Marshes in April 1940 and suggested that the small commission that Saunders was trying to earn could give them a "peck of trouble."

By June of 1948, Mitchell could proudly say that Chile had sold 61,171 legal copies of *Gone with the Wind* (Pyron, pages 421; 430–431; 502, note 7).

*China.* The country of China caused Margaret Mitchell some worry. She discovered an advertisement for a pirated copy of *Gone with the Wind.* The introduction to the illegal copy of the Chinese edition noted that she was "a perfect housekeeper." Furthermore, the introduction described Mitchell as "pure, benevolent, filial and obedient to her husband" (Pyron, pages 422–423; Harwell, *Letters*, page 403).

The exact numbers sold in China and Japan were difficult to determine because of the illegal sales and printings; it seemed, however, that in both countries hundreds of copies had been sold (Pyron, page 431).

*Cuba.* The effort to prevent the illegal sales and printings of *Gone with the Wind* was a non-ending battle for the Marshes. *Diario de la Marina* was publishing — without permissions — regular installments of Mitchell's novel.

The Marshes found it necessary to hire people to send out to countries with pirated editions. In many cases, the Marsh employees were able to force the publishers who were illegally printing copies of *Gone with the Wind* to cease and desist immediately; in addition, the workers were often able to negotiate a contract, even though it was "after the fact."

*Czechoslovakia.* In August–November of 1947 Mitchell was able to report 5,000 copies sold in the Slovakian language. By the end of 1948, she indicated there had been 84,000 copies sold in the Czech language (Pyron, pages 422–434, 443).

*Gone with the Wind* served as an inspiration to many countries, but particularly to the countries of Czechoslovakia and France. Margaret Mitchell commented on this in her letter of September 6, 1945, to Malcolm Crowley, who was preparing a literary history of the United States. "I found it very interesting, too, that while many critics in the United States based their criticism upon the love story or the narrative, European critics evaluated it on a different basis. In practically every European country critics wrote at length of the 'universal historical significance.' Each nation applied to its own past history the story of the Confederate rise and fall and reconstruction.... Czechs wrote not only of their troubled past but of their fears of the future, and I had letters from that country just before it went under (Nazi domination), saying that if the people of the South had risen again to freedom the people of Czechoslovakia could do likewise" (Wiley).

Mitchell expressed concern for the Czechoslovakian publisher of *Gone with the Wind*. On July 26, 1949, she told Dr. Wallace McClure of the State Department that the publishing company was "nationalized." She knew that the head of the company was still alive and was still at liberty. Mitchell noted, however, that she did not know how long this might be true (Harwell, *Letters,* page 424).

*Denmark. Gone with the Wind* was a popular seller in Denmark. The first printing of the fall 1937 edition numbered 10,000 copies. In eleven days the publisher had sold all 10,000 copies. The book went into a second printing, with the publisher estimating the eventual sales of 40,000 copies. The publisher informed her that no other book had ever sold that many copies.

By 1948, Mitchell was able to report that Denmark (with a population of fewer than one million people) had sold 90,000 copies of her work.

*Estonia.* Mitchell heard that a company in Estonia was intending to publish *Gone with the Wind.* Mitchell and Saunders were preparing their course of action, but it was a moot point. Mitchell and Saunders never found out if there was a published volume because Russia invaded Estonia.

*Finland.* Through April of 1948 Finland sold 50,000 copies of *Gone with the Wind* (Pyron, pages 421, 423–426, 430–431, 433–434, 453).

*France.* Mitchell would find that translations and copyright issues in France would consume much of her time and effort. Rewarding to her, however, was the story of how her book benefited the people. A Southerner living in France told her that the French people had distributed the novel through the underground and passed it on with one another.

When the resistance movement in Europe began to find inspiration in the reactions of the South to federal occupation in Mitchell's novel, the Nazis banned *Gone with the Wind.* The "bootlegged" copies of Mitchell's novel sold for $60 in France during the 1940s; some people had been shot for possessing the novel. Margaret remarked: "It made me proud and happy to know that something I wrote could give pleasure and comfort to French people during the occupation" (Wiley).

Not all of her overseas correspondence involved problems. She was pleased with the 1939 French edition of her novel and took note of the "delightful sea changes" many of her Southern expressions had undergone in translation. "I was especially amused when Gerald O'Hara ejaculated 'Oo, la la'" (Wiley).

Of great concern to Margaret, however, was dealing with the unauthorized sequel of *Gone with the Wind* that France issued. Side effects of her overwork were exhaustion and stress; she also contracted a bronchial infection (Pyron, 423–426, 430–434, 453, 512 note 17).

*Germany.* Mitchell's *Gone with the Wind* had sold well in Germany before World War II. The edition printed in Hamburg sold more than 250,000 copies. After the war, Dr. Henry Goverts, her publisher, reminded her that their pre-war contract was still binding, and he reminded her of the bank that held her payment.

Mitchell's problems with Germany, however, were thorny. Federal law made it difficult to trade with Germany before peace was final. The State Department had one set of rules, but the United States Office of Military Government had another. To compound the problems, Hamburg was in the British Occupation Zone. The rules seemed to change often and their interpretation often depended upon who was offering the counsel (Pyron, pages 426–429). She teased George Brett that they might be guilty of collaborating with the enemy before the signing of the peace treaty. She speculated that they might face a firing squad (Harwell, *Letters,* pages 285, 287–289).

Still, sales were good in Germany. By 1948, she was able to report that German sales had reached 368,629 (Pyron, page 431). The German people seemed to relate to the feelings of bitterness that followed the end of the Civil War in the United States; they compared that bitterness to the feelings that the German people felt in 1918 (Wiley).

*Great Britain.* On May 21, 1936, Mitchell received a $5,000 check for the film version of *Gone with the Wind.* She also signed the contract with British Macmillan for their publication of her work. Harold Macmillan — who would become a future prime minister of Great Britain — was heading the British Macmillan Company at the time. (Although the names of the British publishing company and the New York firm were similar, there was no relation between the two.)

Macmillan Publishing Company in the fall of 1936 returned all foreign copyrights to Margaret Mitchell. The British firm had printed 716,048 books by December of 1945; she had no report, however, of the actual number of copies sold in Great Britain (Pyron, pages 324, 326, 418, 420, 426, 431).

*Greece.* Margaret Mitchell found it necessary to report to Marion Saunders, who helped her with foreign copyright, that a newspaper in Greece had serialized *Gone with the Wind* without permission to do so. Saunders began working with the Greek counsel in New York immediately. The Greek press relented and began negotiations on the royalties owed to Mitchell (Pyron, pages 423, 430).

*Holland.* In 1937 Mitchell discovered that, without authorization, a Dutch publishing firm had produced its own version of *Gone with the Wind*. The Dutch novel was a "handsome, three-volume set" (Wiley). Ziud-Hollandsche Uitgevers Mij-AHUM (a shortened name for the firm) and Mitchell went to court. Margaret lost (Pyron, pages 431, 449–453).

She expressed her position to Joseph Henry Jackson in a letter on April 19, 1938. "Ordinarily I am a mild individual, but my blood is up on this matter, and I intend to take it through every court in Holland" (Harwell, *Letters,* page 197). Undeterred by her first loss, Margaret continued her battle with Holland for ten years in court after court. She sought legal counsel through Cadwalader, Wickersham and Taft, Macmillan's legal firm. Upon the advice of the firm, she retained a new attorney in Holland.

Margaret realized that the world was on the eve of war. She wrote to Dr. William McClure with the State Department in Washington on December 9, 1939. "John and I have so often discussed the probable effect of the war on the treaty in which all of us are so interested. We've also discussed the possibility that the threat of war may make the Dutch courts a little more kindly toward American citizens. Of course, such an idea is a long shot, but if the Dutch fear the Germans and want the assistance of America[,] perhaps they may show a little justice to an American caught in their courts" (Harwell, *Letters,* page 288).

On May 1, 1940, Germany invaded Holland. Margaret continued the legal process. She still had not achieved the restitution she demanded. The High Court of Justice in The Hague ruled finally in Margaret Mitchell's favor on February 14, 1941. The High Court called for a retrial. Macmillan's firm of Cadwalader, Wickersham, and Taft, and J. A. Fruin, Macmillan's legal counsel that was helping Margaret in the battle, suggested a settlement in the amount of $1,000 as cash restitution. Before the final negotiations were complete, however, the Japanese bombed Pearl Harbor. America's entry into the war made the communications between the Dutch and the American litigants difficult. Still the case continued (Pyron, pages 449–452).

In December of 1941 Margaret Mitchell and John R. Marsh visited with Marjorie Kinnan Rawlings, author of *The Yearling*. The three talked about how both *Gone with the Wind* and *The Yearling* were the two best-selling novels of recent years and how Holland had pirated both works. They hoped that the passage of a treaty would prevent such pirating for future authors (Walker, page 448).

On September 17, 1945, Margaret Mitchell earned 28,000 florins for royalties and 500 florins for costs. She was dissatisfied.

First, she had received no formal notice of the settlement. Second, the Dutch publisher — without her knowledge or her permission — had sold "publication rights" to a Flemish firm for a Belgian edition. The company in Belgium could produce a cheaply bound, cheaply printed edition if it desired.

The Flemish books first appeared in December of 1945. Margaret inspected a copy with interest. There was no proper copyright imprinted on the flyleaves. The volumes were inexpensively prepared.

She found that the Dutch editions of *Gone with the Wind* also lacked proper copyright. Margaret directed her anger against Holland, ZHUM, her lawyer Fruin, and even Cadwalader, Wickersham and Taft. The law firm of Macmillan Company, in turn, became angry with Margaret Mitchell — not with Fruin or with the pirates.

When at last Margaret's money was released, Fruin deducted his fees from the funds. Margaret complained to the Cadwalader, Wickersham and Taft, but they took Fruin's part. Margaret's brother Stephens wrote a furious letter to Cadwalader, Wickersham and Taft. Stephens and she released her New York attorney and Fruin from her employ (Pyron, pages 449–452).

Margaret was at last able to tell Macmillan Publishing Company on December 8, 1948, that the contract was going much better, and that "adjustments and concessions were made between me and the former pirate, the settlement money made over to me has been paid, and I've even gotten almost all the royalty money due me up to the present paid to me, too. Of course, I'll never collect one fiftieth of the amount of money I spent on this lawsuit, but still it's encouraging to get what I have gotten, which is considerable" (Pyron, pages 451–452).

As a result of the Dutch case, the public could begin to realize how seriously Margaret Mitchell demanded what she considered her rights and her privileges. Holland had sold 48,549 copies by June of 1945 (Pyron, pages 431, 449–453). The case that had occupied Margaret Mitchell for about a decade was finally settled in her favor. The publisher, Wiley reported, "apparently harbored no hard feelings over the matter: For years after Mitchell's death, the publisher sent tulip bulbs to be planted on her grave."

*Hungary*. As Russia moved into the country of Hungary, some of the printing presses and the newspaper critics became silent. Margaret reported that she was so fearful for the lives of her publishers that she was often afraid to communicate with them for fear of causing them trouble; the Russians had openly opposed her novel *Gone with the Wind* on several occasions. Margaret feared that something she might say in a letter might be misconstrued by the Soviet censors and might cause the liquidation of a publisher. Despite these problems, *Gone with the Wind* sold 56,902 copies by February of 1947 (Pyron, pages 431, 442–443).

*Italy.* There were 81,132 copies of *Gone with the Wind* sold in Italy by June of 1948 (Pyron, page 431).

*Japan.* In 1939 Margaret Mitchell discovered a publisher in Japan was illegally publishing copies of *Gone with the Wind*. By the time she received any reply from her correspondence to him, he had already sold 150,000 copies.

Although Japan was not required by treaty to honor copyrights in America, Margaret turned the incident over to Marion Saunders. Margaret, however, never received a single penny from the piracy of her novel in Japan — even with the help of Saunders (Pyron, pages 422, 430–431, 453).

On July 28, 1939, Mitchell wrote to Dr. Wallace McClure of the Department of State about her communications with Japan. The publisher in Japan had informed her that her volume had sold 150,000 copies. He was willing to tell her that her novel had outsold even Pearl S. Buck's *The Good Earth* (1931); Margaret had learned that Buck had never received even a nickel in royalties from her Japanese publisher. Only one book had outsold *Gone with the Wind*; that was *Wheat and Soldiers* by Katsunori Tamai in 1939.

Mitchell said in the letter to McClure that the publisher had asked her to remember that Japan was at war; paying royalties was difficult at this time for the publishing company. Saunders, Mitchell explained, had responded by explaining that the royalty scale was ever increasing — not decreasing (Harwell, *Letters,* pages 284–286).

On October 9, 1939, Mitchell wrote again to McClure. This time she informed him that after Saunders's correspondence with the Japanese publisher, she had received a "very pretty silk kimona [*sic*]" (Harwell, *Letters,* page 287). A few days later, Mitchell received "a Japanese doll nearly three feet high in a red lacquer and glass case about four feet high" (Harwell, *Letters,* pages 287–288). Mitchell described this doll in a humorous manner in the October 9, 1939, letter to McClure. "If ever there was a white elephant this doll and its case is the elephant. There is no place in our apartment where it can be conveniently put. Again I wrote formally, thanking the publishers, and again Miss Saunders wrote them suggesting cash. I was somewhat puzzled as to why I had received these gifts. Saturday I received a letter from the translator, writing in behalf of the

Margaret Mitchell in her American Red Cross uniform confidently poses with "Miss Oh So Solly," her Geisha doll from a Japanese publisher who never paid her royalties. Mitchell donated the doll to a Red Cross fund-raising auction. (Courtesy of the James G. Kenan Research Center at the Atlanta History Center.)

**Margaret Mitchell appears here in her apartment on a footstool in front of a bookcase holding her books and foreign translations of *Gone with the Wind*. (Catalogue Number: 792. Photographer: Ken Rogers. Courtesy of the Atlanta-Fulton Public Library System's Special Collections Department.)**

publisher, and this letter explained everything. They wanted a picture of me standing by the Japanese doll so that they could use it for publicity purposes. A nation with so much gall certainly should go far. Needless to say, they will not get the pictures" (Harwell, *Letters,* page 288). Mitchell donated the Japanese doll to the American Red Cross for an auction. The *Atlanta Constitution* ran a story about the auction on August 2, 1942 (Harwell, *Letters*, page 288).

*Latvia.* Marion Saunders continued to please George Brett of Macmillan Publishing Company most of the time. Saunders generated a foreign contract in Latvia in the fall of 1938. By June of 1948 this contract had resulted in the sale of 2,453 copies of *Gone with the Wind* (Pyron, pages 421, 431).

*London.* On Sept. 29, 1936, Macmillan and Company, Limited, published *Gone with the Wind* in London. Whereas 10,000 copies had been printed in America as a first printing, the first printing in London was a modest 3,000 copies. The book was a success, however. Over the next two years, more than 150,000 copies sold in England.

*Norway.* Margaret Mitchell told a reporter of *Harper's* that through 1939 her book had sold 47,356 copies in three volumes in Norway (Pyron, page 431).

*Palestine.* Keeping track of foreign copyrights and foreign royalties was almost impossible for Margaret Mitchell, Marion Saunders, and John R. Marsh. In an interview with a reporter of *Harper's*, Mitchell indicated that she knew that an edition of her book existed in Palestine, but the war in the Middle East had prevented her from obtaining reports from the sale of this edition. (Pyron, page 431)

*Poland.* Mitchell was pleased to learn that her

book *Gone with the Wind* had proved useful to the underground during German occupation. The underground used the volume for "morale-building purposes" (Pyron, page 434).

Mitchell, however, had no sales figures in pre-war Poland "because my publisher was liquidated." The numbers she did have, however, indicated a sales volume through March of 1948 of 5,500 copies (Pyron, page 431).

The Poles seemed to relate to the sectionalism in *Gone with the Wind*. They compared this division to the partitioning of their country in World War II (Wiley).

*Puerto Rico.* In the spring of 1940, Marion Saunders began pestering George Brett to allow her Chilean publisher to sell his Spanish translation of *Gone with the Wind* in Puerto Rico. Brett flatly refused. He argued that Puerto Rico was a territory of the United States and was Macmillan "turf"—regardless of the language. Saunders disagreed strongly. She accused him of cheating Margaret out of some of her royalties and argued that there was a market for a Spanish translation in Puerto Rico. Despite these disagreements, however, Saunders's performance was acceptable to the Marshes (Pyron, page 421).

*Romania.* Through March of 1947, Romania reported sales of 20,000 copies of *Gone with the Wind*. Communication with the country and with Mitchell's publishers there had been difficult during World War II (Pyron, page 431).

*Spain.* Mitchell shared with *Harper's* that sales of *Gone with the Wind* in Spain through 1947 had totaled — to her reckonings— 25,047 copies (Pyron, page 431).

*Sweden.* *Harper's* was able to inform the public that sales of Margaret Mitchell's two-volume novel in Sweden by the end of 1947 topped 67,363. *Harper's* was eager to run a story on the epic sales of this American author abroad (Pyron, page 431).

*Switzerland.* Margaret found questions about foreign copyrights and foreign editions seemed to fill her mail almost every other day. Even after the end of World War II, problems continued. Her publishers in the American Zone faced a critical paper shortage and could not publish her work easily. They began to request permission to complete their work in Switzerland.

Publishing in Switzerland meant that the companies and she had to negotiate a new series of copyright issues—and more. Furthermore, in many cases the work had to be fed through the channels of the United States Office of Military Government. Although tempted to give up, she persisted with these legal concerns. By the fall of 1948, she was able to claim twelve-year sales of

368,629 copies by her German publishers (Pyron, page 429).

*Ukraine.* The maze of copyright became even more puzzling with the entry of requests to the Macmillan Publishing Company from an Austrian publisher for permission to publish a Ukrainian translation of *Gone with the Wind*. Brett wrote to Mitchell about these communications; he told Mitchell that he and others were curious as to why these requests even came to them. *Gone with the Wind* was not even permitted within the Soviet boundaries by the Russians. Why would an Austrian publisher even want these permissions? Brett told Mitchell that Macmillan had figured out that the Austrian firm intended to sell these translations in Canada; Canada had a large population of Ukrainians (Pyron, pages 429–430).

*Yugoslavia.* Through March of 1948 the number of foreign sales for Yugoslavian translations of *Gone with the Wind* amounted only to 4,563, according to Mitchell's records. This was probably the fewest number of copies of Mitchell's book sold in any foreign country.

Yet the negotiations involved an extraordinary amount of work. Many of the foreign countries assumed the work was in the public domain. Mitchell negotiated, mediated, sought translators, argued, and enlisted the help of the Office of War Information in Belgrade, the United States Embassy, Stephens Mitchell and other lawyers, and also opinions from Marion Saunders and Macmillan Publishing Company.

The reviews of her book in Yugoslavia were actually critiques. The Communists wrote that Margaret Mitchell was trying to re-introduce slavery into the United States; Margaret Mitchell argued, however, that the Communists were fearful of the South because Southerners were conservative and would oppose communism (Pyron, pages 431–432; 442–443).

**See also American Red Cross; Berne Convention; Dixon, Thomas; Hoyle, Steve; plagiarism; Rawlings, Marjorie Kinnan; Saunders, Marion;** *The Traitor* **and young Margaret Mitchell.**

## foreign copyrights/translations and Margaret Mitchell

Mitchell was proud of her personal collection of foreign editions of her novel *Gone with the Wind*. In a color photograph on the cover of the December 14, 1947, edition of *The Atlanta Journal Magazine*, she appears in her apartment and is seated on a footstool in front of her bookshelves. The bookcases behind her hold dozens of foreign translations of *Gone with the Wind*. John R. Marsh (who died in 1952) willed the books in Margaret Mitchell's personal collection to the Atlanta–Fulton County Public Library. The photograph in the Atlanta-Fulton County Public Library, however, indicates that the image had appeared in an issue of the *Atlanta Constitution* — not in the December 14, 1947, edition of *The Atlanta Journal Magazine* (Wiley).

### foreign copies/translations and museums in the Atlanta area

Two Atlanta-area museums currently feature displays of foreign editions of *Gone with the Wind*. The first is the Road to Tara Museum in Jonesboro. The second is the Marietta *Gone with the Wind* Museum: Scarlett on the Square. The Margaret Mitchell House and Museum houses some foreign editions of the novel from the collection of the Atlanta History Center. In addition, the Atlanta-Fulton Public Library on Margaret Mitchell Square in downtown Atlanta has some of the author's foreign editions on display in its Special Collections Department on the fifth floor; John R. Marsh had willed these copies to the library (Wiley).

### formal release date of *Gone with the Wind*

The formal release date of Margaret Mitchell's book *Gone with the Wind* was June 30, 1936. By the end of the first week, Mitchell had received more than 300 copies in the mail to autograph; most of the first senders had expected her to pay for the return of the book (Edwards, page 187; Walker, pages 341–343).

### France, sales of *Gone with the Wind* see foreign copyrights/translations and fair trade laws

### Frank, Leo

Perhaps the best-known victim of a lynching in Georgia was Leo M. Frank, a white, Jewish manager at the National Pencil Company in Atlanta. Charged with the murder of a young female factory worker, Frank was in the state penitentiary in Milledgeville, Georgia. When Frank received life imprisonment instead of a death sentence, an angry mob lynched him in August of 1915. This case and the resulting lynching "generated the formation of the modern Ku Klux Klan [on Stone Mountain], and produced the Jewish Anti-Defamation League, two organizations that exist to this day" (Hepburn, 24).

*Related books, plays, and films.* Leo Frank's death as a result of his supposed murder of an employee of the Atlanta Pencil Company has been the subject of many books, including *The Leo Frank Case* by Leonard Dinnerstein in 1968 and *A Little Girl Is*

*Dead* by Harry Golden in 1965, a Broadway play, *Parade*, a musical by Jason Robert Brown in 1998, and a movie, *The Murder of Mary Phagan*, a 1988 television movie with Jack Lemmon. The lynching of Leo Frank "foreshadowed the 1915 rebirth of the Ku Klux Klan at Stone Mountain" (Hepburn, page 24).

*The stand of Eugene Muse Mitchell on the Leo Frank case.* In his capacity as a lawyer, Margaret Mitchell's father, Eugene Muse Mitchell, wrote a brief in defense of Leo Frank after Frank was accused of murder. After the conviction of Leo Frank, Eugene Muse Mitchell wrote a letter to the Atlanta newspaper urging an appeal of Frank's conviction; Mitchell was at that time president of the Georgia Bar Association. This period in time was "as haunting for Jews in Atlanta as the 1906 race riots were for blacks" (Taylor in *Before Scarlett*, page xi).

*Maybelle Stephens Mitchell and the lynching of Leo Frank.* Maybelle Stephens Mitchell, Margaret Mitchell's mother, was incensed at the lynching of Leo Frank. She had been upset also when politician Tom Watson had campaigned in Georgia and espoused views that were against Jews, African Americans, and Catholics. Maybelle Mitchell cofounded the Catholic Layman's Association, which helped to combat religious intolerance (Taylor in *Before Scarlett*, page xi–xii).

*Margaret Mitchell and the Ku Klux Klan.* With parents who opposed prejudice, it is no wonder that Margaret Mitchell did not condone the activities of the KKK. Instead she actively pursued the rights and advocated good medical care for African Americans during her lifetime. She helped pay for the medical education of several African American students, helped obtain good medical care for Bessie Berry Jordan, and worked to improve the hospitals.

*See also* Grady Hospital, Jordan, Bessie Berry; Ku Klux Klan; Mays, Benjamin; Randall, Alice.

### Friendship Baptist Church

With its establishment in 1862 and its independent organization in 1866, Friendship Baptist Church became Atlanta's first black Baptist autonomous congregation. The congregation worshiped in a boxcar from Chattanooga, Tennessee, at first; the car's primary purpose was to serve as the first classroom of what was to become Atlanta University. The organizers of the school and the leaders of Friendship entered into a contract stating that they would share the facility for worship services and for education.

As the membership began growing rapidly, the congregation needed a larger facility. The congregation of Friendship Baptist Church moved to a building on the corner of Haynes and Markham streets in Atlanta. Later the church moved to its present location on Northside Drive.

When Morehouse College began its move from Augusta to Atlanta, it used the building of Friendship Baptist Church for classes. In 1881 Spelman College utilized the basement of Friendship Baptist Church. The colleges and Friendship Baptist Church maintain close ties.

Friendship — the Baptist "Mother Church" in Atlanta — has close affiliations with the World Baptist Alliance, the American Baptist Churches, and the Progressive National Convention. This church was the one to which Bessie Jordan belonged and to which she brought Margaret Mitchell, John R. Marsh, Stephens and Carrie Lou Mitchell, and Harold Latham on the evening that the 1937 Pulitzer Prize became public ("Friendship Baptist Church").

*See also* Pulitzer Prize; Pulitzer Prize novel for 1937 and Margaret Mitchell's response.

## fur coat

Despite the success of *Gone with the Wind* in sales, Margaret Mitchell and John R. Marsh continued to live on a modest scale and invest wisely. Her one extravagance was a fur coat. During the couple's trip to Florida, someone stole the coat from their apartment. Margaret did wear the coat several times before its theft; she even had a photo taken while she was wearing it (Edwards, page 295).

## Gable, (William) Clark (1901–1960)

William Clark Gable was born February 1, 1901, in Cadiz, Ohio, to William H. Gable, an oil driller and farmer, and Adeline Hershelman Gable. Clark was left in the care of his maternal grandparents after the death of his mother when he was seven months old.

When William Gable remarried in 1903, Clark went to live with Jennie Dunlap, his stepmother, and his father. Clark attended two years at Edinburg High School before leaving with a friend to work at an Akron tire factory.

Clark saw the play *The Birds of Paradise*. Fascinated by the costumes and the scenery, Clark decided to become an actor. To help achieve this end, he took a job as a backstage callboy. This job with a local stock company was unsalaried.

After the death of his stepmother in 1919, Gable joined his father in the oil fields of Oklahoma. In 1922 he left the oil fields and joined the Jewell Players, a traveling theater company. Two months later the group folded in Montana. An almost penniless Gable hitchhiked to Portland, Oregon. After working odd jobs, Gable joined director Josephine Dillon's Portland acting group in 1924. Dillon and Gable married on December 13, 1924.

Gable found work in his chosen career. He worked as a film extra in Hollywood. Then he toured in a production of *Romeo and Juliet*. He found a part in Lionel Barrymore's production of *The Copperhead* before going to Broadway.

In 1928 Gable won good reviews and a positive reaction from the audience for his performance in Sophie Treadwell's play *Machinal*. The same year that Gable's first marriage ended in divorce (1930), he married Texan socialite Rhea Langham.

His acclaimed role as Killer Mears in the 1930 stage production of *The Last Mile* in Los Angeles brought him the role of the "heavy" in the 1931 film *The Painted Desert*, which starred William Boyd (1931). His debut as leading man came in 1931; he played opposite Joan Crawford in the film *Dance, Fools, Dance*. Twelve film roles — mostly for MGM — in 1931 earned him the title of star. He appeared opposite such stars as Greta Garbo, Jean Harlow, and Carole Lombard.

At the end of 1931, Gable suffered exhaustion and was admitted to the hospital.

He refused to accept another role as a "gigolo." To teach him a lesson, MGM loaned him out to Columbia Studios for a Frank Capra comedy: *It Happened One Night* (1934). Gable won the Academy Award for his performance. He was outstanding the same year as Fletcher in MGM's *Mutiny on the Bounty* (1935).

For the rest of the decade, he appeared in a whole series of major films — including *Gone with the Wind* (1939). Although his biographers call his role as Rhett Butler as his greatest performance, he did not win an Academy Award for it.

After his second divorce, Gable married Carole Lombard on March 29, 1939. She attended the 1939 Atlanta premiere of *Gone with the Wind* with him. She died in a plane crash less than three years later; she had been on a bond-selling tour.

At the age of 41, Clark Gable joined the Army Air Force as a private. Gable made a training film on aerial gunnery for his country and flew on five bombing missions over Germany. By the time of his discharge in June of 1944, Gable had achieved the rank (temporary) of major.

Gable immediately and successfully resumed his film career after his discharge from the military. His fans were eager for his return to the screen. Gable married again on December 20, 1949. This marriage to Lady Sylvia Ashley lasted only until 1952. Gable also divorced MGM. As a free-lancer, he carried the highest price in the industry. On July 11, 1955, Gable married again; this time his bride

Living on a modest scale, Mitchell's one extravagance was a fur coat. She wore it a few times before someone stole the coat from her apartment. (Courtesy of the Atlanta-Fulton Public Library System's Special Collections Department.)

was Kay Williams Spreckels. The two had known each other since the 1930s. They had one son.

Gable's last film was *The Misfits* (1960). Two days later he suffered a heart attack and died.

Gable had appeared in sixty-seven films. Between 1932–1942 he was one of the top ten stars in income. In 1945, after his three-year absence from films while he was in service, he remained one of the top ten males stars ("[William] Clark Gable").

*See also* **American Academy of Motion Picture Arts and Sciences; Lombard, Carole.**

### Gable, Clark, and Margaret Mitchell

Clark Gable met with Margaret Mitchell at the Press Club Tea Party that the Atlanta Women's Press Club sponsored during the 1939 Atlanta premiere of *Gone with the Wind*. He said that he found her the most fascinating woman he had ever met. He posed with her at the premiere.

*See also* **Atlanta Women's Press Club Tea Party.**

### Gainesville, Georgia

Margaret Mitchell was overwhelmed after the release of her novel *Gone with the Wind* in June 1936. Strangers appeared unannounced at her door; people approached her on the streets; the phone rang constantly; and mail arrived in bags. On July 2, 1936, Margaret tried to escape: to Gainesville, Georgia.

Mitchell stayed a few days in a hotel in Gainesville. She wrote several letters during this time. One was to Julia Collier Harris— the daughter-in-law of Joel Chandler Harris and the writer of a column for the *Chattanooga Times*. In the letter of July 8, 1936, Mitchell explained to Julia that the trip to Gainesville was to try to find "a place where telephones don't ring and photographers don't materialize with the first cup of coffee of the morning" (Harwell, *Letters*, page 25).

By July 9, 1936, Mitchell was writing to J. Donald Adams, editor of the *New York Times Book Review*. She seemed to realize there was no place that she could go where she was not recognized, so she returned to Atlanta.

*See also* **Adams, J. Donald; Harris, Julia Collier.**

### Gardner, Pyne, and Gardner

One significant feature of Georgia Hall/Grady Hospital is the fact that its designer was Eugene C. Gardner (1836–1915) of Springfield, Massachusetts. For twenty-five years, Eugene Gardner was an independent architect. In 1889 he admitted his son George C. Gardner and another architect, George Pyne, to his Springfield practice. Eugene came to Atlanta in 1889–1891 for his health, and

while he was in Georgia, a solicitation came to design Grady Hospital.

Gardner was one of the best-known and most influential architects in Springfield. In addition, he published alone eight books on architecture. Early in his life Gardner was a teacher and a mason. Gardner's career began as a school teacher and as a mason. His earliest domestic structures were noted for their masonry ornamented brick and stonework, which he used in Grady Hospital.

Grady was not Gardner's first hospital design. In 1889, he had designed the Springfield Hospital. An undocumented claim in many of his biographies is that he designed buildings in nearly every state of the United States.

Georgia Hall/Grady Hospital became a landmark in Atlanta. It easily met all the ordnances of the city ("Grady Memorial Hospital: The New Georgia Encyclopedia").

### Geechee

The dialect of Geechee was used by the African Americans in the area around Savannah and the Golden Islands. Its history goes back to the time when shiploads of African Americans came to the plantations of Golden Islands to be sold. These slaves maintained their original language because they were isolated from others. In the novel *Gone with the Wind* Mammy uses Geechee, which varies from the dialect of many of the other African Americans. Margaret Mitchell encountered the dialect on a trip she and John took to Savannah to a conference of the Georgia Writers Association (Walker, page 193).

*See also* **dialect in *Gone with the Wind*; Gullah; Peterkin, Julia Mood.**

### Georgia-Pacific Tower

The rose granite Georgia-Pacific Tower occupies the site where the Loew's Grand Theatre once stood. The historic theater was the site of the 1939 World premiere of the film *Gone with the Wind* (Snyder, Karen K. "Searching for Margaret Mitchell").

Located at 133 Peachtree Street, Northeast, in Atlanta, the Georgia-Pacific Tower took 3 years for construction. Loew's Grand Theatre burned in 1978, for unknown reasons; in 1979 construction began on the Georgia-Pacific building and theater. It opened as offices in 1982.

With 52 floors of office space, the structure was one of the tallest in Atlanta. Architects from Skidmore, Owings, and Merrill firm that opened in Chicago in 1936 designed the building. Such tall towers were not new to them. The architects had designed the John Hancock Center, the second tallest building in the world, in 1969. Another well-known building of theirs was the Sears Tower in 1973; this structure remained the tallest in the world for twenty years ("Skidmore, Owings, and Merrill").

The Georgia-Pacific Tower has a design like that of stairs; the "steps" stagger down to the pavement below. Inside (2011) are the world headquarters of Georgia Pacific, the downtown branch of the High Museum of Art, the consulate general of the United Kingdom (Suite 3400), and various other tenants.

In 2008 the first tornado hit downtown Atlanta since the weather bureau began keeping records for Atlanta in the 1880s. *The Atlanta Journal-Constitution* reported on March 14, 2008, that the storm had killed 2 and pummeled the downtown area (Tim Eberly and Paul Shea). The Georgia-Pacific Tower survived the storm with only some windows being blown out of their casings.

## Georgia Power Company/Georgia Railway and Electric Light Company

The company now known as Georgia Power has been important to the State of Georgia for more than a century. It was important also to the lives of John R. Marsh and of Margaret Mitchell.

*Early History.* In the 1880s Atlanta citizens began to receive electrical service. The history of their power incorporates several name changes.

*Georgia Electric Light Company of Atlanta.* Chartered in 1883, Georgia Electric Light Company of Atlanta first began providing service in 1884. For the next 35 years, Henry M. Atkinson headed the company, which primarily provided for street railway transportation and street lighting. Most businesses did not have electrical power at the time.

*Georgia Electric Light Company.* The small power business began to grow, but its name became shorter, Georgia Electric Light Company, in 1891. The same year the company built a steam-electric generating plant on Davis Street.

*Georgia Railway and Electric Light Company.* Atkinson and the Atlanta streetcar businessman Joel Hurt began to compete to gain the franchises for steam heat, streetcars, and electricity in Atlanta. In 1902, Atkinson bought out Hurt; the result was Georgia Railway and Electric Company.

Attorney Preston S. Arkwright became president of Georgia Railway and Electric Company about 1902. He remained in this executive position until his 1946 death. With the accession of new power companies, the company became Georgia Railway and Electric Company — "Georgia Power" in everyday usage (Calhoon).

The company was using the name Georgia Railway and Electric Company when John R. Marsh went to work there in 1922. It was still using that name when Marsh left for health reasons in 1947.

*Georgia Power.* Georgia Power soon subsumed Atlanta Gas Light Company, Atlanta Water, the Atlanta Water and Electric Light Company, and the Morgan Falls hydroelectric plant. These mergers brought about name changes in the company also; Georgia Power has moved also into nuclear power plants. Usually known best as Georgia Power, the company continued to flourish in 2011 (Calhoon; *Georgia During the Great Depression*, pages 171–174).

*Georgia Railway and Electric Light Company and the Great Depression (1929–1941).* During the Great Depression the federal government began to emphasize bringing electricity to homes that had never before had power (*Georgia During the Great Depression*, pages 173–174). Georgia Power Company also emphasized its role in promoting electrification. The company organized sales teams to travel to the rural areas with specially outfitted kitchen coaches (i.e., cars and trailers). The sales personnel in these coaches demonstrated electrical home appliances to those who did not have easy access to shopping in large towns and cities; they also tried to sell the appliances that they were demonstrating.

Georgia Railway and Electric Light Company ("Georgia Power Company") did not profit from selling the items. The company did, however, profit somewhat from the increased use of electricity among Georgia residents and from service fees it collected when it repaired their electrical products. Appliance purchasers benefited from the convenience of the appliances and from the company's repair services when an item fell into disrepair (Calhoon).

*Later History.* The last half of the 21st century was generally a turbulent period for power companies across the nation. Large construction programs, large equipment inventories, an oil embargo, construction and use of nuclear plants, and exorbitant inflation followed by a recession resulted in uncertainty.

When costs rose across the nation, many construction projects halted. Employees lost their jobs. Sell-outs abounded. Still, Georgia Power seemingly grew stronger for its trials. (Calhoon).

*Commitment to employees.* Throughout its history, Georgia Railway and Electric Light Company ("Georgia Power") has asserted its commitment to its employees and to the community. This was evident in its treatment of John R. Marsh when he was helping Margaret Mitchell with editing the manuscript for *Gone with the Wind.* He was employed as the head of the communication and public relations department of Georgia Power. Preston

S. Arkwright, the president of Georgia Power Company, was particularly lenient with Marsh about his arrival time in the mornings after John had edited the manuscript of *Gone with the Wind* all night long for many weeks at a stretch. Arkwright also encouraged Marsh to take a leave of absence.

Margaret Mitchell Marsh herself was not an employee of the company. Still Georgia Power typically paid her expenses to accompany her husband and to serve as hostess for some social sessions that Georgia Power sponsored. This was particularly true of the conventions of the Georgia Press Association that Margaret enjoyed attending and that her husband needed to attend in his position.

*Ponce de Leon Park and Stadium.* To generate further business for the railway, the company developed the beautiful Ponce de Leon Springs as a park for visitors in 1907. More people began riding the street cars to the park, which was just east of downtown. The old wooden stadium burned in 1923, just after John R. Marsh went to work there. A concrete structure replaced the old one.

**See also** Arkwright, Preston Stanley; Georgia Press Association; Ponce de Leon Park.

## Georgia Press Association

Because of his role in communications at Georgia Railway and Electric Light Company (later Georgia Power Company), John R. Marsh belonged to the Georgia Press Association. He and his wife had been attending the yearly conferences of the association ever since the first one in Macon in August of 1928 (Walker, page 182). Margaret had met Sue Myrick of the *Macon Telegraph* at the first convention.

*Georgia Press Association and Margaret Mitchell as hostess.* Margaret Mitchell accompanied John R. Marsh to the annual meetings of the Georgia Press Association. She liked serving as a hostess for Georgia Power in gatherings in their hotel room and socializing with the attendees.

In the summer of 1933 the Marshes attended the meetings in Louisville, Georgia, near Augusta. Their role at the 1933 meeting included opening their hotel room to late-night visitors and dispensing booze in paper Dixie cups. Edwards described the scene: "Newspaper people sat on beds and on the floor, drinking corn and discussing job printing and the future of literature, and exchanging gossip and off-color jokes. Peggy loved it, downing as much corn as the most hardened of newspapermen.... [P]ress men and women alike found her an especially 'grand fellow'" (Edwards, page 159). The couple served these "refreshments" during the time that Georgia had statewide prohibition (*Georgia During the Great Depression*, page 53).

John described his wife as a "genuinely valuable helpmate on such occasions and [she] has helped me in the ensnarement of several editors" (Walker, page 183). The general opinion was that Mitchell could draw others to her and could entertain well. Georgia Power/Georgia Railway and Electric Light Company began to pay Margaret's expenses to the Georgia Press Club conventions and to other occasions at which she and John could represent the power company (Walker, pages 192–193).

Harold Martin, a columnist for *The Atlanta Constitution*, wrote to Yolande Gwin to describe a memory of Margaret Mitchell during a conference of the Georgia Press Association. Martin's memories indicate the joy that Mitchell took in her impersonations and the pleasure that others took in watching her performances: "Did you ever see Margaret Mitchell make like she had a good mouthful of snuff? She could pooch out her lower lip with her tongue, and the effect was both accurate and hilarious.... [D]uring the Georgia Press Ass'n meetings in Athens, and we were all in somebody's room in the hotel ... she did it" at the behest of some in attendance (Gwin, page 134).

The Marshes also benefited from these trips. They were able to visit historic sites and preserve the dialect they encountered across the state. They researched and later recorded these dialects in the novel *Gone with the Wind* (Walker, pages 192–193).

*Georgia Press Association and recognition of Margaret Mitchell.* During the annual meeting of the Georgia Press Association in 1936, Margaret Mitchell received an invitation to speak at a banquet in her honor. The convention for 1936 was in Milledgeville on June 10–12, even before *Gone with the Wind* went on sale. Instead of attending the convention as John's wife, in 1936 Margaret achieved celebrity status (Edwards, page 201).

**See also** Georgia Power Company/Georgia Railway and Electric Light Company; Gwin, Yolande; Myrick, Sue.

## Georgia Soldiers' Home

In 1939 the Georgia Soldiers' Home in Atlanta was only a ten-minute ride from the site of the first public showing of *Gone with the Wind*: Loew's Theater in Atlanta. Four residents of the home received private invitations to attend the Atlanta premiere of the movie. Clark Gable made sure that they were in seats where they could see and hear well as the movie ran.

## Georgia Women of Achievement

The mission of Georgia Women of Achievement is to recognize and honor women (1) who are native to or identified clearly with the State of Georgia, (2) who have made extraordinary contributions within their fields of endeavor, and (3) who will inspire future generations to utilize their own talents. In 1994 Margaret Mitchell became the new inductee ("Georgia Women of Achievement").

## Georgia Writers Hall of Fame

The University of Georgia's Year 2000 millennial celebration included the establishment of a new public awards program and a permanent online exhibit. To honor the state's most influential writers, the University of Georgia Libraries intended the Georgia Writers Hall of Fame to include a public awards program and a permanent online exhibit. In addition, the organizers conceived the Hall of Fame as a means to introduce others to the unparalleled Georgia literature collections, its literary source materials, and its reference library.

Nominees for the Georgia Writers Hall of Fame must be Georgia natives or have produced substantial work during or just after residence in the state. When the Hall of Fame officially opened in April 2000, the judges chose twelve famous writers from Georgia's history as charter members. These two members may serve terms of three years as ex officio members of the panel of judges. The purpose of the award is to recognize Georgia writers—past and present. Their work must reflect the character—land and people—of the state. Margaret Mitchell was a charter member of the Hall of Fame ("Georgia Writers Hall of Fame").

## Georgian Terrace Hotel (tourist and residential)

Built in 1911, the Georgian Terrace Hotel at 659 Peachtree Street, NE (Corner of Peachtree and Ponce de Leon Avenue) was advertised as a tourist and residential facility. Annie Fitzgerald Stephens—Margaret Mitchell's grandmother—resided here for a while.

It was also the 1921 site in which the debutante Mitchell shocked polite society by performing an Apache dance—all the rage in Paris. Her performance partner, A. Sigmund Weil, was her escort to the charity ball. Probably as a result of both the dance and her argument about the uses of the revenue of the league, the Junior League blackballed Margaret from membership the next year.

Years later, when the Junior League held a costume ball the night before the world premiere of *Gone with the Wind*, Mitchell declined their invi-

Confederate Soldiers' Home, Atlanta, Ga.

Four Confederate veterans from the Atlanta Confederate Soldiers' Home received special invitations to attend the Atlanta premiere of *Gone with the Wind*. Clark Gable made certain the veterans had seating where they could see and hear without problems. The card was printed by I. F. P. Company, Atlanta, Georgia, no longer in operation.

The Georgian Terrace, Tourist and Residential, Atlanta's New Million Dollar Hotel, Peachtree and Ponce de Leon Avenue, Atlanta, Ga.

Advertised as a residential and a tourist million-dollar hotel, the Georgian Terrace is at Peachtree and Ponce de Leon. Many stars used it during the Atlanta premiere of *Gone with the Wind*. Margaret Mitchell may have given Harold Latham the manuscript of what would be *Gone with the Wind* in the hotel lobby. Grandmother Stephens went there when she became angry with Margaret. The card was printed by I. F. P. Company, Atlanta, Georgia, no longer in operation.

tation to be the guest of honor. Some residents speculated that the reason was the snub the league had given her in 1921.

The Georgian Terrace Hotel may have been the site for another significant event in the life of Margaret Mitchell and in the world's literature. It may have also been here in the lobby that Mitchell handed over her manuscript of what would be *Gone with the Wind* to Harold Latham, editor-in-chief and vice president for Macmillan. (Edwards, page 3). Other people close to Mitchell give differing accounts, however.

Advertisements for the Georgian Terrace Hotel indicate that it was a luxury million-dollar hotel that opened in 1911. The Georgian Terrace was the site where many celebrities stayed during the three-day premiere of *Gone with the Wind* in December of 1939.

*See also* addresses directly related to Margaret Mitchell; Ansley Hotel; Baugh, Margaret Eugenia; Biltmore Hotel; Latham, Harold Strong; Rich's Department Store.

**Germany, sales of *Gone with the Wind*** *see* **foreign copyrights/translations and fair trade laws**

## Glasgow, Ellen

The fictional works of Ellen Glasgow (1873–1945) generally represent the period from the Civil War to World War II. The books are not just works of history but social histories of a particular period — especially as that time period relates to Virginia; Glasgow often reflected on the political economy in her writings. As a Southern writer, she varied from the typical approach to literature by not treating the North, the rich, and the African Americans as the antagonists; rather she believed one's enemies came from within.

Born in Richmond, Virginia, to a father who "never committed a pleasure" and a mother who had a "laughing spirit," Glasgow came from a family that was not always happy; she reflected on this in her works. Under her private tutors she obtained a good education despite her deafness. Cruelty, greed, and intolerance were the real adversaries of mankind, she believed. Her novels led Southern fiction away from the accepted lies that the enemy was the North, the nouveau riche, or black people; her nineteen novels showed that the foe was not without but within.

After her mother's death, Glasgow published her first novel —*The Descendant* (1897)— anonymously.

The woman who knew love but never married followed it with seventeen novels. She earned the Pulitzer Prize for *In This Our Life* (1941), her last novel. Her last book before her death (1945) was a critical writing: *A Certain Measure* (1943) ("Ellen Glasgow").

*Glasgow, Ellen, and Margaret Mitchell.* On October 25, 1940, Margaret Mitchell and her husband John R. Marsh left Atlanta in a new model Mercury to see friends in Richmond, Virginia. Along the way, they were going to visit James Branch Cabell. Cabell, the nephew of Ellen Glasgow, was the author of *Jurgen: A Comedy of Justice* (Edwards, page 296).

Margaret called the Glasgow home and asked to visit while they were in Virginia. She was unaware that Ellen had suffered several heart attacks, and she found Glasgow in bed. Margaret described her in a letter of November 11, 1940, to Herschel and Norma Brickell as being "pretty and full of pep" although she was flat on her back and had a slight cough. She told the Brickells that Glasgow "was all the nice things you have told me she was." She mentioned that Glasgow "has no stuffiness and [exhibits] graciousness that has no condescension" (Harwell, *Letters*, pages 320–322).

The next year Ellen Glasgow wrote to Margaret Mitchell after Margaret sent her a telegram congratulating her on winning the 1942 Pulitzer Prize for *In This Our Life*. Ellen wrote: "I have a charming recollection of your flitting in and spending an hour by my bedside" (Edwards, page 296).

## Goddard, Judge Henry W.

Judge Henry W. Goddard presided over the 1937 suit brought against Macmillan Publishing Company (publisher of the 1936 *Gone with the Wind*) by Susan Lawrence Davis, author of *Authentic History of the Ku Klux Klan, 1865–1877* (1924). Susan Lawrence Davis "had demanded an injunction, accounting damages from the Macmillan Company … on the grounds that Miss Mitchell's story was a plagiarism of … *Authentic History of the Ku Klux Klan, 1865–1877*." Davis sought an injunction and $5,000 damages (Stout, page 1). Edwards calls the suit a 6.5 billion dollar suit (page 263). Walker calls the writer bringing suit *Sarah Lawrence Davis*, not *Susan Lawrence Davis*. Walker refers to her as *an elderly eccentric*.

Walker notes several charges that Davis specified:

1. That Margaret Mitchell had used a Confederate gray for the cover. She noted that her cover, too, was gray in color.

2. That Margaret Mitchell had stolen some Civil War phrases, in particular *scalawag* and *carpetbagger* (Walker, pages 366–367).

3. That Mitchell had stolen place names, historical events, and the names of real people from her book An *Authentic History of the Ku Klux Klan, 1865–1877*.

Davis wanted to settle outside of court. Macmillan refused. Mitchell herself wanted a trial; she wanted the publicity that would accompany a trial to show that she had not bought off anyone and that the charges were not substantiated (Walker, page 368).

Judge Henry W. Goddard dismissed the Davis suit on July 30, 1937; he observed that the charges were unsubstantiated. He ruled that *Authentic History of the Ku Klux Klan, 1865–1877* "contains no plot or story. *Gone with the Wind* is in part historical and a fictional story laid in and about Atlanta, Georgia" (Stout, pages 1–2).

Goddard noted that because both writers grew up in the South, there would inevitably be some similarity in their language. He observed, however, that the styles were not the same. He also stated that the descriptions and the conditions that Margaret Mitchell wrote about were entirely her own. Goddard noted that Mitchell had not used the literary labor of Susan Lawrence Davis (Stout, pages 1–2).

Before the trial, Judge Goddard received the charge to read both books and to note particularly the language and the style of each. Goddard observed that the events related to the Ku Klux Klan are public domain; no one person has exclusive rights to their use (Stout, pages 1–2).

Mitchell was happy when the suit ended. She noted that she had never seen or heard of *Authentic History of the Ku Klux Klan, 1865–1877* until Davis brought the suit; furthermore, she was unable to find a copy at a book store. At last she found a used copy in New York and had just then begun dipping into parts of it; she admitted, however, that she had not read it all at that point (Stout, pages 1–2).

*See also Authentic History of the Ku Klux Klan, 1865–1877; Davis, Susan Lawrence.*

## *Gone with the Wind* (African American and Communist Party reactions)

After the publication of *Gone with the Wind* in 1936, Margaret Mitchell still had concerns in 1937. Some African Americans were criticizing her novel; some were objecting to Selznick's filming *Gone with the Wind*.

The *Daily Worker*, a newspaper that the Communist Party published in New York City, was adamant in its criticism of both the film and the book. The staff wrote to David O. Selznick to voice their concerns. Those associated with the paper threatened to boycott the film; the writers suggested even worse repercussions than boycotting if the film was offensive.

Selznick was very concerned about what was happening. He asked some African American reporters to preview the film. He was determined not to offend Jews or African Americans (Walker, pages 356–357).

Walker quotes Margaret Mitchell in a letter she wrote to Herschel Brickell on April 8, 1937. "They [the staff of the *Daily Worker*] referred to the book as an "incendiary and negro baiting" book. Personally I do not know where they get such an idea for, as far as I can see, most of the negro characters were people of worth, dignity and rectitude—certainly Mammy and Peter and even the ignorant Sam knew more of decorous behavior and honor than Scarlett did" (Walker, page 357).

### Gone with the Wind (authorship questions)

In the will of John R. Marsh, he noted that Margaret Mitchell had "placed upon me the duty of destroying her papers if she should die without having done it. She did so die, and I have tried to fulfill the obligation. As a part of the painful job, I have destroyed the original manuscript of her novel *Gone with the Wind* and all related papers, proof sheets, notebooks, notes, et cetera, except as described below.

"Peggy left me discretion as to the disposal of her papers. I have decided that some of the 'Gone with the Wind' papers should be saved, as a means of authenticating her authorship of her novel. If some schemer were to rise up with the claim that her novel was written by another person, it would be tragic if we had no documentary evidence and therefore were unable to beat down the false claim. So I am saving these original 'Gone with the Wind' papers for use in proving, if the need arises, that Peggy and no one else was the author of her novel.

"I have placed these papers in a sealed envelope, in my safety box in the vault of Citizens and Southern National Bank, Marietta Street, Atlanta. They are to remain sealed unless a real and actual need for them arises for the purpose stated. If such a need never arises, the envelope and contents are eventually to be destroyed unopened. I desire the legatees and trustees to whom I have bequeathed these papers to preserve [in] this envelope, sealed, for the stated purpose. I also authorize them to break the envelope, and I place upon them the duty to use the said papers in defending the good name and literary reputation of my wife as the one and only authentic author of 'Gone with the Wind,' if her authorship of the novel should be seriously challenged.

"The material in the envelope includes the following 'Gone With the Wind' papers:

"(1) The original manuscript of certain chapters, typewritten by my wife, and with many corrections and changes in her handwriting. Also two or three drafts of some chapters, showing their development and changes as she rewrote and rewrote.

"(2) Several proof sheets carrying her handwriting and mine.

"(3) Several chronologies prepared by my wife while the book was being written.... (This quoted material from items 3 through 6 from the Codicil to the Will of John R. Marsh is on page 92 under the heading *Gone with the Wind* (verifying accuracy). The Codicil resumes with item 7.)

"(7) A few of the large manilla [*sic*] envelopes in which she kept the chapters of her book during the years she was writing it. Each envelope contained all of her material relating to a certain chapter, her various rewrites of it, reference notes, et cetera. The envelopes are labeled in her handwriting and have notes scribbled on the outsides of them, as ideas came to her of changes and corrections.

"With this material, I am confident it can be proved not only that my wife, Margaret Mitchell Marsh, wrote 'Gone with the Wind,' but that she alone could have written it.

"Upon my death, I give to my wife's brother, Stephens Mitchell, the sealed envelope and its contents herein referred to, during his lifetime, and upon his death to the Citizens and Southern National Bank, Atlanta, Georgia, as permanent trustee. The said sealed envelope shall be kept in the vault of said bank and its successors after my death." (The remainder of the Will of John R. Marsh and its Codicil is in this *Encyclopedia of Margaret Mitchell* under the heading Will of John R. Marsh.)

### Gone with the Wind (book title)

A favorite poem of Margaret Mitchell was one by Ernest Dowson. Titled "Non Sum Qualis Eram Bonae Sub Regno Cynarae," the poem includes a line in that third stanza that reads, "I have forgot much, Cynara! gone with the wind" ("Non Sum Qualis Eram Bonae Sub Regno Cynarae"). Margaret Mitchell suggested the title "Gone with the Wind" to John; he particularly liked it. Harold Latham, editor-in-chief and vice president at Macmillan Publishing Company, referred to the still untitled manuscript as "A MS of the Old South" (Walker, page 215).

At times Margaret Mitchell herself referred to the manuscript as "Tomorrow Is Another Day." She sometimes shortened it to "Another Day" before learning from a friend Sam Tupper (who frequently wrote book reviews and had worked with both John R. Marsh and Margaret Mitchell) that a book by the title of *Another Day* had recently been published. Next Margaret considered "Tomorrow and Tomorrow," "There's Always Tomorrow," "Tomorrow Will Be Fair," and "Tomorrow Morning." She sent all these titles as suggestions to Lois Cole (Edwards, page 182).

"Gone with the Wind" was not the only tentative title that Margaret Mitchell's novel carried. In 1935 Margaret sent Lois Cole a list of twenty-two tentative titles, including "Jettison," "Ba! Ba! Blacksheep," "Not in Our Stars," "None So Blind," "Gone with the Wind," and "Bugles Sang True."

Margaret Mitchell placed an asterisk and a note beside "Gone with the Wind"; Mitchell indicated that she would agree with any of the titles that Cole recommended but she indicated that she liked that one best (Walker, pages 227–228).

Margaret had used the phrase "gone with the wind" in her manuscript. After the burning of Atlanta when Scarlett O'Hara was fighting to get to Tara, Margaret had written: "Was Tara still standing? Or was Tara also gone with the wind which had swept through Georgia?" (page 262).

Latham liked "Gone with the Wind" best. He also liked the new name of the title character, Scarlett, better than the original name of the character, Pansy (Edwards, pages 182–183).

## *Gone with the Wind* (criticisms)

Margaret Mitchell wrote in a September 6, 1945, letter to Malcolm Crowley, who was preparing an American literary history: "I found it very interesting, too, that while many critics in the United States based their criticism upon the love story or the narrative, European critics evaluated it on a different basis. In practically every European country critics wrote at length of the 'universal historical significance.' Each nation applied to its own past history the story of the Confederate rise and fall and reconstruction. French critics spoke of 1870 (the Franco-Prussian War), Poles of the partitioning of their country, Germany of 1918 and the bitterness which followed, Czechs wrote not only of their troubled past but of their fears of the future, and I had letters from that country just before it went under (Nazi domination), saying that if the people of the South had risen again to freedom the people of Czechoslovakia could do likewise" (Wiley).

## *Gone with the Wind* (genesis)

In the spring of 1926 Margaret Mitchell was involved in a car accident. Her only injury was an injured ankle. It was the same leg that she had injured in her two riding accidents— one with the horse Bucephalus.

During the months that she was bedridden, her husband John brought her reading material from the library. Finally John told her she had exhausted the library and she would have to write her own book; he even brought her several hundred pages of copy paper in the early days of 1927. Margaret began *Gone with the Wind* that year. It finally appeared in print in 1936 (Edwards, pages 240–243).

***See also*** Bucephalus.

## *Gone with the Wind* (influence on legislation)

1. price-maintenance laws. In New York City, especially, department store and book stores began to engage in price wars on *Gone with the Wind* to lure buyers into their establishments. Some stores were selling the book for less than they had paid for it. Macmillan had set the selling price for *Gone with the Wind* at $3.00. Macy's was selling the book at a discounted rate. Macmillan said that even the publishing company itself could not sell *Gone with the Wind* at the price of $1.51 that Macy's was charging for the books in its department stores.

George Brett, Jr., with Macmillan noted that no other publisher had ever before had to act to maintain its prices on its books. In August of 1937 President Franklin Delano Roosevelt signed into law the Tydings-Miller bill, also known as the Fair Trade or the Price Protection Act.

2. The "Margaret Mitchell Law" was another result of the book *Gone with the Wind*. Mitchell had to pay enormous taxes in 1936 and 1937 because of her royalties on *Gone with the Wind*. These taxes fell due at once from work spread across the many years it took to write the book. To help alleviate this injustice, a revenue law — Code Section 107-C — passed Congress in 1952 (Walker, pages 353–355).

3. Foreign copyright was another issue that Margaret Mitchell helped to resolve.

***See also*** foreign copyrights; Tydings-Miller Bill.

## *Gone with the Wind* (production of film)

The 1939 film is a historical epic adapted from Margaret Mitchell's 1936 Pulitzer-Prize winning novel. Produced by David O. Selznick and directed by Victor Fleming from Sidney Howard's screenplay, the film — like the book — is set in the American South in the 19th century. The movie, which stars Vivien Leigh, Clark Gable, Olivia de Havilland, Leslie Howard, Hattie McDaniel and others, gives a Southern point of view of both the American Civil War and Reconstruction.

The film *Gone with the Wind* earned 8 competitive Academy Awards and 2 honorary Academy Awards. This record stood for 20 years. The American Film Institute in its inaugural list of the Top 100 Best American Films of All Time ranked *Gone with the Wind* as number four. The film — which ran 3 hours and 44 minutes, plus an additional intermission of 15 minutes— was one of the longest sound films up until 1939; it was one of the first major Technicolor films and won the first Academy Award for Best Cinematography.

*See also* **American Academy of Motion Picture Arts and Sciences.**

### Gone with the Wind (sales of book)

The book *Gone with the Wind* gained almost immediate popularity upon its publication in 1936. By January of 1937 sales had surpassed one million copies; this was more than double what Margaret Mitchell had expected.

In the spring of 1937, the American Booksellers Association presented its annual prize for the best fiction of the previous years. This prize went to *Gone with the Wind*. The award enhanced sales even further.

In May of 1937 Margaret Mitchell received the Pulitzer Prize for the best fiction of the previous year. Another award and its publicity further enhanced sales volume. *Gone with the Wind* has sold more than 28 million copies in more than 37 countries since its 1936 publication ("Gale Notable Literature and Its History: *Gone with the Wind*").

*See also* **American Booksellers Association annual award.**

### Gone with the Wind (special editions)

The novel *Gone with the Wind* has appeared in many different editions through the years. Below is a description of two of the newest editions.

The 60th Anniversary Edition of *Gone with the Wind* was designed to coincide with the anniversary of the 1936 release of the novel and went into print in 1996. Pulitzer Prize-winning novelist for *Tales of the South Pacific* (1947) James Michener prepared the Introduction. The author of the Preface (1996) was Pat Conroy, a Southern writer with strong ties both to Atlanta and to the book *Gone with the Wind*.

Conroy writes how his mother read him the whole novel over the period of a year when he was five. He credits his becoming a novelist to Mitchell's novel. He also explains the tremendous impact the novel had on him and his family. Conroy writes

his preface as a tribute to the book and its author. He acknowledges the crucial role of the Georgia Writers Hall of Fame honoree Margaret Mitchell in his life; Conroy was a fellow Georgia Writers Hall of Fame honoree.

Conroy recalled his mother's pointing out historical landmarks as she drove him to Sacred Heart School. She shared her experience of standing in the crowd at the Atlanta premiere of *Gone with the Wind* with her son and showed him where it had happened. On weekends they visited Stone Mountain, discussed the generals on the carving, found the site where the car had struck Margaret Mitchell, and located her gravesite (Preface to 60th Anniversary Edition of *Gone with the Wind*).

75th Anniversary Edition of *Gone with the Wind*, with the Preface by Pat Conroy and the Introduction by James Michener.

### Gone with the Wind USPS Postage Stamp (United States Postal Service)

A stamp issued in 1998 by the United States Postal Service shows cover of *Gone with the Wind* by Margaret Mitchell.

The stamp bearing an image of the cover of the book *Gone with the Wind* appeared in 1998. The 32-cent stamp was first issued in Cleveland, Ohio, at the foot of the Terminal Tower Building. "Artist Howard Paine used the cover of the first edition *Gone With the Wind* for the stamp; he placed a Southern magnolia on the left and a Confederate sword on the right. The inscription on the back of the stamp reads: 'Margaret Mitchell's 1936 novel *Gone with the Wind* portrayed the Old South during the Civil War and Reconstruction. It was a number one bestseller for two years and continues to be sold throughout the world. Celebrate the Century—1930s'" (Davis and Hunt, page 74).

### *Gone with the Wind* (verifying accuracy)

Mitchell went to great lengths to ensure the accuracy of information in her novel. John R. Marsh included some very specific documents among the information he saved after the death of the author. This information in the codicil to his will explains the extreme means that Mitchell had employed to ensure precision, and what he had preserved from her papers to attest to her diligence in this matter. According to his will, these documents include:

"(3) Several chronologies prepared by my wife while the book was being written, giving events in the book and historical events side by side, to keep them in step; ages of various characters with relation to other characters; pregnancies and other time-important situations. These [*sic*] were one of the means by which Peggy achieved her remarkable success in avoiding errors in her book.

"(4) A few samples of the mass of notes she made in collecting data and information for her book. She kept these notes in large manilla [*sic*] envelopes labeled in her handwriting "Notes on Reconstruction," 'Miscellaneous References,' et cetera. In saving some of this material, I also noted down the total amount of material in the envelopes in the sealed envelope reads, 'from Envelope labeled "Miscellaneous References"—which contained 37 sheets, handwritten, mostly on both sides. Also various letters. Amount saved—6 sheets and 4 letters.'

"(5) Lists she made up of items to be checked for accuracy, and material she dug up in answer to her questions.

"(6) She was especially diligent about accuracy in the sections of her book about the Atlanta Campaign. The story of the fighting is told simply in the book, but she did a large amount of research in order to get it simple, and accurate. Included are some of her research notes, chronologies, her items to be checked further. Also notes made by her father and brother, who were asked by her to read the manuscript and let her know of any errors they found" (codicil to the Will of John R. Marsh, pages 1–2).

### Gordon, John Brown

John Brown Gordon was one of the five Confederate generals whom Gutzon Borglum was supposed to carve on Stone Mountain. Margaret Mitchell as a reporter for the *Atlanta Journal* produced an article on each of the five for publication. This first article in the series by Mitchell appeared on November 29, 1925; readers received it so well that Margaret received the assignment to lengthen the other articles in the series.

General John Brown Gordon carried the nickname the "Bayard of the Confederacy." His statue on horseback stands at the entrance of the Atlanta Capitol. Gordon was a native Georgian. He was born on July 6, 1832, in Upson County and graduated from the University of Georgia in 1852; his admittance to the law profession came a few months later.

When war came, he entered the "Raccoon Roughs" as a private. By 1861 he had advanced to lieutenant colonel. At Sharpsburg, he assumed command when the commanding officer suffered severe wounds. He gave the order: "No man who could still keep his saddle must leave the field." Wounded himself four times, he refused to dismount. When he received the fifth shot, he fell unconscious. Gordon continued to distinguish himself in battle after battle and to earn promotions for his gallantry. General John Brown Gordon led the last charge at Appomattox for the South and Lee's army.

After the war, General John Brown Gordon entered politics. He served in the Senate (1873) for one term. He next served as general counsel to LandN railroad and later as a builder with the Georgia Pacific railway.

He was Georgia governor in 1866 and 1888. From 1890 until 1896 he again served in the Senate. He served as the first elected commander of the United Confederate Veterans Organization from 1890 until his death in 1914. His most famous lecture was "The Last Days of the Confederacy."

Margaret Mitchell said he was "a gallant gentleman and perfect soldier, who added to his four years on the battlefield thirty years of selfless service in civil life for the good of his state" (Mitchell, *Margaret Mitchell: Reporter*, pages 258–264).

### Grady, Henry Woodfin

Born in 1850 in Athens, Georgia, Henry Woodfin Grady moved from Rome, Georgia, to Atlanta in 1872. Grady had been serving as editor of the *Rome Daily* newspaper. In Atlanta, he joined Alexander St. Clair–Abrams and Robert A. Alston as the editor and co-owner of the *Atlanta Daily Herald*. In an editorial on March 14, 1874, Henry Grady used the term "New South." The *Atlanta Daily Herald*, a rival of the *Atlanta Constitution*, only lasted four years.

Grady became an outstanding orator and a memorable editor of the *Atlanta Constitution*, from 1879 to 1889. He promoted harmony between the North and the South, encouraged industrialization, and advanced the concept of economic independence.

He was a passionate lecturer and journalist with an innovative message. He advocated the investments of the industrial North in the Southern economy; important to him also was a proper healthcare facility for Atlanta. Dubbed "the Spokesman of the New South," Grady carried his message in the late 19th Century. His aim was to bring prosperity to a South hurt by the Civil War. As editor of the *Atlanta Journal-Constitution*, he was in a position to advance his message and to help bring politicians with similar agendas to office.

A baseball fan, Grady helped establish Southern baseball as a popular sport. He encouraged the establishment of a hospital in Atlanta. In effect, he pointed Atlanta in the direction it has followed since reconstruction. Grady died on December 23, 1889.

In his 39 years, Grady was able to help his city and the surrounding area accept the changes that made Atlanta the hub of the South. One of the ways Atlanta continues to honor Grady is through the hospital that bears his name ("Henry Grady: A Georgia Biography"; "Georgia Hall: Original Grady Hospital"). Grady's statue appears prominently in Atlanta.

*See also* Doyle, Alexander; Grady Statue.

### Grady Hospital

Grady Hospital is a brick structure at 36 Butler Street, SE, now a landmark in Atlanta. The main architect for the facility constructed between 1890 and 1892 was Eugene Gardner of the firm of Gardner, Pyne, and Gardner.

Originally called Georgia Hall, the structure was in a residential community, for the most part. It was, however, near Atlanta Medical College, which had received its charter on February 14, 1854. In the days to come the medical facilities and the commercial structures in the area increased. In 1912 the city bought the remaining residences on the block.

Before this building, Atlanta had only one hospital of any size. Founded in 1880, St. Joseph's Infirmary served the entire city. It would not treat indigent patients, and it was a private facility. Grady Hospital — a municipal hospital advocated by Henry Woodfin Grady — helped to change that.

Exactly one year after Grady's death (December 23, 1890), many attended the laying of the cornerstone of the hospital to bear his name. The newly constructed building was ready for the arrival of the first patients on June 1, 1892.

Eighteen employees and 100 beds — 50 for African Americans and 50 for whites — were ready for the admitted. The new facility included one operating room and an amphitheater for students and staff. In 1899 a patient paid $1.09 in daily costs. Just before World War I, a second building provided separate hospitals, clinics, quarters for nurses, and emergency rooms for African Americans and whites. In addition the hospital now had a children's ward, a maternity ward, a laundry, a morgue, and a kitchen. A series of extended corridors connected all these units.

GRADY HOSPITAL, SHOWING NEW ADDITION, ATLANTA, GA.

This postcard of Grady Hospital shows the Butler Street facility and the building added before 1920. (C. T. American Art and Imperial Post Card Company of Atlanta.)

*Grady Hospital and its administration.* Four periods in the administration/funding of Grady Hospital are evident.

1. A board of trustees governed Grady Hospital from 1892 to 1921. Funding came from the city, private fundraising, and donations from private citizens. In May 1915 Emory University acquired the Atlanta Medical College; Emory housed the Emory School Medicine not on its campus but in a building across the street from Grady Hospital.

2. A politically appointed council committee governed Grady Hospital between 1921 and 1931. These committee members served one-year terms but could serve more than one term. The source of official funding was local revenues.

3. In 1931 a citizens' board of trustees governed Grady Hospital. For the first time, Grady Hospital had access to federal funds.

4. Beginning in 1945 the Fulton/DeKalb Hospital Authority was in charge of the active management of all municipal hospital facilities. The counties that used the hospital assumed some of the expense for Grady Hospital.

It was during this last period that Margaret Mitchell entered Grady Hospital in August of 1949. She was treated for five days for injuries sustained when a car struck her on Peachtree Street before her death. Mitchell donated to the education of many African American medical students during this period of administration of the hospital.

The first hospital training school for nurses in the State of Georgia received its charter here on March 25, 1898. Grady Hospital also became the teaching hospital for the Morehouse School of Medicine ("Grady Memorial Hospital: The New Georgia Encyclopedia").

*Grady Hospital architecture.* The architectural style of Grady Hospital is significant. The building shows the influence of Romanesque style architecture, even though the architect usually describes the structure as being "Italiante."

Although the original brick and frame wards, the out-buildings, and many of the connecting corridors were destroyed for a parking lot in 1959, the exterior of the main building remains intact.

Usually identified as belonging to the Richardson Romanesque style, the original Grady Hospital has definite characteristics of the style.

1. Massive scale.

2. Round arches over the doors, the windows, and the porches.

3. The use of stone and brick as the primary building materials.

4. Corners made of the construction material, not applied to the surface.

5. The frieze at the entrance portico has *The*

*Grady Hospital* in a floral motif. This motif was probably the inspiration of architect Louis Sullivan.

The early three-story brick building demonstrates the stretcher-bond pattern. The construction rests on a solid granite basement, rising five feet above ground level. The openings in the building vary between rectangular and arched design. The recession of second and third-floor windows, the first-floor extended portico with a set of paired windows and a set of tiered windows (each set divided by engaged oak columns with Georgian Ionic cusps), and a five-story tower add architectural interest and distinction to what could have been a plain, functional building.

Some other features give a unique flavor to Grady Hospital.

1. The original windows on the first and second floor were transom windows with bars.

2. The third floor has four continuous round arch windows featured on either side of a large arched balcony.

3. Brick lintels and granite sills characterize the windows. The granite sill of the second-floor window continues around the perimeter.

4. An egg and art pattern and a carved keystone detail the molding on the granite-faced, rounded arch of the entrance portico.

A new operating room (1903–1904) and the replacement of the bell by chimes were some of the earliest modifications to the original building. A new six-story hospital building in 1913–1914 necessitated the removal of the porte-cochere and the addition of an enclosed corridor to connect the two buildings. Although a new building is present, the original building — with some necessary modifications— remains in use ("Grady Memorial Hospital: The New Georgia Encyclopedia"; "Georgia Hall: Original Grady Hospital").

*Grady Hospital and Margaret Mitchell.* After the 1936 publication of *Gone with the Wind*, Margaret Mitchell began to work with Benjamin Mays, the president of Morehouse College, to sponsor some anonymous scholarships for African American students who were pursuing a medical education. Many of these students took some of their training in Grady Hospital in Atlanta. One of Atlanta's first black pediatricians, Dr. Otis Smith, received the benefit of Mitchell's generosity.

Her final association with the hospital was tragic. In 1949 after being struck by a car, an ambulance took her there. Five days later she died of her injuries in that facility.

***See also*** **accidents; addresses directly related to Margaret Mitchell; Gravitt, Hugh Dorsey; Mays, Benjamin; Smith, Dr. Otis.**

## Grady Statue

To honor the influential newspaper editor Henry W. Grady and his contributions to the city and state, a ten-foot statue of Grady on a marble base has stood near the headquarters of the *Atlanta Journal-Constitution* since 1891. On October 21, 1891, over 25,000 people attended the dedication of the statue titled "Henry W. Grady." Originally on the sidewalk, the statue was later relocated to a nearby intersection for the benefit of viewers.

On November 20, 1929, the city of Atlanta gave another tribute to Grady. The area where the monument stood received the name Henry Grady Plaza. Alexander Doyle (1858–1922) sculpted the monument that includes a bold Grady standing on a marble base. Two women in bronze sit on a bench with footstool; they each hold a wreath with these words: "This hour little needs the loyalty that is loyal to one section and yet holds the other in enduring suspicion and estrangement. Give us the broad and perfect loyalty that loves and trusts Georgia alike with Massachusetts that knows no South, no North, no East, no West; but endures with equal and patriotic love every foot of our soil, every State in our Union. Boston, December 1889."

*See also* Doyle, Alexander.

## Granberry, Edwin Phillips, biographical sketch

Edwin Phillips Granberry (1897–1988) was born in Meridian, Mississippi, lived in the Oklahoma Territory and moved to Florida at age ten. He attended the University of Florida until World War I interrupted his schooling.

He served in the United States Marines until the end of the war and until his tour of duty was complete. In 1920 he enrolled in the University of Columbia. After earning his *artium baccalaureatus* in romance languages, from 1920–1922 he served as an assistant professor at Miami University.

From 1925 to 1930, Granberry served as a private school language teacher. During this time he worked on and had published three novels. His third—*A Trip to Czardis* (1934)—received the O. Henry Memorial Prize. It appeared more than forty times on radio and television broadcasts and in magazine anthologies.

Granberry began to freelance as a book reviewer and as a critic. His 1,200-word review of *Gone with the Wind* in the New York *Evening Sun* (June 30, 1936) brought much pleasure to both Margaret Mitchell and John R. Marsh. The review generated a lifelong friendship among the members of the Marsh and the Granberry families. In 1936, Granberry, Brickell, and Mitchell attended a writers' conference at the Green Park Inn in Blowing Rock, North Carolina.

The review also drew the attention of Hamilton Holt, the president of Rollins College. He offered Edwin Granberry a position as assistant professor of English. Granberry accepted. Granberry's play *The Falcon* debuted at Rollins College in February of 1950. Until his 1971 retirement, Granberry remained the Irving Bacheller Chair of Creative Writing at Rollins.

After his retirement, he began a new profession. With the artist Roy Crane to help, he began co-writing *Buzz Sawyer,* a nationally syndicated comic strip. Granberry's death came on December 5, 1988. The father of three sons, Edwin saved his and his wife's correspondence with John R. Marsh and Margaret Mitchell. His son Julian Granberry would later compile the correspondence into the volume *Letters from Margaret* ("Edwin Granberry").

*Granberry, Edwin, and Margaret Mitchell.* Edwin Granberry wrote a review of *Gone with the Wind* just after its release; the review pleased John Marsh. When it became necessary for someone to write a biographical sketch of Margaret Mitchell, John selected Granberry for the task. Granberry intended the article for *Collier's,* a weekly magazine from 1888 to 1957. Marsh himself reviewed Granberry's article several times before its publication.

*See also* Blowing Rock Writers' Conference; Brickell, Herschel; biographical articles on Margaret Mitchell (selected); Granberry, Julian; Green Park Inn.

## Granberry, Julian

Julian Granberry is the son of Edwin and Mabel Granberry. He is an anthropologist and linguist.

Julian knew Margaret Mitchell from the time he was seven years old in 1936 until she died in 1949. The letters that his parents saved were from both John R. Marsh and his wife Margaret Mitchell.

Julian Granberry was able to link these letters in such a way as to give the reader continuity and show the friendships among the family members in his book *Letters from Margaret* (2001). After knowing her for more than a decade, he was able to sum up her life at the end of the book: "This was the Margaret Mitchell whom the Granberry family knew. A vivacious Southern lady with a verve for life and all that it brought. As my father said, 'one of the brightest, the most scintillating, and most compassionate spirits we have ever known.' Though it may seem that she is gone, she has, as Finis Farr said, 'just stepped out of the room.' Margaret was, to those who knew her, as close as one could get to humanity itself" (page 130).

*See also* Granberry, Edwin.

## Grant, Lemuel P. (1817–1893)

Lemuel P. Grant was a railroad engineer who served Atlanta during the Civil War (1861–65) by designing its fortifications. After the war, he became successful in his business and donated the animals for the zoo and most of the land for Grant Park, Atlanta's first park, which the city named in his honor.

Grant had been born in Frankfort, Maine, but he came to Atlanta to survey for the Atlanta and LaGrange railroad lines in 1849. Grant incorporated several railroads—including the Georgia Western (1854) and the Georgia Air Line (1856). He became president of the Georgia Railway (1848) and the Southern Pacific (1858) in addition to serving as the superintendent of both the Atlanta and West Point and the Montgomery and West Point Railway.

In 1850 Grant was able to donate ten acres for use by the Southern Central Agricultural Society for a fair; the Atlanta City Council donated $1,000 for housing for the fair's exhibits. In 1855 with the permanent location made available by Grant, Atlanta became the permanent host of the fair; before this donation by Grant, Atlanta had competed with Savannah, Macon, and Athens for the job. The city council even bought another fifteen acres for the society to use as long as Atlanta held the fairs. Atlanta served as host until the Civil War began.

Grant Park would become the home of the Atlanta Cyclorama, which Margaret Mitchell loved to visit. At the Atlanta premiere of *Gone with the Wind* in 1939, Clark Gable was impressed with the Cyclorama and *The Battle of Atlanta*.

Grant also helped to review the city charter in 1873 and to name the streets in 1867. He served on the Atlanta City Council in 1872, as a Fulton County Commissioner in 1886, as water commissioner in 1879, on the board of education, and helped petition for the West View Cemetery in 1874. In 1893 his interment was in this cemetery (Galloway, Tammy H. "Lemuel P. Grant").

*See also* Atlanta Cyclorama; Atlanta premiere of *Gone with the Wind*; *Battle of Atlanta* painting; Civil War in Margaret Mitchell's education; Grant Park.

## Grant Park

Grant Park was important to the life and education of Margaret Mitchell. It was here that she visited the Cyclorama and viewed *The Battle of Atlanta* painting. It was here that Clark Gable visited when he came to the Atlanta premiere of *Gone with the Wind*. It was here that he made a suggestion for an addition to the diorama inside the Atlanta Cyclorama and later his figure was added.

Atlanta resident Lemuel P. Grant offered the 100 acres that would become Grant Park to the City of Atlanta in the spring of 1882. The execution of the deed came on May 17, 1983. The street boundaries of the park today are Atlanta Avenue, Sidney Street, Cherokee Avenue, and Boulevard. Grant Park would become the first city-owned, public park.

Important in the early park development was Atlanta merchant Sidney Root. Root, a lover of nature and trees, had suggested to prosperous railroad man Lemuel Grant that the city could use the land well.

The land itself was of historic significance. At Boulevard and Atlanta Avenue was the crown of a hill. In 1864 a Confederate battery held this as a commanding position; the site had contained entrenchments and Old Fort Walker.

Atlanta Mayor John B. Goodwin (1850–1921) served Atlanta as mayor from 1883 to 1885 and from 1893 to 1895. Goodwin named Sidney Root (1824–1897) as superintendent, construction supervisor, and president of Grant Park. Root served the park until his 1897 death. Lemuel P. Grant served as a commissioner for the park.

Soon after assuming the park ownership, the City of Atlanta spent $1,500 to improve the grounds. The city had extended its corporate limits to include the park by 1885. As soon as the city took over ownership, it spent $1,500 to improve its grounds. By 1885 the city had extended its corporate limits to include the park.

George Hillyer (1835–1927) served as Atlanta mayor from 1885 to 1887. In his annual address to the Atlanta City Council, Hillyer identified L. P. Grant Park (Grant's Park, as it was commonly known) as a source of pride. Hillyer said the industrious, hardworking citizens of Atlanta and their visitors deserved such a place of recreation.

In 1889, Grant Park became the home of a zoo. Atlanta lumber dealer George V. Gress had purchased a bankrupt circus for the railroad cars and the wagons. He made Atlanta a gift of the animals, which formed Atlanta's first municipal zoo.

As a result of Grant's additional generosity in the gift of the animals, the City of Atlanta purchased some additional acreage. On April 4, 1890, Grant Park included 131.5 acres.

George Valentine Gress and Charles Northen purchased *The Battle of Atlanta* a few years later. In 1892 this cycloramic painting became a part of the exhibit in the circular structure in Grant Park.

Atlanta architect John Francis Downing designed a new building to hold the painting that John ("Blackjack") Logan commissioned to show his charge in the Battle of Atlanta after the fall of General James B. McPherson. In 1921 the move was complete.

Again in 1979, the painting and the circular building received renovation after a major storm hit Grant Park. The building reopened in 1982.

Lakes were an important feature of Grant Park. Lake Abana and Willow Brook were natural features. An added lake — Lake Loomis— joined Lake Abana in 1888; later the two merged. In 1900 an enlargement and reconstruction made the four-acre Lake Abana into a six acre lake with two islands. In 1902 swimming equipment, boating equipment, and a pavilion became popular features.

Constitution Spring and several other mineral water springs were other prominent features of Grant Park. When Willow Brook and Constitution Spring became contaminated, water from the city's reservoir filled Lake Abana starting in 1906. Other popular additions to Grant Park included (1917) a 500 foot by 200 foot pool and Asa G. Candler's collection (1935) of 84 wild animals and 100 birds.

Grant Park has had other changes through the years, including the draining of Lake Abana, the addition of acreage and a carousel (1966), and the removal of the early pavilions. The 131.5 acre park remains an important part of Atlanta. In 2001 it averaged two million visitors each year (Galloway, Tammy H. "Grant Park").

*See also* Atlanta Cyclorama; Atlanta premiere of *Gone with the Wind; Battle of Atlanta* painting; Downing, John Francis; Grant, Lemuel P.; Logan, John Alexander "Blackjack"; McPherson, James Birdseye.

## Gravesites of Margaret Mitchell's Immediate Family

Burial sites for most of Margaret Mitchell's immediate family members are in Oakland Cemetery, Atlanta, Georgia.

*Marsh, John Robert (1895–1952).* John Robert Marsh, the second husband of Margaret Munnerlyn Mitchell (1900–1949), was born October 6, 1895, in Maysville (Mason County), Kentucky. Marsh was the son of Millard Filmore Marsh and Mary Troup Marsh. He died on March 5, 1952; his interment — like his wife's— was in Oakland Cemetery in Atlanta, Georgia ("John R. Marsh: Find-a-Grave").

*Mitchell, Alexander Stephens (1896–1983).* The second son of Maybelle Stephens Mitchell (1872–1919) and Eugene Muse Mitchell (1896–1944), Alexander Stephens Mitchell (called "Stephens") was born in January 14, 1896, in Atlanta. Stephens was the older brother of Margaret Munnerlyn Mitchell (1900–1949). A first-born child, Russell Stephens Mitchell, (1894–1894) preceded Stephens and Margaret in birth and death.

Stephens, a graduate of the University of Georgia, was— like his father before him — a lawyer. Stephens married twice. In 1927 he wed Caroline Louise Reynolds (1902–1950), nicknamed Carrie Lou. The couple had two surviving children: Eugene Muse Mitchell (1931–2007) and Joseph Reynolds Mitchell.

After Carrie Lou's death in 1950, her interment was in Atlanta's Oakland Cemetery. Stephens Mitchell remarried in 1952. His new bride was Anita Benteen (1902–1978). Alexander Stephens Mitchell died in 1983. His interment was in Oakland Cemetery in Atlanta ("Mitchell, Alexander Stephens: Find-a-Grave").

*Mitchell, Anita Benteen.* Anita Benteen Mitchell (1902–1978) became the second wife of Alexander Stephens Mitchell (1896–1983) in 1952. Stephens's first wife, Caroline Louise Reynolds (1902–1950), had passed some two years before. Anita Benteen Mitchell was born and died in Atlanta. She was the daughter of Frederick Benteen. Her burial was in Oakland Cemetery in Atlanta, Georgia ("Anita Benteen Mitchell: Find-a-Grave").

*Mitchell, Caroline Louise Reynolds.* Caroline Louise "Carrie Lou" Reynolds Mitchell (1902–1950) was born in Augusta, Georgia. She was the first daughter born to lawyer Joseph Shewmake Reynolds (1869–1935) and his wife Frances Pauline "Fannie" Hansberger Reynolds (1866–1956) of Augusta, Georgia. The Magnolia Cemetery in Augusta was the final resting place of both Joseph Shewmake Reynolds and Frances Pauline "Fannie" Hansberger Reynolds. Carrie Lou's siblings were the artist William Glascock Reynolds (1903–1967) and Mary Josephine Reynolds Powell (1905–1987, Mrs. Henry Russell Powell).

On 3 May 1927, Carrie Lou Reynolds married Alexander Stephens Mitchell (1896–1983), called Stephens, a prominent Atlanta lawyer and historian and brother of Margaret Mitchell (1900–1949).

Caroline Louise Reynolds preceded her husband in death. She left behind two sons, Eugene Muse Mitchell (1931–2007) and Joseph Reynolds Mitchell. The interment of Caroline Louise Mitchell, her husband Stephens, and her son Joseph Reynolds Mitchell are all in the Oakland Cemetery in Atlanta ("Mitchell, Caroline Louise: Find-a-Grave").

*Mitchell, Clara Belle Neal Robinson (1854–1912).* The widow Clara Belle Neal Robinson became the second wife of widower Russell Crawford Mitchell (1837–1854). They had two children together before his death in 1905 and her death in 1912. The Oakland Cemetery in Atlanta was the site of her interment ("Mitchell, Clara Belle Neal Robinson: Find-a-Grave").

*Mitchell, Deborah Margaret Sweet (1847–1887).*

Deborah Margaret Sweet Mitchell was born in 1847 in Quincy, Florida. The daughter of William Charles Sweet (1817–1898) and Mary Ann McKenzie (d. 1873), her paternal grandparents were the Rev. Gospero Sweet (1771–1856) and Ann Munnerlyn Sweet (1794–1841); the family name *Munnerlyn* suggests the origin of Margaret Mitchell's middle name.

As Confederate soldier Russell Crawford Mitchell (1837–1905) was recovering from wounds he had received at that Battle of Sharpsburg (Antietam), he met Deborah. After his convalescence, he went back to the war. He and Deborah married after the war when he returned to Florida for her on August 10, 1865.

The two went to Atlanta when R.C. quarreled in Florida with a Northerner. They remained in Atlanta, and Deborah bore 11 children before her 40th birthday. One of these children was Eugene Muse Mitchell (1866–1944); Eugene and Maybelle Stephens Mitchell had three children — one of whom was Margaret Munnerlyn Mitchell.

Deborah Sweet Mitchell died from consumption in 1887. Her burial was in Oakland Cemetery ("Mitchell, Deborah Sweet: Find-a-Grave").

*Mitchell, Eugene Muse (1866–1944).* The father of Margaret Munnerlyn Mitchell, Russell Stephens Mitchell, and Alexander Stephens Mitchell and the husband of Maybelle Stephens Mitchell, Eugene was born on October 16, 1866, in Atlanta (Fulton County), Georgia. His death on June 17, 1944, occurred in Atlanta.

He was the son and Russell Crawford Mitchell (1837–1905) and Deborah Margaret Sweet Mitchell (1847–1887). Eugene's daughter Margaret Mitchell fondly remembered sitting on the lap of Russell Crawford Mitchell (her grandfather) and hearing his stories of the Civil War. Margaret's grandmother Deborah Sweet Mitchell told her stories about the home front during the Civil War.

Eugene's wife was Mary "Maybelle" Isabelle Stephens (1872–1919), a suffragette and the mother of Margaret Mitchell (1900–1949). Their two boys were Russell Stephens Mitchell (1894–1894) and Alexander Stephens Mitchell (1896–1983). The interment of Eugene Muse Mitchell — a prominent Atlanta attorney — was in the Oakland Cemetery in Atlanta ("Mitchell, Eugene Muse [1866–1944]: Find-a-Grave").

*Mitchell, Eugene Muse (1931–2007).* Named for his paternal grandfather, Eugene Muse Mitchell became an economist for the government. Like his brother, Joseph Reynolds Mitchell, he eventually was an heir to the estate of Margaret Mitchell and John R. Marsh.

Even though Eugene Muse Mitchell died in Farmington Hills, Michigan, his interment was in Oakland Cemetery in Atlanta. Virginia Mitchell, Eugene Muse Mitchell's wife, and his brother, Joseph Reynolds Mitchell, survived him ("Eugene Muse Mitchell [1931–2007]: Find-a-Grave").

*Mitchell, Mary Isabelle ("Maybelle") Stephens.* Born in 1872 to John Stephens (1833–1896) and Annie Fitzgerald Stephens, who died in 1934, Maybelle Isabelle Stephens Mitchell married Eugene Muse Mitchell (1866–1944) after she left a convent in Canada. Eugene and Maybelle had three children: Russell Stephens Mitchell (1894–1894), Alexander Stephens Mitchell, and Margaret Munnerlyn Mitchell (1900–1949). Maybelle Mitchell died from influenza and pneumonia in 1919; her interment was in Oakland Cemetery in Atlanta; this was the interment site of her husband, her sons Russell Stephens Mitchell and Alexander Stephens Mitchell, her daughter Margaret, and many of her relatives ("Maybelle Isabella Mitchell: Find-a-Grave").

*Mitchell, Russell Crawford (1837–1905).* The fifth of nine children born to the Reverend Isaac Green Mitchell (1810–1881) and Mary Ann Dudley (1808–1859) of Georgia, Russell Crawford ("R. C.") was a Confederate soldier who enjoyed talking to his granddaughter Margaret Mitchell about the war and showing her the scar across his head. Russell Crawford Mitchell's family moved to Atlanta soon after its founding. He suffered severe wounds at the Battle of Antietam.

Initially a lawyer by trade, R. C. Mitchell met and married Deborah Margaret Sweet (1847–1887) after the war's end (1865). They soon moved back to Atlanta. They had eleven children before Deborah died before age 40; one of these children was Eugene Muse Mitchell, the father of Margaret Munnerlyn Mitchell.

R. C. became one of the richest men in Atlanta after starting a lumber mill and going into real estate. He served as Atlanta mayor for a while also.

R. C. married a second time (1888) to Clara Belle Neal Robinson in (1854–1912). They had two more children. In 1900 R. C. retired after a street railway accident. His retirement furnished him more time with Margaret and his other grandchildren.

Russell Crawford Mitchell died in 1905. His burial was in Oakland Cemetery in Atlanta ("Mitchell, Russell Crawford: Find-a-Grave").

*Mitchell, Russell Stephens.* Russell Stephens Mitchell (1894–1894) was the first-born child of Eugene Muse Mitchell (1866–1944) and Mary Isabelle "Maybelle" Stephens Mitchell (1872–1919). The burial place for the infant was Overland Cemetery in Atlanta, the burial cemetery for his sister, Margaret Mitchell, and many others of their immediate family ("Mitchell, Russell Stephens").

*Stephens, Annie Fitzgerald (1844–1934).* Annie Fitzgerald Stephens, the maternal grandmother of Margaret Munnerlyn Mitchell, lived in Atlanta near her daughter, Maybelle, and her son-in-law, Eugene Muse Mitchell (1866–1944). Annie lived long after her husband, John Stephens (1833–1896). The burial of both was in Oakland Cemetery in Atlanta ("Stephens, Annie Fitzgerald: Find-a-Grave"; Pyron, page 20).

*Stephens, Captain John (1833–1896).* Born in Ireland, John Stephens came as a young man to Augusta, Georgia, where his brother was a merchant. John graduated from Tennessee's Hiawassee College and went to work as postmaster for four years.

John enlisted in the 9th Georgia Infantry Regiment. He rose to captain and spent much of the war near Atlanta. He married (1863) Ann/Anna Elizabeth "Annie" Fitzgerald (1844–1934). She was a daughter of Philip Fitzgerald (1798–1880) and Eleanor McGhan Stephens (1818–1893) of Rural Home, Clayton County, Georgia.

John and Annie had twelve children, one of whom was Mary Isabelle "Maybelle" Stephens (1872–1919). Maybelle married Eugene Muse Mitchell; one of their children was Margaret Munnerlyn Mitchell. John Stephens, Margaret's maternal grandfather, died (1896) before Margaret Mitchell was born (1900); the gravesite of John Stephens is in Oakland Cemetery in Atlanta ("Stephens, John: Find-a-Grave").

### Gravitt, Hugh Dorsey (1919–1994)

Hugh Dorsey Gravitt was the driver of the car that struck Margaret Mitchell. Gravitt was born in 1919. His "Find-a-Grave" listing indicated that his burial site is unknown ("Gravitt, Hugh Dorsey: Find-a-Grave").

Gravitt, of Covington, Florida, died on Friday, April 15, 1994. His funeral was held in Cumming, Florida, on the following Sunday. The funeral home officials, his family, and friends withheld all details of his death and his burial site ("Hugh Gravitt, Driver Who Killed Margaret Mitchell"). His death announcement was in the *Orlando Sentinel* on April 22, 1994.

*Charges after the accident.* Twenty-nine-year-old Hugh Dorsey Gravitt's arrest came soon after the accident. The charges against him included drunken driving, speeding, and driving on the wrong side of the road. Because the death of Margaret Mitchell did not occur until five days later, the driver of the car that struck her did not automatically receive a charge of involuntary manslaughter.

*Gravitt's prior convictions.* Gravitt had received more than 20 citations in the ten years prior to the accident that took Margaret Mitchell's life.

*Another accident before beginning his sentence.* The judge gave Gravitt a week to get his affairs in order before beginning to serve his eighteen months for involuntary manslaughter. Before beginning his sentence, however, Gravitt had another traffic accident. He was driving his car with his wife inside as a passenger. His car — the same one that had struck Margaret Mitchell — hit a truck. Both Gravitt and his wife suffered injuries ("Final Days Margaret Mitchell, U.S. Author"). Gravitt would not serve the entire term; a parole entitled him to earlier release.

### Great Britain, sales of *Gone with the Wind* *see* foreign copyrights/translations and fair trade laws

### The Great Depression

The Great Depression was a severe economic slump resulting from the 1929 failure of the stock market. It covered the 1930s and the beginning of the 1940s.

It was during the Great Depression that Margaret Mitchell's *Gone with the Wind* appeared in print. The novel was an inspiration to many who read it and who were experiencing "hard times"; these people in the midst of the Great Depression identified with Margaret Mitchell's characters and the difficulties they endured.

After the Great War, known later as World War I, most of the nation experienced during the 1920s seven years of economic expansion, unprecedented by any other period in American history. The rules of the decade for many parts of the country were personal extravagance, labor saving devices, materialism, unwise investments, new social codes, chewing gum, and motion pictures ("World War I Statistics" from Georgia Department of Veteran Services and U.S. Department of Veteran Affairs; Davis, *Georgia During the Great Depression*, page 5).

Although white women in other parts of the nation could vote, white women in Georgia could not vote until 1922. Maybelle Mitchell, however, did not see her dream come true.

Atlanta began to organize a nationwide advertising campaign to advance its image. Between the years 1926 and 1929, 679 new firms located in the city. With the firms came the people. The population of Atlanta increased from 200,616 in 1920 to 270,366 by 1930 ("Georgia Population").

The capital city of Atlanta soon became the hub for many insurance companies, businesses, banking firms, and, of course, Coca-Cola. During this period of expansion, Atlanta became the convention and cultural center of the South; it housed a symphony orchestra, musical performers specializing in all genres of music, and several colleges—for African Americans and whites alike.

Georgia, however, did not collectively enjoy the "good times." For some the Jazz Age soon ended—or failed to begin. In the decade of the 1920s and the 1930s the rural areas especially began to feel the pinch of hard times. The people of Georgia and the nation could identify with the hardscrabble Reconstruction era in *Gone with the Wind* and with their own hard times in the 1920s-1930s.

Cotton prices dropped from the 35 cents per pound in 1919 to 17 cents per pound in 1920. The price of cotton seed declined from $31 per ton in 1919 to $10 per ton in 1920. Corn prices fell from $1.07 a bushel to 66 cents a bushel. At no time during the next two decades would farm prices reach their pre-war level. For the State of Georgia — primarily an agricultural state with its textile industry based on cotton — this price drop spelled disaster (Coleman, page 263; Davis, *Georgia During the Great Depression*, pages 8–9).

As if the price drops were not trouble enough, the drought of 1924–27 brought further problems and foreshadowed the further hardships to come. The U.S. Geological Service reported that this drought in the 1920s had "a profound influence on industrial and agricultural conditions in Georgia" ("Water Resources of Georgia"; Davis, *Georgia During the Great Depression*, page 9).

Rural Georgia received another blow: the arrival of the boll weevil. First appearing in 1913 in southeast Georgia, the destructive insect began to spread over the state. By 1919 the weevil was devastating the cotton farmers. Thousands of rural families faced hunger and destitution. The drought helped reduce the population of the boll weevil, but the dry weather also reduced yields and income from other crops such as corn (Coleman, page 263; Davis, *Georgia During the Great Depression*, page 9).

There came a time near the end of the 1920s when production of many goods far exceeded national demands, when the American government adjusted tariffs, when the foreign market for American manufactured goods and foodstuffs decreased, when foreign countries did not meet their deadlines for repayment of money borrowed from the United States, when some European countries began to recover and no longer needed aid from the United States, and when other parts of the nation that had prospered in the Roarin' Twenties also began to feel the first pinch of the Great Depression. Many Georgians, however, noticed "nothing new"; lean times had long been with them.

Across the nation investors began to take even greater chances. The stock market began to pulsate and tremble. The long, rolling downward slide gained momentum (McElvaine, *The Great Depression*, page 46).

The morning of Thursday, October 24, 1929, brought panic to the nation. Traders exchanged more than 12 million shares in a single day. The crash of the stock market followed on October 29, 1929 — Black Tuesday: a sixteen-million-share day. The loss quickly reached more than $30 billion. *The Variety* report on October 19, 1929, summed up the collapse in its headline: "Wall Street Lays an Egg." The Great Depression had officially begun (Biles, page 120; Davis, *Georgia During the Great Depression*, page 11).

Following the Stock Market Crash, throughout the nations both laborers and the unemployed were finding their lives and homes threatened from all sides. Citizens responded in a variety of ways.

Some despondent Americans resorted to suicide. Most of these suicides did not occur with the crash of the stock market in 1929, contrary to common belief. The Metropolitan Life Insurance Company reported that 14 people per 100,000 took their own life in 1929; in 1931, however, 20.5 per 100,000 did so. In 1932 17.4 persons per 200,000 committed suicide (McElvaine, *Down and Out*, 18; Time-Life Editors, 25; Davis, *Georgia During the Great Depression*, pages 11–12).

The public usually associates Black Thursday (October 24, 1929) with the beginning of the Great Depression in America, but the South and parts of Georgia already knew "hard times." While much of the rest of the nation reveled in "The Roaring Twenties," Southern laborers mired in debt and fought bank foreclosures on their land and assets. Many Georgians were already acutely aware of the "maldistribution of wealth" that McElvaine blames as a leading cause of the Great Depression (*The Great Depression*, 38).

*The 1930s.* The 1920s had symbolized, for much of the nation, a new woman, a new era, and unprecedented economic expansion. The following decade would be a marked contrast for many.

During the Great Depression stocks dropped. Banks closed. Industries failed. Lenders foreclosed. Jobs decreased. Workloads increased. Salaries dropped. Farmers borrowed, accumulated debts, went without, took out mortgages, and sold land and family possessions. They — along with other unemployed Georgians searching for jobs — felt fear.

Even nature seemed to turn on the people. Droughts and floods ravaged the land. Disease and malnutrition escalated. Despair prevailed. Even the well-to-do knew of the pain and suffering about them. Hard times had come (Davis, *North Carolina During the Great Depression*, pages 8, 238–239).

**Greece, sales of *Gone with the Wind*** *see* **foreign copyrights/translations and fair trade laws**

### Green Park Inn

Upon the invitation of Edwin Granberry, Margaret Mitchell and some other writers attended a writers' conference in Blowing Rock, North Carolina.

To reach Blowing Rock from Atlanta, Margaret took a train from Atlanta to Hickory, North Carolina, and continued to Blowing Rock, arriving July 13, 1936, and registering at the Green Park Inn.

*The Green Park Inn.* The Green family in Blowing Rock owned extensive acreage; local residents referred to their holdings as "Green Park." Green Park originally included its own United States Post Office; a portion of this facility remains in the "history room" of the inn.

Some other important figures who have registered at the inn have included Annie Oakley, J.D. Rockefeller, Eleanor Roosevelt, Calvin Coolidge, and Herbert Hoover.

In 1982 the Green Park Inn achieved its place on the National Register of Historic Places. It is one of the last of the "Grand Manor Hotels" in North Carolina. It is one of the oldest operating resort hotels.

In May of 2010 Eugene and Steven Irace (two New York hotel "affection-ados") purchased the Green Park Inn. During the summer and early fall, they repaired and modernized the infrastructure

and the systems and entirely refurnished it. The new owners "bought American" for most of the remodeling. Much of the furniture carried the "Thomasville" brand, manufactured in nearby Lenoir, North Carolina, or High Point, North Carolina ("Green Park Inn").

*See also* **Blowing Rock Writers' Conference; Granberry, Edwin.**

### Gress, George Valentine (1847–1934)

George Valentine Gress was born in Sullivan County, New York, but he would become an outstanding citizen of Atlanta in the days to come. His gift of animals to the city in 1889 was the foundation of the Grant Park Zoo. Gress's purchase of the Cyclorama in 1893 and its presentation to the city in 1898 were important civic-minded actions. Because of Gress's actions, *The Battle of Atlanta* had its preservation ensured. It was the world's best-known cycloramic painting.

Gress's conditions for giving *The Battle of Atlanta* to Atlanta were that the city repair the painting and improve its housing. These expenses amounted to $4,066.17; with an admission charge of 10 cents per person, the city hoped to regain its investment and perhaps even make a profit. The repairs were complete in time for a reunion of Confederate veterans in Atlanta. During the first week of operation, the admissions totaled $1,000, even though veterans had free admission.

Atlanta erected a fireproof building in 1919 to house the painting; its architect was John Francis Downing. A diorama was complete by 1936 ("Atlanta Cyclorama and Civil War Museum: History").

*Evolution of* The Battle of Atlanta *that Gress purchased.* William Wehner and his artists had painted

The Green family opened the Green Park Inn in Blowing Rock, North Carolina, in 1882. It has been a popular resort for more than a century. Margaret Mitchell stayed at the inn during a writers' conference after the publication of *Gone with the Wind*. (Courtesy of the Green Park Inn.)

*The Battle of Atlanta* and stored it with the Miller family. Because of legal concerns, Wehner, however, had to surrender *The Battle of Atlanta* to the Millers in 1888. In 1890 the Millers sold *The Battle of Atlanta* to Paul Atkinson of Madison, Georgia. Atkinson sold it to H. H. Harrison of Florida. After a snow storm caved in the roof of the wooden building holding the painting, Harrison decided to sell *The Battle of Atlanta*.

Ernest Woodruff bought the damaged painting in 1893 and sold it at auction to George Valentine Gress and Charles Northen. Gress and Northen asked for housing for the painting in one of the city's parks. Atlanta agreed, and Gress made the donation.

*See also* Atlanta Cyclorama; *Battle of Atlanta* painting; Civil War in Margaret Mitchell's education; Downing, John Francis; Grant Park.

## Grosvenor Hotel

Margaret Mitchell sometimes stayed in the Grosvenor Hotel on her visits to New York. One such occasion was when she and her brother Stephens Mitchell went to New York to negotiate contracts with Macmillan Publishing Company on July 28, 1937.

The Grosvenor Hotel was at 35 Fifth Avenue and Tenth Street. Its advertisements indicate it was "a quiet hotel of distinctive charm" (Walker, page 302–303).

## Grove, Edwin Wiley (1850–1927)

The public remembers Edwin W. Grove primarily for his fight against malaria and for his establishment of the Grove Park Inn in Asheville, North Carolina. It was at the Grove Park Inn that Berrien Kinnard ("Red") Upshaw and Margaret Mitchell spent their honeymoon.

Grove was born in 1850 in Bolivar, Tennessee. He formed the Paris Medicine in 1886. Grove married two times: Mary Louisa Grove (1855–1884) and Gertrude Matthewson Grove (1866–1928). He died in Asheville, North Carolina, but his burial plot was in Paris City Cemetery, Paris, Tennessee, near his birth place ("Edwin Wiley Grove: Find-a-Grave").

Edwin Grove had a vision of a resort to serve the emotional needs of its patrons. Asheville, North Carolina, would be the location of the inn that he envisioned.

Grove intended the Grove Park Inn to be an up-to-date inn that was convenient, clean, and quiet. He saw it as a place for tired people who were not ill but who wanted sanitary surroundings, good food, luxurious rooms, and peace. He requested that all guests speak in hushed tones and that all employees wear rubber soled shoes. Patrons who spoke in loud voices received notes asking them to lower their voices.

To preserve cleanliness, Grove required em-

EAST ENTRANCE, GROVE PARK INN, ASHEVILLE, N. C. B-571

This is an early postcard-photograph of the East Entrance of the Grove Park Inn, built by Edwin W. Grove. (Courtesy of the Public Relations Department, Grove Park Inn, Asheville, North Carolina.)

ployees to wash all coins before giving them to the guests. Employees could give only new bills when they made change. Grove required employees to boil all silverware, glasses, and dishes two times before the guests used them (Davis, *North Carolina During the Great Depression*, pages 223–224).

The Grove Park was an important resort to the state, the nation, and the world. By the end of the 1920s it had become the most popular resort in the nation for wealthy Americans.

To stay at the Inn, one had to secure reservations months in advance. Fred Seely — the son-in-law of owner Edwin W. Grove — had to approve any new guests. Certain traditions became a feature; for instance after performances, the guests received washed apples and a sheet of thin gray paper for the core. It was truly, as Seely always said, "a place where guests could get away and rest."

Some important guests who stayed at the Grove Park Inn at various times from its opening until the time of the Great Depression included William Howard Taft (president from 1909 until 1913); Woodrow Wilson (president from 1913 until 1921); Margaret Mitchell and her first husband, Berrien Kinnard ("Red") Upshaw, on their honeymoon beginning September 3, 1922; Calvin Coolidge (president from 1923 until 1929); Herbert Hoover (president from 1929 until 1933); and Franklin Roosevelt (president from 1933 until 1945). Other patrons included John Edgar Hoover, FBI director from 1929 until 1972; the magician Harry Houdini; the inventors Thomas A. Edison and Henry Ford; humorist Will Rogers; and tire producers Harvey Firestone and son.

*Edwin W. Grove and his Malaria-Relief Tonic.* Edwin W. Grove had earned the money necessary to begin the Grove Park Inn through his tonic for malaria relief. By mixing iron, lemon, and sugar with quinine, Grove had developed a tasteless medicine for the treatment of malaria; he called his medicine Grove's Tasteless Chill Tonic. It sold for 50 cents a bottle and carried Edwin's own guarantee: no cure, no pay (Davis, *North Carolina During the Great Depression*, page 147).

The tonic even became a standard issue item to troops, going into malaria-infested lands ("Edwin Wiley Grove: Find-a-Grave"). When more bottles of his Tasteless Chill Tonic sold than bottles of Coca-Cola, Grove quickly became a millionaire (Davis, *North Carolina During the Great Depression*, page 147).

## Gullah

Margaret Mitchell became quite interested in the dialects among the African Americans in the South. She tried to replicate these various dialects precisely in her manuscript.

After the death of her Grandmother Stephens in 1934, Margaret Mitchell and her husband, John R. Marsh, took a trip to Savannah, Georgia, to a meeting of the Georgia Press Association. The dialect of the African American population in the Savannah area struck them as quite different from the Gullah dialect around Charleston, South Carolina. Mitchell began to study both in detail (Walker, page 192).

*See also* Geechee.

## gumption

Margaret Mitchell long remembered a lesson on gumption that Maybelle Mitchell gave on Margaret's return home from her first day of school at North Boulevard School. Margaret told her mother that she hated arithmetic and did not want to go back to school. (On page xx of *Before Scarlett*, Mary Rose Taylor mentions Margaret Mitchell's attending Forrest Avenue School when she learned the lesson from her mother.)

Mrs. Mitchell's "response was to bare her daughter's rear and give her a good whacking with a hairbrush" (Edwards, page 25). Next, she ordered Margaret into their horse-drawn carriage. Margaret long remembered hanging on to the seat as her mother drove at a fast clip. They drove toward Clayton County on the Jonesboro Road.

Maybelle Mitchell only slowed the buggy down when they reached the former plantation houses. Maybelle explained that the homes — in ruins — were once the homes of wealthy, fine people; the homes had been in neglect since Union General William Tecumseh Sherman came through the area. She indicated that some of the people who had lived there were in ruins also.

Maybelle Mitchell pointed Margaret's attention to the other side of the road. The houses were old also, but the occupants had tended the homes and surroundings well (Edwards, pages 25–26). The thing that made a difference in the lives of the people who survived having their world explode right under them, Mrs. Mitchell explained, was *education* or *surviving* or — as most sources indicate — *gumption*. Mrs. Mitchell told Margaret that education, common sense, survival, and gumption were particularly important for women — who should be like buckwheat.

Maybelle Mitchell told Margaret matter-of-factly that she would return to first grade the next day without question. She also warned her daughter that some day Margaret's world, too, would explode under her; she would be armed with education and gumption.

The two drove slowly home. Margaret raised no protest to school on the way home or in the days to come (Edwards, pages 25–27).

John Wiley quotes Margaret Mitchell on the subject of *gumption*, or survival. "What makes some people able to come through catastrophes and others, apparently just as able, strong and brave, go under? It happens in every upheaval. Some people survive; others don't. What qualities are in those who fight their way through triumphantly that are lacking in those who go under? I only know that the survivors used to call that quality 'gumption.' So I wrote about the people who had gumption and the people who didn't" (Wiley).

*See also* **buckwheat people.**

## Gwin, Yolande

Yolande Gwin was a writer and society editor for the *Atlanta Journal-Constitution* (before and after the merger of the two newspapers) for a total of fifty years. Gwin was the first of the Atlanta reporters to get an interview from Margaret Mitchell and to receive an advance copy of *Gone with the Wind*.

The interview, which John Marsh described in a letter to Lois Cole on February 9, 1936, was more social than literary; the two women visited comfortably. Marsh told Cole that Gwin referred to Mitchell as "this clever young writer" (Edwards, page 189).

Margaret Mitchell wrote to Gwin on June 28, 1936, after she and John had read Gwin's review of *Gone with the Wind* in print. Mitchell said she was "still blushing about the ankles" with happiness at the flattering review. Margaret reminded Gwin that she — as author of the article — would have to answer on Judgment Day to the Recording Angel for the perjury in the article; Margaret did, however, promise "to put in a good word for you" if she were there (Gwin, page 40).

Margaret also had something to say about Gwin's reference to her as a "young author." Margaret reacted by saying that she had "passed the broiling stage and the frying stage and [was] rapidly approaching the roasting and broiling stage" (Mitchell on June 28, 1936, to Yolande Gwin and quoted in Gwin, page 40).

Gwin created a name for herself in journalism. On December 1, 1983, Georgia Governor Joe Frank Harris issued a proclamation acknowledging Yolande Gwin as an outstanding journalist, commending her contributions to journalism and recognizing the honor she had brought to herself and to the state (Gwin, page 187).

Much about the personal life of Yolande Gwin is unknown. This absence of personal information about her is also a subject in an article about her ("Chamblee54: Google Goose Chase").

## Hamilton, Charles

Charles Hamilton was a character in the book and movie *Gone with the Wind*, Melanie Hamilton Wilkes's brother. He became the first husband of Scarlett O'Hara. Hamilton dies in service during the Civil War; he dies not from battle injuries but from measles and pneumonia — after Scarlett becomes pregnant.

## Hanson, Elizabeth I.

Elizabeth I. Hanson was the author of *Margaret Mitchell* (1991). Hanson's work was one of the earliest biographies of the Georgia writer.

Joseph Millichap evaluated Margaret Mitchell's biographies that had been prepared before 1991, including Hanson's. Millichap wrote that Hanson's work "provides an insightful analysis of Mitchell's life in relation to her great work."

Hanson's work provides critical introductions to Mitchell. It includes chapters on each stage of Mitchell's life — childhood and family, young adulthood and first marriage, second marriage and career in journalism, writing *Gone with the Wind*, and Mitchell's relations to southern literature, other writers, and the film version of *Gone with the Wind* (Joseph Millichap).

## Harris, Joel Chandler (December 9, 1848– July 3, 1908)

Author Joel Chandler Harris worked for and published in the *Constitution* in Atlanta. He still found time to record his "Remus" tales. Harris's reproduction of the dialect of the African Americans in the Macon area was flawless (Steven Gale, pages 169–172). Harris's desk at the *Constitution* is now located at his home, which he called the Wren's Nest. His desk from the newspaper office ranks as one of the most famous pieces of Atlanta's newspaper history — along with a table and chair that Margaret Mitchell used there (Farr, page 60).

Like Harris, Margaret Mitchell and John R. Marsh meticulously perfected and replicated the regional dialects of the various characters in *Gone with the Wind*. When the Macmillan copy editors changed Margaret's and John's carefully spelled and worded dialogues, Margaret refused to agree to the changes.

## Harris, Julia Collier

Julia Collier Harris was the daughter-in-law of Joel Chandler Harris. She wrote a weekly column for the *Chattanooga Times*. In that position, Julia had received an advance copy of *Gone with the Wind*; Collier had written Margaret a personal letter to predict that the novel would be a huge success. She warned Margaret to guard against being consumed by the publicity and the demands that would come with the sales of *Gone with the Wind*.

Margaret Mitchell received the advice eagerly. On the day before the publication of *Gone with the Wind* (June 29, 1936), Mitchell wrote to Julia to thank her for the review of her novel and for the personal letter that Julia had written to her. Margaret wrote that she did not welcome the publicity that Julia predicted might accompany the book. "I did not realize the being an author meant this sort of thing, autographing in book store, being invited here and there about the country to speak, to attend summer schools, to address this and that group at luncheon. It all came as a shock to me and not a pleasant shock. I have led, by choice, so quiet and cloistered a life for many years.... Being in the public eye is something neither of us care about but what good does it do to say it? ... How comforting it was to read your words—how pleasant to know that some one like you felt like John and I, upon this subject. I feel that I had a strong rock on which to stand if someone of your stature refuses, then I, too, can refuse [to speak and attend all the events]" (Harwell, *Letters*, pages 17–18). Margaret Mitchell wrote to Julia Collier Harris many times after this June 19, 1936, letter.

*See also* **Gainesville, Georgia.**

## Harris, Julian

Julian Harris (1874–1963) was the executive editor of the *Chattanooga Times* and the son of Joel Chandler Harris. Julian wrote to John R. Marsh to tip him off in advance that Margaret Mitchell had won the Pulitzer Prize for the most distinguished novel. John's letter from Harris came to him at his office. John called Margaret to share the important news. Mitchell later told Julian Harris that John had to read the news to her three times before it sank in what had happened (Brown, page 149).

Mitchell also corresponded occasionally corresponded with Julian Harris's wife, Julia Collier Harris. Julia, the daughter-in-law of Joel Chandler Harris, was the author of a column in the *Chattanooga Times*.

*See also* **Harris, Julia Collier.**

## Harrison, H. H.

The history of Margaret Mitchell's beloved painting *The Battle of Atlanta* in the Atlanta Cyclorama is a complicated one. H. H. Harrison of Florida bought the painting from Paul Atkinson of Madison, Georgia. Harrison intended to exhibit the work at the World's Columbian Exposition in Chicago.

Harrison found, however, that building a structure in Chicago would be cost prohibitive. Ernest Woodruff bought the painting at auction from Harrison in 1893 after a heavy snowfall caved in the roof of the structure where the painting was on display. Woodruff sold *The Battle of Atlanta*, in turn, to George Valentine Gress and Charles Northen. The complicated story of *The Battle of Atlanta* continued; its location, however, in Atlanta, Georgia, remained the same ("Atlanta Cyclorama and Civil War Museum").

*See also* **Atkinson, Paul; Atlanta Cyclorama; *Battle of Atlanta* painting; Gress, George Valentine.**

## Hartsfield, William Berry (1890–1971)

This mayor (1937 to 1941 and 1942 to 1962) was born in Atlanta in 1890, to Victoria Dagnal and her tinsmith husband Charles Green Hartsfield. During his last year in high school, he dropped out of school to take a secretarial course at Dixie Business College. He began clerking for various firms and married the Western Union operator Pearl William on Aug. 2, 1913; they would have two children.

By reading in the library and clerking with the law firm of Rosser, Slaton, Phillips and Hopkins, William B. Hartsfield studied law. In 1917 he was able to pass the Georgia bar examination. For the remainder of his life, he would declare that the Atlanta Public Library was his alma mater.

As a successful lawyer, William B. Hartsfield was able to meet and to establish friendships with the business leaders of Atlanta. The powerful city leaders accepted Hartsfield into their inner circles.

Hartsfield loved the City of Atlanta and aviation. He won election to the Atlanta City Council in 1923 and received a prompt appointment to the new Aviation Committee for the city. Hartsfield was able to negotiate the land acquisition from Asa Candler for a municipal airport; he also negotiated Atlanta as a federal designation as a transfer and a terminal point on the first of the New York–Miami and Chicago-Jacksonville air routes.

Although Hartsfield served in the Georgia General Assembly from 1933 until 1936, he determined his true place was with Atlanta and local government. In 1936, he entered Atlanta's mayoral race. The campaign was full of vicious attacks. Incumbent Mayor James L. Key accused Hartsfield of dishonesty in business, submitting bribes, and of not paying his obligations. Hartsfield accused Key of using the police for political purposes, of overseeing a shoddy jail, and of vetoing bill to make Confederate Memorial Day a holiday for Atlanta.

When William B. Hartsfield took office on January 4, 1937, *Gone with the Wind* was selling well in Atlanta's department stores and bookstores after its publication in 1936. He found other things, however, that were not so pleasant. Atlanta was so deep in debt that city employees were not being paid; instead they were receiving certificates that promised payment at a later time. He found an inefficient, dishonest police administration; Atlanta had a bad reputation for gambling and for prostitution.

Hartsfield began his work by trying to strengthen the financial foundations of the city; he tried to anticipate the revenues and to budget realistically. He appointed new administrators to oversee the police force and — with him — to demand a crack-down on Atlanta's night spots and on gambling.

Mayor Hartsfield was able to refinance Atlanta's payroll with the support of the city bankers and with the support of Robert W. Woodruff, the head of the Coca-Cola Company. By the end of his term, he had successfully reformed the police department and other city agencies.

William B. Hartsfield found a way to bring recognition to Atlanta and to himself. He began a campaign to bring the 1939 premiere of David O. Selznick's film *Gone with the Wind* (based on Margaret Mitchell's novel *Gone with the Wind*) to Atlanta. This event was one of the most celebrated occasions of the golden era of Hollywood. Atlanta and the premiere were the national focus of the newspapers, magazines, radio, and newsreels. Mayor Hartsfield was in the national spotlight during the days and nights of parades, balls, the film premiere, and the appearances of the major Hollywood stars.

Hartsfield did not win the 1940 mayoral election despite his campaign to bring the film premiere of *Gone with the Wind* to Atlanta and despite the success of his policies for the city; hindsight indicated he had not focused enough on campaigning again for the position. Atlanta citizens cast more than 22,000 votes for the candidates; William B. Hartsfield lost by only 83 votes to Candidate Roy LeCraw. Analysts, however, suggested that the police officers on motorcycles hiding behind billboards to reinforce the new 25-mile-per-hour speed limit throughout the city had dissatisfied the voters and had turned the election against Hartsfield.

In April of 1942, however, LeCraw resigned from office to enter the military. Hartsfield returned to office as a result of the special election of May 1942. For the next twenty years he held the office of mayor of Atlanta.

Atlanta became a leader of southern cities after World War II — in part because of Hartsfield's leadership. He maintained close associations with business leaders in the community; these ties ensured that governmental policies would support businesses. Hartsfield ended each fiscal year with a surplus, yet he recommended and oversaw major improvements to infrastructure.

Atlanta's population exceeded one million people by 1959. Part of this increase was the fact that Hartsfield had initiated a campaign to increase the city limits from 35 to 118 square miles. Primarily because of their having to pay city taxes, suburban homeowners had opposed this annexation by the state legislature of additional land into the city limits.

A high priority goal that Hartsfield set was developing and improving the runways, the lighting, and the approaches to the Atlanta Municipal Airport. Under his watch, Atlanta emerged as an air transportation hub in the Southeast; this distinction helped reinforce the status of Atlanta as a vital financial and commercial center of the region.

After the United States Supreme Court declared in 1944 that African Americans must be included in the voting primaries, Hartsfield began to pay attention to these citizens and business leaders — a segment of the population that he had not regarded in the past. He managed to lead the City of Atlanta through the racial policy changes without the turbulence that marked other Southern cities during the Civil Rights era.

In 1948 he appointed the first black officers to the police force. In 1951 he welcomed to Atlanta the convention of the National Association for the Advancement of Colored People. In addition to working to integrate the public transportation system of buses and trolleys (1957), he supervised the 1961 integration of the city schools; Atlanta ended its school segregation without the violence and turmoil that characterized integration in many other Southern cities.

The business community in Atlanta supported the racial policies that the federal courts and Hartsfield had espoused. The city frequently used a phrase to attest to the partnership of business and the leaders of the African American community; this popular expression was a city "too busy to hate."

Hartsfield's first marriage was destined for divorce. He knew this marital situation and his involvement with another woman would hurt his chances of continuing in public office. On June 7, 1961, he announced his decision not to seek re-election; on February 20, 1962, his divorce became final. On July 11, 1962, he married the young widow Tollie Bedenbaugh Tolan and later adopted her son.

William Berry Hartsfield died on February 22, 1971. One week later — on what would have been Hartsfield's eighty-first birthday — the name of the airport in Atlanta became the William B. Hartsfield Airport in his honor. In July the name of the William B. Hartsfield Airport changed again. Because Eastern Airlines had begun flights to Jamaica and Mexico, the airport name became the William B. Hartsfield Atlanta International Airport. Eastern had initiated the William B. Hartsfield International Airport's first international service ("Hartsfield Atlanta Airport in the Early 1970s"; "William Berry Hartsfield" in *Dictionary of American Biography*; "William Berry Hartsfield" in *Gale Biography in Context*).

*See also* Coca-Cola.

## Hartsfield-Jackson Atlanta International Airport

Located on what was once Atlanta Speedway, a racetrack built in 1909 by Coca-Cola founder and former Atlanta Mayor Asa Candler, the Hartsfield-Jackson Atlanta International Airport is now one of the busiest airports in the world. Candler purchased the flat, swampy land in 1909 for $77,674.28. The track, also known as Atlanta Motor Speedway, Candler Raceway, Automobile Speedway, and Atlanta Raceway, cost $400,000 to build. The track opened on November 9, 1909, and proved unsuccessful; it closed after one season.

Asa Candler began to use the flat area that had been the race track for air races and air shows. Gradually, Candler began to add motorcycle and car races back on the field. When the government began to offer airmail service, Atlanta began to search for an appropriate field for the planes. William Hartsfield, a city alderman, suggested Candler Field. In 1925 Candler offered Atlanta a 5-year, rent-free lease on the 287 acres for use as an airfield. As part of the agreement, it was to be called Candler Field in honor of Asa Candler. Mayor Walter Sims signed the lease.

On September 15, 1926, a Florida Airways mail plane, flying to Atlanta from Jacksonville, Florida, used Candler Field. When Pitcairn Aviation (1928) and Delta Air Service (1930) — now Eastern Air Lines and Delta Air Lines — began service, Atlanta became their hub. By 1930, the airport in Atlanta had become the third busiest airport in the nation. Only New York and Chicago exceeded Atlanta in the number of regular daily flights. In March of 1939, Candler Field opened its first control tower. This opening was just before the Atlanta premiere of *Gone with the Wind*.

In October 1940, the U.S. government declared Candler Field a military airfield. The Works Project Administration built two additional runways and extended the existing runways at Candler Field in 1941–1942. The base took on the additional mission of the medical examinations and the processing of prospective aviation cadets.

The United States Army Air Force was able to operate its airfield jointly with Candler Field. The Army Air Force used the field to service transient aircraft and to maintain some of the planes. During World War II, the field set a record with 1700 takeoffs and landings in one day; this made it the busiest airfield in the world.

The Atlanta Army Airfield closed after the end of World War II. Delta Airline, however, continues to use the office and hangar from World War II. In 1946 Candler Field became Atlanta Municipal Airport. Today, Candler Field bears the name Hartsfield-Jackson Atlanta International Airport, one of the world's biggest and busiest airports ("The History of Atlanta Airport"; "Airport History: Hartsfield-Jackson Atlanta International Airport").

An interesting but difficult to substantiate legend states that Candler Field figured prominently in the festivities of the Atlanta premiere of the film *Gone with the Wind*. When Mayor William B. Hartsfield had learned that the plane with many of the stars was arriving early, he had gone to the newly-opened control tower and begged the pilot of the plane carrying Clark Gable and some of the other stars to circle Stone Mountain; this detour would give the Atlanta dignitaries a little more time to get the flowers and the ceremonies ready.

*See also* **Atlanta premiere of *Gone with the Wind*; Atlanta Municipal Airport; Candler Field.**

## Harwell, Richard Barksdale

Richard Barksdale Harwell (1915–1988) was born in Washington, Georgia. In addition to his three books on Margaret Mitchell, Harwell has edited 27 other works and written some 30 other pieces.

His works dealing specifically with Margaret Mitchell and *Gone with the Wind* (book and film) — in addition to the three books listed earlier — include *Technical Adviser: The Making of Gone with the Wind* (The Hollywood Journals of Wilbur G. Kurtz, Atlanta Historical Society, 1978); *Susan Myrick, White Columns in Hollywood: Reports from the GWTW Sets* (Mercer University Press, 1982); his work with Darden A. Pyron on *Recasting Gone with the Wind* (University Presses of Florida, 1983); and *GWTW: The Screenplay* (Macmillan, 1980). Many of his additional works relate also to the South and the Confederacy.

In addition to serving as a librarian at Smith College (where Margaret Mitchell attended in 1918–1919), Harwell held the position of archival consultant at four institutions. He served at eighteen other libraries (mostly college and university libraries), including the University of Rangoon, the

University of Mandalay, the University of Jordan, and the University of Baghdad. His awards included a doctor of letters from New England College (1966); the Distinguished Service Award, the Atlanta Civil War Round Table (1983); and the Nevins-Freeman Award, Chicago Civil War Round Table (1984).

Although Harwell was a historian, bibliographer, biographer, editor, librarian, researcher, and scholar, he preferred to think of himself first as a librarian — the field in which he had worked the longest and earned his living. He served in that capacity for 44½ years.

Harwell found his collection of Margaret Mitchell letters to be his most satisfying project. Stephens Mitchell finally decided Harwell should publish the letters; their publication was "probably the most worthwhile thing I've done" ("Richard Barksdale Harwell").

*Harwell, Richard Barksdale and Margaret Mitchell.* Richard Barksdale Harwell wrote three volumes about Margaret Mitchell and her work. These volumes included *The Big Book: Fifty Years of Gone with the Wind; An Exhibit at the Madison-Morgan Cultural Center, From the Collection of Richard Harwell, April 4–May 25, 1986* (1986); *Gone with the Wind As Book and Film* (1983); and *Margaret Mitchell's Gone with the Wind Letters, 1936–1949* (1976).

Millichap evaluated some of the biographical publications on Margaret Mitchell. He looked particularly at Harwell's *Gone with the Wind Letters, 1936–1949.* He observes that the letters Harwell gathered were mainly written after the publication of the book and after the completion of the film. Millichap considers Harwell's collection, nevertheless, to be valuable. It still provides the reader with insight into the "conception, writing, editing, and publishing" of *Gone with the Wind.* Although Margaret Mitchell requested that many of the remaining documents be destroyed after her death, Mitchell allowed these letters to remain. Millichap believes that Mitchell did not designate these valuable letters for destruction because "they deal with the more public side of her life and work. They also provide a basis for a consideration of more private issues. Harwell's edition is scholarly, and his insights about the cross-identification of Mitchell, Scarlett, and their mutual hometown of Atlanta, possibly began the novel's recent critical evaluation as an important text" (Millichap).

## Heine, F. W.

The Prussian War veteran Frederick William Heine (1827–1921) was one of the German artists with experience with cycloramas and with battle itself that William Wehner selected to bring to Milwaukee, Wisconsin. Wehner selected Heine as the chief supervisor of Atlanta's cycloramic painting: *The Battle of Atlanta,* one of young Margaret Mitchell's favorite historical landmarks. August Lohr would supervise the landscape of the painting. William Wehner hired three main landscape painters, five main figure painters, and two primary animal painters.

First, Heine, Lohr, and several other artists came to Atlanta in 1885 to study the location of the battle. They set up a 40-foot wooden tower at the intersection of the Georgia Railroad and Moreland Avenue and made sketches of many details; they also began correlating existing landmarks with reports and military maps. As they worked atop the tower, the artists had visits from both Union and Confederate veterans and from residents who had information to contribute. A translator helped the artists to understand the helpful recollections that these trustworthy sources were sharing; after all, they were present at the time.

The technical advisor to these German artists was Theodore Davis, who had been a staff artist with *Harper's Weekly* during the Civil War and had witnessed and sketched many battles — including the Battle of Atlanta. His experiences and knowledge contributed significantly to the painting, particularly to the authenticity of both the landscape and the military action ("Atlanta Cyclorama and Civil War Museum").

***See also*** Davis, Theodore.

## Henker, Sophie

Margaret Mitchell made several close friends at Smith College, in addition to her roommate Ginny Morris. Her other friends included Madeleine Baxter, Helen Atkinson, and Sophie Henker. Sophie Henker shared Margaret's love of horses. Because she lived in nearby Amherst, Sophie went home for weekends at times. Margaret visited in Sophie's home on several occasions. Sophie introduced Margaret to several Amherst men, and she was accepted into their social circles. Margaret, however, remembered that she was engaged to Clifford Henry (Edwards, page 60).

## Henry, Clifford West (1896–1918)

After America entered World War I (1917–18), the Red Cross and other hosts and hostesses often invited Atlanta girls — especially those who had attended or were attending Washington Seminary — to attend the dances and other social events for the young men at Fort Gordon, Georgia.

Margaret Mitchell was a frequent guest at these parties, and at one of them eighteen-year-old Margaret Mitchell met twenty-two-year-old Lieutenant Clifford Henry, who was a bayonet instructor at Camp Gordon and a wealthy and socially prominent New Yorker. The two fell in love. When Henry found out that he was to receive a transfer overseas, the two became secretly engaged and made plans to marry as soon as they were able ("Margaret Mitchell and Clifford West Henry").

Margaret's Yankee lieutenant was a good listener. He could recite poems to her and could quote Shakespeare for her. She was intrigued by his knowledge of literature.

After Clifford's departure, Margaret began to adjust to her new school: Smith College. Margaret had four good friends at "Ten Hen." They were Ginny Morris, Sophie Henker, Madeleine Baxter, and Helen Atkinson. Because they had much in common, they all got along well.

On September 11, 1918, Ginny brought Margaret a letter from Clifford Henry; he was at Saint-Mihiel. On the very next morning — September 12 — the American army attacked the German troops during a dense fog. Within two days, the Americans had routed the Germans; the cost had been a dear one: 8,000 lost lives.

During the attack, Clifford assumed command when his captain became disabled. Bomb fragments from a German plane hit Clifford in the leg and stomach. As he lay in a hospital bed, he received the Croix De Guerre. He died on October 16. Margaret was devastated ("Margaret Mitchell Biography").

*See also* **Atkinson, Helen; Baxter, Madeleine; Henker, Sophie; Nixon, Ginny Morris; Ten Henshaw.**

## Historical Jonesboro

The founding of Historical Jonesboro dates from 1968. The purpose of the establishment was to save "the buildings, the furnishings, and written documents that reflected the heritage of Clayton County, GA. Buildings had to be moved to a secure location and the site selected was designated as the Margaret Mitchell Memorial Park. This was done to honor the famous author of *Gone with the Wind*, because Clayton County was not only the setting for Tara but also her great-grandfather's plantation…. The crown jewel of the property is the Stately Oaks Plantation House, which was built in 1839 and is a true example of plain Greek Revival architecture. It is believed to be one of the inspirations for Margaret Mitchell's beloved Tara.

"All who share the love of history and preservation are encouraged to visit and tour the grounds and buildings of Historical Jonesboro/Clayton County, Inc." ("Welcome to Stately Oaks Plantation").

*See also* **Tara, Stately Oaks Plantation.**

## Hoar, Jay S.

Jay S. Hoar was obsessed with the veterans of the Civil War and wanted to know about the lives of the last remaining vets. After more than 12,000 letters, he was able to locate and interview the last 38 of them. The result of his work was a three volume set — more than 2,000 pages. Two volumes were for the last of the Union veterans; one volume was for the last surviving Confederate vets, including the four who attended the premiere of *Gone with the Wind* (the film) in Atlanta (Skelton, Kathryn).

## Hodge, Edwin

The Atlanta attorney Edward Hodge was the first (1883) publisher of *The Atlanta Journal*, where Margaret Mitchell would work. In 1887, Hodge sold the paper to fellow attorney and future Georgia governor Hoke Smith.

## Holbrook, Carrie

One of the women in the employment of Eugene Muse Mitchell (1866–1944) and his daughter Margaret was Carrie Holbrook. Carrie came in two days a week to do the laundry after the death of Maybelle Mitchell (Edwards, page 66).

After Margaret Mitchell married John R. Marsh, Carrie took their laundry and brought it back to them one day a week. Like Bessie Berry Jordan, Carrie Holbrook remained loyal to Margaret Mitchell — and she to Bessie and Carrie.

In the 1940s — when Carrie had been with John and Margaret for over twenty years — she became very ill. Doctors determined that Carrie was dying of cancer. The Holbrook family would not accept charity; they asked "Miss Peggy" to find Carrie a hospital in which she could die comfortably. Because Carrie Holbrook was African American, many hospitals did not want to accept her.

Margaret Mitchell appealed to Our Lady of Perpetual Help Hospital. She pled with the charitable hospital to accept Carrie Holbrook as a paying patient. Their rule had been that patients be friendless and without means to pay. They finally accepted Carrie; she died three days after her admittance.

John had been sick, but as soon as he was better, Margaret began a new project. She began to work to secure better hospital care for African Americans. She began to raise funds to build a non-charitable hospital as soon as John was able for her to spend some time away from him. She was instrumental in selling the plans for such a facility to Fulton-DeKalb Hospital Authority and to the Fulton County Medical Society. Once they approved the project, Margaret made the first donation: $1,000 (Edwards, pages 66, 80, 148, 321).

**Holland, sales of *Gone with the Wind*** *see* **foreign copyrights/translations and fair trade laws**

### honorary citizenship in Vimoutiers, France (1949)

On July 15, 1949, just before her death the next month, Margaret Mitchell wrote to Dr. Wallace McClure, her contact at the State Department in Washington, D.C. Mitchell had received notification that she had been elected an honorary citizen of Vimoutiers, France. She had some specific questions about this honor. She was not sure whether she was elected or the exact procedure that brought this about. She knew only that the mayor and the council of Vimoutiers bestowed this citizenship on her.

She was aware "that an American citizen in government service, or in the armed services, may not accept decorations from a foreign government, or gifts, et cetera, except under special rulings. My

brother can find nothing in the Code concerning private citizens" (Harwell, *Letters,* page 402). Mitchell was also concerned whether she would offend if she elected not to accept the citizenship.

The little village had been bombed "almost out of existence by our air corps during the invasion." This bombing was in error (Harwell, *Letters,* page 402): "Our Ninth Air Force gave Vimoutiers all it had, killing a great many of the citizens, maiming others, leveling their schools, municipal buildings, hospitals and many homes. The people of Vimoutiers did not complain, and still have not complained, for they knew that liberations came with the air force. Through a French refugee air corps boy, who is the son of the Mayor of Vimoutiers, I came to know about the little town" (Harwell, *Letters,* page 402).

Vimoutiers appealed to Mitchell to try to get it "adopted" by some American organization or some American city. After many unsuccessful attempt to oblige, Margaret at last was able to help with the

Margaret Mitchell and Bessie Jordan pack relief parcels for post-war Europe, November 1947. (Collection number 786. O'Neal. Courtesy of the Atlanta-Fulton Public Library System's Special Collections Department.)

adoption. At a recent convention, the Pilot Club International voted to affiliate itself with Vimoutiers (Harwell, *Letters,* page 402).

McClure received Margaret Mitchell's letter about her honorary citizenship in Vimoutiers; he responded. On July 26, 1949, Margaret wrote an acknowledgment of "the decision of the Legal Advisor's Office ... that I could accept the honor. Naturally, I have been very pleased about it and am very anxious to accept it" (Harwell, *Letters,* page 423).

Mitchell indicated that she packed food, vitamins, and clothing at night for Europe — and especially France. She indicated that she had hoped that the packages that she and Bessie Jordan packed would get to the places for which they were intended.

## Hotel Ansley  *see*  Ansley Hotel

## Hotel Biltmore  *see*  Biltmore Hotel

## Hotel Grosvenor  *see*  Grosvenor Hotel

## Howard, Branch

Branch Howard was a lawyer friend of the Mitchell family who represented Margaret in her divorce from Berrien Kinnard "Red" Upshaw. It was filed June 17, 1923. The deposition that Margaret had sworn to after Upshaw had beaten her on July 10, 1923, was the evidence submitted. Branch swore to the validity of the deposition. Margaret waived alimony, but she asked for the restoration of her maiden name and the annulment of the marriage.

Even though Eugene Muse Mitchell believed that the marriage between his daughter-in-law and Upshaw had demeaned the Mitchell family name, he was opposed to a divorce. He was not representing his daughter — nor was his son — despite the abuse she had suffered. Divorce until this time was unheard of in the Mitchell family; it was against the Catholic religion, the religion of the Fitzgeralds, Margaret's maternal family.

The jury foreman stated that a divorce was in order. The restoration of the family name and an annulment, however, was not applicable. On October 16, Branch Howard accompanied her to another hearing. This time the jury granted Margaret's petition (Edwards, pages 102–103, 109–110).

## Howard, Leslie (1893–1943)

The actor, director and producer Leslie Howard was best known for his film roles as a gentle, civilized English man. His most famous role was as Ashley Wilkes in *Gone with the Wind* (1939). His father, Frank Stainer, was Hungarian-Jewish; Leslie's first language was German. Stainer married Lilian Howard, a barrister's daughter in London.

Leslie grew up in Vienna but took his college education from Dulwich College in London. Stainer intended his son to follow him as a stockbroker, but Leslie already had his mother's affinity for drama. Adopting his mother's maiden name, Leslie appeared onscreen in the 1914 film *The Heroine of Mons,* directed by his uncle Wilfred Noy.

Although he had never ridden a horse, Leslie joined the 20th Hussars during World War I. He served on the Western Front, but as a result of shell-shock in 1916, he received a discharge. He married the same year and began pursuing films in earnest.

In the 1920s he began producing and acting in some minor films. Sound films made Leslie valuable because he had a trained voice and had already appeared successfully in some Broadway productions.

Howard's debut in sound films came in 1930 with *Outward Bound,* a talkie based on a successful stage production. Another notable screen role included *The Petrified Forest* (1936) with the little-known Humphrey Bogart, whom he selected as his co-star. Howard could bargain quite easily because he already had received a nomination for a Best Actor Oscar for his role in *Berkeley Square* (1933). Humphrey became a good friend with Leslie and even named his daughter Leslie after the friend who helped launch his screen career.

Howard made his breakthrough on British films with the 1935 hit *The Scarlet Pimpernel.* In the British film *Pygmalion* (1938), Howard made his directorial debut; George Bernard Shaw adapted his own play for the movie. Leslie Howard received his second Best Actor Oscar nomination for *Pygmalion.* He became one of the first of the British stars to enlist in the war effort. He made such propaganda films as *From the Four Corners* (1941).

He directed his first film, *"Pimpernel" Smith,* in 1941. This film was reminiscent of *The Scarlet Pimpernel* but with a World War II setting. The same year he played in *49th Parallel.* Howard would direct two more films: *The First of the Few* (1942) and *The Gentle Sex* (1943).

In 1943 the Luftwaffe shot down the plane carrying Leslie Howard over the Bay of Biscay. He was supposedly flying home from a lecture tour that may have been a cover for a mission for the British intelligence. Howard's plane may have been mistaken for one carrying Winston Churchill, or Howard himself may have been the intended target. One writer said of his death, "Certainly, Nazi propaganda chief Josef Goebbels was well aware of his importance to the British people as the very embodiment (both onscreen and off) of all they stood for and all that was worth cherishing about their values. His shockingly sudden death was widely regarded as a national tragedy" ("Screen Online: Howard, Leslie [1893–1943]").

*Howard and the Atlanta premiere of Gone with the Wind (December 13–16, 1939).* Leslie Howard was unavailable to attend the Atlanta premiere of *Gone with the Wind.* England had just entered World War II, and Howard had joined the cause.

## Howland, William S.

William S. ("Bill") Howland was with the Nashville *Banner* when Margaret Mitchell's *Gone with the Wind* was ready for publication. Margaret wanted him to have a review copy. She wrote Lois Cole that Bill would "write a glowing review 'regardless of how rotten' the novel was and 'cram it down' his book editor's throat" (Brown, 50).

## Hoyle, Steve

Steve Hoyle was a main character in Thomas Dixon's *The Traitor.* Sixteen-year-old Margaret Mitchell assumed the role of Steve Hoyle in her own production of Dixon's novel.

Margaret Mitchell's father — Eugene Muse Mitchell (1866–1944) — and her mother — Maybelle Mitchell (1872–1919) — lectured their daughter sternly on violation of copyright after they observed her performance; she had not credited author Thomas Dixon for his work in her production. Margaret Mitchell would remember the lesson the rest of her life.

Steve Hoyle was the rich, handsome young character in *The Traitor.* Another main character is the lawyer John Graham, who is the North Carolina Grand Dragon of the Ku Klux Klan and who has recently suffered disbarment and the loss of his family home as a result of the corrupt Judge Hugh Butler. The drunken, angry Graham seeks revenge only to find himself infatuated with Judge Butler's daughter Stella.

Judge Butler summons federal troops to locate the members of the Ku Klux Klan. John Graham disbands the North Carolina Ku Klux Klan at a final dress parade; Graham declares their work finished.

Hoyle, however, challenges Graham's decision to disband. Hoyle forms a new organization, which begins to terrorize the local citizenry. After Judge Butler's murder, John Graham becomes the chief suspect.

The conclusion of *The Traitor* is that rebellion and revolution are not the answers to regeneration. Rather the novel's conclusion is that hope comes from human relationships (Kirkpatrick, Mary Alice).

***See also*** **Berne Convention; Dixon, Thomas;** fears of Margaret Mitchell; plagiarism; ***The Traitor*** and young Margaret Mitchell.

**Hungary, sales of *Gone with the Wind*** *see* **foreign copyrights/translations and fair trade laws**

### *I Remember Margaret Mitchell* (1987)

Yolande Gwin collected the many memories of the friends of Margaret Mitchell into the book *I Remember Margaret Mitchell* (1987) (Gwin, page 19). Included in the book are such people as Eleanor Roosevelt, soldiers with whom Margaret corresponded during World War II, and Yolande Gwin herself.

***See also*** **Gwin, Yolande.**

### illnesses and health concerns of Margaret Mitchell

Walker suggests that Margaret Mitchell may have begun to use illness as a protective device after the death of Maybelle Mitchell in 1919 and after Margaret's return from Smith College to her father's Atlanta home at the end of the school year. Margaret wrote often to Allen Edee from July 1919 until December 1921; she often wrote about her injuries and illnesses. The maladies that she wrote about to Edee included "flu, colds, sprains, bone injuries, back pain, an inordinate number of accidents, and emotional depression." Walker indicated that Margaret feigned illness to avoid attending the Junior League Ball during the 1939 Atlanta premiere of the film *Gone with the Wind* (Walker, page 57, 76).

Walker notes: "One thing is clear; her preoccupation with her health did not start until after she came home to Atlanta. Even then, she managed to stay well while she was relatively content and busy doing things she enjoyed" (Walker, page 58).

Pyron also observes that Margaret Mitchell's health problems began soon after her return to Atlanta after she left Smith College and after the death of her mother and Clifford Henry (Pyron, page 110).

Some of Margaret Mitchell's health concerns and illnesses follow.

*Abdominal surgeries.* Margaret Mitchell suffered from appendicitis in 1919 and had surgery for abdominal adhesions in 1920. Mitchell found the decade of the 1940s opening with her again having abdominal surgery for adhesions. She postponed the surgery until after the Atlanta premiere of December 1939 and after the holiday season (Pyron, pages 319, 411; Walker, page 58).

*Allergies.* Margaret found herself plagued with allergies and hives. The summer of 1945 found her particularly allergic to many things. In August of 1948, Margaret Mitchell had to report to the Augusta city hospital for emergency treatment. Another flare up of allergies occurred in March 1949. John R. Marsh attributed the onset to be a result of the dye in some vitamins she had begun taking (Walker, pages 478, 498, 502).

*Ankle injuries.* Ankle injuries plagued Mitchell for most of her life. Shortly after her return to Atlanta after one year at Smith College, she injured her leg and ankle in an accident while horseback riding — perhaps with Berrien Kinnard ("Red") Upshaw — on Stone Mountain, in 1920 (Edwards, page 69). This was not her first injury — or only — injury to her ankle and leg.

1. John Marsh was able to report to his mother by letter on January 20, 1925, that except for an ankle injury, Margaret Mitchell's health had been good (Walker, page 115).

2. Shortly after the marriage of John Marsh and Margaret Mitchell on July 4, 1925, Margaret continued to have trouble with her left ankle; the couple found that the specialists were a drain on their limited budget. John brought home a second-hand Remington typewriter to lift her spirits. In the alcove of "The Dump"— their first apartment together — she began a story of the Old South that became *Gone with the Wind* (Walker, page 30).

3. Margaret continued to have trouble with her ankle, but she did not refer to it. Finally in early spring of 1926 she wrote about the ankle to Henry Marsh, John's brother. She wrote that she had had — at the suggestion of her doctor — some teeth extracted, her tonsils removed, and a special diet to stop the "toxic flow" (Pyron, page 209).

Margaret could no longer walk except with the aid of orthopedic shoes and crutches. The doctor had the idea that something "was poisoning her ankle" (Walker, page 45). Margaret's ankle had gone "bad again for no apparent reason, swelled up and all of that. It was really serious because it was supposed to be well and a recurrence in a spot where you've got arthritis isnt [sic] so good. The doc slipped me the pleasant news that I'd probably get a permanently stiff ankle out of it" (Walker, page 145).

Margaret elaborated on her condition also to her sister-in-law Frances Marsh in the spring of 1926. Margaret wrote that her feet hadn't "touched the floor in three weeks except on one glorious day that the doc told me he *might* have to fuse two ankle bones together and make it solid for life. I felt somewhat depressed, came home, bought a quart of rye, and took three drinks, threw away my crutches, and getting a taxi went calling on all my friends. I had a lovely five hours. I didn't even

know I had a bad foot until I sobered up when John came home and he, poor angel, kindly sat up all night rubbing the blamed thing" (Pyron, page 209).

For the time-being, however, Frances and Henry Marsh did not know about the massive project — a novel — that was occupying Margaret Mitchell's time.

*Back problems.* During the first week of May 1920 Margaret Mitchell complained to Allen Edee about her mishaps. She told him that she had "either torn a ligament or misplaced or displaced, whichever it may be, a joint in my hip — sacroiliac something-or-other" (Peacock, page 94).

Eight weeks later she indicated again to Allen Edee that she had been swimming when she jumped into shallow water and her foot kicked a brick; she broke her foot. "Like a fool, I didn't have it set, and danced and swam, drove and hiked for all I was worth, which didn't improve it a-tall. Finally it gave out and so did I" (Peacock, page 98).

After a car accident on November 22, 1934, John Marsh observed that his wife had been bedridden for three months. All winter she used a therapeutic girdle. Removing the girdle for even a short time caused the pain and nausea to return. This persisted for six months (Pyron, pages 293–294).

After Mitchell received a letter of praise from Harold Latham in May of 1935, she responded directly. "Thank you again for your encouraging words. I'm sure they'll have a more healing affect [sic] on my back than all the braces, electrical treatments, and operations the doctors devise.... We hope you unearth a Pulitzer prize winner here so it will be necessary for you to come back to Atlanta and stay awhile" (Walker, page 201).

The editing process had been hard on her back (Walker, page 233). John R. Marsh elaborated on just how hard to Lois Cole. "The reason why she has been in bed the past two weeks is the fact that getting the book delivered to you involved the most serious and the most prolonged strain she has had to undergo in many years. She hasn't yet recovered from the injuries to her back which she received in the automobile accident.... Sitting up for hours at a time, day after day, over a period of weeks, typing, editing the MS, handling heavy reference books, etc., was about the worst possible thing she could have done. It was a marvel to me that she held out as long as she did ... and then her ailments got her down and the doctor ordered her to bed. The doctor thinks she may yet have to have an operation — one which she might have had a couple of months ago except for the book — and her whole operation at least until after the proofs are read and the job is finished. It won't help her resting a bit, if she thinks that Macmillan is making plans based on her coming to New York when she may not be able to come" (Walker, page 234).

After over exerting herself in the fund raising campaign for the USS *Atlanta,* Margaret Mitchell left Atlanta for Johns Hopkins in Baltimore on March 20, 1943. She was going to undergo surgery to fuse some vertebrae. She did not return to Atlanta until April 19, 1943. She counted these four weeks "the most horrible of her life" (Pyron, page 406).

Even three weeks after the surgery, she could barely move for the pain. Margaret was "severely disabled." She cried during her phone conversations with John and expressed to him that her left foot, her neck, and her shoulders were still extremely painful (Walker, pages 455–458).

Mitchell's physician at Johns Hopkins University found that she had a ruptured vertebral disc also. This information came to John R. Marsh on June 1, 1943 (Pyron, page 405). The doctor offered to perform another surgery on her when ten weeks after the surgery, she could still not sit on a hard chair. Dr. Dandy even came to Atlanta to see her. She refused to consider the additional surgery at that time.

Mitchell began going to the doctor in Atlanta for vitamin B-1 shots. She was convinced that they relieved her back pain and her arthritis (Pyron, pages 456–562, 478).

*Blindness.* After Stephens Mitchell and Margaret Mitchell finished some copyright negotiations with Macmillan on July 28, 1937, Margaret Mitchell went to spend a few days with the Herschel and Norma Brickell.

Margaret was tired, but she ate a light supper with the Brickells, talked with them until late, and went to bed. She did not sleep well away from home. When she was dressing the next morning, she went completely blind for a few seconds. The Brickells took her to their own doctor, who determined the episode was the result of continued eyestrain.

Margaret left for Atlanta as soon as she could board a train. Her own doctor attributed the episode to broken blood vessels, which had caused hemorrhages. He warned Margaret that the condition could re-occur; he advised her to rest completely for two weeks in a dark room. He told her for twenty-one days she was not to write letters or to take phone calls.

John R. Marsh wrote to the Brickells that he thought the rest was helping her. "The first day or two in a darkened room with nothing to do, hour by hour, but twiddle her thumbs was pretty terrible, but after that she began to relax, some of the tightly wound springs inside her mind began to unwind from the steadily increasing tension of the past several months" (Walker, pages 303–304). Margaret's eyesight had deteriorated. Walker reported that Margaret was wearing thick glasses by 1945 (Walker, page 478).

*Boils.* Margaret wrote to Lois Cole in October of 1935 after Lois had asked her for some photographs. Margaret explained that because of the anxiety she experiences in completing the manuscript and researching its minute details, she had broken out in boils on her scalp. To treat these boils, her doctor had had to shave spots on her scalp. Trying to get a good photograph and not expose the boils and bare places was almost impossible, but she would try (Walker, page 225).

*"Breast cancer."* In October-November of 1928 Mitchell expressed to her sister-in-law Frances Marsh Zane her fear that she had breast cancer. Margaret had severely bruised her breast about 1926 when she had bumped into the bed post. The breast had continued to give her problems and concern over the intervening months. She was relieved each year when she had not received a diagnosis of breast cancer. At last, in the fall of 1928, "the terror of self-induced malignancy lifted" (Walker, pages 231–232).

*Bursitis.* In June of 1945 Mitchell suffered a new affliction. She developed bursitis in both shoulders. She had to wear her right arm in a sling for several weeks (Walker, page 478).

## impersonators

Margaret Mitchell and John R. Marsh were often furious with women who pretended to be Margaret. These women would often circulate rumors about Margaret. Margaret vented her frustrations in a letter to Herschel Brickell on July 6, 1937: "If I can just catch one and fry her ears in deep fat, it will give me great pleasure…. I wonder why people do this. God knows, it's no fun *really* being Margaret Mitchell so what possible fun could there be in pretending to be Margaret Mitchell?" (Walker, page 313).

Margaret continued to fume about her impersonators. Some were making a profit of as much $20 on her autograph. She expressed her anger at these impersonators by writing to Herschel Brickell on May 25, 1938: "They have signed autographs, given lectures, gotten drunk, picked up gents and done other things not salutary to mention on paper. To date I have been unable to catch a one of them, which is a source of great regret to me" (Walker, page 377).

One particular person that plagued Margaret Mitchell and John R. Marsh was a woman who impersonated Margaret and opened charge accounts in Margaret's name in stores across the country. John R. Marsh hired the Pinkerton National Detective Service to help him locate this woman whom others described as being "very fond of men."

While the Pinkerton Service was in his employ, Marsh had them help him put an end to the rumor that Margaret wrote *Gone with the Wind* in Albert's French Restaurant on University Place and Eleventh Street in Greenwich Village (Walker, page 468).

As if the swindlers using her name were not enough to concern her, a rumor from Jonesboro confronted her also. These local plantation owners were advertising their family home as the real Tara; they were making money by selling admission tickets. To apprehend the Jonesboro residents who were falsely advertising their property, Margaret even went so far as to don a pair of dark classes and drive around; she hoped to find the "liars of the first water" (Walker, page 378).

Rather than dismissing the stories of her impersonators, Margaret Mitchell seemed to collect the horrific tales. John R. Marsh retained the Pinkerton detectives for several years to make sure his wife felt safe and to try to end these distractions.

***See also*** **accidents; Acorn Cottage; addresses directly related to Margaret Mitchell; Brickell, Herschel; Bucephalus; Grosvenor Hotel.**

## Irving Thalberg Memorial Award

The Irving Thalberg Memorial Award was named for the head of the Production Division of Metro-Goldwyn-Mayer. It was Thalberg (1899–1936) who helped earn MGM's reputation for sophisticated films. David O. Selznick, producer of *Gone with the Wind*, was a recipient of the award in 1939.

Irving Thalberg had the nickname "boy wonder." He was born in Brooklyn, New York, to William and Henrietta Thalberg; his parents were German Jewish immigrants. Thalberg had rheumatic fever as a child and was left with a bad heart; he was sick a lot of the time.

Promptly after his graduation from high school, Irving went to work for the Universal Pictures' New York office. The company in the 1920s had the title Universal Film Manufacturing Company; it would later become Louis B. Mayer's film company. Twenty-year-old Thalberg was head of production.

When Universal Film Manufacturing Company became Metro Goldwyn Mayer, Thalberg became vice president and supervisor of production. At the time, the studio was producing 50 films a year. Thalberg was married to the actress Norma Shearer. He died at the age of 36. For someone so young with a relatively short career, he obviously was a "wonder boy" ("Oscar Awards: Irving Thalberg Memorial Award").

The presentation of the Irving Thalberg Memorial Award occurs periodically — but not yearly — at the Academy Awards ceremonies.

*Recipients.* The Irving Thalberg Memorial Award is reserved for producers of films. The inscription reads, to "Creative producers, whose bodies of work reflect a consistently high quality of motion picture production."

In 1939 David O. Selznick was the third producer to receive the coveted award. He was preceded by only Darryl F. Zanuck (1937) and Hal B. Wallis (1938). Another award was not presented until 1941, when Walt Disney earned the distinction.

*Trophy.* A bust of Irving Thalberg is the form of the award presented to the outstanding producer for that year; the trophy is separate and apart from the Oscar statuettes and awards presented yearly. It is not, presented necessarily the same year as the film. A person cannot receive the Irving Thalberg Memorial Award two times ("Oscar Awards: Irving Thalberg Memorial Award"). Other recipients include Francis Ford Coppola, George Lucas, Steven Spielberg, and Alfred Hitchcock ("The Irving G. Thalberg Memorial Award").

*See also* Academy of Motion Picture Arts and Sciences.

**Italy, sales of *Gone with the Wind*** *see* **foreign copyrights/translations and fair trade laws**

## Jackson Street (179)

Margaret Mitchell (1900–1949) lived her whole life in Atlanta. In 1903, she and her family moved to 179 Jackson Street; this was the third house in which Mitchell would live, and the second house on Jackson Street.

The Victorian Style, two-story, brick house at 179 Jackson Street had twelve-rooms. The Mitchells would live at this address until they moved to Peachtree Street in 1912.

## Jackson Street (187)

In 1902 Eugene and Maybelle Mitchell moved their children to this residence at the southeast corner of Jackson and Highland Avenue; the house at 187 Jackson Street was larger than the 296 Cain Street residence in which Margaret Mitchell had lived until 1902. Walker notes that this residence remained the Mitchell family home only until 1903, when they moved to 179 Jackson Street (Walker, page 27).

Edwards gives the address of Margaret Mitchell's second home as 177 Jackson Street, not 187 Jackson Street. This varies from the 187 Jackson Street address that Walker gave. Edwards's account varies from Walker's, which uses Stephens Mitchell's memoir in the University of Georgia Archives as its basis (Edwards, page 17; Walker, page 27).

## Japan, sales of *Gone with the Wind* *see* foreign copyrights/translations and fair trade laws

## Jim Crow laws

The Jim Crow laws were the local and state laws enacted between 1876 and 1965 to enforce the "separate but equal" doctrine of segregation — especially in the South. Because of these Jim Crow laws, Hattie McDaniel decided not to come to Atlanta for the premiere of the *Gone with the Wind* film in December of 1939.

The treatment of non-whites and their separate facilities were usually inferior. Even the United States military, the public schools, public transportation, restaurants, drinking fountains, and public places were governed by these Jim Crow laws. With the ruling in the 1954 court case *Brown v. Board of Education*, school segregation was no longer legal. The Civil Rights Act of 1964 and the Voting Rights Act of 1965 overruled remaining Jim Crow laws ("Jim Crow Laws").

One of the persons who helped bring about integration was the Atlanta native Martin Luther King, Jr. This pastor of the Ebenezer Baptist Church followed his father's footsteps to the pulpit. He was also one of the young people who performed in the choir during the Atlanta premiere of the film *Gone with the Wind* in December of 1939.

*Jim Crow laws within the State of Georgia.* Segregated drinking fountains, movie theaters, waiting rooms, restaurants, and restrooms were typical of much of Georgia and the South during the lifetime of Margaret Mitchell. Public conveyances had their own rules for waiting rooms and for seating within vehicles. Segregation and Jim Crow laws persisted for years to come. The multiracial society in Georgia was a negative for encouraging migration to the state.

Discrimination of Georgians toward groups other than blacks was also common. Members of the Jewish faith often felt the scorn and discrimination of others. Sometimes this discrimination led to violence and even lynching.

*Lynchings.* Georgia frequently led the nation in lynching between 1889 and 1930. The statistics are, of course, unreliable, but the estimate is that at least 450 lynchings occurred during this time period. The victims were usually blacks (Coleman, page 286). Hepburn reports 531 lynchings between 1882 and 1968 in Georgia (Hepburn, page 24).

Between 1882 and 1968 there were 4,742 black lynchings in the nation. Congressman John Lewis calls the period "one of the darkest and sickest periods in American history ... not so long ago" (Allen, page 7).

Photographers often recorded the lynchings and sold the images to others, to publications, and to postcard companies for re-sale. After Allen purchased postcards of the lynching victims, the result was his book *Without Sanctuary: Lynching Photography in America.* "In America everything is for sale, even a national shame. Until ... I came upon a postcard of a lynching, postcards seemed trivial to me.... Studying these photographs has engendered in me a caution of whites, of the majority, of the young, of religion, of the accepted.... Hundreds of flea markets later, a trader pulled me aside and in conspiratorial tones offered to sell me a real photo postcard.... That image of Laura [Nelson hanging from a bridge] layered a pall of grief over all my fears.

"I believe the photographer was more than a perceptive spectator at lynchings. Too often they compulsively composed silvery tableaux (natures mortes) positioning and lighting [of] corpses as if they were game birds shot on the wing. Indeed, the photographic art played as significant a role in the ritual as torture or souvenir grabbing — creating a sort of two-dimensional biblical swine, a receptacle for a collective self. Lust propelled the commercial reproductions and distribution of the images, facilitating the endless replay of anguish. Even dead, the victims were without sanctuary" (Allen, pages 204–205).

Eleanor Roosevelt openly supported anti-lynching laws. She wrote on March 19, 1936, to Walter Francis White, the executive secretary of the NAACP about her concerns. Mrs. Roosevelt said she had talked with President Franklin Delano Roosevelt and mentioned to him that "it seemed rather terrible that one could get nothing done." She wrote of his response that "the difficulty is that it is unconstitutional apparently for the federal government to step in the lynching situation. The government has only been allowed to do anything about kidnapping because of its interstate aspect, and even that has not yet been appealed so they are not sure that it will be declared unconstitutional.

"The president feels that lynching is a question of education in the states, rallying good citizens, and creating public opinion so that the localities themselves will wipe it out. However, if it were done by a Northerner, it will have an antagonistic effect.... I am deeply troubled about the whole situation as it seems to be a terrible thing to stand by and let it continue and feel that one cannot speak out as to his feeling. I think your next step would be to talk to the more prominent members of the Senate" (Letter, Eleanor Roosevelt to Walter White detailing the First Lady's lobbying efforts for federal action against lynchings, 19 March 1936).

While all the cruelties that were going on, Margaret Mitchell was working to secure good health care for African Americans in Atlanta. She helped Bessie Berry Jordan to obtain the treatment she needed and would later help several African American students to pursue a medical education.

*Jim Crow laws, lynchings, and Leo M. Frank.* Perhaps the best-known victim of a lynching in Georgia was Leo M. Frank, a white, Jewish manager at the Atlanta Pencil Company.

Frank was in the state penitentiary in Milledgeville, Georgia; his charge was the murder of a young female factory worker. When the governor changed Frank's death sentence to life imprisonment, twenty-five men took him from jail and hanged him in Marietta, Georgia. The actions of this mob became significant for the state of Georgia and the nation in the days to come; the case of Leo Frank and his lynching "generated the formation of the modern Ku Klux Klan, and produced the Jewish Anti-Defamation League, two organizations that exist to this day" (Hepburn, 24).

*See also* Atlanta premiere of *Gone with the Wind*; Dixon, Thomas F. Jr.; McDaniel, Hattie; Ebenezer Baptist Church; Frank, Leo; Jordan, Bessie Berry; King, Martin Luther, Jr.; Mays, Benjamin; Randall, Alice; *The Traitor* and young Margaret Mitchell.

## "John Brown's Body"

This poem by Stephen Vincent Benét made an impact upon Margaret Mitchell. She indicated to others that the magnificent poem had generated in her "writer's block."

Frank Daniel — who worked at the *Atlanta Journal Sunday Magazine* at the same time that Margaret Mitchell was on staff there — was working on a review of Stephen Vincent Benét's "John Brown's Body" when he visited with Margaret Mitchell in her home; she was working on the manuscript of what would eventually become the novel *Gone with the Wind*. When Daniel began reading to Margaret from Stephen Vincent Benét's book, she stuck her fingers in her ears and would not listen. The work was giving her writer's block (Edwards, page 146).

*See also* Benét, Stephen Vincent; Daniel, Frank.

## Johnson, Ira Joe

The Reverend Ira Joe Johnson was a 1973 graduate of Morehouse College. Johnson and William Pickens (class of 1948) teamed together to write a biography of Benjamin Mays (past president of Morehouse) and his association with Margaret Mitchell. The book carries the title *Benjamin E. Mays and Margaret Mitchell: A Unique Legacy in Medicine.*

The Rev. Ira Joe Johnson grew up in Dry Branch, Georgia, in Twiggs County. He was influenced by Benjamin Mays (Morehouse College president), Martin Luther King, and stories about Margaret Mitchell and her dedication to the causes of others. He was reminded of the premiere of *Gone with the Wind* (the film) and King's participation in the event, which occurred some twelve years before Johnson's birth.

Johnson was 17 when he met Martin Luther King, Jr., on March 23, 1968. The Reverend King was speaking at New Zion Baptist Church. Twelve days later, King died from gunshot wounds in Memphis, Tennessee. As a result of these experiences, Johnson devoted his life to promoting civil rights, including working in several government positions related to civil rights.

In 2011 Ira Joe Johnson intended to attend the dedication of the new Martin Luther King, Jr., Memorial in Washington, D.C. Hurricane Irene, however, forced the postponement of the dedication events originally scheduled for August 28 ("Local Minister to Kick off Trip to MLK Memorial Event").

Johnson and Pickens in *Benjamin E. Mays and Margaret Mitchell* compare Mitchell with Dr. Martin Luther King, Jr., in some favorable ways. The two writers note that she "joined hands with the son of proud, tenacious, God-fearing former slaves of South Carolina over fifty years ago with the singular mission of financially assisting Morehouse College students in their quests to become doctors.... [T]wenty-two years before Dr. King's [*I Have a Dream*] speech, Margaret Mitchell had not only set down at the table of brotherhood, but at Morehouse she had picked up the check" (Johnson and Pickens, page 1). Johnson made some comparisons between Margaret Mitchell and her nephew Eugene Muse Mitchell (1931–2007). He found them similar on several issues.

*See also* Mays, Benjamin; Mitchell, Eugene Muse (1931–2007); Pickens, William G.

## Jones, General James R.

In December of 1939, during the time of the Atlanta premiere of *Gone with the Wind*, General

James R. Jones was residing at the Georgia Soldiers' Home; this facility was only a ten-minute ride from the Loew's Grand Theater. Jones was one of the last of Confederate veterans across the nation.

Of the four Confederate veterans who were special guests of Clark Gable at the first showing nationwide of *Gone with the Wind*, ninety-five-year-old General James R. Jones was the oldest and the most talkative. Jones had volunteered to kiss any woman present.

Jones commented at the end of the film that the pictures looked just like the Civil War had looked. His opinion seemed to be that *Gone with the Wind* was accurate (Rosenburg, x–xi).

*See also* **Atlanta premiere of *Gone with the Wind* (film); Gable, (William) Clark; and Martin, Harold.**

## Jonesboro, Georgia

Jonesboro Mayor Hugh Dickson and the United Daughters of the Confederacy staged their own event in recognition of the Atlanta premiere of *Gone with the Wind*. On December 11, 1939, the town re-enacted the flight of film characters Rhett, Scarlett, Melanie, Wade Hampton, Prissy, and the newborn Beau from Atlanta the night the munitions site burned. Dickson dubbed the entire affair Jonesboro's biggest day in history ("City of Jonesboro").

*See also* **Dickson, David Hugh.**

## Jonesboro Road during the premiere of *Gone with the Wind*

On December 11, 1939, Jonesboro staged its own event to celebrate the premiere of *Gone with the Wind* (the film). A wagon with characters representing Scarlett, Rhett, Melanie, Wade Hampton, Prissy, and the newborn Beau left Atlanta for the town of Jonesboro. Mayor Hugh Dickson declared the arrival of the wagon in Jonesboro as "Jonesboro's biggest day in history!" ("City of Jonesboro").

*See also* **Atlanta premiere of *Gone with the Wind* (film).**

## Jonesboro Road in the Education of Margaret Mitchell

When Margaret Mitchell came home from her first day in school, she declared that she hated arithmetic, and she was not returning to school. Her mother made her get in the carriage and took her down Jonesboro Road. She pointed out the dilapidated housing of the residents who were without education, common sense, survival skills, or gumption.

*See also* **buckwheat; gumption.**

## Jordan, Bessie Berry

Bessie Berry Jordan was the cook for the Mitchell family. After the marriage of John R. Marsh and Margaret Mitchell, the young couple had Lula Tolbert to help them (Farr, page 71). (Pyron spells her name *Loula* on page 220.) When Lula died, Eugene Muse Mitchell sent Bessie Berry Jordan to work for the couple.

*Appearance and demeanor of Bessie Berry Jordan.* Anne Edwards describes the physical appearance, the personality, and the character of Bessie Berry Jordan: "Bessie was a lean, handsome woman, ten years older than Peggy. A wise, religious person, she brought Peggy closer to the church than any member of her family had succeeded in doing. Bessie also believed strongly in the sanctity of marriage and that a man must be catered to, and Peggy was influenced by her convictions" (Edwards, page 149). Walker describes Jordan in similar terms. "A loyal and devoted friend, Bessie remained with them for the rest of their lives" (Walker, page 151).

Jordan was always enthusiastic and eager to help her employers on whatever they needed. Bessie even helped Margaret Mitchell pack relief parcels.

*Bessie Berry and Margaret Mitchell (1919).* When Margaret Mitchell returned to Atlanta after the end of her first year at Smith College, she intended to help her father, Eugene Muse Mitchell, with the household affairs because of the death of her mother, Maybelle Mitchell, in January of 1919.

Margaret found that to manage the household finances wisely, she would have to let some of the paid help go. She kept only Carrie Holbrook as laundress, Bessie Berry (later Jordan) as cook, fifteen-year-old Cammie as house girl (no last name given), and Charlie (no last name) for other services (Edwards, page 65).

*Bessie Berry (Jordan) and the Marshes.* Margaret Mitchell and John R. Marsh married on July 4, 1925. After Margaret Mitchell Marsh's ankle injury, Margaret's father Eugene Muse Mitchell (about 1926) "sent Bessie Berry Jordan, his housekeeper and cook, around to the Marshes' apartment to help out" (Walker, page 151). The situation initially had not been so easy. "Bessie left the house on Peachtree Street to work full-time for Peggy. It was an extravagance for the Marshes, but Lula Tolbert had quit and neither Peggy nor John was able to take over the household chores. Peggy was not fond of cooking and felt she simply could not manage the shopping. According to Bessie, although her love and dedication to 'Miss Peggy' knew no bounds, her first weeks in the Marsh household were less than pleasant" (Edwards, page 147).

Bessie wrote to Medora Fields Perkerson. Bessie confided that although she had worked with Margaret's father, she felt frightened around Mr. Marsh. She even described the first weeks as "hard and frightful. I were so afraid of Mr. Marsh until my clothes would seem to slip like a tight window shade at his appearance" (Edwards, page 147).

Perhaps the small size of "The Dump"— 550 square feet—facilitated the close relationship that developed between Bessie and the Marshes. Bessie usually remained in the kitchen while Margaret worked at the typewriter.

*Bessie Berry, Bessie's daughter Deon, and the Marshes.* The good relationship of the Marshes and Bessie extended to Bessie's daughter Deon Jordan. Deon and her mother would ride the streetcar to the Marshes' home each morning, often before 7:00 A.M.; later in the morning, Deon would ride the streetcar at the corner to school. In the afternoon, Deon would return to the Marshes' apartment and stay with her mother until Bessie was ready to go home for the night. The Marshes were happy to have Deon and Bessie in their home. Deon indicated that Margaret Mitchell always told her mother to get what she and Deon wanted for their supper; she always reminded Deon and Bessie that they did not have to eat what the Marshes were eating (Walker, page 180).

*Bessie's illnesses.* Margaret Mitchell was very open about her concern for Bessie in a letter to Harold Latham on July 17, 1935. She told Harold that "the black jewel of our kitchen" had contracted meningitis. Mitchell told him that she had been spending all her time in the charity ward at the hospital checking on Bessie and "savaging the interns" (Walker, page 204). The hospital wards had separate facilities for the patients according to their color.

*Bessie Jordan, Friendship Missionary Baptist Church, Margaret Mitchell, Harold Latham, and the Pulitzer Prize.* On the night May 3, 1937— the evening of the day that Margaret Mitchell had received the telegram announcing that she had won the 1937 Pulitzer Prize for her 1936 book— Margaret Mitchell, John R. Marsh, and Harold Latham were seated in the auditorium of the Friendship Baptist Church in Atlanta. They had all assembled to hear Bessie Berry Jordan sing in her church choir. The media was frantic trying to find Margaret Mitchell to interview her, but her location in the church was never discovered (Walker, pages 359–360).

Edwards indicates that Latham was a "devotee of Negro spirituals." She states that Latham, John, and Margaret were actually attending a late-evening choir practice at Friendship Baptist Church—not a performance (Edwards, page 268).

*Bessie Berry Jordan, the Marshes, and Berrien Kinnard ("Red") Upshaw.* On October 24, 1932, the day that President Franklin Delano Roosevelt vis-

ited Atlanta, Margaret heard loud voices. She hurried to the living room to find that Bessie Jordan had answered the door and that Berrien Kinnard ("Red") Upshaw, Margaret's first husband, had pushed past Bessie. Bessie, however, stood guard and refused to allow Red to be alone with Margaret.

Red explained that he was just passing through; he asked for a loan. It took Margaret about ten minutes to talk him out of the house. She never revealed if she loaned him the money (Edwards, page 158).

*Bessie Berry Jordan and the post-publication of* Gone with the Wind *(the book).* The day after the publication of *Gone with the Wind,* Bessie recorded the results on that day — and for months to come. Bessie indicated that the telephone rang every three minutes until midnight and once an hour until morning; every seven minutes a telegram arrived. A group of at least ten people waited outside the apartment day and night. Mail arrived in satchels; books to be autographed — usually without return postage — were usually part of the daily haul (Edwards, pages 208, 211).

Margaret Mitchell wrote to Edwin Granberry that Bessie Jordan answered the telephone for her and shielded her from most callers. Margaret described vividly Bessie's answering the telephone "gently in that cooing voice of hers. 'No, Mam, I can't tell you whether or not Miss Scarlett got the Cap'n back or not. No Mam, Miss Peggy she don't know either. Yes, Mam, I've heard her say a hundred times she didn't have no idea than the next 'bout what happened to Miss Scarlett after she went home to Tara!'" (Edwards, page 252).

*Bessie Jordan and the death of Margaret Mitchell.* John R. Marsh was at home at the time that Margaret Mitchell died in Grady Hospital. Bessie Jordan learned of the death of her employer before John learned his wife had died.

Bessie was concerned about John's appearance and prepared his lunch. She insisted that John finish eating before anyone told him the news. Stephens revealed the news to him (Edwards, page 335).

Bessie Jordan would later learn that Margaret Mitchell had made a small provision for Bessie in the will. Margaret Mitchell's will — written in Margaret's own hand — read: "I want Bessie Jordan to be given $500 (five hundred dollars) in addition to the house" (Margaret Mitchell, "Will of Margaret Mitchell, November 21, 1998"). Margaret asked also that Deon Ward, Bessie's daughter, receive $500 (Margaret Mitchell, "Will of Margaret Mitchell, November 21, 1998").

*Bessie Jordan and John R. Marsh after the death*

*of Margaret Mitchell.* Margaret Mitchell had never wanted a house; she had been content to live in the apartments with John. John, however, had always wanted a house.

Just before Christmas of 1949, after Margaret Mitchell Marsh's death in August of 1946, John Marsh moved into a one-story cottage with an apartment attached to it. Bessie Jordan helped with the move, and John arranged for her to live in the apartment.

About 11:00 P.M. on May 5, 1952, Bessie heard John call for help. She rushed to his side and found him very sick, having a heart seizure. She helped him to bed, called the doctor, summoned an ambulance, and remained with him until help came. John died, nevertheless (Edwards, pages 337–338). By contrast, Pyron indicates that Bessie Jordan found John R. Marsh dead on Monday morning, May 5, 1952 (Pyron, page 463).

"The Will of John R. Marsh" stated in Item First: "I give and bequeath to Bessie Jordan and Deon Ward, who have been the faithful servants of myself and my late wife, $1000.00 each in fee simple" (John R. Marsh, "Codicil to the Will of John R. Marsh, July 26, 1951").

*Tribute to Margaret Mitchell by Bessie Jordan.* Margaret Mitchell seemed to feel a deep loyalty to Bessie Jordan and her family. This dedication was returned by Bessie Jordan and her kin.

In 1936 *The Atlanta Journal* published a tribute to Mitchell that Jordan had written: "She nursed us when we were sick. She gave clothes, she gave us trips North and South, she gave my granddaughter a trip to New York in 1948 and had given her school clothes in July of 1949. I have not spent one week in her service that I did not receive a gift of some kind. She was a friend to everybody" (Pyron, page 415).

Jordan said Mitchell always thought of others before herself. She called Mitchell a "home missionary" and "a good Christian." She drew analogies from the scriptures to describe Margaret Mitchell: "She Fed the Hungry. / She gave drink to the Thirsty. / She clothed the Naked. / Sheltered the out of doors. / Ministered to the Sick and in Prison" (Jordan as quoted in Pyron, pages 415–416).

## Junior League

Founded in 1916 with only 45 members, the Junior League of Atlanta was the host organization for the 1921 debutantes, of which group Margaret Mitchell was a member. Focuses of the Junior League included both volunteering and improving the health, the education, and the welfare of children and women.

Some of the services of the Junior League in the early days included instruction in household arts for women through its Domestic Science Institution, offering Red Cross courses to help with war relief and the establishment (1918) of a hot lunch program with milk to needy children in Cabbagetown (East Atlanta). The organization is still in operation ("About the Junior League of Atlanta, Inc.").

Margaret Mitchell, however, was not accepted into the Junior League. Speculation was that her Apache Dance performed at the Georgian Terrace Hotel and her arguing with the group's use of funds triggered her rejection.

*See also* Apache dance; Georgian Terrace Hotel.

## Junior League Charity Ball on December 14, 1939

During the Atlanta premiere of *Gone with the Wind*, the Junior League hosted a ball for the night of December 14, 1939, in the Atlanta Municipal Auditorium.

The auditorium had a floor the size of a football field, but it still could not house everyone who wanted to attend the ball with Kay Kyser leading the orchestra. Ozzie Nelson's orchestra played for those who could not go to the ball.

Margaret Mitchell, however, did not accept an invitation to the Junior League Ball. Whether her absence was because of her reluctance to make public appearances, because of her rejection by the Junior League in 1921, or because of some other reason, others could only speculate — if they cared to do so.

Marianne Walker was a biographer of Margaret Mitchell. Walker indicated that Margaret feigned illness to avoid attending the Junior League Ball (Walker, page 57, 76). The real reason for her absence was only known by Mitchell.

*See also* Apache dance; Atlanta Municipal Auditorium; Atlanta premiere of *Gone with the Wind*; Georgian Terrace Hotel; Kyser, Kay; Weil, A.S.

## Kennedy, Frank

Frank Kennedy was a character in *Gone with the Wind*, both the book and the film. Kennedy — a middle-aged merchant — was the second husband of Scarlett O'Hara. In a first version of *Gone with the Wind* Kennedy dies from pneumonia.

In reviewing the manuscript — probably in 1933 — Margaret decided the drama and the plot "sagged." Margaret used the Ku Klux Klan to remove Scarlett's husband. Mitchell's biographer Darden Pyron indicates that Professor Charles Everett, who had reviewed the manuscript, "objected to the Ku Klux Klan episode in the book" (Pyron, page 312).

Pyron indicates that Margaret Mitchell at that time indicated that she preferred the second version with the Ku Klux Klan dispatching Kennedy after he went to defend his wife, who had been frightened on a buggy ride at night (Pyron, page 312).

On the other hand, Edwards indicates that in a letter of July 7, 1935, to Harold Latham, Mitchell had stated that she preferred the version of the manuscript that had Frank Kennedy dying of illness. Mitchell did not like the version that included the Ku Klux Klan as well (Edwards, page 168).

Latham wrote to Mitchell on July 30, 1935. He commented on his preference in the two versions of the Frank Kennedy death. "And now I'll tell you a secret. I myself rather prefer the Ku Klux Klan ending to the other. I let [Professor Charles] Everett say his say on that subject, but I don't altogether agree with him. I think your reason [believing the plot sagged] for the K.K.K. episode is a good one. I don't feel that the book sags anywhere — not for one chapter or one page — but I do think this K.K.K. material adds color and excitement, etc. So here, as in the case of other matters, follow your judgment" (Walker, pages 207–208).

### King, Martin Luther, Jr., (1929–1968)

Martin Luther King, Jr., was born Michael Luther King, Jr., in a house in Atlanta, Georgia. His father had also been born Michael Luther and had legally changed his name to Martin Luther. As his father had done, Michael Luther later changed his name; he was now Martin Luther King, Jr.

Both the grandfather and the father of Martin Luther King, Jr., were pastors at Ebenezer Baptist Church in Atlanta. The tenure at Ebenezer Baptist Church of young King's grandfather had lasted from 1914 to 1931; his father's tenure continued from 1931 until 1974. Martin Luther King, Jr., served as co-pastor from 1960 until his death from assassination in 1968.

*King, Martin Luther, Jr., at the 1939 Atlanta premiere.* A young Martin Luther King, Jr., performed at the 1939 Atlanta premiere of *Gone with the Wind.* As a member of the Ebenezer Baptist Church Choir, he sang at the Junior League Ball held at the Atlanta Auditorium on Thursday, December 14, 1939.

The Margaret Mitchell House and Museum, displays a photograph of the choir at the Atlanta Auditorium on the evening of December 14, 1939. Dr. Martin Luther King, Sr. — the father of Martin Luther King, Jr., and the pastor of the Atlanta Ebenezer Church on Auburn Avenue — holds a guitar in the photograph. In the choir, ten-year-old Martin Luther King, Jr., wears a white hat.

Many in the African American community expressed their displeasure at the participation of the Ebenezer Baptist Church at the premiere and at the appearance of Dr. Martin Luther King, Sr., at the event. The pastor, however, explained that he had no misgivings about his participation or that of his congregation; he said anything one did could carry a political interpretation (Richardson, Nigel).

### KKK *see* Ku Klux Klan

### Kling, Joe

Joe Kling was a copyeditor at the *Atlanta Journal* when Margaret Mitchell went to work there in December 22, 1922. Joe later would marry Rhoda Williams (Kling); Rhoda would serve as a typist for Margaret Mitchell when Macmillan Publishing Company sent the manuscript for what would be *Gone with the Wind* back to Mitchell for retyping and editing.

Joe, Rhoda, Margaret, and John became close friends. It was Joe who delivered the invitations to Margaret's private service at her death. Joe and Rhoda made sure that John was not without friends in the days to come (Walker, page 507).

### Kling, Rhoda Williams *see* Williams, Rhoda

### Kobernaut, G. M.

G. M. Kobernaut was the associate warden of the Atlanta Federal Prison, where Margaret Mitchell sponsored a yearly contest for the inmates who wrote in the *Atlantan*. Kobernaut encouraged inmates to participate in this contest.

*See also Atlantan.*

### Ku Klux Klan (KKK)

The Ku Klux Klan is a secret society formed after the Civil War in the Southern U.S. to assert white supremacy through acts of terrorism. It has opposed granting civil rights to African Americans and has also been anti–Semitic and anti–Catholic.

In 1924 Susan Lawrence Davis published *Authentic History of the Ku Klux Klan, 1865–1877.* She used as a basis for much of her work the information she had obtained from her father and from other Klan members. Her volume concerned the original Ku Klux Klan, not the clan after its "rebirth" in the 1920s. She would later charge Macmillan Publishing Company with plagiarism because of information in *Gone with the Wind*; the suit was not directly against Margaret Mitchell.

The first Ku Klux Klan had "ceased activities"

after the Civil War partly because of "the restoration of 'white supremacy'" and partly because of federal legislation from the Republican Congress of the United States. Concerned about the loss of Republican strength in the South and outraged by the actions of the KKK, Congress took action after the close of the Civil War.

Congress's first action was reviewing an investigation of the Klan. Next, the Congress passed the Force Act of 1870, the Federal Election Law of 1871, and the 1871 Ku Klux Klan Act. These laws declared that secret societies were illegal. The laws also suspended the writs of habeas corpus "in disorderly areas," increased penalties for violation of the Fourteenth and Fifteenth Amendments, and gave military commanders more control over elections (Lefler, 1963, page 470).

The KKK became active again after the beginning of the 20th Century. D. W. Griffith's 1915 film *The Birth of a Nation* had as its basis the Thomas Dixon novels *The Clansman* (1905) and *The Traitor*. The film appeared in Atlanta in December of 1915. The silent movie presented the Klan as an honorable institution and became popular across the state — and elsewhere. These novels were also the sources of Margaret Mitchell's performance for which her parents punished her for plagiarism.

*KKK and vigilante groups.* With the rebirth of the KKK, vigilante groups began to form. Margaret Mitchell witnessed these mob activities in Atlanta in 1906 and in 1919–1921. She even included mob activities in her book *Gone with the Wind*; the death of Scarlett's second husband, Frank Kennedy, occurred when he and others tried to take revenge activities into their own hands (Mitchell, *Gone with the Wind*, pages 524–540).

Margaret Mitchell's/Scarlett O'Hara's feelings about the Klan become evident when Scarlett finds out that her husband, Frank Kennedy, is a member of the Klan. "He had promised her he would have nothing to do with the Klan. Oh, this was just the kind of trouble she had feared would come.... And who would have thought that spiritless old Frank would get himself mixed up in the hot-headed doings of the Klan?" (Mitchell, *Gone with the Wind*, page 533).

*KKK and lynchings.* Lynchings in Georgia and elsewhere increased with the rebirth of the KKK in 1915 on Stone Mountain. Perhaps the best known of these KKK lynchings was that of Atlanta Pencil Factory owner Leo Frank.

*See also* **Authentic History of the *Ku Klux Klan, 1865–1877*; Davis, Susan Lawrence; Dixon, Thomas; Frank, Leo; *The Traitor* and young Margaret Mitchell.**

### Kurtz, Wilbur G.

Kurtz was the historical consultant for the film *Gone with the Wind*. Both he and his wife, Annie Laurie Kurtz, attended the Atlanta premiere of the film *Gone with the Wind*. They also attended the party hosted by Margaret Mitchell and John R. Marsh at Apartment #3 in the Della Manta Complex on December 13, 1939.

Wilbur Kurtz performed a service for the Atlanta Cyclorama. He helped to prepare an addition — the diorama — for the *Battle of Atlanta*. His payment came through the Works Progress Administration ("Wilbur Kurtz").

In addition, Kurtz wrote a history of the Eternal Flame of the Confederacy. He found time to advise Margaret Mitchell on some of her historical questions also.

*See also* **addresses directly related to Margaret Mitchell; Atlanta premiere of *Gone with the Wind*; Della Manta; Eternal Flame of the Confederacy.**

### Kyser, Kay

Kyser, a North Carolina native, began his first radio show, *Kay Kyser's Kampus Klass*, in 1937; later this show became the network show *Kay Kyser's Kollege of Musical Knowledge* in 1938. During his career Kyser would have 35 top ten recordings and 11 number one records. His number one songs during the 1930s included "The Umbrella Man" and "Three Little Fishies"; these upbeat songs helped the nation forget the problems of the Great Depression. Kyser's later songs— like "The White Cliffs of Dover," "He Wears a Pair of Silver Wings," "Praise the Lord and Pass the Ammunition," and "Till Reveille"— encouraged the nation during World War II (Davis, *North Carolina During the Great Depression*, pages 193–194).

Kay Kyser assisted Atlanta Mayor William B. Hartsfield and the governors of the five Southern states in greeting the crowds for the Atlanta premiere of *Gone with the Wind*. Kyser played for the Junior League Charity Ball on the night of December 14, 1939 (Davis, *North Carolina During the Great Depression*, pages 193–194). Kyser would also perform at a dance on Friday night, December 15, 1939, for those who could not purchase tickets to the premiere. The Friday night event would be in the same location — the Atlanta Auditorium — with the same decorations as the Thursday Charity Ball; tickets for this alternate on December 15, 1939, event sold rapidly.

Guests at the Junior League Ball on December 14 found Confederate flags and colors draping the Atlanta Municipal Auditorium. Above the marquee was a fifteen-foot replica of the municipal seal and motto—*Atlanta Resurgens*.

The auditorium, whose floor was the size of a football field, had laurel, swags, and smilax decorating its walls. Because the City Auditorium could not house everyone who wanted to attend the ball, Ozzie Nelson's orchestra played for those who could not go.

Claudette Colbert—a movie star who wanted to attend the festivities but who was not directly involved in the movie *Gone with the Wind*—dressed in red velvet for the Kay Kyser event. Carole Lombard, Clark Gable's wife, arrived in black velvet. Olivia de Havilland, however, did not arrive promptly; no escort had come to the Georgian Terrace Hotel to take her to the ball. The story of her entrance at the ball is a part of her entry.

Margaret Mitchell was not in attendance. Some suggested that she was "reluctant to market herself or display herself for the delectation of the hoi polloi." Others said that the rejection of the invitation came because in the past the Junior League had refused her membership in their organization (Farr, page 5; Edwards, page 283).

*See also* Atlanta Municipal Auditorium; de Havilland, Olivia; Georgian Terrace Hotel.

## Lamp Lighting Ceremony on December 14, 1939

A major event of December 14, 1939—one day in the three-day Atlanta premiere events of the film *Gone with the Wind*—was a lamp lighting ceremony at 10:15 A.M. The central feature for this ceremony was a lamp post from the Civil War period. The lamp represented "an eternal flame of the Confederacy" (Bridges, pages 43–44).

## Latham, Harold Strong

Harold Strong Latham was the editor-in-chief and vice president from Macmillan who received the manuscript of what would be *Gone with the Wind* from its writer, Margaret Mitchell.

*Harold Strong Latham and Margaret Mitchell.* The Macmillan editor who came to Atlanta and received Margaret Mitchell's manuscript on April 11, 1935, after a luncheon at Rich's was Harold Latham. Sources vary as to which hotel lobby Margaret Mitchell delivered the manuscript. Some indicate the hotel was the Georgian Terrace Hotel. Even in Latham's *My Life in Publishing* (1965), he does not solve the mystery.

*Margaret Mitchell is goaded into submitting her work to Harold Latham.* The stories about how "a child" goaded Margaret Mitchell into delivering the manuscript of *Gone with the Wind* to Harold Latham abound. In a car after the Rich's luncheon,

a young woman cried out from the backseat of the vehicle.

"I wouldn't take you for the type who would write a successful novel!" (Edwards, page 9). This remark upset Margaret—who was driving—so much that she slammed on the brake. The young woman continued talking. "That confirms my opinion. You lack the seriousness necessary to be a novelist" (Edwards, page 10). Margaret delivered her manuscript to Harold Latham shortly after that experience.

*Harold Latham, John R. Marsh, and Margaret Mitchell form a friendship.* Margaret trusted Latham in almost all matters. Latham was with the Marshes when the public learned that she had won the Pulitzer Prize for *Gone with the Wind* (1936). The media was unable to locate them because they were with Bessie Berry Jordan at Friendship Baptist Church.

*Biography of Harold Latham (1887–1969).* Born in 1887, Harold Strong Latham graduated in 1909 from Columbia University. The following Monday he entered the doors of Macmillan Company as a full-time employee. At that time Latham worked mainly in Macmillan's advertising and accounting departments. Latham liked writing the circulars and the jacket copies, but he did not enjoy the accounting work as much. He wanted to edit.

Latham even tried to produce his own literary magazine. When the Macmillan editor Edward C. Marsh found out about Latham's efforts, he called Latham into his office. Marsh told Latham if he wanted that much to be an editor, Latham should come to work in the Editorial Department at Macmillan.

Early in 1910 Latham began working as an editorial assistant. In 1920 he became editor-in-chief of the trade department and a director of the firm. Later he would serve as vice-president.

Before World War I, writers often delivered their manuscripts directly to the publisher. After World War I, when the number of printed materials increased, editors began to scout the territory for manuscripts.

In 1935 Harold Latham decided it was a good time for Macmillan to conduct its first scouting tour; the Great Depression was subsiding. Latham decided to conduct the tour himself—in the South: Atlanta. George P. Brett, Sr., the chair of the firm, agreed with Latham's plan. It was on this trip that Latham found the manuscript that would become *Gone with the Wind* (Farr, pages 89–95).

*See also* Rich's Department Store, Georgian Terrace Hotel.

*Harold Latham and My Life in Publishing.* Before his 1969 death, Harold Latham's 1965 book *My Life in Publishing* appeared in print.

*See also* Ansley Hotel, Atlanta premiere of *Gone with the Wind*; Biltmore Hotel; Georgian Terrace Hotel; Jordan, Bessie Berry; *My Life in Publishing*; Rich's Department Store.

## Latvia, sales of *Gone with the Wind* *see* foreign copyrights/translations and fair trade laws

## lawsuit of Susan Lawrence Davis against Macmillan Publishing Company

In 1924 Susan Lawrence Davis had published *Authentic History of the Ku Klux Klan, 1865–1877*. She used as a basis for much of her work the information she had obtained from her father and from other Klan members.

Davis brought a lawsuit against Macmillan Publishing Company because she said its publication *Gone with the Wind* plagiarized her *Authentic History of the Ku Klux Klan, 1865–1877*. The suit was dismissed.

*See also Authentic History of the Ku Klux Klan, 1865–1877*; Davis, Susan Lawrence; Goddard, Judge Henry W.

## Leigh, Vivien

Vivien Leigh auditioned for the role of Scarlett O'Hara *Gone with the Wind* in an unusual time and place: at the filming of the burning of the munitions plant in Atlanta that was simulated in Culver City; Scarlett O'Hara had a stand-in actress representing her in the buggy that passed before the fire. O'Hara and the other characters in the carriage were in silhouette in the filming and in the actual film. David O. Selznick's brother Myron had brought Leigh to the set and introduced her to David as his Scarlett O'Hara (Shavin and Shartar, page 20).

*Vivien Leigh's biography.* Vivian Mary Hartley's birth was on November 5, 1913, in Darjeeling, India; her father was a Yorkshire broker. She received her education in convents in England and throughout Europe. Vivian Hartley (later Vivien Leigh) received her inspiration from schoolmate Maureen O'Sullivan; she launched her career in acting by enrolling in 1932 in London's Royal Academy of Dramatic Art.

Vivian married Herbert Leigh Holman the same year; he was a British barrister. Vivian began using his middle name and a changed spelling of her first name for her stage name: *Vivien Leigh*.

Her first film was *Things Are Looking Up* (1934),

a British production. She made several more low-cost British movies. In 1935 she appeared in her first stage production: *The Green Sash*. "Although she possessed a weak stage voice at this point in her career, her stunning stage presence and beauty were impossible to ignore" ("Vivien Leigh").

In 1935, although she was still married, she began an affair with Laurence Olivier, a married British leading man. The two appeared together in *Fire Over England* (1937) and *21 Days* (filmed in 1937). In 1938 Leigh auditioned for and won the role of Scarlett O'Hara in *Gone with the Wind* ("Vivien Leigh").

Olivier came to Atlanta in 1939 for the premiere of *Gone with the Wind*. Although not publicly announced, the engaged couple Leigh and Olivier were special guests at the Nunnally private residence in Atlanta. Room accommodations records for the Georgian Terrace Hotel, however, list Laurence Olivier in Room 523 (Herb Bridges, *Gone with the Wind: The Three-Day Premiere*, page 67).

Leigh was in attendance at the tea party held by the Atlanta Women's Press Club at the Piedmont Driving Club. The party on Friday, December 15, 1939, was in the afternoon before the night premiere of *Gone with the Wind*.

In 1940, Leigh married Olivier. In 1944, while filming *Caesar and Cleopatra* (released in 1946),

Vivien Leigh wore an elegant hat when she attended the Atlanta Women's Press Club tea party at the Piedmont Driving Club on December 15, 1939. The photograph made the front page of the Saturday *Atlanta Constitution*. (Courtesy of the Atlanta-Fulton Public Library System's Special Collections Department.)

Leigh suffered an accident that resulted in a miscarriage. Some biographers of Leigh trace her struggles with manic-depressive psychosis to this incident; others indicate that she showed signs of her illness in the late 1930s. She suffered also from tuberculosis, but she continued to work.

Vivien Leigh won two Academy Awards. Both were for Southern belles: Scarlett O'Hara in *Gone with the Wind* and Blanche DuBois in *A Streetcar Named Desire* (1951).

Although suffering from mental and physical instability and plagued by her deteriorating marriage to Olivier, Leigh delivered excellent performances in the films *The Roman Spring of Mrs. Stone* (1961) and *Ship of Fools* (1965). She won a Tony Award for her role in the 1963 Broadway musical *Tovarich*. Her marriage to Olivier ended in divorce in 1960. Leigh also starred in the New York stage production of Anton Chekhov's *Ivanov* (1966). She was rehearsing for a role in Edward Albee's *A Delicate Balance* when she was found dead in her London apartment on July 8, 1967 ("Vivien Leigh").

*Vivien Leigh and Clark Gable on a postage stamp for the United States Postal Service.* On March 23, 1990, the United States Postal Service issued a 25-cent postage stamp bearing the image of Vivien Leigh and Clark Gable: "Designer Thomas Blackshear designed this stamp with portraits of Clark Gable as Rhett Butler and Vivien Leigh as Scarlett

The 25-cent stamp from the United States Postal Service bears an issue date of March 23, 1990, and shows Clark Gable ("Rhett Butler") and Vivien Leigh ("Scarlett O'Hara") with Tara in the background. It is part of the Classic Films Series. (Courtesy of United States Postal Service)

O'Hara (the original stars) with Tara (the O'Hara home) in the background" (Davis and Hunt, *Women on United States Postage Stamps*, pages 125–126).

*See also* **Atlanta premiere of *Gone with the Wind*; Brown, Katharine "Kay"; fire scene filming for *Gone with the Wind*; Georgian Terrace Hotel; Nunnally home.**

### Leigh, W. Colston

Harold Latham contacted Leigh Bureau of Lectures and Entertainments and suggested that Margaret Mitchell would be a perfect person for a transcontinental tour for the 1936–1937 seasons. The company that had booked such celebrities and artists as Eleanor Roosevelt was interested.

W. Colston Leigh contacted Margaret Mitchell on March 27, 1936, and offered her a tour for late 1936 — with the possibility of a tour for 1937–1938. Mitchell, however, had little interest. The Macon Writers Club had invited her to speak in January. She had not even responded to the invitation.

Lois Cole with Macmillan knew about Margaret Mitchell's aversion to public appearances. Cole wrote to Margaret and tried to explain the importance of accepting Colston Leigh's invitation. Cole described Leigh as being one of the most powerful names in the field of lecturing; no one could make more money for the writer than Colston Leigh (Brown, pages 54–56).

Mitchell was not persuaded. She wrote to Colston Leigh on April 9, 1936. Brown quotes this letter in her book *Margaret Mitchell's Gone with the Wind*. "I have made only one speech in my life and that was last week, and, God helping me, I never intend to make another. I am small, unimpressive, afflicted with stage fright, and have a loathing for a crowd of strangers.... I'm not a speaker. I'm not yet a writer and may never be one if the critics don't like me" (Brown, page 56). Although her letter only served to whet the interest of Leigh, Mitchell was not to be convinced (Brown, pages 54–55).

### *Letters from Margaret* (2001)

Edwin Granberry and his wife Mabel Granberry were good friends with John R. Marsh and Margaret Mitchell from 1937 until 1949. Edwin Granberry was careful to preserve the letters from the couple.

The Granberrys had three sons. One was Julian Granberry, who knew Margaret Mitchell and John R. Marsh from 1937 (when he was seven) until 1949 (when he was twenty). Julian — an anthropologist and linguist — compiled these letters into a volume, complete with his observations from direct experience. The result appeared in print in 2001 with the copyright of Edwin Granberry, Jr., and Julian Granberry (*Letters from Margaret*, 2001).

*See also* **Granberry, Julian; Green Park Inn.**

## "Little Sister"

Margaret Mitchell's first published story was "Little Sister." The short story appeared in the yearbook *Facts and Fancies* of Washington Seminary during Margaret's junior year. Eva Paisely — who, as a teacher, "lived on the side of angels," according to Mary Rose Taylor — was Margaret's English teacher that year; Paisely encouraged Margaret in her writing. This was probably Margaret's first published writing.

The plot of "Little Sister" centers around a young American girl who witnesses the murder of her parents in Mexico. She also hears the horrifying sounds of her older sister being raped by bandits during the episode (from "Foreword" by Taylor, Mary Rose, in Jane Eskridge's "*Before Scarlett: Childhood Writings of Margaret Mitchell*, ix–xii).

*See also Before Scarlett: Childhood Writings of Margaret Mitchell*; **Eskridge, Jane; "Sergeant Terry"; Taylor, Mary Rose.**

## Llorens, Joseph Victor, Sr.

Joseph Victor Llorens's first employment was as a bartender in a downtown Atlanta saloon. Joseph began drawing sketches of the customers; he found this more interesting than "drawing beer." The customers, too, liked his work.

When young Joe drew F. C. Fisher, Fisher liked the work. Fisher was one of the South's early designers of stained glass; he told Joseph to have Mr. Llorens come to see him. When Joseph's father arrived in Fisher's stained glass studio in Atlanta, they began to talk about young Joe's artistic talents. They discussed the importance of learning a trade to use all one's life. Fisher asked to train young Joe — with Mr. Llorens's permission. Mr. Llorens agreed, and young Joe's career began.

First, Joe began outlining letters on the stained glass. Next he learned to design crowns and crosses. When Fisher left the following year (1906), Joe secured a job with the Empire Glass Company. When he had learned the phases of stained glass–making, Joe opened a business on Edgewood Avenue in 1912. He later built his own studio.

Llorens's windows embellish churches and other buildings. Thousands of his works are adorn structures in the United States, the West Indies, and Mexico. Joe considered his best work to be the Ascension Window in the Peachtree Presbyterian Church, Atlanta, Georgia.

Llorens helped to create the diorama in the foreground of *The Battle of Atlanta* inside the Atlanta Cyclorama. He worked with Weis C. Snell and Wilbur Kurtz to create the three-dimensional objects. Their payment came from the Works Progress Administration — and from their own satisfaction with the completed project. They used plaster, concrete, paint, earth, and earth coloring. Their finished product included six thousand leaves of plaster and hundreds of figures and equipment from plaster. Llorens also gave advice on the filming of *Gone with the Wind*. He particularly helped with the tree set for the film.

Soon the family business would grow. Frank D. Llorens, Sr., and Frank D. Llorens, Jr., joined ("Master Craftsmen of Stained Glass Windows: Joseph Victor Llorens, Sr."). After serving in World War II, Joseph Victor Llorens, Jr., began working with his father. He served as president of Llorens Stained Glass Studio for 35 years.

In 2005, Llorens sold Llorens Stained Glass Studio to his grandson, Ken Hardeman. Llorens Studio became Hardeman Fine Art Glass ("Hardeman Fine Art Glass").

## Lochridge, Edward Pain

Shortly after 8:00 P.M. on August 11, 1949, Margaret Mitchell was hit by a car driven by Hugh D. Gravitt. When help arrived, Edward Pain Lochridge was the intern inside the Grady Ambulance No. 1.

Edward was the son of Lethea Turman Lochridge, who had been a classmate of Margaret Mitchell. She had been a member of the Debutante Club the same year that Margaret had been a member (Farr, page 228).

*See also* **accidents.**

## Loew's Theatre

Loew's Grand Theatre at 157 Peachtree Street in Atlanta was the chosen site for the premiere of *Gone with the Wind*. Margaret Mitchell and many other dignitaries attended.

In the late 1860s the local Mason group in Atlanta had bought the land that would later house the Mason Hall at 157 Peachtree Street. When the Masons were unable to pay for their venture, the land and the shell of the building reverted to the original owner: Laurant DeGive, a Catholic lawyer who had come from Belgium in mid–1800.

DeGive converted the hall into the first building constructed for theatrical purposes in Atlanta. The edifice opened in 1893 and took the name DeGive Grand Opera House.

DeGive remodeled (1923) the DeGive Grand Opera House to provide a building to serve Atlanta (and later the world) as a movie theater and for certain other performances. The recently renovated facility at the intersection of Peachtree and Pryor provided 2,700 seats. Gilded and carved woodwork decorated the theater whose name had changed to Loew's Grand Theatre to reflect the lessee: Loew's Films. Incandescent lighting for the stage was a popular new feature in the innovative Atlanta facility (McInerney, Rita).

Loew's, named for Marcus Loew, dates from 1904 and Loew's Films. Loew's—Metro-Goldwyn-Mayer Studio's parent company—was the oldest operating North American theater chain until a later merger with AMC Theatres in 2006. Loew's would serve as the distributor of *Gone with the Wind* ("1920s Film History: Foundations of the Prolific Film Industry").

Loew's Grand Theatre in Atlanta became a part of the National Register of Historic Places in 1977. Damage by fire in 1978 hastened its demolition later in that year. Atlanta's Houston Restaurant at 2166 Peachtree Street recycled and used many of the bricks from the Loew's in its construction. ("Cinema Treasures: Loew's Grand Theatre, Atlanta, Georgia.") The Tabernacle, an Atlanta church that later became a concert hall, prominently displays the chandelier from the Loew's Grand Theatre ("Tickets to Go: The Tabernacle").

## Logan, John Alexander "Blackjack"

John Alexander Logan served two terms in the United States Senate: the 1871 term and the 1874 term. In 1874 Logan was a vice-presidential candidate. It was during this campaign that Logan commissioned the famous painting *The Battle of Atlanta*. This painting later became the focal point of the Atlanta Cyclorama and a favorite visiting place for Margaret Mitchell and her family.

Logan had fought as a civilian at Bull Run; he was not a member of the Union forces, but he had pro-Union sentiments. He joined the forces and rose to major general. Logan fought in eight major campaigns, distinguished himself at Vicksburg, and was commander of the entire Union forces at the Battle of Atlanta.

## Lohr, August (1843–1919)

August Lohr was a German landscape artist who traveled and painted in the Americas. His best-known work to those in the Atlanta area was his *Battle of Atlanta*.

Lohr actually painted the cycloramic painting in Milwaukee, Wisconsin, at American Panorama Company and in its studio. Established in 1883, the company produced two cycloramic paintings with the Civil War as their theme. The first was *The Battle of Missionary Ridge* (1883–84); the second was *The Battle of Atlanta* (1885–86); the company also produced a series of panoramic works with biblical themes.

The manager of the company was William Wehner, who had traveled to Europe to find artists with the skills needed to prepare the cycloramic paintings. Wehner selected F.W. Heine (a Prussian army veteran) and August Lohr (a landscape painter) as the supervisors.

Lohr, Heine, and several other artists came to Atlanta in 1885. They erected a 40-foot wooden tower near the intersection of Moreland Avenue and the Georgia Railroad and identified and mapped the landmarks needed for the painting. Others with helpful information came to the tower. The artists stored their equipment in the Fred Koch house at 282 Moreland Ave. S.E.

*The Battle of Atlanta* went on display first in Detroit (1887), then on tour (1888). While on tour, the title of the painting was *Logan's Great Battle*. *The Battle of Atlanta* remains in Atlanta ("Atlanta Cyclorama: The Story of the Painting").

**See also** Atlanta Cyclorama; Atlanta premiere of *Gone with the Wind*; Candler Field; Downing, John Francis; Gable, (William) Clark; Grant Park; Gress, George Valentine.

## Lombard, Carole (1908–1942)

Carole Lombard was the wife of Clark Gable. She attended the December 13–15, 1939, premiere events with her husband. Lombard and Gable arrived at the ball sponsored by the Junior League in the Atlanta Auditorium on December 14, 1939; Lombard was elegant in black velvet.

The master of ceremonies of the Junior League Ball was Major Clark Howell, the editor and publisher of the *Atlanta Constitution*. He captivated the audience when he introduced Clark Gable as "Carole Lombard's husband" (Farr, page 7).

Born Jane Alice Peters in 1908, Carole Lombard at five years old demanded to play football with the neighborhood team in Fort Wayne, Indiana; she was not obliged. In 1914, Carole went to California with her mother after her parents' separation. Her mother Bessie always remained her best friend.

After junior high, Carole left school. She was a frequent participant in ballroom dancing exhibitions at Hollywood's Coconut Grove. An executive from Fox Studio discovered seventeen-year-old Carole and gave her a screen test. She made several comedies and various films for Pathe and Paramount.

After making the film *Man of the World* with William Powell, Carole and Powell married in 1931. They divorced after 28 months, but they remained friends and even made the film *My Man Godfrey* together in 1936.

It was 1936 before Lombard and Gable became romantically involved. Carole accepted an invitation to a Hollywood costume party; the invitation said that guests should dress in white. Ambulance attendees carried Carole on a white stretcher into the party from the white ambulance. It was at this "White Ball" that Lombard and Gable renewed their friendship. They married in March of 1939 — before the December 1939 Atlanta premiere of *Gone with the Wind*—and settled on an estate in the San Fernando Valley.

After the entry of the United States into World War II in 1941, Gable accepted the chair of the Hollywood Victory Committee. He arranged for Lombard to begin a selling tour in January 1942; she was to end the tour on January 15 in Indianapolis.

On January 16, 1942, Carole and her mother boarded a plane to California. Twenty-three minutes after refueling in Las Vegas, all the 23 passengers died when the plane struck the side of a mountain. Gable joined the search for the bodies. He placed Carole and her mother in Forest Lawn Cemetery in Glendale, California. Clark Gable joined them in 1960 ("Biography: Carole Lombard").

*See also* Gable, (William) Clark; Kyser, Kay.

## Los Angeles premiere of *Gone with the Wind* (the film)

The Atlanta premiere of *Gone with the Wind* (the film) occurred on December 13–15, 1939. Two other premieres followed — one in New York on December 19, 1939, and the other in Los Angeles on December 28, 1939. The Los Angeles premiere was in the Carthay Circle Theatre.

*See also* Astor Theatre; Atlanta premiere of *Gone with the Wind* (film); Capitol Theatre; Carthay Circle Theatre; New York premiere.

## *Lost Laysen*

Despite the common belief that Margaret Mitchell wrote *Gone with the Wind* as her only novel, that is not true. Mitchell wrote other novels— one of which is *Lost Laysen*; she composed it when she was only sixteen (Springfield-Greene County Library District). Hubbard states that she was fifteen at the time (Hubbard).

Mitchell's good friend Henry Love Angel kept a complete copy of this novella — small novel — that she had given him. He also saved some of her letters to him and some of their photographs. The novel *Lost Laysen* became a 1996 publication of Scribner Publishing Company, about 60 years after the publication of *Gone with the Wind*. Debra Freer edited

the book *Lost Laysen* and verified the authenticity of the materials that she included. The Mitchell Estate, the Road to Tara Museum in Jonesboro, and the family of Henry Love Angel all approved its publication ("*Lost Laysen*: Book Review").

The novella itself has only four chapters. The pages published by Scribner have wide margins; the story itself has page numbers from only 66 to 123.

The first Scribner edition bears the copyright date of 1996 — to correspond with the 60th anniversary of *Gone with the Wind* ("*Lost Laysen*: Book Review").

*Lost Laysen: Its Setting, Its Characters, and Its Plot.* Set on a South Pacific island, *Lost Laysen* is a fast-moving story of honor and love. The work took her less than a month to prepare. Springfield-Greene County Library District calls *Lost Laysen* "a national treasure."

Courtenay Ross— the feisty, independent heroine of *Lost Laysen*—carries the name of Margaret Mitchell's real-life best friend at the time. In the novel Courtenay is engaged to a young American man, who loves Courtenay enough to follow her to the remote South Pacific to persuade her to return to the United States and to marry him.

There is some additional conflict in the book, however. An Irish boatsman named Charley also finds himself attracted to the young woman (Springfield-Greene County Library District).

*See also* Angel, Henry Love; Road to Tara Museum; Ross, Courtenay; Wiggins, Patsy.

## Love, Lucille Thompson

Lucille Thompson Love, with the assistance of Mary Ellen DeBarbieri Kozuck and Linda Bourgeois Davidson, prepared the book *Remembering Margaret Mitchell* (1992). The book has as its basis the correspondence between Lucille Alladio Busey and Margaret Mitchell from about 1938 until about 1943.

Busey was a founder of the Margaret Mitchell Library in Fayetteville, Georgia. *Remembering Margaret Mitchell* includes a history of the founding of the Margaret Mitchell Library. The library is the only institution on which Margaret Mitchell allowed her name during her lifetime. The 188-page book is a publication of the Ellen Ross Publishing Company in Huntsville, Alabama ("*Remembering Margaret Mitchell, Author of Gone with the Wind*").

## Lukeman, Augustus

On April 1, 1925, Augustus Lukeman took over the Stone Mountain carving project that Gutzon Borglum had begun and that Margaret Mitchell had written about for the newspaper. Lukeman blasted Borglum's carving of Robert E. Lee from the side of the mountain and began a scene that was to feature three men: Robert E. Lee, Jefferson Davis, and Stonewall Jackson.

A popular but difficult-to-document story involves Stone Mountain and the 1939 premiere of the film *Gone with the Wind*. It goes that a heavy tailwind threatened to make the arrival time of stars Vivien Leigh, Olivia de Havilland, the Selznicks, and the others on the Eastern Airline plane earlier than expected. When the welcoming committee realized that the arrival of the celebrities was imminent and that the floral arrangements were not at the airport, Atlanta Mayor William B. Hartsfield contacted the newly-constructed control tower and asked the pilot to detour around Stone Mountain. He asked the pilot to show the honored guests the monument under construction.

On May 20, 1928, the Venable family reclaimed the property where Lukeman had been preparing the carving. By the date of repossession, Lukeman had completed only the figures of Lee and Davis. On July 4, 1964, carving resumed on the Stone Mountain Confederate Memorial under the direction of Walker Hancock.

The list of the above-average works of Henry Augustus Lukeman is long. Some of his most notable works include statues of President McKinley in Adams, Massachusetts; of Christopher Columbus for the Custom House in New York; of Franklin Pierce for Concord, New Hampshire; and of Jefferson Davis for Statuary Hall in the United States Capitol.

One of Lukeman's last projects was not a pleasant one for him. After Gutzon Borglum had worked eight years on a carving for Stone Mountain near Atlanta, Georgia, Lukeman took over the project that Borglum had abandoned after quarreling with its sponsors. Some observers criticized Lukeman's accepting the position; Borglum himself protested Lukeman's actions. Lukeman was distressed and abandoned the project soon after finishing the work on Lee.

Lukeman held many honors. He earned membership in 1898 to the National Sculpture Society and the Architectural League of New York. He earned an associate (1909) in the National Academy of Design. His work in the 1904 Louisiana Purchase Exposition, St. Louis, earned him a bronze medal.

Lukeman credited others for their influence. He noted Thompson for helping him with technique; he acknowledged French for helping him to achieve grace in his sculptures.

Lukeman married in 1933 when he was about 62. He married Mrs. Helen Bidwell Blodgett of Stockbridge, Massachusetts, where he had a summer home and studio. Lukeman died of heart disease in 1935 — only two years after his marriage. His burial is in Stockbridge ("Henry Augustus Lukeman").

*See also* Borglum, Gutzon; Stone Mountain.

## Macmillan Publishing Company and *Gone with the Wind*

Macmillan Publishing Company was the publisher of Margaret Mitchell's *Gone with the Wind*. Lois Cole, an associate editor in the Atlanta office, was instrumental in encouraging Mitchell to submit her manuscript to Harold Latham, editor-in-chief (later vice-president).

Latham visited Atlanta in April of 1935. It was the first scouting trip that Macmillan had tried. Latham decided to try the scouting approach himself; he made the first trip for the company.

Cole invited Margaret Mitchell, Harold Strong Latham, and others to attend a luncheon at Rich's Department Store in Atlanta. Margaret did not take her manuscript to give to him at that time.

It was after the luncheon that Margaret gathered the envelopes that held the separate chapters, in random order, of her book. She called Harold Latham and asked if she could bring the manuscript to him in the lobby of his hotel. She arrived shortly before 6:00 P.M. as he was preparing to leave Atlanta that night (Farr, pages 89–95).

Cole mentioned that Mitchell took the unorganized envelopes holding the chapters to Latham in the lobby of the Biltmore Hotel. Margaret Baugh, Anne Edwards, and Marianne Walker, however, suggest that Margaret Mitchell delivered the envelopes bearing the chapters to different hotels, including the Georgian Terrace and the Ansley Hotel. No definitive location for the manuscript delivery, therefore, is available (Brown, page 16; Edwards, page 3; Walker, page 198).

*Macmillan, its employees, and Margaret Mitchell.* Several, but not all, of the Macmillan employees below had direct contacts with Margaret Mitchell.

1. Daniel Macmillan (1813–1857) — director of Macmillan and Company from 1850 to 1857.

2. Alexander Macmillan (1818–1896) — director of Macmillan and Company from 1857 to 1889.

3. Maurice Frederick (director 1889) and George Alexander.

4. George Edward Brett — director of marketing and sales for the New York branch of Macmillan and Company (the headquarters of Macmillan in the United States) beginning in August of 1869 until 1890.

5. George Platt Brett — joined his father George

Edward Brett in 1874 at Macmillan; in 1890 he began serving as director after his father died.

6. George Platt Brett, Jr.—followed his father as director of Macmillan and Company after his father retired in July of 1936; George Platt Brett, Jr., served as director until the early 1960s.

7. Lois Dwight Cole — editor/office manager.

8. Harold Latham — received manuscript of *Gone with the Wind*.

*Macmillan Publishing Company and Its History.* This was originally an English publishing company established as D. and A. Macmillan in 1843. The two brothers Daniel and Alexander Macmillan were born to a Scottish farmer; Daniel was born in 1813, and Alexander was born in 1818.

Daniel went to work for a bookseller and bookbinder in Irvine, Scotland, after he completed his primary school education. Alexander, after his primary school education, taught school before he joined a firm of booksellers in Glasgow.

At the age of 20, Daniel went to work at a bookstore specializing in classical authors and located close to Cambridge University. The university students began to respect Daniel as a well-read and reliable guide to publications. Daniel worked for a bookseller in London; Alexander soon joined him.

The two brothers opened their own establishment in London. In 1843 they produced *The Philosophy of Training*, their first publication. The publication advocated establishing additional colleges for teachers in Britain.

The Macmillan brothers regarded their work as more than a way to earn a living. Daniel once wrote to another dealer that the book business was a way to destroy confusion and to create harmony and beauty in the world. The brothers still had to earn their livelihood and remain good businessmen in the process.

Daniel and Alexander closed the London business after one year, borrowed some money from the Cambridge churchman Archdeacon Hare, and set up a business in Cambridge. The Macmillan brothers became advocates of Christian Socialism, a reform movement. Their publications in this period reflect their liberalism in church reform and their belief in universal education in Great Britain. As a result of the beliefs of Daniel and Alexander and their strategic location near Cambridge University, Macmillan Publishing Company became a leading book, textbook, and educational publisher. In 1850 the establishment adopted the name Macmillan and Co. The first important publications were Charles Kingsley's *Westward Ho!* (1855) and Thomas Hughes's *Tom Brown's School Days* (1857).

After Daniel's death in 1857, Alexander became the director of Macmillan and Co. He remained in that position until 1889. With its success in marketing fiction, the company was able to open a second branch in London.

The sociable Alexander found his shop in London the setting for "feasts of Talk, Tobacco, and Tipple." Every Thursday night England's most brilliant writers assembled there to socialize, smoke, and drink. Tennyson, T. H. Huxley, and Herbert Spencer were regular guests; they also contributed to the monthly journal that Alexander Macmillan began in 1859: *Macmillan's Magazine*. The journal remained in operation until 1909 — a period of fifty years.

Macmillan and Co. continued under the direction of Alexander Macmillan. Its published writers included Lewis Carroll, Matthew Arnold, William Gladstone, George Meredith, Walter Pater, Christina Rossetti, Lord Tennyson, Thomas Hardy, W. B. Yeats, and Rudyard Kipling.

Macmillan and Co. continued to produce textbooks for students and *Macmillan's Magazine*. The company also published the medical journal *The Practitioner* and the science journal *Nature* (still in publication). Alexander's son George and his two nephews Frederick and Maurice helped with the enterprise; Frederick assumed the chair of the operation after Alexander's 1889 retirement.

As early as 1859, Alexander had recognized the American publication market. He retained the agents Scribner and Welford. In 1867 Alexander came to the United States for eight weeks and met with U.S. president and distinguished writers. Alexander Macmillan envisioned an international publishing house.

Alexander set up a New York branch office. In August of 1869, he hired the young Englishman George Edward Brett as the sales and marketing director of the headquarters for the United States. Brett opened the New York Office at 63 Bleecker Street; the New York Office, however, would begin its own publishing until some thirty years afterwards.

George Edward Brett's son George Platt Brett joined the firm in 1874. He became director of Macmillan and Co. in 1890, after his father died. He remained as director of what had become the Macmillan Company in New York (1896) until his retirement, which was in July of 1936.

At that time George Platt Brett, Jr., took over as director. (His period of serving as director and president of the New York office of Macmillan began after the June 1936 publication of *Gone with the Wind*.) The younger Brett remained in this position until the early 1960s. The Brett family, then, exercised control of the American offices of Macmillan from the creation of these offices in 1869 until the early 1960s; this was a span of a century. Few other families in American business can match such a record.

The split of the Macmillan Company in New York and Macmillan and Co., Ltd., of London occurred in 1951. In 1959 Crowell-Collier Publishing Company began buying up shares of Macmillan; the two companies merged in December 1960 under the Crowell-Collier name. In 1963 Raymond C. Hagel replaced Bruce Y. Brett, the last of the family to serve as president of Macmillan; Hagel served as CEO until 1980. Macmillan did reassume its name during this time period ("Macmillan, Inc.").

The history of the company is complex after that date which is also after the time of Margaret Mitchell and the scope of this book. One might note, however, that Macmillan and Co. in Toronto produced the first "foreign" copy of *Gone with the Wind*.

*See also* addresses directly related to Margaret Mitchell; Ansley Hotel; Baugh, Margaret Eugenia; Biltmore Hotel; foreign copyrights/translations and fair trade laws; Georgian Terrace Hotel; Latham, Harold Strong; Rich's Department Store.

### March Hare Tea Shop

This tea shop in downtown Atlanta was in the basement of the Haynes Building at 2½ Auburn Avenue — one block from Peachtree Street. The tea shop entered prominently in the courtship of John R. Marsh and Margaret Mitchell (Walker, pages 8–9).

*See also* "The Rabbit Hole."

### Margaret Mitchell: American Rebel

To commemorate the life of Margaret Mitchell, to mark the 75th anniversary of the publication of *Gone with the Wind*, and to celebrate 50 years of Georgia Public Broadcasting, Pamela Roberts and Georgia Public Broadcasting released the program and the video/DVD *Margaret Mitchell: American Rebel* on June 29, 2011.

The Collector's Edition — available to the public through Georgia Public Broadcasting in Atlanta — features interviews with historians, biographers, and those with personal connections to Margaret Mitchell; images and papers from the Atlanta History Center; dramatic re-enactments; an interview with Pat Conroy, who wrote the Introduction to a special edition of *Gone with the Wind*; and a review of the 1939 Atlanta premiere of the *Gone with the Wind* (the film) and of Pulitzer Prize night in the year 1937.

*See also* Atlanta premiere of *Gone with the Wind*; Conroy, Pat; Roberts, Pamela.

### Margaret Mitchell and African Americans

Many viewers of the film *Gone with the Wind* were uncomfortable with the use of the word Nigger and seeing the portrayal of African Americans as "happy slaves." In addition, many Americans expressed concern that at the Atlanta premiere of *Gone with the Wind* Hattie McDaniel and Butterfly McQueen — two principal African American actresses — felt uncomfortable in attending because of segregation laws.

Equally notable — and equally controversial — was the presence of the Ebenezer Church Choir. This group wore the attire of slaves in a performance at the Atlanta Auditorium.

Russell Caldwell — a guide at the Margaret Mitchell House and a relative of Berrien Kinnard ("Red") Upshaw — notes that Margaret Mitchell had some specific concerns about the book *Gone with the Wind*. Caldwell quotes Mitchell — according to the article by Nigel Richardson — as having said: "The one thing I've always wanted to avoid is the stirring up of old hates and prejudices, because I wrote my book with no hate and no prejudice."

More information on Margaret Mitchell's support of the African American community, especially in Atlanta, is now available. This support was mainly possible through the sales of her novel *Gone with the Wind*. Caldwell notes also the time and aid that she was able to give to people in Atlanta, and through the American Red Cross to the world. Caldwell said rendering aid to African Americans in the 1930s and 1940s "was highly irregular at the time, her being a prominent white woman. She gave money anonymously to set up a clinic and 50 scholarships to Morehouse College. It was all done under the radar" (Richardson).

*See also* Atlanta premiere of *Gone with the Wind*; Ebenezer Baptist Church; Jim Crow laws; Margaret Mitchell Chair in the Humanities at Morehouse College; Mays, Benjamin.

### Margaret Mitchell Chair in the Humanities at Morehouse College

In 2002 Morehouse College in Atlanta, the alma mater of Martin Luther King, Jr., received $1.5 million from Margaret Mitchell's nephew Eugene Muse Mitchell.

Eugene Muse Mitchell — a namesake of the father of Margaret Mitchell — presented the generous check to Walter E. Massey in 2002. A special ceremony on the Morehouse campus in Davidson House marked the occasion. Eugene Mitchell designated the donation for the establishment of the

Margaret Mitchell Chair. The chair for the Division of Humanities and Social Science celebrated the commitment of Margaret Mitchell to literature, to scholarship, and to humanity ("Morehouse College Receives $1.5 Million from Nephew of Late *Gone with the Wind* Author Margaret Mitchell").

Three years later — in 2005 — Eugene Mitchell made another gift to Morehouse College. Just as Margaret Mitchell had secretly paid for the tuition for dozens of African American medical students (in collaboration with Morehouse President Dr. Benjamin E. Mays), Eugene Mitchell had asked to donate a gift for scholarships at Morehouse (Vejnoska).

*See also* **Mitchell, Eugene Muse (1931–2007); Morehouse College.**

## Margaret Mitchell House and Museum

In September of 1991, the former news anchor Mary Rose Taylor announced the "Save the Dump" campaign. Taylor began to raise money to restore Apartment #1, the first home of John R. Marsh and Margaret Mitchell and the site where Mitchell began *Gone with the Wind*.

*Margaret Mitchell house and fire #1.* On September 17, 1994, a fire destroyed the top two floors of the building that housed Apartment #1. The basement unit, however, remained intact. Investigators ruled that the fire was the work of arsonists.

Some rumors indicated that a real estate developer had set the fire as a result of believing that the property would not be more profitable. Other speculations suggested that the fire was racially motivated and that the fire had been an objection to *Gone with the Wind*. There were ultimately no arrests by the police.

The fire, however, seemed to draw attention to Mary Rose Taylor's project. When Daimler-Benz — the German automobile producer — learned of Taylor's work and of the fire, it contributed $5 million to the project as a goodwill donation to Atlantans.

Taylor set her mind, her will, and her back to the effort to preserve Apartment #1. Taylor determined that the Margaret Mitchell House — like Atlanta — "would rise out of the ashes." Taylor announced that the Margaret Mitchell House would be open for the 1996 Summer Olympics in Atlanta (Brown, Ellen F. "Writer's House: The House that Lived").

*Margaret Mitchell House and fire #2.* In May 1996, just before the Olympics opened in Atlanta on July 19, and shortly before the official "unveiling" of Apartment #1 in the Margaret Mitchell House Museum, arsonists again found their target. Most of the apartment building was reduced to rubble, but once more Apartment #1 had somehow escaped damage (Brown, Ellen F. "Writer's House: The House that Lived").

Taylor and Apartment #1 prevailed. Today as a part of the Atlanta History Center, the Margaret Mitchell House Museum is an important destination of many visitors to Atlanta. Because *Gone with the Wind* is still popular at home and abroad, thousands of tourists from many different locales eagerly visit the Margaret Mitchell House Museum each year.

*The Margaret Mitchell House opening.* Ellen F. Brown, author of *Margaret Mitchell's* Gone with the Wind, was able to report that Apartment #1 opened on May 16, 1997, as the Margaret Mitchell House, the "Birthplace of *Gone with the Wind*" (Brown, Ellen F. "Writer's House: The House that Lived").

The official dedication ceremony included Georgia Governor Zell Miller, Atlanta Mayor Bill Campbell, representatives from founding patron Daimler-Benz, students from the Margaret Mitchell Elementary School in Atlanta, and the keynote speaker: Tom Wolfe. The house entertains over 50,000 visitors a year from all fifty states and the District of Columbia; visitors from over 70 foreign countries have also come to the Margaret Mitchell House.

*Margaret Mitchell House and the 75th Anniversary of* Gone with the Wind. In 2011, the Margaret Mitchell House was the central focus of the 75th anniversary of the publication of *Gone with the Wind*. The Atlanta History Center, which now operates the Margaret Mitchell House Museum, assisted in hosting and planning the celebratory activities (Brown, Ellen F. "Writer's House: The House that Lived").

*See also* **addresses directly related to Margaret Mitchell; The Dump; Taylor, Mary Rose; foreign copyrights/translations and fair trade laws.**

## Margaret Mitchell Law

Margaret Mitchell's *Gone with the Wind* influenced public policies and regulations about books.

One important legal result of Margaret Mitchell and her novel *Gone with the Wind* was a modification of tax law that the public commonly calls the "Margaret Mitchell Law." Mitchell was scheduled to pay enormous income taxes in 1936, 1937, and each year thereafter because of the phenomenal sales of *Gone with the Wind* even though the novel took years to write.

The Margaret Mitchell Law, Code Section 107-C, was a result of her initiative. Its passage, however, did not come until 1952 — after her 1949 death. The legislation called attention to the fact that some taxpayers had to pay large taxes on a lump sum of money or income received in one year for work performed over several unpaid years. These wage earners were often self-employed; they asked not to be free from tax but that the total amount be averaged over the years of work that they earned them (Walker, page 354, Farr, pages 232–233). Mitchell's personified request called attention to the problem of some self-employed persons, in particular.

*See also* Berne Convention; foreign copyrights/ translations and fair trade laws.

## Margaret Mitchell Memorial Park

Although Margaret Mitchell never lived in Jonesboro and presumably never targeted a particular plantation in Jonesboro for her novel *Gone with the Wind*, Historical Jonesboro/Clayton County, Inc. has established Stately Oaks as a tourist site for visitors seeking to find Tara.

Stately Oaks is 15 miles south of downtown Atlanta. Costumed tour directors and MP3 guides direct the visitors who have come to the residence with its white columns. These guides discuss the links that Jonesboro has with the author, with *Gone with the Wind*, and with the Atlanta campaign during the Civil War.

Also on the grounds, tourists can rest in the rocking chairs or on the provided benches. They can visit the 1896 store called Juddy's Country Store, go inside the one-room schoolhouse, enter a tenant house and the separate log kitchen, and observe a well house all on the property. Historical Jonesboro/Clayton County, Inc. owns Stately Oaks.

The founding of Historical Jonesboro dates from 1968. The intention of the corporation was to save the buildings, the furnishings, and the written documents that were rapidly disappearing and that reflected the history of the area.

The selected site for the preservation and restoration attempt was Margaret Mitchell Memorial Park. If the representative buildings were not already on the site, the necessary moving made the historic area possible. The Stately Oaks Plantation House, which dates from 1839, is the central focus of the Margaret Mitchell Memorial Park. The house is a true example of plain Greek Revival architecture ("Stately Oaks Plantation").

## Margaret Mitchell Museum

The Margaret Mitchell Museum in Atlanta is at 990 Peachtree Street, NE. It is part of the one-hour, docent-led tour of the Margaret Mitchell House.

The tour begins with a short film titled "It May Not Be Tara." The film, which is a local production, includes a short summary of Margaret Mitch-

ell's life and the effort involved in preserving Apartment #1, where *Gone with the Wind* began. Visitors tour the house, Apartment #1, and the Museum Shop, where they can purchase gifts, souvenirs, mementos, and collectibles.

December 15, 1999 — the 60th anniversary of the Atlanta Premiere of *Gone with the Wind* — marked the opening of an additional museum. This feature highlights the 1939 Atlanta premiere of *Gone with the Wind* and focuses on the filming of the movie. The memorabilia include items from the collection of Herb Bridges, and even the Tara doorway of the movie set ("Margaret Mitchell House and Museum of Atlanta: Travel Guide").

*See also* addresses directly related to Margaret Mitchell; Atlanta premiere of *Gone with the Wind*; The Dump; Tara.

## Margaret Mitchell Safety Council

The death of Margaret Mitchell brought national concern about laws governing drunken drivers and about safety regulations. In addition to news about Margaret Mitchell's condition and about the accident, editorials in newspapers across the country focused attention on safety issues. To examine the records and qualifications of taxi drivers, Atlanta established a safety board called The Margaret Mitchell Safety Council; this council later became the Georgia Safety Council. Margaret Mitchell's life — and her death — had made a difference to others (Walker, page 513).

## Margaret Mitchell Square

Located at the intersection of Peachtree Street, Forsyth Street and Carnegie Way is a public memorial to Margaret Mitchell. The memorial is so unpretentious that many tourists pass the site without recognizing its importance. Such anonymity might be acceptable to Margaret Mitchell, who disliked both calling attention to herself and speaking in public.

The tributes at Margaret Mitchell Square include an inscription on a marker and a cascading fountain with a sculpture. The sculpture is representative of the columns of Tara. Near the square is the Central Library; this library — started by Margaret Mitchell's father, Eugene Muse Mitchell (1866–1944) as the Carnegie Library — now contains a variety of materials which relate to Margaret Mitchell.

If one crosses Peachtree Street from Margaret Mitchell Square, the Georgia Pacific Building will be in view. The Georgia Pacific Building now stands where Loew's Theater — the site of the 1939 Atlanta premiere of *Gone with the Wind* (the film) — once stood.

Margaret Mitchell Square with the cascading fountain at the far left and the columns of Tara before it. (Courtesy of Tara Perisco; tpersico@hotmail.com)

Only a block away from the square is Atlanta's famous intersection: Five Points. Margaret Mitchell refers to Five Points in her book *Gone with the Wind* (Frommer's, "Searching for Margaret Mitchell").

*See also* addresses directly related to Margaret Mitchell; Atlanta–Fulton County Public Library; Georgia Pacific Tower; Loew's Grand Theatre.

### Marsh, Ben Gordon (1899–1954)

Ben Gordon Marsh was John R. Marsh's youngest brother. Upon their father's death in 1904, eight-year-old John was given the responsibility of helping his grandmother care for five-year-old Ben Gordon. John felt some responsibility for his brother throughout his life.

In 1928, Ben Gordon and his wife Francesca Renick Marsh visited with John and Margaret. Francesca was three months pregnant with what would be their only child: a boy named Renick ("Renny"). Francesca mentioned to Margaret her desire for seven children and fourteen dogs (Walker, page 177).

Even in 1928, John was still protective of his brother Ben Gordon and sister-in-law Francesca. When John learned that Ben Gordon and Francesca were driving into Atlanta and not taking a train, John and Margaret insisted that their guests call them when they reached the city limits. John and Margaret volunteered to escort them through the "dangerous traffic."

During the visit when the two brothers went for a walk, John shared with Ben Gordon that he believed his wife had psychosomatic problems. John indicated that the book that his wife was writing had improved her health more than the medical care that she had received had done (Walker, page 178–179).

As did the other siblings, Ben Gordon felt a strong family loyalty. At the death of Margaret Mitchell, Ben Gordon and their brother Henry were there to be with John during the service (Walker, page 508).

Frances Marsh Zane visited with her brother John R. Marsh for an extended period of time after the death of Margaret Mitchell. Their sister

Katharine Marsh Bowden stayed with John for a month after Margaret's death. When she left, Ben Gordon and his wife Francesca left Lexington to spend time with John and, hopefully, to ease his grief and to see after his health. The close relationship of the couple with the widower John continued (Walker, page 513).

John's will provided for Ben Gordon Marsh. His part was to be equal to that of John's other siblings: Henry, Katharine, and Frances.

*See also* will of John R. Marsh.

## Marsh, Frances *see* Zane, Frances Marsh

## Marsh, Francesca Renick

Francesca ("Frank") Renick Marsh was the wife of Ben Gordon Marsh, John's younger brother. Francesca and Margaret became good friends. Their correspondence was by mail much of the time because she and Ben Gordon Marsh lived in Lexington.

Francesca and her family took great pride in knowing the author Margaret Mitchell. Francesca loved to tell the story about how her mother bragged to her friends that she had an advance copy of *Gone with the Wind*. When her friends inquired about how Mrs. Renick had gotten an advance copy, Mrs. Renick would brag that she was "the mother-in-law of the brother-in-law of the author" (Walker, page 263).

Francesca and Ben Gordon wanted to ease John's grief after the death of Margaret. John's sister Frances Marsh Zane stayed with John for a while after Margaret's death. When Frances returned home, Ben Gordon and his wife Francesca left Lexington to spend time with John. The close relationship of the couple with the widower John continued (Walker, page 513).

*See also* Marsh, Ben Gordon.

## Marsh, Henry (1893–)

Henry Marsh, the oldest child of Millard Fillmore Marsh and Mary Toup Marsh, was eleven when his father died in 1904. As did the others in the Marsh household, Henry stayed in contact with the rest of his family even though many miles might separate them.

In 1912 Henry, who was enrolled in the University of Kentucky, moved from a boarding house into an apartment. The new lodging place was halfway between the town of Lexington and the campus. The new facility would be less expensive for John and Henry to share. Henry would later remark that John and he had little contact during this time. John was busy with school and was going out with Kitty Mitchell (Walker, page 47).

Henry made his career in ballistics and chemistry. He was a scientist. In an interview with Anne Edwards for her *Road to Tara,* Frances stated that he did not have an understanding of people that John had. He was more of a scientist (Walker, page 41).

As was typical of the Marsh clan, a strong family bond persisted. At the death of Margaret Mitchell, brothers Henry and Ben Gordon were present to be with John during the service (Walker, page 508).

John's will provided for Henry Marsh. His part was to be equal to that of John's other siblings: Ben Gordon, Katharine, and Frances.

*See also* Mitchell, Kitty; will of John R. Marsh.

## Marsh, John (1895–1952)

John Robert Marsh was born in Maysville, a small northern Kentucky town. Before John was three he developed a life-threatening case of scarlet fever; this was before the days of antibiotics.

John's mother sent the other children next door to her family home. Her mother, Sara Jane Kercheval Kenman Toup, her maiden sister Molly Kenman, and a bachelor brother lived there.

Mary Toup Marsh spent her days caring for John, reading to him, playing games with him, and making puppets out of socks and rags. Every morning and every evening, Mary Toup Marsh would go to the window that faced her mother's home. She would hold her son John in one arm and with her other arm she would perform a puppet show for the amusement of her other children.

John's illness left him with abnormal hearing and a weakened heart. Because he was often ill, he read and wrote. He even helped to teach his younger sister Frances and his brother Ben Gordon to read and write (Walker, page 41).

*John Marsh as a bread-winner at an early age.* John and his brother Henry helped to support his mother, their brother Ben Gordon Marsh, and their sister Frances after their father — who had worked with the local newspaper — died of a heart attack in 1904. John worked at a clothing store much of the time.

John's employer helped to pay for John's education at the University of Kentucky. He graduated in 1916 with a degree in English. He had a fellowship to pursue a degree at the University of Kentucky and taught two classes in English composition while he pursued his graduate degree; he also wrote for newspapers — including the *Lexington Leader* — until World War I began. John served in France (Walker, pages 48–54).

After his discharge from the army after serving two years, Marsh continued to work for the

Lexington newspaper. He moved to Atlanta and worked for the *Georgian* there. On one of the law enforcement raids of a moonshiner's still, one of the officers gave John—who was working on the news report—a confiscated .32-caliber revolver. Walker reports that this was the loaded pistol that Margaret would later keep by her bed each night until the death of Berrien Kinnard ("Red") Upshaw (Walker, pages 49–50).

Both Pyron and Edwards, however, note that Margaret herself bought the pistol. Farr gives no evidence of the source of the pistol (Pyron, page 194; Edwards, page 103; Farr, page 57).

*John Marsh and his first encounters with Margaret Mitchell.* John had been in Atlanta for about a year and was established in his job with the newspaper when he first met Margaret Mitchell. John's niece Mary Marsh Davis indicated that her uncle had fallen in love with Margaret Mitchell the first time that he saw her. John claimed that the November 21, 1921, encounter was "a soul-shaking, terrifying experience" (Walker, page 11).

Margaret's father, Eugene Muse Mitchell, and her brother Stephens Mitchell had not liked the type of young men that Margaret had been bringing home. They seemed to be the play-boy, fraternity type. John seemed different.

John believed that Margaret was different. He wrote to his mother about his "new Sweetie" and told his mother that she was the "only girl that interests him." John turned down an offer to work with the *Lexington Leader* in order to stay closer to Margaret. The two dated regularly (Walker, page 14–16).

*John R. Marsh, Berrien Kinnard "Red" Upshaw, and Margaret Mitchell: A Triangular Relationship.* The relationship between John R. Marsh and Margaret Mitchell seemed to change when Berrien Kinnard ("Red") Upshaw returned to Atlanta around the end of March in 1922. John seemed to have a premonition about Red and Margaret when he saw them seated together at the Rabbit Hole.

John continued to date Margaret—but so did Red. In fact, they sometimes dated her on the same night. To complicate things further, John and Red were roommates in an apartment that John had been renting; John's new roommate had come at the suggestion of Margaret Mitchell, who seemed to string both young men to believe she cared for each more than the other.

*John R. Marsh as best man.* Just when John R. Marsh was working up the nerve to ask Margaret to marry him, Red proposed marriage to Margaret—and she accepted. To complicate things even more, Margaret asked John to serve as the best man. On September 2, 1922, Margaret and Red married in a formal ceremony at the home of Eugene Muse Mitchell; John Marsh fulfilled his duties as best man (Walker, pages 77–82).

*John Marsh and work outside of Atlanta.* When John realized that Margaret Mitchell was going to marry Red Upshaw, he quit his job with Georgia Power and went to work in Tuscaloosa for Legare Davis, a freelance publicity agent. John was heading the funding for the building campaign for the University of Alabama. The announcement of the first news story on the campaign reached the papers on July 30, 1922. On this day, he also wrote to his mother to tell her that Margaret's engagement to Red was in the day's paper.

By the end of September after the early September wedding of Red and Margaret, Margaret was already writing complaining letters to John about her new husband. Some of these letters bore John's address in Washington, D.C. Soon Marsh left his position in Tuscaloosa and went to work at the Associated Press office in Washington, D.C. By December, Margaret Mitchell was begging John to return to Atlanta to encourage Red—a known bootlegger—to stop drinking (Edwards, pages 86–88).

*John Marsh as mediator between Margaret and Red.* Indeed John did return to Atlanta to assist the couple however he could. No sooner than his arrival, however, he received a phone call telling him that the Upshaws were on the way to his hotel and that they had decided to divorce.

The next morning, a "hung-over" Berrien Kinnard ("Red") Upshaw arrived at the Mitchell home. Red informed Margaret that he was going to Asheville, North Carolina, where he had a job prospect. He told her that he never planned to return to Atlanta and that she could pursue a divorce anytime she wished (Edwards, pages 88–89).

Red Upshaw returned to Atlanta unexpectedly on July 10, 1923. His abuse caused Margaret to lose time from work and sped up her divorce proceedings (Edwards, pages 102–103).

*John R. Marsh helping Margaret Mitchell in job search.* After the Upshaw marriage was over, John contacted Medora Field Perkerson, with whom he had worked at the *Atlanta Journal Magazine.* He let her know that Margaret Mitchell was now available for employment. Both Angus Perkerson—the editor of the magazine—and his wife Medora Field Perkerson were in favor of her employment (Edwards, pages 90–94).

*Renewed relationship of John R. Marsh and Margaret Mitchell.* In June of 1924 Margaret Mitchell visited John in Washington, D.C. She expressed her love and concern for him; he expressed his love for her also (Walker, page 111).

John began to see Margaret regularly—often in

a helpful role. Finally, on Sunday night, January 18, 1925, he asked Margaret to marry him; he found favor with her. On January 19, 1925, he asked — and received — Eugene Muse Mitchell's consent. They all settled on a Valentine's Day date for the ceremony. The day after obtaining Eugene Muse Mitchell's consent for the marriage, John became ill. Margaret wrote to her future sister-in-law on February 2, 1925, to explain John's ailment.

*Margaret Mitchell's and John R. Marsh's relationship interrupted by John's illness.* Margaret Mitchell described John's sickness as a "hiccoughing flu," which caused him to hiccough every other breath. She said that the affliction was not painful but that it had interfered with his sleeping and recovery. John's hiccough attack was to last forty-two days. He would become the only one on record at the time to have had an attack that lasted that long and to have survived.

On January 31, 1925, Margaret checked Marsh into St. Joseph's Infirmary. He was given oxygen and placed under observation (Pyron, pages 197–199). John remained hospitalized until the end of March — long after their February 14, 1925, intended wedding date had passed. Margaret described the discharged patient as looking "like a famine victim" (Pyron, page 200).

John had learned that the hiccoughs may have been a result of the epilepsy. He asked Margaret if they could set a date for the wedding in the future when they would know more about his condition and treatment. During the next two months, John recuperated at his home, an apartment that would later bear the nickname "The Dump" (Edwards, pages 111–113).

*John R. Marsh and Margaret Mitchell's wedding.* On June 15, 1925, the couple John R. Marsh and Margaret Mitchell applied for a marriage license. John and Margaret set their wedding date as July 4, 1925 (Edwards, pages 113–115).

They married at 5:00 P.M. on July 4, 1925. The site of their vows was the Unitarian-Universalist Church on West Peachtree Street. Augusta Dearborn and Medora Field Perkerson served as Margaret's attendants; Dearborn was the bridesmaid and Perkerson was the matron of honor.

John R. Marsh had as best man Frank L. Stanton, Jr.; Frank was the son of the Georgia poet Frank Stanton, who wrote the lyrics for "Mighty Lak a Rose."

In her papers in the files of the University of Georgia, Medora Field Perkerson wrote that the weather was hot as a usual July day. Medora helped Margaret dress in an upstairs bedroom at Eugene Muse Mitchell's two-story home with its white columns and cool, high-ceilinged rooms. Margaret

wore a knee-length georgette gown. The pansy-purple gown was in high style in 1925. Medora wrote: "That afternoon she had the glow that makes all brides beautiful. Hers was a beauty with an elfin touch, a Puckish smile and that incalculable quality called charm.... Peggy didn't want a slow-drag wedding and we stepped lively down the aisle. Afterwards we all raced to their small apartment" (Perkerson, in her papers at the University of Georgia, as cited in Walker, pages 124–125).

*Wedding reception of John R. Marsh and Margaret Mitchell.* The friends of John R. Marsh and Margaret Mitchell catered their wedding reception at the Crescent Avenue apartment that John had been renting. "The Dump" would now be the home of the married couple.

On July 5, 1925, Margaret and John boarded a train to the mountain region of Georgia. The couple spent their honeymoon in at the lovely, secluded Linger Longer Lodge. Their cabin was one that the Georgia Power Company owned and used by its publicity department to entertain editors and executives (Walker, pages 124–125).

*John R. Marsh's later illnesses.* John Marsh's health was never good. Before the age of three, two serious illnesses almost killed the boy. His sister Frances believed the illnesses and the gentle care he received help make him the giving, sensitive, loving person he was (Pyron, page 187). Pyron described John in this way: "He was dyspeptic: strange digestive problems plagued him constantly. Nameless ailments sapped his strengths all his life, but some of them bore terrifying names, like "myocardial infarction." Long before his massive heart attack, however, he regularly spent vacations in the hospital between bouts of sickroom care at home. In no way did his life resonate more with his beloved's than in their tears and failings in physical health. It proved an extraordinary bond, critical to their union" (Pyron, page 185).

1. John's hiccoughs after his engagement to Margaret Mitchell in December of 1924 resulted in several weeks of hospitalization and of a diagnosis of epilepsy. Because of this diagnosis, the engaged couple decided never to have children in order not to pass the disorder to another (Edwards, pages 118–119).

2. John entered the Veterans' Hospital for a complete physical examination after his release from the hospital and after the bout with hiccoughs subsided. The doctors surprised him with their conclusion: the battle with hiccoughs was a result of his military service and were psychosomatic in origin. Although he had not actually served in the trenches, witnessing so many mangled men dying in his medical unit and hearing the unending

115—U. S. Veterans Hospital No. 48, Atlanta, Ga.

As a veteran, John R. Marsh received treatment at the Veterans Hospital in Atlanta. This 1944 postcard shows Government Hospital number 48, which had 285 beds and cared for veterans of all wars. (Curteich-Chicago [C. T. Art Colortone] Postcard and R. and R. News, Atlanta, Georgia.)

sound of explosives had caused a severe nervous condition; this information was on his medical records and was on his discharge papers. The government was willing to pay him a pension each month for his "service-oriented psychosomatic illness."

Even though Margaret and John would have a limited income, John did not want to take the pension. Stephens Mitchell — in his capacity as a lawyer for John — advised John not to take the small monthly pension. Stephens indicated that some people might attach a stigma to one having a mental or emotional disorder. He advised John to struggle on financially without the compensation from the United States Army. Stephens thought that the diagnosis might someday "be misunderstood and embarrass you" (Edwards, pages 118–119).

John did not accept the compensation. The Marshes continued happily along their way without the additional funds.

3. John faced hospitalization again in May of 1927 after Stephens Mitchell's May 3, 1927, marriage to Caroline Louise Reynolds. John's weight had dropped from 163 to 145 in the previous weeks; the cause was unknown. He became weak, and the doctors could not determine a cause. He could

not lift his head from the pillow without severe nausea.

John remained in the hospital until June. The doctors could not explain the illness, but they suspected undulant fever. After two weeks of resting at home following his weeks of hospital care, John was finally able to resume his work at Georgia Power (Edwards, pages 142–143).

4. John's seizures from what the doctors had diagnosed as epilepsy began to evidence themselves again. Speculation was that John's two full-time jobs— editing *Gone with the Wind* and working full time at Georgia Power — had perhaps hastened the recurrence of the seizures. Most of the seizures had not required hospitalization, but Margaret felt guilty because her book may have caused such a strain on John's health (Edwards, pages 226–227).

5. In September of 1937 a rumor began to fly about John's health. A Hollywood column reported that John R. Marsh was a victim of shell shock suffered from his service during World War I; the rumor even suggested that John had a nervous disorder. John and Margaret never determined the source of this rumor.

Margaret wrote to their friend Edwin Granberry and told him about the incident. Edwin was teaching at Rollins College in Winter Park, Florida. They

THE CLOISTER, SEA ISLAND BEACH, GEORGIA

3863-29

John R. Marsh and Margaret Mitchell stayed in 1945 at Georgia's exclusive Cloister on Sea Island. (C. T. American Art, Chicago.)

accepted an invitation to visit Mabel and him while they were there staying in their hotel and relaxing later in the year (Edwards, pages 237–238).

6. Edwin and Mabel invited John and Margaret to come to a small party they were giving on Christmas Eve in 1936. Margaret informed them that John might suffer a small seizure. If she had to place a spoon between John's lips during a seizure, Edwin and Mabel should try to distract the guests. Fortunately no such occasion arose (Edwards, pages 257–258).

7. John R. Marsh entered the hospital soon upon his return to Atlanta; it was necessary for him to undergo a hemorrhoid operation. Both John and Margaret were embarrassed about the condition and neglected to report why John was in the hospital. Their silence about the matter caused many to speculate about his condition and conceive it as being worse than it really was (Edwards, page 259).

8. John's health condition did not improve. By the spring of 1938 the strain of working on the copyright issues of *Gone with the Wind*, of having helped Margaret to finish editing the book, and of continuing to work full time had resulted in exhaustion. By the fall of 1938, John weighed 132 pounds. His labored breathing and his low energy level worried Margaret and others about him.

9. John managed to remain out of the hospital

during the 1939 Atlanta premiere of *Gone with the Wind*. Margaret spent three weeks in the hospital in January of 1940 recuperating from surgery for abdominal adhesions.

John, however, seemed to be in more precarious health than Margaret. He was running high fevers and feeling listless. The doctors suspected undulant fever and hospitalized him. Tests did not confirm a diagnosis. For six weeks he was extremely weak, but no one seemed to know what was wrong with him (Edwards, pages 293).

10. In December of 1945 John was feeling tired. He had suffered high fevers and weakness since June. Again the doctors were mystified. Margaret and he decided to get away for a few days. They went to the Cloister Hotel at Sea Island for a few days. John went to bed as soon as they reached the hotel.

Within an hour John suffered a severe heart attack. The hotel had no doctor. Sea Island had no doctor. Margaret Mitchell was able to secure the station wagon belonging to the Cloister and take John R. Marsh to Brunswick, Georgia. Even though he gained prompt admittance to the hospital, he nearly died the next day — Christmas Day. Slowly he began to progress (Edwards, pages 318–320, 321–322).

It was three weeks, however, before he was able

to endure the trip back to Piedmont Hospital in Atlanta. In November of 1948, Edwards described Marsh as being "at death's door" (Edwards, page 328).

By the spring of 1949 the world of Margaret Mitchell and John R. Marsh was still small. Occasionally John felt able to cross the street and to have dinner at the Piedmont Driving Club. Sometimes they would even ask that their meal be brought to them at their home by a waiter at the Driving Club (Edwards, page 330).

*John R. Marsh and the death of Margaret Mitchell.* John R. Marsh and Margaret Mitchell had planned to attend a movie on the evening of August 11, 1949, at the Peachtree Arts Theater. The movie was *A Canterbury Tale.*

A car driven by Hugh D. Gravitt struck Margaret as they crossed Peachtree Street. John held her in his arms and crooned, "My poor, poor Baby." He requested that the ambulance take her to Grady Hospital, to which Margaret had made sizeable donations.

John wanted to remain at her side, but occasionally the staff persuaded him to leave for a little rest. When she died on August 15, 1949, John R. Marsh was not the first to know.

John had gone home for a meal, to dictate a letter to his family, and to rest because the doctors were contemplating surgery for Margaret after lunch. Bessie Berry Jordan was preparing his lunch when Dr. W. C. Waters from Grady Hospital called to tell John that Margaret had died. Bessie did not allow John to take the call or to receive visitors until she had served his lunch; Bessie later told others that she did not hear even a whimper from John when Stephens shared the news with him. John later went about preparing the memorial service and the burial (Walker, page 506–507).

*Burning the papers of Margaret Mitchell on August 18, 1939.* Walker indicates that the day after the funeral, John R. Marsh and Bessie Jordan began carrying Margaret Mitchell's papers that they intended to destroy to the back yard of Della Manta apartment house; they also took the clothing and the shoes that Margaret Mitchell had worn the night she was struck by the car. The two would burn these items in a wire basket (Walker, page 511).

This account differs from that of Edwards. Edwards indicates that Eugene Carr, the custodian of the Della Manta Apartments, helped Bessie Jordan and John R. Marsh take the papers to the basement of the 1258 Piedmont Avenue apartment building. The trio burned the papers in the furnace there (Edwards, page 336).

Wherever the destruction of Mitchell's papers occurred, their demise was at her instruction in November of 1948. The five-page, longhand document does not indicate that her papers are to be burned. She did, however, convey this request orally to her brother Stephens (Edwards, page 328; Walker, page 500; Farr, page 226). John followed these oral instructions from Margaret Mitchell to Stephens Mitchell.

*John R. Marsh's will of August 24, 1939, as it relates to Margaret Mitchell.* Only a few days after the burial of Margaret Mitchell John R. Marsh wrote a new will and signed it. As did those about him, he, too, must have wondered if his heart would survive the shock. He left all rights of all kinds and all royalties from *Gone with the Wind* to Stephens Mitchell, Margaret's brother. In the case of Stephens dying before John, John gave these rights and royalties to Stephens's two sons.

The Atlanta–Fulton County Public Library, founded originally as the Carnegie Public Library in Atlanta by Eugene Muse Mitchell and others, received the awards and mementos belonging to Margaret Mitchell. These items included Mitchell's typewriter. Other items relating to Mitchell included a ten thousand dollar donation to Grady Hospital, where Mitchell stayed before her death, and one thousand dollar donation to the Margaret Mitchell Library in Fayetteville, Georgia (Walker, page 509 and the Will of John R. Marsh).

*Walker Terrace Home of John R. Marsh.* On Christmas Eve of 1949 John R. Marsh moved into a house on Walker Terrace. The house had an attached apartment. Bessie Berry Jordan would live in the apartment so that John could have the help he needed. It was in this Walker Terrace home that John R. Marsh would die (Edwards, page 337).

*John R. Marsh's Death on May 5, 1952.* John R. Marsh had had several visitors on the weekend preceding Monday, May 5, 1952. He sat up reading for a while. At 11:00 P.M. Bessie heard him calling for help.

John had a heart seizure. Bessie got him to bed and called the doctor and an ambulance. She remained at his bedside until help arrived. It was too late for John. His will left instructions on what he wanted to happen next (Edwards, pages 337–338).

## Marsh, (Mrs.) John R.

Despite her marriage to John R. Marsh on July 4, 1925, Margaret Mitchell did not follow the accepted custom of changing her last name to that of her husband's. On the front door of "The Dump" she tacked two calling cards: "Mr. John R. Marsh" and "Miss Margaret Mitchell." Margaret Mitchell still loved to shock (Walker, page 132).

Her writings were under the name Margaret

Mitchell. Her autographs followed the same style. Although she had used the names Margaret Upshaw and Peggy Upshaw for a while after her marriage to Berrien Kinnard ("Red") Upshaw, she followed no such pattern after her second marriage.

## Marsh, Katharine *see* Bowden, Katharine Marsh

## Marsh, Mary Toup

In 1889 at the age of twenty-three, Mary Toup married Millard Fillmore Marsh, who had moved to Maysville, Kentucky, from "the Kentucky hinterland of his birth." The thirty-four year-old lawyer also served as editor of *The Maysville Bulletin* (Pyron, pages 186–187).

The Toup family lived on the main residential street in Maysville in a big Victorian house. Millard considered himself as "marrying up." The Marshes moved next door to the Toups. The Marshes had five children. In 1904 Millard Fillmore Marsh died at age forty-nine; Walker attributes his death to a case of typhoid fever. John R. Marsh had just turned eight (Walker, pages 40–41).

Mary Toup Marsh was a devoted parent. John, her second son, was severely ill before he reached the age of three. The other children were fond of saying that she healed him with her love. In an interview with Frances Marsh Zane for *Courier-Journal Magazine* (1987), she noted that the love of Mary Toup Marsh shaped the man John, who was "sensitive, always giving to others some of that life-giving love he had received from her."

All five of Mary Toup Marsh's children won academic honors and put themselves through school. These five also went to graduate school (Pyron, pages 186–188).

*Mary Toup Marsh's round robin letters.* Mary Toup Marsh encouraged a warm, loving relationship among her children and with herself. She wanted her children to remain close to each other throughout her life. To foster the independence and ensure the loyalty, she started something she called "round robin letters" when they began to move away from home. She used this communication system for more than twenty years, until her death in 1950 (Walker, page 43).

With the "round robin letters," Mary Toup Marsh would write a letter and send it to the oldest child. That child would read it and enclose it with a letter to the next oldest family member. This process of communication kept the family in touch.

John wrote an emotional letter to his mother on Thanksgiving Day of 1923. It included the following: "I do have you to be thankful for and there's no harm in telling. As I get older and see other families and other young people who have grown up in other families, I come more and more to appreciate my own" (Walker, page 43).

The bonds among the family members were readily apparent. When John R. Marsh had a heart attack on a trip to Sea Island on December 24, 1945, his siblings Henry, Gordon, and Frances arrived to visit him in the hospital in Brunswick (Walker, page 484).

*Mary Toup Marsh's correspondence from John before his marriage.* John R. Marsh was very open with his mother about his love for Margaret Mitchell and about her choosing Berrien Kinnard ("Red") Upshaw instead of him. He admitted missing her and wishing she had been present to share his feelings, in a September 6, 1922, after Margaret Mitchell's marriage earlier in the month: "Dearest Mother, there were many times when I wanted you terribly. No one else could have taken your place…. [S]ince *you* weren't here and no one else could take your place I went through it with my head up and barrels of cheerio for the entertainment of the mob. We're all children even when we grow up, I suppose, and we don't want nobody else but our mothers some times" (Pyron, pages 191–192).

*Mary Toup Marsh's letters from John announcing his marriage plans.* In January of 1925, John wrote to his mother to tell her of his upcoming marriage. The couple planned to live in their own apartment — not in the Mitchell house as his father-in-law wanted; he explained to his mother their need for their own place. John continued to write his mother loving letters through the years (Pyron, pages 198, 201).

In 1928 Mary Toup Marsh paid her son and his wife a visit. She brought her granddaughter and namesake Mary with her. John rented an apartment for their guests. Their relationship was warm (Walker, page 53).

*Care of Mary Toup Marsh.* John Marsh and his brother Henry supported their mother Mary Toup Marsh after she moved to Wilmington, Delaware, in her later years. The two also supported their sister Frances until her 1927 marriage (Walker, page 171).

Their expenses in caring for their mother was a financial strain on both young men. Still, when John was able to do so, he wanted to share his and Margaret's good fortune with her. Their first large purchase after the payments for *Gone with the Wind* came in was for John's mother. They not only purchased an automobile for her, but they also engaged a chauffeur. Margaret and John paid for this driver to take her wherever she wanted to go and whenever she wanted to go for the rest of her life (Walker, page 306).

Like Margaret Mitchell and John R. Marsh, Mary Toup Marsh had health problems. She let John know that she had fallen and injured her hand (Walker, page 481).

John R. Marsh provided for his mother in his will.

## Marsh, Millard Fillmore (1855–1904)

In 1889 at the age of thirty-four, Millard Fillmore Marsh married twenty-three-year-old Mary Toup. A lawyer and editor of *The Maysville Bulletin*, Millard had moved to Maysville from "the Kentucky hinterland of his birth." Millard often referred to the union as "marrying up" (Pyron, pages 186–188).

The couple had five children: Katharine, Henry, John, Frances, and Ben Gordon. Both Millard and his wife Mary Toup encouraged education for their children.

In 1904, forty-nine-year-old Millard Fillmore Marsh died suddenly. He had become very ill on the day after Christmas with what appeared to be a mild attack of typhoid fever.

The area residents admired the editor of the local newspaper for his intelligence and his unselfishness. The modest man had so many friends that at his funeral service on the bitterly cold Sunday afternoon of January 1, 1905, they filled the church to overflowing.

*The Evening Bulletin* on December 30, 1904, described Millard Fillmore Marsh as a "good, kind, gentle Christian man, generous to a fault and greatly beloved by his colleagues." His service was in the Christian Church in Maysville, Kentucky (Walker, pages 40–41).

## Martin, Harold

Harold Martin wrote of the 1939 Atlanta premiere of *Gone with the Wind*. In his own book Richard Barksdale Harwell quoted from Martin's description of the event. Much of Atlanta agreed with Martin's assessment of the occasion as being "Atlanta's Most Brilliant Event."

## Maud

Margaret Mitchell adopted another kitten after the one that she and John dubbed *Count Dracula*. The couple called this new kitten *Maud*.

Maud had come to them from a neighbor, Mrs. West. Mrs. West had rescued Maud from a sewer, and she brought the little animal to the back door of the Marshes' apartment (Walker, page 495). Thinking the animal might be a good sickroom companion for John, Margaret took in the pet in 1946 (Farr, page 218).

Earlier, John had talked to Mr. West, who had told him about a woman with a questionable reputation. John — in jest — named their new kitten *Maud*. Margaret, too, grew fond of John's pet.

The couple told the *Atlanta Journal* — at the suggestion of Margaret's personal secretary Margaret Baugh — that the cat had received its name from Maud in Alfred Lord Tennyson's writing, rather than from a woman who worked in a house of ill repute. Margaret even posed for a 1947 photograph with Maud. The *Atlanta Journal* used this photograph of Maud and Margaret — probably her last photograph before her death in August of 1949 — on the cover of the *Sunday Magazine* of December 14, 1947 (Walker, pages 495–495).

About the time that John Marsh was ready to move into his home on Walker Terrace in 1950, Maud became lost. John offered a generous award for Maud's return, but it was without success. John particularly missed the cat because of his loss of Margaret a few months before. The Atlanta papers carried the disappearance of Maud on their front pages. Maud never reappeared (Walker, page 515).

***See also*** **Count Dracula.**

## Mauldin, Bill

Margaret corresponded with many of the overseas soldiers. In a May 1945 cartoon appearing in newspapers throughout the nation, the Pulitzer Prize–winning artist Bill Mauldin showed a soldier "Somewhere in Italy" licking his pencil and writing a letter to "Miss Mitchell." Margaret thanked Mauldin in a May 14, 1945, letter (now housed at the University of Georgia) for mentioning her name in the same breath as these men who serve. She commented that Mauldin's cartoon had "raised her stock with youngsters to extravagant heights" (Edwards, page 311).

## Mays, Benjamin

As president of Morehouse College, Benjamin Mays worked with Margaret Mitchell to provide anonymous scholarships to Morehouse students. Ira Joe Johnson and William G. Pickens wrote about Margaret Mitchell's contributions in their book *Benjamin E. Mays and Margaret Mitchell: A Unique Legacy in Medicine*.

***See also*** **Johnson, Ira Joe; King, Martin Luther Jr.**

## McCaig, Donald

The trustees for the estate of Margaret Mitchell selected Donald McCaig to prepare a sequel to *Gone with the Wind*. Originally, they had negotiated with Pat Conroy — who had prepared the preface to the 60th Anniversary Edition of *Gone with the Wind* — to write the sequel. The parties involved, however, did not arrive at a satisfactory arrangement. After their failure to reach an agreement with Conroy, the trustees selected McCaig to write the book after they read his own Civil War novel, *Jacob's Ladder*. McCaig is perhaps best known for his work with *All Things Considered* on National Public Radio, but he has more than a dozen honors and noteworthy books of fiction, nonfiction, and poetry to his credit.

The 60-plus-year-old McCaig abandoned in 1971 his lucrative profession in New York advertisement to live on a sheep farm he and his wife, Anne, had established. The rural ranch where they raised sheep and trained border collies was near Williamsville, a Virginia town of 16 in Highland County. McCaig admitted his income dropped 90 percent in the first year, but he supplements his income by renting as a writer's retreat a shepherd's cottage—complete with outdoor toilet—on the farm; in the early 2000s he speculated that any farmer in the area would do well to earn $10,000 per year.

St. Martin's Press published his *Rhett Butler's People*, the second sequel to *Gone with the Wind*. The publisher ordered an advance run of 1,000,000 copies upon its publication (Fedo).

*See also* **Ripley, Alexandra; *Scarlett: The Sequel*.**

## McDaniel, Hattie

One of those cast members who was conspicuously absent from the 1939 Atlanta premiere of *Gone with the Wind* was Hattie McDaniel. Hattie played "Mammy" in the film, but she did not attend any premiere events in Atlanta on December 13–16, 1939.

McDaniel would, however, attend the Academy Awards ceremonies in February of 1940. At this event she would receive an Oscar for Best Supporting Actress; she would be the first African American to receive such a tribute from the American Academy of Motion Picture Arts and Sciences.

McDaniel cited her reason for not attending the 1939 Atlanta premiere of *Gone with the Wind* as being the segregation laws in Georgia at that time. She would not be able to stay in the hotels where the "white" cast and crew members stayed. The Loew's Theatre would not allow her to sit with the other cast members. Other conspicuously absent cast and crew members were Victor Fleming and Leslie Howard, who played Ashley Wilkes in the film ("Hattie McDaniel." *Encyclopedia of World Biography*).

*Margaret Mitchell telegrams Hattie McDaniel during the 1939 Atlanta premiere of Gone with the Wind.* Margaret was concerned to find that Hattie

On January 25, 2006, the United States Postal Service issued a postage stamp honoring Hattie McDaniel in its Black Heritage Series. McDaniel appears in the dress she wore when she received an Academy Award for her role in *Gone with the Wind*.

McDaniel would not be attending the 1939 Atlanta premiere of *Gone with the Wind*. Unlike the other African American cast members, McDaniel had at least received an invitation. McDaniel had simply chosen "not to visit the segregated city, where she could not stay in the same hotel nor eat at the same table with the white actors." Mitchell's thoughtful, sincere telegram to McDaniel stated how sorry she was that "Mammy" would not be attending the premiere (Walker, page 423).

*Hattie McDaniel's (1898–1952) biography.* Hattie McDaniel was born in Wichita, Kansas, in 1898. She was the thirteenth child of Susan Holbert McDaniel and Henry McDaniel, a Baptist minister. Hattie's first performances were in church choirs when she was just a child.

The McDaniel family moved to Denver, Colorado, when Hattie was 15 years old. When she was 18, she won an award for drama; the Women's Christian Temperance Union sponsored the event. Her older brother Otis took her on tour; her parents, however, objected to her performances with his tent show.

McDaniel may have been the first African American to sing on the radio. In the 1920s she sang in the South at fraternal order conventions; in addition she appeared on the vaudeville circuits, in clubs, and in Jerome Kern and Oscar Hammerstein's *Show Boat*.

McDaniel wanted to work in films. She began by going to Hollywood in 1932 and working as an extra. She appeared in sixty films over the next seventeen years— one of which was *Gone with the Wind*. Even though she received an Academy Award — the first African American to do so—for her role, she had to augment her income with vaudeville tours.

McDaniel appeared on such radio programs as *Amos 'n' Andy*, *Eddie Cantor*, and *Rudy Vallee*; she also starred as Beulah on *Fibber McGee and Molly*. Later McDaniel starred in the television series *The Beulah Show*. She found, however, that she had breast cancer after only three episodes of the program.

Hattie's congenial, subservient demeanor in films, in radio, and in television did not reflect her moderate activism. She chaired the African American wing of the Hollywood Victory Committee, helped organize entertainment events for black troops, and promoted education fund-raising for African Americans. She brought — and won — a racial discrimination suit related to her purchase of a house in the 1940s ("Hattie McDaniel." *Dictionary of American Biography*).

Hattie McDaniel had three husbands. Howard J. Hickman, her first husband, died in 1915; they had been married four years. Her second marriage to Nym Lankford lasted from 1922 until 1938; the marriage ended in divorce. Her third husband was Larry C. Williams, an interior decorator; she divorced him in December 1950 after their wedding in June of 1949 ("Hattie McDaniel." NNDB).

Hattie McDaniel's star appears on the Hollywood Walk of Fame. One of her last wishes before her death from breast cancer was that her ex-husband Larry Williams receive $1 after her death; the bulk of her $10,000 estate was to go to her actor-brother Sam "Deacon" McDaniel ("Hattie McDaniel." *Dictionary of American Biography*).

Even though McDaniel wanted her burial in Hollywood, the rules prevented her burial in the segregated cemeteries at that time. In 1999, however, Hattie McDaniel's wish came true with the erection of a pink-and-gray monument to her in the Hollywood Forever Cemetery. Her other monuments include the 200 films in which she appeared and the "now unlocked doors for African Americans that she helped open" (Davis and Hunt, page 127).

*The United States Postal Service honors Hattie McDaniel with a stamp.* The United States Postal Service issued a 39-cent stamp to honor Hattie McDaniel. The stamp was a part of the Black Heritage Series; also in the series is Dr. Martin Luther King, Jr.

## McFedyen, Bernice

Bernice McFedyen and Margaret Mitchell's longtime friend Courtenay Ross married in October of 1920. He was in the military in 1922 when Margaret Mitchell and Berrien Kinnard ("Red") Upshaw married; both he and his wife were in the Philippines at the time and did not attend the wedding.

## McFedyen, Courtenay Ross *see* Ross, Courtenay

## McPherson, James Birdseye (1828–1864)

Union General James McPherson lost his life in the Battle of Atlanta and was featured in Atlanta's famous cycloramic painting called *The Battle of Atlanta*.

McPherson was top in his class at West Point from 1849 to 1853; Robert E. Lee was president of the academy at that time. Secretary of War Jefferson Davis was the commencement speaker in 1853 when McPherson graduated.

After McPherson graduated, West Point hired him as an engineering instructor. Later he received different assignments: supervising river improvements, harbors, and seacoast defenses on the coasts of the Atlantic and the Pacific Oceans.

During the Civil War, McPherson commanded the XVII Corps during the Battle of Vicksburg. He received a furlough to return to Baltimore to marry Emily Hoffman, but General Grant recalled him to help plan the attack on Atlanta.

McPherson received orders to command the Army of Tennessee during the planning and conducting of the Battle of Atlanta. Some Confederate rebels, however, shot and killed the 35-year-old McPherson ("James Birdseye McPherson").

## Memorial Day

John Alexander Logan commissioned the cycloramic painting *The Battle of Atlanta*, a favorite display of Margaret Mitchell. Margaret would study the painting on display in Atlanta and identify the points and people portrayed.

He has another achievement to his credit. He helped to begin the national holiday of Memorial Day. As a veteran of the Civil War, Logan acknowledged the sacrifices of others. His action in beginning the holiday reminds others to recognize those who died in serving their country ("Memorial Day History").

***See also*** **Atlanta Cyclorama;** *The Battle of Atlanta* **painting; Logan, John Alexander "Blackjack."**

## Miller, Edmund

Edmund Miller lived at the Georgian Terrace

OFFICERS ROW, FORT MC PHERSON, ATLANTA, GA.

Fort McPherson in Atlanta took its name from James Birdseye McPherson; this is Officer Row. With her volunteer work with the American Red Cross, Margaret Mitchell often hosted events for the soldiers of Fort McPherson. (I. F. P. Company, Atlanta, Georgia.) (The company is longer in operation.)

Hotel. When no car came to take Olivia de Havilland to the ball on December 14, 1939, Miller secured a hotel car for her and accompanied her to the ball. Their entrance to the affair was unconventional; more about this arrival is available in the entry for de Havilland (Farr, pages 6–7).

### Mitchell, Alexander Stephens (1896–1983)

Alexander Stephens Mitchell was the second child of Eugene Muse Mitchell and Maybelle Stephens Mitchell. Born in Atlanta in 1896, Stephens never knew his older brother Russell Stephens Mitchell (1894–1894), who died in infancy. His younger sister was Margaret Munnerlyn Mitchell (1900–1949). (These genealogical facts are consistent in most reference sources. An exception, however, is Edwards's *Road to Tara*, where she refers to Alexander Stephens Mitchell as "Stephens Alexander Mitchell" on page 16 and throughout the book.)

*Occupation and activities of Alexander Stephens Mitchell.* Stephens Mitchell attended elementary school with his sister Margaret Mitchell for a few years. With a six-year age difference, however, he soon found himself separated from her in education. The two remained close friends for life.

Stephens Mitchell attended the University of Georgia. He pledged Beta Delta Chapter of Delta Tau Delta fraternity. Stephens, like his father, Eugene Muse Mitchell, entered the law profession; both Mitchell men practiced in Atlanta.

Alexander Stephens Mitchell served as president of the Atlanta Bar Association and as the editor of the *Atlanta Historical Society Bulletin*. Stephens was a member of the Catholic Layman's Association, a member of the Sacred Heart Catholic Church in Atlanta, and a part of the Vincentian Society (Society of St. Vincent De Paul). He was interested in history and the church; he often gave of his time and of his service to charitable causes. Stephens served as a first lieutenant in the 326th Regiment of the United States Army during World War I.

*Alexander Stephens Mitchell and Caroline Louise Reynolds (1902–1950).* Alexander Stephens Mitchell and Caroline Louise ("Carrie Lou") Reynolds married on May 3, 1927. The daughter of Joseph Shewmake Reynolds and Fannie Hansberger Reynolds, Carrie Lou was originally from Augusta; her family moved to Atlanta in 1916. The noted artist Glascock Reynolds (1903–1967) was Carrie Lou's brother.

*The surviving children of Alexander Stephens Mitchell and Caroline Louise Reynolds Mitchell.* Carrie and Stephens Mitchell's two children who survived childbirth were Eugene Muse Mitchell (1931–2007) and Joseph Reynolds Mitchell.

*The second marriage of Stephens Mitchell.* After the death of Caroline Louise Reynolds Mitchell

(1902–1950), Stephens Mitchell married Anita Benteen (1902–1978) in 1952. Again, Stephens survived his wife ("Alexander Stephens Mitchell").

*Stephens Mitchell's death and burial.* Alexander Stephens Mitchell died on May 12, 1983. His burial — like that of his mother, his father, his brother-in-law, and his sister — was in Oakland Cemetery in Atlanta. Later his son Eugene Muse Mitchell would also be buried in the Oakland Cemetery in Atlanta ("Alexander Stephens Mitchell").

### Mitchell, Anita Benteen (1902–1978)

Anita Benteen Mitchell (1902–1978) was the daughter of Civil War Veteran Frederick W. Benteen and Catherine L. Benteen. Anita married Alexander Stephens Mitchell on June 26, 1952. Her burial plot is in the Oakland Cemetery in Atlanta ("Anita Benteen Mitchell").

### Mitchell, Caroline Louise Reynolds (1902–1950)

Caroline Louise Reynolds ("Carrie Lou") married Alexander Stephens Mitchell. She was the daughter of Joseph Shewmake and Fannie Hansberger Reynolds. Carrie's brother Glascock Reynolds (1903–1967) was a noted artist ("Caroline Louise Reynolds Mitchell").

### Mitchell, Carrie

Carrie Mitchell — not to be confused with "Carrie Lou" Mitchell, Stephens Mitchell's wife — did the ironing for John R. Marsh "for years" before John married Margaret Mitchell. After the marriage of Margaret Mitchell and John R. Marsh, Carrie continued to iron for the couple (Walker, pages 150–151).

### Mitchell, Deborah Margaret Sweet (1847–1887)

Deborah Sweet Mitchell was born in Gadsden County, Florida, in 1847. The daughter of William Charles Sweet (1817–1898) and his wife Mary Ann McKenzie Sweet (d. 1873), Deborah married Russell Crawford Mitchell (1837–1905). She and Russell were the grandparents of Margaret Mitchell and Alexander Stephens Mitchell.

At the time Deborah met her future husband, he was recovering from severe wounds received at the Battle of Sharpsburg (Antietam) in Thomasville, Georgia. It was the scars and ridges from these wounds that a young Margaret Mitchell would trace on his head during their visits.

Russell had attended Bowdon College. He practiced law in Texas until the war. After convalescing in Thomasville, R.C. returned to battle and fought until the end. At the end of the war, he returned to Florida and married Deborah Margaret Sweet on August 10, 1865.

After Russell had some personal disputes in Florida, he returned to his home in Atlanta. Deborah soon joined him there. He asked her if she wanted to remain in Atlanta or try to make their fortune in Texas. She preferred Atlanta.

The choice seemed to be a good one for them. Russell started with a lumber mill and then went into real estate. He became a wealthy man and even served as mayor of Atlanta.

Deborah gave birth to eleven children, the eldest of whom was Eugene Muse Mitchell (1866–1944). Eugene was a prominent historian and lawyer in Atlanta. He was the father of Russell Mitchell, Alexander Stephens Mitchell, Margaret Mitchell (1900–1949) and the husband of Mary Isabel "Maybelle" Stephens Mitchell (1872–1919). Margaret had taken her first name from her grandmother Deborah's middle name; her own middle name *Munnerlyn* came from the last name of some of her other family members.

Early in her life, Deborah Mitchell developed consumption. She died from the disease just after the age of 40. The contagious disease killed several of her children also. The gravesite for Deborah Margaret Sweet Mitchell is in Atlanta's Oakland Cemetery ("Deborah Margaret Sweet Mitchell").

### Mitchell, Eugene Muse (1866–1944)

Eugene Muse Mitchell (1866–1944) was the oldest of the eleven children of Deborah Margaret Sweet (1847–1887) and Confederate veteran Russell Crawford Mitchell (1837–1905).

Eugene Muse Mitchell was a respected Atlanta attorney and a prominent historian who was born and died in Atlanta. Like many of the others in his close family, his gravesite is in the Oakland Cemetery, Atlanta, Georgia.

Eugene Muse Mitchell married "Maybelle" Stephens of Atlanta in 1893. The couple had three children: Russell Stephens Mitchell (who died in infancy in 1894), Alexander Stephens Mitchell (1896–1955); and Margaret Mitchell (1900–1949).

*Eugene Muse Mitchell (1866–1944) and his young daughter Margaret Mitchell.* Eugene Mitchell believed his first role was as a provider for his family. His life was largely one of work. He also believed that he had community responsibilities and served on many boards and in many organizations. Eugene Mitchell, therefore, was away from home most of the time.

Mitchell loved his family, but he rarely expressed his love toward his children. He was quiet, reserved, and — according to his daughter — "brilliant" (Pyron, pages 15–16, 27, 37–38).

Eugene Muse Mitchell and Margaret Mitchell sit and look at her newly published *Gone with the Wind*. (Courtesy of the Atlanta-Fulton Public Library System's Special Collections Department.)

Once, when Maybelle Mitchell was away, Eugene chose to discipline his daughter himself. Margaret had written a play based on Thomas Dixon's *The Traitor.* She had not, however, given any recognition to Dixon or his book. "Not only did Eugene scold her harshly, he also gave her quite a spanking, so that, as Margaret went on to explain, 'I would never forget I must not take what wasn't mine,' and that 'plagiarism was exactly the same as stealing'" (Edwards, page 32).

*Eugene Muse Mitchell, Margaret Mitchell, and her courtship by Berrien Kinnard "Red" Upshaw.* Both Eugene Mitchell and his son Stephens were unimpressed with Margaret's beau Berrien Kinnard ("Red") Upshaw. Regardless, they decided the way to make sure that Margaret married Upshaw was to object to him; therefore they remained silent.

Margaret's father, however, emphatically objected to Upshaw when Margaret told him of their wedding plans. His objections did not prevent his daughter's going ahead with the ceremony and his giving Margaret away in the wedding ceremony.

Mitchell was even more upset about the relationship of his daughter and her husband after the marriage. Eugene was so distressed over the "inadvisable situation" that he took to his bed (Farr, pages 57–57).

*Eugene Muse Mitchell, Margaret Mitchell, and John R. Marsh.* Margaret Mitchell lived most of her life until 1925 with her father until she married John R. Marsh. Eugene Mitchell was more accepting of John R. Marsh than he had been of Berrien Kinnard ("Red") Upshaw.

*Eugene Muse Mitchell, Margaret Mitchell, and* Gone with the Wind. After the publication of *Gone with the Wind*, Eugene Muse Mitchell posed with his daughter and the new book. He looks pleased as he holds the book and stands close to his daughter ("Mitchell, Eugene Muse Mitchell [1866–1944]").

In an April 30, 1936, letter to Lois Cole, however, Margaret Mitchell reports a very different story. Margaret said her father reported that it seemed to him that "a sensible organization" [like the Book-of-the-Month Club?] might choose *Gone with the Wind* as one of its selections. Margaret said that her father had read her entire copy of *Gone with the Wind*. In her letter to Cole, Margaret quoted him as saying that "nothing in the world would induce him to read the book again and that nothing in the world except the fact that [Peggy] was his child induced him to read it originally" (Edwards, page 195).

Margaret valued her father's opinion. When John returned home, Margaret was despondent. She told him that her book was going to fail miserably as a book club selection. The failure of her book was going to embarrass Latham and everyone who had supported her efforts. John simply said that Margaret was "a fool" (Edwards, page 195).

## Mitchell, Eugene Muse (1931–2007)

Eugene Muse Mitchell, the son of Alexander Stephens and "Carrie" Reynolds Mitchell and the nephew of the author of *Gone with the Wind*, died at age 76 of multiple illnesses in 2007 in Farmington Hills, Michigan, where he resided. A retired government economist, Eugene Muse Mitchell requested his gravesite be in Oakland Cemetery, At-

lanta, Georgia — like that of many of his family — including his parents, grandparents, and the author Margaret Mitchell.

The obituary for Eugene Muse Mitchell reflects on Eugene the man. The article states that Mitchell's burial site was near Margaret Mitchell, "whose celebrity far exceeded his, yet whose penchant for quiet philanthropy in Atlanta he shared" ("Eugene Muse Mitchell [1931–2007]").

Ira Joe Johnson, author with William G. Pickens of the book *Benjamin E. Mays and Margaret Mitchell: A Unique Legacy in Medicine* (1996), commented on the philanthropy of this nephew of Margaret Mitchell: "Eugene Mitchell was not only a *Gone with the Wind* heir…. He also inherited his famous aunt's compassion for helping blacks and the poor with a quiet grace and dignity" (Ira Joe Johnson, as cited in the *Atlanta Journal Constitution* and quoted in "Eugene Muse Mitchell [1931–2007]").

Eugene Muse Mitchell received his name from his grandfather, Eugene Muse Mitchell (1866–1944). The younger Mitchell's parents, grandparents, one sister, and one brother died before him.

Virginia, his wife, and Joseph, his brother, survived him. Joseph and Eugene were the only surviving children of Margaret Mitchell's brother Stephens Mitchell. An attorney, Stephens managed the rights to his late sister's masterpiece until his own death in 1983. At that time, Eugene and Joseph became the heirs.

The younger Eugene Muse Mitchell donated $1.5 million in 2002 to Morehouse College to endow a chair in the humanities in Margaret Mitchell's name ("Morehouse College Receives $1.5 Million from Nephew of Late *Gone with the Wind* Author Margaret Mitchell"). In 2005 he quietly made another donation to Morehouse (Vejnoska).

At the 2007 death of Eugene Muse Mitchell, Dr. John E. Maupin, Jr., president of Morehouse School of Medicine, made a statement about the deceased: "From quietly giving support to black students (2005) to an endowed scholarship that bears his aunt's name (2002), Eugene Mitchell made it possible for Margaret Mitchell's legacy to continue to help train minority physicians, leaving an impact on the Morehouse School of Medicine that will endure" (Vejnoska).

*Eugene Muse Mitchell (1931–2007) Estate.* Alexander Stephens Mitchell had created in the mid–1970s two trusts for his two sons, Joseph and Eugene. All the profits from royalties of *Gone with the Wind* would go into the trusts.

Stephens Mitchell had asked Paul Anderson, Sr. — his former law partner — to serve on a three-person committee with his two sons. The committee would direct the trust and would serve to protect and exercise the copyright. Several sequels have already been considered by the committee; these considerations— to name a few — include the publication of *The Wind Done Gone, Rhett Butler's People,* and *Scarlett* (Vejnoska).

Eugene, Joseph, and the Trust Company Bank, as executor of Stephens Mitchell's estate, also considered whether Jane Bonner Peacock should publish the letters (1919–1921) of Margaret Mitchell to Allen Edee in the form of a book: *A Dynamo Going to Waste* (1985). Eugene Muse Mitchell (1931–2007), Joseph Mitchell, and Trust Company Bank gave her the rights to go ahead with her project (Mitchell, Edee, Peacock, "Acknowledgments," *A Dynamo Going to Waste* [1985]).

A second book (1994) that the executor and committee approved— among others— was *Benjamin E. Mays and Margaret Mitchell: A Unique Legacy in Medicine.*" Co-authored by William G. Pickens and Ira Joe Johnson, the Mitchell Trusts Committee granted them permission to use Margaret Mitchell and Benjamin E. Mays' correspondence in the volume (Vejnosky).

Still another consideration of the executor and committee was the use of Margaret Mitchell's early writings in a volume by Jane Eskridge, with added information from Mary Rose Taylor. The resulting volume edited by Jane Eskridge was *Before Scarlett: Childhood Writings of Margaret Mitchell* (2000) (Vejnosky).

*Eugene Muse Mitchell (1931–2007), Historic Oakland Foundation, and Oakland Cemetery, Atlanta, Georgia.* Jill Vejnoska described Mitchell as being a "quiet, almost shy man by most accounts" who "made a gift that spoke volumes to Oakland Cemetery in 2004."

Vejnoska quotes Beaumont Allen, chair of the board of advisers of the Historic Oakland Foundation, regarding the donation. "He didn't really say, 'I want this to be anonymous,' he just said, 'Please don't make a big deal out of this,' Beaumont Allen … said of Mitchell's $667,000 donation. About Mitchell's wish to be buried at Oakland, Allen said, 'I do think he's coming home to be with the rest of the Mitchell family'" (Vejnoska).

David Moore, the executive director of the Oakland Cemetery, noted that most of the money that Mitchell gave to the Historic Oakland Foundation went toward the endowment of Oakland Cemetery. Moore believed that the message Mitchell's endowment sent was almost as important as the amount of the donation. Moore observed: "Giving directly to restoration efforts and operations is wonderful, but an endowment endures" (Vejnoska).

*Eugene Muse Mitchell's funeral and burial.* Although Eugene Muse Mitchell died on August 8, 2007, the final service was not until August 18. The services were at the Cathedral of Christ the King on Peachtree Road. His burial site was in Oakland Cemetery, Atlanta; this was the burial site of his father, grandfather, mother, and aunt ("Mitchell, Eugene Muse [1931–2007]").

## Mitchell, Joseph

This son of Alexander Stephens Mitchell still resides in Atlanta (2011). Stephens had one other son: Eugene Muse Mitchell. Joseph Mitchell has not been a public figure.

At the death of John R. Marsh and Stephens Mitchell — the older brother of Margaret Mitchell — a committee composed of Joseph Mitchell, Eugene Muse Mitchell, and the Trust Company Bank served as executor of Stephens Mitchell's estate. The committee made many difficult decisions (Mitchell, Edee, Peacock, "Acknowledgments," *A Dynamo Going to Waste* [1985]).

## Mitchell, Kitty

John R. Marsh had a sweetheart before Margaret Mitchell. Like Margaret, Kitty, too, was red-haired. From Bowling Green, Kentucky, Kitty studied at the University of Kentucky; it was there that John met her (Walker, page 47).

As he had done with Margaret, John began to proof Kitty's articles. Kitty's ambition was to become a writer and to return to her hometown to write on women's issues. John, evidently, planned to remain with her (Walker, page 49).

When the military shipped John R. Marsh to France, he wrote to his mother expressing his interest in Kitty. He told Mary, his mother, not to worry about the women overseas and him; he reminded her that one particular Kentucky girl (Kitty!) had made him forget that there were other women in the world (Walker, pages 52, 88).

According to Edwards, John had believed that he and Kitty were engaged. While he had been in France and England, however, Kitty married a businessman in Cuba. She had gone to Havana to live (Edwards, pages 83–84).

John wrote to Kitty to tell her of his love for Margaret a few weeks before his marriage to Margaret on July 4, 1925. Kitty did not reply immediately. Finally she wrote to tell John about her marriage and relocation. She congratulated him on his impending marriage (Edwards, pages 116, 117). Edwards indicates that Kitty Mitchell "had not had the depth of feeling for John that he had had for her" (Edwards, page 118).

In a September 1922 letter to his mother, just after Margaret's wedding to Berrien Kinnard

("Red") Upshaw, John wrote to his mother that he loved Margaret Mitchell more than he had ever loved Kitty (Walker, pages 52, 88). In May of 1928 Kitty contacted John. Walker indicates that 1928 was ten years after John had heard from her last (Walker, page 174). Edwards, however, had spoken of Kitty's congratulatory note to John just before his 1925 wedding. The 1925 correspondence made the period of ten years without contact impossible (Edwards, pages 116–117).

Kitty was writing to tell him that she and her ten-year-old son would be coming through Atlanta on their way to Bowling Green, Kentucky. She wanted to visit with John and his wife. When she arrived, Kitty was elegantly dressed. Her meticulously-groomed appearance and her expensive jewelry hinted at a prosperous environment.

Margaret, on the other hand, was concerned about her own appearance when she met their guests for the first time. She herself had gained weight and was wearing orthopedic shoes. She had no money for clothes at the time; Margaret wore the blue dress that her sister-in-law Frances Marsh Zane had given her (Walker, pages 174–175).

Kitty did not just "pass through"; she stayed a month with them in Atlanta. Her son became ill while she was there; the child was hospitalized for several weeks and Kitty remained with him. Margaret, John, and Kitty never saw each other after this, but the three of them continued to correspond (Walker, page 175).

*See also* Zane, Frances Marsh.

## Mitchell, Margaret Munnerlyn (1900–1949)

Margaret Munnerlyn Mitchell was born in Atlanta, Georgia; she was the youngest child of Eugene Muse Mitchell (1866–1944) and Mary Isabel ("Maybelle") Mitchell (1872–1919). Her maternal grandparents were John Stephens (1833–1896) and Annie Fitzgerald Stephens (1845–1934). Her paternal grandparents were Confederate veteran Russell Crawford Mitchell (1837–1905) and Deborah Sweet Mitchell (1847–1887).

Margaret Mitchell's two older brothers were Alexander Stephens Mitchell (1896–1983) and Russell Stephens Mitchell (1894–1894). All three children of Eugene and Maybelle Mitchell were born in Atlanta.

*Margaret Mitchell's elementary/high school education.* Margaret Mitchell completed her elementary school education in the public schools of Atlanta, Georgia. Talking with Civil War veterans, listening to Russell Crawford Mitchell's stories, and visiting historic sites in the Atlanta area increased her education. She completed high school at Washington Seminary.

*Margaret Mitchell's nickname.* Some people called *Margaret Munnerlyn Mitchell* by her given name only. Others began to use the nickname *Peggy Mitchell* when Margaret was about to enter high school. Still others used her nickname at times—but not at all times. Margaret Mitchell used the byline *Peggy Mitchell* for some of her articles; for other articles *Margaret Mitchell* was her byline.

*Margaret Mitchell's first engagement.* Margaret Mitchell became engaged to Clifford Henry during the summer before her first year at Smith College. One of Henry's stations was Camp Gordon, Georgia; Margaret Mitchell met him at a local event for the military. Clifford died in France in October of 1918 while Margaret was at Smith College.

*Margaret Mitchell's higher education (1918–1919).* Mitchell completed one year at Smith College, in Northampton, Massachusetts. She enrolled at Smith during 1918–1919. She came back to Atlanta, Georgia, after the end of the year to help her father after the death of her mother. She continued to attend events at Smith College even in her later years.

*Margaret Mitchell's mother dies.* In addition to the death of Clifford Henry in the fall of 1918, Margaret endured the loss of her mother, Mary Isabel/ Isabelle "Maybelle" Stephens Mitchell, who died of influenza in January of 1919. Margaret Mitchell returned to Atlanta to help her father at the end of the 1918–1919 year at Smith College.

*Margaret Mitchell's first marriage.* Margaret Mitchell and Berrien Kinnard ("Red") Upshaw married on September 2, 1922. Margaret changed her name to *Margaret Upshaw* for only a brief period of time. John R. Marsh served as best man in the ceremony.

*Margaret Mitchell's employment.* In 1922 Mitchell began working as a professional writer for the *Atlanta Journal.* At various times, she used the names *Margaret Mitchell, Peggy Mitchell,* and *Peggy Upshaw* for her stories. She was willing to try many things for a story. Patrick Allen collected some of her newspaper columns and stories in *Margaret Mitchell: Reporter* (2000).

*Margaret Mitchell's divorce and maiden name.* After the divorce of Margaret Mitchell and Red Upshaw on June 17, 1924, Margaret reverted to her maiden name. She sometimes used the name *Margaret Munnerlyn Mitchell* and sometimes the nickname *Peggy Mitchell.*

*Second marriage of Margaret Mitchell.* Margaret Mitchell and John R. Marsh married on July 4, 1925. They moved to 17 Crescent Avenue, Apartment #1—"The Dump"; Margaret placed two calling cards on the door: *Miss Margaret Mitchell* (on top) and *John R. Marsh* (below). Their marriage endured until Margaret Mitchell's 1949 accidental death.

*Margaret Mitchell and* Gone with the Wind *(the*

The United States Postal Service issued a one-cent postage stamp on June 30, 1986, honoring Margaret Mitchell. The stamp issue date was on the fiftieth anniversary of the publication of her book *Gone with the Wind*.

book). The writing of the manuscript for *Gone with the Wind* was an arduous affair. The impetus for the work may well have come from an accident that Margaret Mitchell suffered.

Harold Latham obtained the manuscript from Margaret Mitchell (probably at the Georgian Terrace Hotel). Macmillan offered her a contract.

*Speech at the Atlanta premiere of the film Gone with the Wind on December 15, 1939.* Margaret Mitchell's speech at the Loew's Grand Theatre on the night of the Atlanta premiere of the film *Gone with the Wind* was an unusual thing for Mitchell to do—not only because a premiere of a book based on her novel was a one time event but also because Margaret Mitchell did not usually make speeches and public appearances.

Attending the premiere — among others — was Harold Martin, a reporter for the *Atlantan Georgian*. In his article (later published in Richard Harwell's *Gone with the Wind as Book and Film*), Martin describes Mitchell as "small" and having "a white face and big eyes; Martin notes that at the time — just after the showing — Mitchell "appeared to be under a tremendous strain" (Harold Martin, page 149).

Martin includes Mitchell's speech as a part of his article, aptly titled "Atlanta's Most Brilliant Event." Margaret had begun her speech by thanking the audience — at least three-fourths of whom she considered friends—for their consideration and for their friendship. She acknowledged the importance of their friendship in adversity, but she expressed gratitude also for the friendship she had found during the "incredible success" that she had expe-

rienced; she addressed her appreciation to those present and to those that had been unable to attend: "the man at the grocery, the boys at the filling station, the folks on the newspapers" (Harold Martin, page 149).

Martin quotes Mitchell's words about the film: "Of this picture, I feel that the only expression adequate for use is that [we] have just come together through a great emotional experience.... I know I'm not the only one whose eyes have been wet tonight" (Harold Martin, page 149).

Mitchell commented publicly — and humorously — about David O. Selznick, "the man who made this picture" (Harold Martin, page 149). "All of you, I know, heard the jokes about the search for Scarlett — 'I'll see the picture when Shirley Temple gets old enough to play the role,' and all that sort of comment. But I want to pay my tribute to David O. Selznick for his stubbornness and determination in getting the Scarlett he wanted. He wanted a perfect cast, and to my mind, he got it." Margaret Mitchell made a sincere request to her audience: "be kind to my Scarlett" (Harold Martin, page 149).

*Margaret Mitchell's accidental death.* Mitchell seemed prone to accidents from an early age. She had a fear of cars. It is ironic that her accidental death was a result of her being struck by Hugh D. Gravitt.

*Margaret Mitchell on a United States postage stamp.* The United States Postal Service honored Margaret Mitchell on the fiftieth anniversary of the publication of *Gone with the Wind* by issuing a one-cent stamp in her honor. The ceremonies to accompany the issuance were at the Omni International Hotel in Atlanta, Georgia. The stamp is brownish vermilion in color. The Bureau of Engraving and Printing did the engraving. The stamps are in a pane of 100 and are perforated 11; they are in a plate block of 4 and a ZIP block of 4. Rona Adair designed the stamp. Errors include stamps without tagging (Davis and Hunt, page 256).

## Mitchell, Mary Isabel ("Maybelle") Stephens (1872–1919)

In 1892, "Maybelle" Stephens — the daughter of John Stephens (1833–1896) and Annie Fitzgerald Stephens (1844–1934) — became the wife of Eugene Muse Mitchell (1866–1944). The couple had three children — Russell Stephens Mitchell, Alexander Stephens Mitchell, and Margaret Mitchell.

*Mary Isabel ("Maybelle") Stephens Mitchell (1872–1919), death, and burial.* Mary Isabel ("Maybelle") Stephens Mitchell died in January of 1919 as a result of influenza. Margaret Mitchell took a train home to see her mother, but Maybelle died before Margaret's arrival. Margaret Mitchell's brother Alexander Stephens Mitchell, a first lieutenant in the 326th Regiment during World War I, had just returned from France. Maybelle's services were at Sacred Heart Catholic Church, of which she was a member. The burial was in Oakland Cemetery, Atlanta, Georgia ("Mitchell, Maybelle Isabelle Stephens: Find-a-Grave").

*Mary Isabel ("Maybelle") Stephens Mitchell's education.* Maybelle Mitchell graduated first in her class from the Atlanta Female Seminary, which has since closed. She graduated also from the Villa Maria Convent in Quebec.

*Mary Isabel ("Maybelle") Stephens Mitchell and her activities.* In 1893 Maybelle married the attorney and historian Eugene Muse Mitchell (1866–1944). Maybelle was interested in educational and intellectual movements in Atlanta. She served as president of a prominent women suffrage organization and of the Women's Study Club. She also served her church in many ways ("Mitchell, Maybelle Isabel Stephens: Find-a-Grave").

*Mitchell, "Maybelle" Isabel Stephens and the community's assessment of her.* The obituary of Maybelle Mitchell that appears at "Mitchell, Maybelle Isabelle Stephens: Find-a-Grave" indicates the high esteem of Maybelle in the community: "A woman of splendid education and of brilliant qualities of mind, as well as of a most lovable personality; she was always popular and always welcome in all efforts in which women were interested."

*Survivors of "Maybelle" Isabelle Stephens Mitchell.* Maybelle Mitchell had many survivors. These relatives included her husband; her mother (Mrs. John Stephens); three sisters, Mrs. Morgan Y. Gress of Jacksonville, Florida; Mrs. Edward Ney Morris of Greenwich, Connecticut; and Mrs. David T. Crockett of Atlanta; John and Alex Stephens, her brothers in Jacksonville, Florida; and her two children: 1st Lieutenant Alexander Stephens Mitchell and Margaret Munnerlyn Mitchell ("Mitchell, Maybelle Isabelle Stephens: Find-a-Grave"; "Obituary of Mary Isabel Mitchell," *Atlanta Constitution,* January 26, 1919, page 5). (Various sources spell "Maybelle" Mitchell's complete name in different ways. For instance her obituary uses *Isabel,* but her foot marker uses *Isabelle.*)

## Mitchell, Russell Crawford (1837–1905)

Confederate veteran Russell Crawford Mitchell was the paternal grandfather of Margaret Mitchell. Although he died when Margaret was only five years old, she remembered visiting him on Sunday afternoons, tracing the path left by a bullet to his head, and listening to him tell Civil War stories (Walker, pages 25–27).

Russell Crawford ("R.C.") Mitchell (1837–1905) was the fifth of nine children born to the Rev. Isaac Green Mitchell (1810–1881) and Mary Ann Dudley Mitchell (1808–1859). The Reverend Mitchell was a Methodist circuit rider.

R.C. lived most of his early life in Georgia. He received his postsecondary education at Bowden College in Georgia. In 1856 R.C. began practicing law in Texas. During the Civil War, he enlisted in the First Texas Infantry and was a part of the Texas Brigade led by Hood. He served under General Lee in many of the Virginia campaigns.

It was in the Battle of Sharpsburg (Antietam) that Russell Crawford Mitchell suffered severe wounds. Mitchell went to his brother's home in Thomasville, Georgia, to recuperate. He met Deborah Margaret Sweet Mitchell (1847–1887) from just across the Florida state line.

R.C. returned to battle after his convalescence. When the war was over, he returned to Florida to marry Deborah Sweet on August 10, 1865 ("Mitchell, Russell Crawford: Find-a-Grave").

*Russell Crawford Mitchell and his profession after the war.* By selling the cotton in which he invested to the North, R.C. made a fortune. After a heated dispute, however, he had to flee Florida. Later, Deborah Sweet Mitchell met him in Atlanta ("Mitchell, Russell Crawford: Find-a-Grave").

Instead of going to Texas, the Mitchell couple stayed in Atlanta, at the request of Deborah Sweet Mitchell. R.C. started a lumber mill in Atlanta and made investments in real estate. "Eventually, he became one of the wealthiest men in the city, and also served as mayor for a time" ("Mitchell, Russell Crawford: Find-a-Grave").

*Russell Crawford Mitchell and his progeny.* Deborah Sweet Mitchell and Russell Crawford Mitchell had eleven children. The oldest of these was Eugene Muse Mitchell (1866–1944); Eugene married Mary Isabel "Maybelle" Stephens, and they had three children — Russell Stephens Mitchell, Alexander Stephens Mitchell, and Margaret Mitchell ("Mitchell, Russell Crawford: Find-a-Grave").

*Russell Crawford Mitchell and his second marriage.* Deborah Sweet Mitchell died from tuberculosis (consumption) at an early age; several of the eleven children belonging to "R.C." and Deborah Sweet Mitchell also died of the disease ("Mitchell, Russell Crawford: Find-a-Grave").

R.C. married Clara Belle Neal — the widow Robinson — on April 5, 1888. They had two children: Clara Emma (1891–1983) and Lillian Leona (1895–1988), in addition to her son Arthur Neal Robinson from a previous marriage ("Mitchell, Russell Crawford: Find-a-Grave").

*R.C. and his later injuries.* Margaret Mitchell's

accident in which Hugh D. Gravitt hit her in August of 1949 caused the older population to remember an earlier event when a close member of the Mitchell family suffered severe injury, had been unconscious like Margaret, and had regained consciousness. R.C. Mitchell had recovered from his injury, and the hope was that Margaret Mitchell would likewise recover from her head injuries, but it was not to be.

In 1900, R.C. Mitchell was seriously injured in a streetcar accident; Atlanta's first streetcar had struck him. He recovered, but he retired from the work world after the accident. As a result of his retirement, he was able to spend time with his grandchildren. He especially enjoyed telling them stories of his Civil War experiences and of Reconstruction. One of his most avid listeners was Margaret Mitchell, the future author of *Gone with the Wind* ("Mitchell, Russell Crawford: Find-a-Grave").

## Mitchell, Russell Stephens (June 3, 1894 – December 13, 1894)

The first born child of Eugene Muse Mitchell and Maybelle Stephens Mitchell died in his first year. Ironically, the first day of the events of the Atlanta premiere of *Gone with the Wind* began exactly 45 years after his death date.

Russell Stephens Mitchell got his first name from his paternal grandfather. His middle name came from the maiden name of his mother, Maybelle Stephens. Russell Stephens Mitchell was the older brother of Margaret Mitchell Marsh and of Alexander Stephens Mitchell. Russell Stephens's siblings, however, were not born until after his death. The child's gravesite is in Oakland Cemetery in Atlanta, where many of his relatives lie ("Mitchell, Russell Stephens: Find-a-Grave").

## Mitchell, Thomas (1892–1962)

The actor chosen for the role of Gerald O'Hara in the movie *Gone with the Wind* had the same surname as did the author of the book on which Selznick based the film. Thomas Mitchell appeared in both *Gone with the Wind* and *Stagecoach* in 1939; he won the Academy Award for his role in *Stagecoach*— not *Gone with the Wind*, as Edwards suggested on page 295.

Actor, playwright, and director Thomas Mitchell was born in Elizabeth, New Jersey, to James Mitchell, a mortician and furniture store owner, and Mary Donnelly Mitchell. Both of his parents had come from Ireland.

The youngest of seven children, Thomas attended St. Patrick's High School in Elizabeth. He appeared in the role of Cardinal Richelieu in his class's graduation play. He had gained some attention with a monologue that he wrote and performed at the age of seventeen in vaudeville houses. In 1928 Mitchell would earn the Roi Cooper Megrue playwrighting prize for his comedy *Little Accident*.

After his 1909 high school graduation, Mitchell secured a job as reporter for the *Elizabeth Daily Journal*. After the paper had to print five retractions in two weeks because of Mitchell's dramatization of events, however, he sought jobs elsewhere, including newspapers in Baltimore, Washington, D.C., Pittsburgh, and Youngstown, Ohio. Mitchell submitted his resignation after he reviewed a play in Youngstown and began pursuing a life on the stage.

His first professional stage appearance was in New York City in 1912. His roles later included appearances in *The Tempest* with Tyrone Power, Sr., and fifty roles between 1914 and 1916 with Charles Coburn's Touring Shakespeare Company. He found jobs in Denver, Omaha, and Springfield, Massachusetts.

Mitchell rejected methods of acting and "living a part." He played a part by reading the playwright's words and performing those words. He wrote in 1961 that an actor who thinks is a "dead duck" ("Thomas G. Mitchell").

Mitchell was able to use many dialects. He could quickly memorize his lines. This enabled him to find roles in many Broadway plays, including the part of Willy Loman in *Death of a Salesman* (1949, 1950). In 1936 Mitchell also began filling roles in Hollywood. Mitchell contracted with Columbia and Samuel Goldwyn. He also free-lanced.

Mitchell appeared in sixty films, on radio, and on television. He also wrote and directed many works. He earned an Emmy as the best actor of the year 1952. The following year he won the Antoinette Perry "Tony" Award for the best male performance in a musical. Mitchell earned also the Donaldson Prize as best actor of 1953.

Married three times and the father of one child, Mitchell served his country in World War I. He died in Beverly Hills, California, in 1962 ("Thomas Gregory Mitchell").

## monkey

As a reporter for the *Atlanta Journal Sunday Magazine*, Margaret Mitchell became accustomed to photographers going with her when she went to gather information for her articles. The photographers enjoyed baiting Margaret, and she rose to the occasion. With her love of animals, Margaret was not hesitant about going backstage at a circus and being photographed with a monkey on September 13, 1924. The newspaper photographers

The newspaper photographers were probably surprised when reporter Margaret Mitchell held a monkey for a photograph at the local circus. (Courtesy of the Atlanta-Fulton Public Library System's Special Collections Department.)

probably did not expect her to hold the monkey in her arms.

*See also* animals; elephant.

## Morehouse College

After her novel was published in 1936, Margaret Mitchell worked with Morehouse President Benjamin Mays to provide some anonymous scholarships for students seeking a medical education at this college for African American men.

From the basement of a church to a 66-acre campus, Morehouse College has grown into an internationally known institute. It was founded by Springfield Baptist Church Augusta Institute, the Augusta Baptist minister, journalist and cabinetmaker William Jefferson White, the minister and former slave Richard C. Coulter, the Reverend Edmund Turney (who had organized the National Theological Institute to educate freedmen in Washington, D.C.), and others. The first president, the Reverend Doctor Joseph T. Robert, ensured that African American men were prepared for the teaching and for the ministry.

In 1879, after moving to Atlanta's Friendship Baptist Church, Augusta Institute became Atlanta Baptist Seminary; later, the Baptist Seminary moved to a four-acre lot in downtown Atlanta. Seminary professor David Foster Estes began serving as its president in 1884 after the death of the former president.

The seminary moved in 1885 to the west end of Atlanta, and, through a gift from John D. Rockefeller, began occupying a site there. The site was where Confederate soldiers staged their resistance to William Tecumseh Sherman's siege of Atlanta in 1864. In 1897 — under the guidance of Dr. George Sale, the third and youngest president (1890–1906) — Atlanta Baptist Seminary became Atlanta Baptist College.

The fourth president (1906–1931), John Hope, the first African American president and a proponent of expanding the curriculum, disagreed with Booker T. Washington's idea of focusing primarily on agriculture. In 1913 Atlanta Baptist College took the name of the corresponding secretary of Northern Baptist Home Mission Society and became Morehouse College.

Dr. Samuel H. Archer (1931–1937) and Dr. Charles D. Hubert (1937–1940) took the helm at Morehouse. In 1940, Dr. Benjamin Elijah Mays took over the leadership position; he was a mentor to Dr. Martin Luther King, Jr., and worked with Margaret Mitchell to advance the medical education of African American students. During his tenure, Morehouse earned full accreditation by the Southern Association of Colleges and Schools (1957) and a chapter of Phi Beta Kappa (1968).

Other effective administrators followed. Morehouse gained an international reputation; the institution established a $29 million endowment, added twelve buildings to the campus, including the Martin Luther King, Jr., International Chapel, and developed programs in cooperation with the Georgia Institute of Technology, the University of Michigan and Boston University. The Morehouse School of Medicine became an independent institution in 1981.

Morehouse's improvements in bricks and mortar, in programs, in endowment, and in reputation have persisted over the years. For the third time, *Black Enterprise* named Morehouse (2004) as the nation's number one college for educating African Americans. In 2006, the college received Dr. Martin Luther King, Jr.'s personal papers ("About Morehouse College").

*See also* 1939 Atlanta premiere of *Gone with the Wind*; Ebenezer Baptist Church; Ebenezer Baptist Church Choir; Johnson, Ira Joe; King, Dr. Martin Luther, Jr.; Mays, Benjamin; Mitchell, Margaret.

## Morris, Ginny *see* Nixon, Virginia "Ginny" Morris

## Movie projector and movies at Marshes' home

Margaret and John loved films. In 1946 when John became extremely incapacitated in their Della Manta Apartment, trips to the theaters were becoming impossible. They decided to rent a 16-millimeter film projector. They liked the old movies especially, and the building custodian Eugene Carr would go to town every day to borrow a film for them to watch.

In a letter to his mother in 1947, John described their first evening with the new projector. He indicated that they had worked for about two hours trying to operate the device. He reported that they had employed "everything including a pickle fork, a jelly spoon, egg beater, a carved backscratcher, an after-dinner coffee spoon engraved 'Chicago World's Fair 1893,' a piece of Jensen silver sent to Peggy by one of her admirers in Denmark" (Walker, page 489).

Finally, John had an inspiration. He employed a "plain ordinary coat-hanger." It worked! John described this as one of his triumphs in recent days (Walker, page 489).

In a letter to Helen Dowdey on February 14, 1947, Margaret reported that "Machine guns rattle every night here or the roar of the motors of 1918 Curtis jennys deafen the neighbors or the ton-toms of 'South of Pago Pago' wake the echoes (Walker, page 489). Their neighbor in the apartment house was Sam Tupper. Sam frequently came over to visit. "Sam says he does not come to see us for love of us but because of the free moving pictures we are showing" (Walker, page 489).

*See also* Carr, Eugene.

### *Mrs. John Marsh ... The World Knew Her as Margaret Mitchell*

This is a two-act, 90-minute play in two scenes. Written by Melita Easters, who lived in Buckhead in Atlanta, the play was a revision of Easters's production of 1991. It has primarily a 1930s setting. It concludes in 1949 when Margaret Mitchell is hit by Hugh D. Gravitt as she is crossing Peachtree on her way to see the movie *A Canterbury Tale* and dies five days later (Bookman).

### "A MS of the Old South"

Before the publication of the novel *Gone with the Wind*, Macmillan Publishing Company assigned the working name "A MS of the Old South" to Margaret Mitchell's work.

*See also* *Gone with the Wind* book title, Latham, Harold Strong; Mitchell, Margaret.

### *My Life in Publishing*

In 1965 — before his 1969 death — the editor Harold Latham of Macmillan Publishing Company wrote of his experiences in the publishing field. Some of the writers with whom he worked were Margaret Mitchell, poet Rachel Field, and novelist Kathleen Winsor (*Forever Amber*). Latham also included in his book some vignettes about such writers as James Michener and Herbert Hoover.

He describes *My Life in Publishing* as "a book of random memories" (page 38). His literary contacts were many and his contributions to literature are vast.

### Myrick, Susan (1893–1978)

Born in Milledgeville, Georgia, "Sue" Myrick and Margaret Mitchell first met at the first conference of the Georgia Press Association in 1928. Sue was the "blond, husky-voiced farm editor of the *Macon Telegraph* and later the associate editor of that same paper." The two women found that they had much in common; their friendship nine years later was still "valuable and fascinating" (Walker, page 182).

Myrick served as the voice coach and an adviser for the film *Gone with the Wind*. Her recommendation came from W. T. Anderson, the editor and publisher of the *Macon Telegraph* and later the *Macon News* for more than 30 years. Anderson emphasized that the Southern-born Myrick had studied the stage, was familiar with Southern dialect, and understood the characters (Walker, page 400).

The Georgia Newspaper Hall of Fame inducted Myrick into its ranks in 1984 for her work on the *Macon Telegraph*. Her nickname became "The Emily Post of the South" ("Susan Myrick").

*See also* Anderson, W.T.

### National Book Award of the American Booksellers Association

The American Booksellers Association presents an annual award for the best fiction of the preceding year. The name of this ABA award is the National Book Award; one should not confuse it with the National Book Association Award. The members of the American Booksellers Association select the recipient whose books they most admire and enjoy selling. *Gone with the Wind*, whose release date was June 30, 1936, was the 1937 recipient of the ABA award for the most distinguished novel (Brown, page 149).

### Nelson, Ozzie (1906–1975)

The celebrated bandleader Ozzie Nelson was a special guest at the 1939 Atlanta premiere of *Gone with the Wind*. The Atlanta Auditorium could not accommodate all the guests who wanted to attend the ball on Thursday, December 14, 1939, when Kay Kyser would conduct the orchestra; the Loew's Grand Theatre could not accommodate everyone who wanted to attend the film premiere in Atlanta on December 15, 1939. Ozzie Nelson's orchestra graciously conducted another in the Atlanta Auditorium on December 15, 1939. The same decorations used on the evening of December 14, 1939, again decorated the Atlanta facility on December 15, 1939 (Pyron, pages 372–180).

The celebrated bandleader was extremely popular during the 1930s— the era of swing — as an orchestra leader, songwriter, and vocalist. Nelson became popular in the 1950s, after the death of Margaret Mitchell, in another venue. He played a father on a television show: *The Adventures of Ozzie and Harriet.*

Ozzie Nelson had always enjoyed entertainment. Born in Jersey City in 1906, Ozzie learned to play the ukulele, and the banjo; he learned also to sing and to play the saxophone. Ozzie and Frank Leithner, a pianist, became part of the Syncopation Four; the quartet played for weddings, club, and parties. When he entered Rutgers in 1923, he played football and joined the boxing team. Next came law school; to earn extra money, he led a small band and coached football.

By 1930 Nelson had his own radio show. The

*New York Daily Mirror* ran a poll, and Nelson—with the help of his manager—came in first. He took a job as leader of a small orchestra in Long Island. Next came more radio shows. Nelson's name had become a well-known one. He added the singer Harriet Hilliard to his big band in 1932. She was only the second female singer featured with an orchestra. They married in October of 1935. Two sons were born, David in 1936 and Ricky in 1940.

In the 1940s he began making records, which sold well. In 1944 the Nelson family started a radio "sit com" that centered on family life. Their feature film *Here Come the Nelsons* (1951) preceded the Nelsons' ABC television show *The Adventures of Ozzie and Harriet* (1952–1967); Nelson was a star and the producer and writer.

Even after the end of the series, Ozzie Nelson continued working as a film and television writer, producer, and director; he also continued making guest television appearances. He produced another syndicated television shows: *Ozzie's Girls*. In 1975 he died from cancer ("Ozzie Nelson").

## New York premiere of *Gone with the Wind* (the film)

Two other premieres of *Gone with the Wind* followed the Atlanta premiere. One was in New York City; the other was in Los Angeles, California. Neither event was the gala affair held in Atlanta.

The New York event was on December 19, 1939. Two simultaneous showings of *Gone with the Wind* in New York were at the Capitol Theatre and at the Astor Theatre.

NBC had begun televising programs in April of 1939 and broadcasting them—to limited audiences, of course. NBC televised the crowds waiting outside the Capitol Theatre to gain entrance to the first New York showing of *Gone with the Wind*.

The Los Angeles premiere was on December 28, 1939, at the Carthay Circle Theatre. Margaret Mitchell attended neither the New York nor the Los Angeles premiere. Other stars attended both.

*See also* **Capitol Theatre and Astor Theatre.**

## *New York World Telegram*

Edwards asserts that after the publication of *Gone with the Wind*, Margaret Mitchell had no other book on the horizon and yet the novelist was still trying to maintain the legend of the novel and herself. Mitchell found a way to do this by quarreling with the *New York World Telegram*, in the opinion of Edwards (Edwards, pages 314–315).

Margaret matter-of-factly wrote on October 23, 1944, to Douglas Gilbert protesting statements in two *New York World Telegram* articles saying

Mitchell had sold movie rights to *Gone with the Wind* for $50,000 after the movie company had read the book in galley proofs only. She protested that no galley proofs of her novel had ever been sold; she had not sold the film rights until July 30, 1936—after the June publication of *Gone with the Wind*. The contention that the movie rights came before the publication of the novel seemed impossible.

Margaret Mitchell also told Gilbert that she never indicated how much she received for the movie rights. She indicated that her novel had already sold between 50,000 and 90,000 copies in the pre-publication period. Mitchell stated further that the book had sold several hundred thousand copies before she signed a movie contract. Margaret concluded her letter by stating she was "far from being hornswaggled by Hollywood[;] the rights to *Gone with the Wind* brought the highest price ever paid for a first novel by an unknown author up to that time" (Harwell, *Letters,* page 383).

## Nixon, Virginia "Ginny" Morris

Margaret Mitchell moved into a second floor room on Ten Henshaw Street in Northampton, Massachusetts, for her first year at Smith College. She occupied the room by herself at first, feeling very much like an outsider until one girl began sharing her room. That girl was Virginia ("Ginny") Morris—later Ginny Morris Nixon (Edwards, page 52).

Ginny was "outgoing, loved by all, and the catalyst of most activities." It was she who finally became the permanent roommate with Margaret, whom her friends had begun calling "Peggy" (Pyron, page 52).

*Ginny Morris brings Margaret Mitchell news of the war in Europe.* Margaret and her fiancé Clifford Henry always wrote regularly. His letters, however, were always a month late because of the overseas mail delivery time required. In October, however, Clifford Henry's letters ceased. The last letter that Margaret received had the date of September 11, 1918. It bore the postmark of Saint-Mihiel.

Ginny brought Margaret the news of a devastating American loss on September 12. American troops and three French divisions had attacked German troops. Eight thousand lives were lost. Margaret immediately called Clifford's parents. They, too, had heard nothing.

The waiting was soon over. The Henrys received a telegram informing them that Clifford had been severely injured by bomb fragments dropped by a German plane after he had taken over for his captain; his superior officer had been disabled in the fighting—much of which had been hand-to-hand.

Clifford had suffered a severed leg and fragments in his stomach.

In his hospital bed, Clifford Henry had received the Croix de Guerre. He had died on October 16, 1918.

*Marriage of Ginny Morris (Nixon).* Ginny would later marry, have a daughter, and become a divorced single parent. She was an employed woman at a time when most women did not work. In addition to serving as a freelance writer, she worked in the publicity department at United Artists.

*Career of Ginny Morris Nixon.* As a freelancer writer and friend, Ginny Morris Nixon was particularly interested in Margaret's novel and its adaptation into a film. They wrote several times about Mitchell's work. Ginny and her author-friend Margaret had much in common. Their friendship, however, was not to last a lifetime (Edwards, page 194, 479).

Margaret Mitchell had long denied that she had patterned the characters in *Gone with the Wind* after real-life people. Freelance writer Ginny Nixon prepared a story about the resemblances between characters in *Gone with the Wind* and certain real-life people. Ginny noted comparisons between Gerald O'Hara in *Gone with the Wind* and Margaret's own father, Eugene Muse Mitchell (1866–1944), between the death of Maybelle Mitchell and Scarlett O'Hara's mother, and between even the letters that Clifford Henry wrote to Margaret and the letters that Ashley Wilkes wrote to Melanie.

In the article Ginny also discussed Sophie Hencke and Madeleine Baxter gathering in Margaret's and her room after classes. She noted Margaret's disregard of Smith's rules and drew attention to Margaret's skill at smoking — at a time when smoking cigarettes was an offense punishable by expulsion. Ginny discussed Margaret's ability to enthrall the others with her stories of the Civil War. Margaret had become agitated at one point and called Ginny "a damn Yankee."

Nixon submitted the article to *Photoplay* — against Margaret's wishes, but Margaret managed to kill the article. The whole episode, however, also killed the friendship between Ginny and Margaret. Ginny did not attend the ceremony when Margaret received an honorary degree from Smith College (Pyron, pages 249, 291, 479).

## Northen, Charles

Margaret Mitchell's beloved painting *The Battle of Atlanta* has a complicated history. Paul Atkinson of Georgia bought the painting from H. H. Harrison of Florida. Ernest Woodruff bought the painting at auction in 1893; Woodruff in turn sold *The Battle of Atlanta* to George Valentine Gress and Charles Northen.

Gress and Northen asked the city to assign space for it in one of Atlanta's parks. Atlanta erected a frame building — and later more substantial structures — in Grant Park. *The Battle of Atlanta* is still a popular attraction through the actions of Gress and Northen ("Atlanta Cyclorama and Civil War Museum").

**See also** Atkinson, Paul; Atlanta Cyclorama; Battle of Atlanta; *Battle of Atlanta* painting; Downing, John Francis; Civil War in Margaret Mitchell's education; Grant Park; Gress, George Valentine; Harrison, H. H.; Logan, John Alexander "Blackjack."

## Norway, sales of *Gone with the Wind* see foreign copyrights/translations and fair trade laws

## Nunnally home

The records of the Georgian Terrace Hotel report that both Laurence Olivier and Vivien Leigh stayed at the hotel during the Atlanta premiere of *Gone with the Wind*. In actuality, Leigh and Olivier may have stayed at the home of investor Hugh P. Nunnally. The white, two-story house — designed by the firm of Frazier and Bodin and completed in 1936 — was on 281 Blackland Road. Its four columns were reminiscent of Hollywood's Tara ("Album: Atlanta History Center").

## Oakland Cemetery (Atlanta)

Oakland Cemetery dates from 1850 when the city purchased six acres for the town of Atlanta. The intention was to develop a cemetery that resembled a rural garden cemetery — an alternative to the crowded, traditional cemeteries. Initially called Atlanta Graveyard or City Burial Place, it received the new name Oakland Cemetery in 1872. Oakland Cemetery had 48 acres by 1872, partly because of the burials resulting from the Civil War.

The National Register of Historic Places added the Oakland Cemetery in 1976. That same year marks the establishment of the Historic Oakland Foundation. The Oakland Cemetery is the burial place for Margaret Mitchell and many of her family members.

When Mitchell's nephew Eugene Muse Mitchell (1931–2007) died, Oakland Cemetery became his burial site. He had quietly donated earlier some $667,000 to the cemetery ("Historic Oakland Cemetery").

**See also** Marsh, John R.; Mitchell, Eugene Muse (1866–1944); Mitchell, Eugene Muse (1931–2007); Mitchell, Mary Isabelle.

This is the gravesite of Margaret Mitchell Marsh and John R. Marsh in the Oakland Cemetery, Atlanta, Georgia. (Courtesy of Zeny Williams, www.beyondthepalace.com)

## O'Hara, Gerald

Gerald O'Hara is the father of Katie Scarlett O'Hara in *Gone with the Wind*. Gerald—played by Thomas Mitchell in the Selznick film—suffers a breakdown when his wife dies. In the book and in the film *Gone with the Wind* Gerald is killed in a horseback riding accident.

## O'Hara, Katie Scarlett

Scarlett was the independent, quick-tempered, emotional mistress of Twelve Oaks Plantation. Her life became woven with that of Rhett Butler's. She was a character in both *Rhett Butler's People* and in *Gone with the Wind*—and perhaps in other writings related to *Gone with the Wind*. In the film *Gone with the Wind*, Vivien Leigh played Scarlett O'Hara.

## Old Timer

To discourage the Western Union operators who were sharing the contents of her telegrams, Margaret Mitchell began using some code names for people in her communications. As she had done since childhood, Mitchell was caring for some stray cats; she and the persons with whom she corresponded began substituting the names of her cats—particularly Wish-Wish and Napoleon—in these messages.

Margaret told her friend Mabel Search, an editor with *Pictorial Review*, in a March 4, 1937, letter that a Western Union operator actually called her at her Georgia home and asked her if she knew anyone with the names of Napoleon and Wish-Wish in New York. Margaret had replied that the two were old, dear friends of hers. The operator made the further comment that these people must be foreigners (Walker, page 355).

When John came home from the hospital in early spring of 1937, he found Margaret had adopted a stray tomcat. She wrote about the cat to Mabel Search. Margaret lovingly called the cat "a tramp" who was "dirty as a stoker." She called the cat *Old Timer* and described him as "a fine, old striped animal, a great ladies' man who as been dropping in for a dish of milk every other night" (Walker, page 355).

Margaret wrote to Herschel Brickell on February 8, 1937: "A couple of weeks ago he came calling with all his rear end chewed and mangled and as fine an infection in his equipment as you ever laid eyes on. I put him in the cat hospital and the veterinarians and I labored vainly to save the above equipment. We saved Old Timer, but, alas, the equipment is gone with the wind. He is at home now being fed on yeast and cod liver oil, for I cannot turn a sick animal out. I fear I will never be able to turn him out for he adores the silk brocade of my rocking chair as it makes such a delightful sound when his claws rip into it. Adopting a cat is a serious manner and apt to change one's life as it means becoming a slave to the creature's insistent desires to go out when he's in and in when he's out. But John and I are succumbing to his charms. He has the most beautiful stand of whiskers you ever saw" (Walker, page 356).

Margaret describes Old Timer's condition as improved in a March 4, 1937, letter to Mabel Search. "He is doing very nicely but there is still some infection in his twickey. If I put ointment on the twickey he licks it off, or else wipes it on the brocade chair. John has refused to let me put a diaper on him [Old Timer]. He says it is shocking enough for a male creature to be bereft of his dearest possessions without having to suffer the final ignominy of a diaper" (Walker, page 356).

After Old Timer vanished, Margaret found the animal called Count Dracula in the summer of 1937 — supposedly to keep John company (Walker, page 495).

**See also** animals; cats; Count Dracula; Dracula; Maud.

### one-cent U.S. postage stamp, 1986

The United States Postal Service (USPS) honored Margaret Mitchell (1900–1949) with a one-cent stamp. The USPS issued the stamp on the fiftieth anniversary of the release of her novel *Gone with the Wind*, published in 1936. The USPS held its first-day ceremonies in Atlanta, Georgia, Margaret Mitchell's birth and burial place (Davis and Hunt, page 256–257).

### Paisley, Eva

Eva Paisley was Margaret Mitchell's English teacher at Washington Seminary. Mary Rose Taylor describes Paisley's role in Margaret Mitchell's life in the book *Before Scarlett: Childhood Writings of Margaret Mitchell*. Taylor believes this instructor—like all teachers—"lived on the side of angels."

Mary Rose Taylor, as director of the Margaret Mitchell House and Museum, was the person primarily responsible for the preservation of Margaret Mitchell's and John R. Marsh's first apartment. Apartment #1 was the place where Mitchell wrote much of *Gone with the Wind* (From "Foreword" by Mary Rose Taylor in Jane Eskridge's *Before Scarlett: Childhood Writings of Margaret Mitchell*, ix).

With Paisley's guidance, Margaret Mitchell saw her short stories published in the school yearbook, *Facts and Fancies*. Margaret's two published short stories were "Little Sister" (during her junior year) and "Sergeant Terry" (during her senior year) (Mary Rose Taylor, *Before Scarlett: Childhood Writings of Margaret Mitchell*, pages ix–xii).

### Palestine, sales of *Gone with the Wind* see foreign copyrights/translations and fair trade laws

### Peachtree Street in Atlanta

Peachtree Street was important to Atlanta and to the life and death of Margaret Mitchell. Below are some of the most significant Peachtree Street numbers.

*659 Peachtree Street, NE (Corner of Peachtree and Ponce de Leon Avenue).* The hotel at the corner of Peachtree and Ponce de Leon Avenue — the Georgian Terrace Hotel — figured prominently into the life of Margaret Mitchell and *Gone with the Wind* (book and film). It may have been in the lobby of the Georgian Terrace Hotel where on April 11, 1935, Margaret Mitchell delivered the manuscript of what would be *Gone with the Wind* to editor Harold Latham of Macmillan Publishing Company (Edwards, page 3). Many of the cast and crew of the film *Gone with the Wind* stayed at the Georgian Terrace Hotel during Atlanta premiere of the film *Gone with the Wind* (December 13–15, 1939).

*806 Peachtree Street, later 17 Crescent Avenue.* Cornelius Sheehan's three-story brick home housed Apartment #1 — Margaret Mitchell and John R. Marsh's first apartment together. After the relocation of the house, it had a Crescent Avenue address and the name Crescent Apartments (Edwards, pages 118–119).

*990 Peachtree Street, Northeast.* The Margaret Mitchell House opened on May 17, 1997, in what had been the Cornelius Sheehan house and later the Crescent Apartment Building; John R. Marsh and Margaret Mitchell had resided in Apartment #1 — "The Dump." The House bears the address 990 Peachtree Street, Northeast — not the old 17 Crescent Avenue or 806 Peachtree Street address.

*1137 Peachtree Street, NE.* The Peachtree Arts Theatre (in operation from the 1940s until the 1970s) was three-quarters of a mile from the resi-

"Peachtree Street, Looking North from Viaduct, Great White Way, Atlanta, Georgia." This postcard was mailed in 1922. (A. M. 32 Union Square, New York. Author's collection.)

dence of John R. Marsh and Margaret Mitchell. As the couple was crossing the street on the evening of August 11, 1949, a car driven by Hugh D. Gravitt struck Margaret Mitchell (Pyron, page 461).

*Peachtree Street (1149, 1401, or 1701).* The immediate family of Eugene Muse Mitchell (1866–1944)—Eugene, Maybelle, Stephens, and Margaret Mitchell—moved in 1912 into the fourth house in which Margaret would live. Margaret lived in the Peachtree home from 1912 until her 1925 marriage to John Marsh—with the exception of the year that Margaret attended Smith College. The house was originally at 1149 Peachtree Street; after the renumbering of the streets, the house number changed to 1401 or 1701 (Walker, page 34; Tommy H. Jones).

Only a plaque showing where the residence once stood now remains. Alexander Stephens Mitchell had the home demolished in 1952.

*See also* addresses directly related to Margaret Mitchell; Atlanta premiere of *Gone with the Wind*; *A Canterbury Tale*; "The Dump"; Gable, (William) Clark; Georgian Terrace Hotel; Grady Hospital; Gravitt, Hugh Dorsey; Leigh, Vivien; Margaret Mitchell House and Museum; Mitchell, Alexander Stephens; Taylor, Mary Rose.

### Peacock, Jane Bonner

An Atlanta native, Jane Bonner Peacock is a graduate of the University of Georgia, where she was a journalism major at the Henry W. Grady

School of Journalism. She and her husband, Atlanta physician, have three grown children. Peacock has written many articles in addition to editing the book *A Dynamo Going to Waste*, a compilation of letters (1919–1921) between Margaret Mitchell and Allen Edee.

*See also A Dynamo Going to Waste*; Edee, Allen.

### "Peggy" Mitchell

Margaret Mitchell sometimes—but not always—used the byline *Peggy Mitchell* on her newspaper articles. After the date of December 31, 1922, she sometimes used the byline *Peggy Upshaw* to acknowledge her marriage to Berrien Kinnard ("Red") Upshaw. After she and Upshaw divorced on June 17, 1924, and during their separation, Margaret used the byline *Peggy Mitchell* or *Margaret Mitchell*. After her marriage to John R. Marsh, she placed a card identifying herself as *Margaret Mitchell*—not *Margaret Marsh*—on their door. She used *Margaret Mitchell* as her pen name henceforth. Margaret's family refused to use the nickname *Peggy* (Edwards, page 66).

### Peggy Upshaw

Margaret Mitchell—who had married Berrien "Red" Kinnard Upshaw on September 2, 1922—used the byline *Peggy Upshaw* on her first article on December 31, 1922, for the *Atlanta Journal Sun-*

*day Magazine.* After she and Upshaw separated, Margaret used the bylines *Peggy Mitchell* or *Margaret Mitchell.*

## Perkerson, Jr., Angus Millard (1888–1967)

Angus Millard Perkerson, Jr., a lieutenant in the First World War, began writing for the *Atlanta Journal-Constitution* newspaper when he was 18. In 1912 he founded the *Atlanta Journal-Constitution Magazine* and served as its editor for forty-four years until his retirement.

Through the *Atlanta Journal-Constitution Magazine,* Angus Perkerson—and later his wife Medora Field Perkerson—encouraged new writers. His magazine carried the writings of many authors who later become respected novelists, including Margaret Mitchell (*Gone with the Wind*), Medora Field (*White Columns in Georgia, Who Killed Aunt Maggie, Blood on Her Shoe*), and Olive Ann Burns (*Cold Sassy Tree*) ("Angus Millard Perkerson, Jr.").

With her life-long desire to write, her confident approach to life, and her affection for Atlanta, Margaret Mitchell's application for a position at the *Atlanta Journal* seems inevitable. In December of 1922, Margaret went to see Angus Perkerson, the editor of the *Atlanta Journal Sunday Magazine* at the time. Perkerson hired Margaret Mitchell as a feature writer.

Margaret Mitchell was a reliable employee; she usually worked 10 hours a day. Between her hiring and when she had to take a leave of absence four years later because of health issues and an ankle injury, Mitchell wrote 129 feature stories. She considered her work comparable to obtaining a liberal education (Christina Lewis).

Angus and Medora Perkerson became good friends with Margaret Mitchell and John R. Marsh. When John had a heart attack on his way to Sea Island on December 24, 1945, Margaret contacted John's family and the Perkersons. They arrived promptly to visit him in the hospital in Brunswick (Walker, page 484).

## Perkerson, Medora Field (1892–1960)

Margaret Mitchell and Medora Field Perkerson—the wife of editor Angus Perkerson and "mainstay" of the *Atlanta Journal Sunday Magazine*—became fast friends when Margaret became an employee. Medora Perkerson was the wife of Angus Millard Perkerson (Farr, page 69).

Medora Field had gone to work at the *Atlanta Journal-Constitution Magazine* in the early 1920s. She married Angus Millard Perkerson, Jr., in 1922. Both of them were Georgia natives: Angus from Atlanta and Medora from Linder.

Like her husband Angus, Medora befriended

and encouraged many young writers. Margaret Mitchell was no exception. Medora Field Perkerson was a writer in her own right. Her volumes included one celebrating the architecture in her home state: *White Columns in Georgia.* Medora also wrote two mysteries: *Who Killed Aunt Maggie?* and *Blood on Her Shoe.*

After Medora's death in 1960, the Georgia Historical Commission placed in 1961 a bronze marker in Linder, the place of Medora's birth. The marker reads: "Medora Field (1892–1960) was born nearby on the site of the present Lindale Baptist Church. In her early twenties she became a member of *The Atlanta Journal-Constitution Magazine* staff, and later was married to Angus Perkerson, its editor. For many years, troubled people sought the sympathetic and sound counsel she gave in her weekly column as 'Marie Rose.' She was the friend of the friendless. Through offices held in her Church, in the Child Service Association of Atlanta and in organizations of writers, she became an influence for good throughout Georgia and beyond its borders.

"Mrs. Perkerson's most notable book, *White Columns in Georgia*, tells the story of her state through its historic houses. Her two other books, *Who Killed Aunt Maggie?* and *Blood on her Shoe*, have Georgia settings" ("Perkerson, Medora Field").

## Peterkin, Julia Mood (1880–1961)

The Southern writer, Pulitzer Prize winning novelist, and friend of Margaret Mitchell was born in Fort Motte (Laurens County), South Carolina, in 1880—twenty years before Margaret Mitchell was born in Atlanta. Julia was born to Dr. Julius Andrew Mood and Alma Archer Mood.

Alma Archer Mood died soon after the birth of Julia. A nurse—"Mauma"—and her father reared the child. Mauma taught her Gullah dialect, Gullah customs, and Gullah superstitions. Later, in a novel, Julia would describe Gullahs as "perfect" and having "tall straight bodies, and high heads filled with sense." Julia appreciated the Southern culture and the South also. She included both cultures in her later writings ("Julia Mood Peterkin").

Dr. Mood enrolled Julia and her sister Laura in Columbia College in Columbia, South Carolina. The two rebellious girls found themselves dismissed with the year. Julius enrolled both Julia and Laura in Converse College in Spartanburg, South Carolina. Julia earned the bachelor's degree in 1896; she studied for another year and received the master's degree. Both young women had a literary bent.

After taking her degrees, Julia returned to Fort Motte. At the age of seventeen, Julia began teaching in a local school near Fort Motte; she usually had fewer than ten students in that farming settlement.

The Peterkin family dominated that rural settlement. The Peterkins owned the Lang Syne Plantation. Julia married William George Peterkin — the heir to the plantation — in 1903. As the plantation mistress, Julia assumed the role of managing the Lang Syne Plantation, which employed 400 to 500 Gullah people and a foreman. Over the next seventeen years, Julia raised her son, traveled, learned farming, and assumed the responsibility for the family's social obligations, which included membership in the "right" clubs and societies; during her lifetime she belonged to such organization as P.E.N., the Daughters of the American Revolution, the Daughters of the Confederacy, the Cosmopolitan Club, and the Afternoon Music Club (Columbia, S.C). Peterkin even learned to create fancy needlework.

"Hard times" threatened about 1920. Julia's husband became ill and permanently incapacitated; Julia had to take control of the plantation. The death of the foreman and a livestock epidemic threatened Lang Syne further. With the encouragement of her father Julius Mood and with her own inner strength — *gumption* — Julia managed to endure and to bring Lang Syne through the troubled times.

For enjoyment and for therapy, Julia began in 1921 to write some sketches of plantation life. Dr. Henry Bellamann — her piano teacher — encouraged her to continue writing and to submit her writings to H. L. Mencken. Mencken accepted one of her sketches for publication in his magazine *Smart Set* ("Julia Mood Peterkin").

Fourteen of what Peterkin called her "crude, really stark plantation sketches" appeared in Emily Clark's literary magazine *The Reviewer*. James Branch Cabell, Alfred A. Knopf, and Alfred Harcourt began to notice her works.

In 1924 Julia Mood Peterkin saw her first book in print: *Green Thursday*, which collected some of her short stories and sketches. Her first novel, *Black April* (1927), received excellent reviews. The following year (1928) her novel — a comedy — *Scarlet Sister Mary*, won a Pulitzer Prize; more than 1 million copies of the novel sold. Another honor came when one of her sketches appeared in *The O. Henry Memorial Prize Stories of 1930*. Peterkin wrote and published also *Bright Skin* (1932) and *Roll, Jordan, Roll* (1933).

From 1933 until the death of William George Peterkin in 1939, however, Julia devoted her time to managing the Lang Syne Plantation. Her ill health and severe droughts occupied her time and energy until her death in Orangeburg, South Carolina, in the 1950s ("Julia Mood Peterkin").

Julia Mood Peterkin and Marjorie Kinnan Rawlings — two Southern women Pulitzer Prize Winners — attended a luncheon with fellow prize winner Margaret Mitchell in December of 1939. The luncheon at Rich's Department Store was just hours before the world's first showing of *Gone with the Wind* on the evening of December 15, 1939 (Pyron, page 377).

It was at this luncheon that a problem arose. Margaret Mitchell missed her chair and landed in pain on the floor. Margaret did, however, manage to attend the premiere, talk with Clark Gable, and deliver her address on the evening of December 15, 1939 (Pyron, page 377).

*See also* Atlanta premiere of *Gone with the Wind*; gumption; Rawlings, Marjorie Kinnan; Rich's Department Store.

## Piedmont Driving Club

In the heart of Midtown Atlanta is the Piedmont Driving Club. The address of the club is 1215 Piedmont Avenue; it is between Piedmont Park and the Atlanta Botanical Garden. The Tudor-style house dates from 1887. The facility was originally a club where the well-to-do could flaunt their fine carriages and drive their prize horses — hence the name *Driving Club*.

The members of the club carry the nickname in Atlanta of "Big Mules." Membership usually has a limit of 1,000; members are usually the "big names" in society and business. In 1977 hefty initiation fees of about $5000 and yearly membership fees of about $1,000 applied. Screening of the applicants was a practice, and the separate but equal tradition was the rule at that time ("The Nation: Where Atlanta's 'Big Mules' Relax").

For several years the club used the adjacent property as a golf course. The city, however, bought the land in 1904 to use as a park. Today the private social group has more than one clubhouse in Atlanta.

*Piedmont Driving Club and Margaret Mitchell.* In 1939 John R. Marsh and Margaret Mitchell Marsh moved from their Russell Apartment, their second home together, to a larger apartment at 1268 Piedmont Avenue in 1939. Their new home — their last together — was at 1268 Piedmont Avenue, which was across the street from the Piedmont Driving Club. Their new apartment — Apartment #3 in the Della-Manta Apartments — later carried the address 1 South Prado.

After one of John Marsh's hospitalizations for his heart condition, his doctor recommended that the seriously-ill John drink some alcohol each day for his heart and circulatory system. Marsh began asking for help to cross the street for daily visits to the Piedmont Driving Club. There he would have a drink and stay for about forty minutes.

The Piedmont Driving Club was also the site of one of Margaret and John's only extravagances. They began occasionally sending across the street to the Piedmont Driving Club for cocktails and their dinner; a waiter would serve them in their own living room in the Della-Manta Apartment Building (Farr, pages 218–220).

It was in their Apartment #3 across the street from the Piedmont Driving Club that Margaret Mitchell Marsh and John R. Marsh hosted a small party for some of the cast and crew of *Gone with the Wind* on the evening of Wednesday, December 13, 1939 — before the Friday, December 15, premiere showing (Edwards, pages 281–283).

It was at the Piedmont Driving Club that the Atlanta Women's Press Club held a tea party on the afternoon of December 15, 1939. Clark Gable and Margaret Mitchell both attended the affair (Edwards, pages 285–286).

*See also* Atlanta premiere of *Gone with the Wind*; Atlanta Women's Press Club; Della-Manta Apartments; Gable, (William) Clark; Piedmont Park.

## Piedmont Park

The grounds adjacent to the Piedmont Driving Club had once served as a golf course; later it was the site for expositions and fairs. In 1895 the land was the site of the World's Fair; the area continued to be a place to use for recreation, relaxation, and fun. During World War II, the land — now called Piedmont Park — often served in additional ways, such as a place for the troops to camp.

Margaret Mitchell and her husband, John Marsh, lived near the park in Della-Manta Apartment #3. In December of 1942 Margaret Mitchell and other area women supported the 2,000 soldiers camping in Piedmont Park. Margaret and the other women attached chevrons, mended uniforms, served meals, and assisted in any way needed (Edwards, pages 311–312).

## pistol

After "Red" Upshaw and Margaret Mitchell visited John Marsh to notify him of their separation, John purchased a pistol for Margaret. From December 1922 or July 1923, Margaret kept the loaded pistol beside her bed until she received a report of his death in January 1949 — just months before her own August death in the accident involving a drunken driver. Pyron notes instead that Margaret herself bought the pistol. Walker, however, gives another source of the pistol Margaret stored (Edwards, page 103; Pyron, page 194; Walker, pages 49–50).

## plagiarism

Plagiarism is using another writer's work or closely imitating those words or thoughts without crediting that author. Plagiarism is— simply put — representing someone else's work as one's own and not paying the owner of the work for its use (*Plagiarism*).

*Plagiarism and Margaret Mitchell.* Margaret Mitchell learned about plagiarism at an early age. The lesson held her in good stead as she researched and wrote *Gone with the Wind* and as others tried to use her work without credit or compensation.

As a teenager, Margaret Mitchell based one of her stage productions on some of Thomas Dixon's books— particularly *The Traitor*— that she had read; his books by that time included *The Leopard's Spots: A Romance of the White Man's Burden* (1902), *The Clansman: An Historical Romance of the Ku Klux Klan* (1905), *The Traitor: A Story of the Fall of the Invisible Empire* (1907), *The Fall of a Nation: A Sequel to* The Birth of a Nation (1916). Margaret played the role of Steve Hoyle in the play; he was a character in *The Traitor*.

Margaret's mother, Maybelle Mitchell, was not at home when her daughter presented the play; the program was one in which young Margaret starred. It was also a program that Margaret wrote, using the uncredited works of Thomas Dixon.

Margaret always remembered the reprimand from her parents and the spanking she endured. Even more important she remembered that using the works of others without credit or compensation was the same as stealing. She worked to protect her copyright of *Gone with the Wind*, a work that she had gone to great measures to ensure that she had "stolen" nothing in creating it (Edwards, pages 31–32).

*See also The Traitor* and young Margaret Mitchell.

## Poland, sales of *Gone with the Wind* *see* foreign copyrights/translations and fair trade laws

## Prink, Susan

Susan Prink was the copy editor for Margaret Mitchell's *Gone with the Wind*. Many letters passed between Mitchell and Prink. Margaret was particularly opposed to Susan's having changed some of the dialect of the African American characters. Margaret refused to give in to her on the changes.

Margaret did surrender to Susan on the matter of quotes around Scarlett's stream of consciousness words. At first, Margaret refused to budge. The pair exchanged four letters before Margaret surrendered.

Another matter the two disagreed upon was Margaret's title page. Because a Mary Mitchell was publishing a book that spring also, Susan asked Margaret to use the name *Margaret Marsh* to avoid confusion. Margaret Mitchell would not comply (Edwards, page 190).

*premiere gown for Margaret Mitchell.* Readers of the *Atlanta Constitution* on December 13, 1939, received a news scoop: a preview of Margaret Mitchell's premiere gown. The description read: "The dress is made of layers of pale pink tulle posed over a foundation of pale pink crepe. The bouffant skirt is topped with a tight-fitting bodice, fashioned in front with a sweetheart neckline…. Rose-colored camellias, those flowers so redolent of the old South, will form her floral adornment, and tiny silver slippers will peek beneath the folds of the bouffant skirt" (*Atlanta Constitution,* December 13, 1939, as cited by Judy Cameron and Paul J. Christman. *The Art of* Gone with the Wind. New York: Prentice Hall Editions, 1989, page 229).

### Puerto Rico *see* foreign copyrights/ translations and fair trade laws

### Pulitzer Prize

The Pulitzer Prize refers to a series of prizes that Columbia University in New York City awards annually. The prize recognizes those who have performed outstanding public service and outstanding achievement in American music, letters, and journalism.

Newspaper magnate Joseph Pulitzer (1847–1911) made the Pulitzer Prizes possible with his gift of $500,000. Since 1917 Columbia University has presented the prestigious awards each May. A Pulitzer Prize Board of university-appointed judges selects the recipients. The number of the prizes and the categories of the prizes have varied through the years, but in 2011 there were six prizes in letters, 14 in journalism, one in music, and four fellowships. The six prizes in letters include fiction by an American author and that pertains to American life, a play by an American author and that pertains to American life, a United States history book, a bi-

ography-autobiography written by an American author, a book of verse prepared by an American author, and a non-fiction work not eligible for inclusion in another category and prepared by an American author ("Pulitzer Prize").

### Pulitzer Prize Novel for 1937 (*Gone with the Wind*) and Margaret Mitchell's response

Harold Latham of Macmillan Publishing Company was with Margaret and John in Atlanta on the night of the public announcement that *Gone with the Wind* by Margaret Mitchell was the 1937 winner of the Pulitzer Prize. Neither John, Harold, nor Margaret was home on Monday, May 3, 1937, when the telegram came. The three were visiting with Margaret's father and attending a choir performance at Friendship Baptist Church in Atlanta when the telegram arrived.

Because John Latham had always lavished such praise on the food that Bessie Jordan prepared for him, she had planned a special event for him when she found he would be coming to Atlanta. Latham had mentioned to Bessie on an earlier visit that he was particularly fond of spirituals; she had arranged a special concert for him that night in her church (Walker, page 359). Edwards, however, indicates that John Marsh, Harold Latham, and Margaret Mitchell attended a choir practice — not a special concert that Bessie had arranged at Friendship Missionary Baptist Church in Atlanta (Edwards, page 268).

Margaret Mitchell notes in a letter to Herschel Brickell on May 9, 1937, some details about the concert — an event that Walker indicates lasted until 1:00 A.M. Margaret told Brickell: "The choir was marvelous and half the congregation turned out. The whole affair was so sweet, so simple and

**Friendship Baptist Church in Atlanta, Georgia, was a church that Margaret Mitchell attended with Bessie Berry Jordan. (Courtesy of Friendship Baptist Church and Helena L. Harper, secretary.)**

dignified and in such good taste. Bessie presided and introduced us (John, Harold, Steve, and Carrie Lou) and we all made little talks. The colored folks were pleased to have us but they didn't slop over. They just took it for granted that naturally Bessie's Madam and Bessie's Madam's publisher wanted to hear them sing and oh, how they sang! One old sister got to shouting and I thought Harold Latham would have a spasm he enjoyed it so much. Anyway, we didn't get home until one A.M. and that's why you didn't get me" (Harwell, *Letters*, pages 143–144).

*Reactions to Margaret Mitchell and* Gone with the Wind *earning the Pulitzer Prize for American Fiction (1937).* The reactions to Margaret Mitchell's winning the award varied. Some critics were delighted with the news; others were dismayed. Some were surprised; others had expected the news of Mitchell's winning. Some critics in the spring of 1937 were expecting the Pulitzer Prize for American fiction by an American author to go to William Faulkner for his novel *Absalom, Absalom!*

Margaret had received advance notice of her selection for the prize. Walker suggests that Harold Latham also knew of Margaret's selection, hence his visit to Atlanta. Walker indicates that he had come "ostensibly to visit the reopened Macmillan branch office there. The actual purpose of his visit was to be with Peggy when she received the official word" (Walker, page 359). Edwards, too, suggests that Latham was in town in the "possibility" that Margaret might win the Pulitzer for *Gone with the Wind*; Edwards indicates also that he had not shared this possibility with the author (Edwards, page 268). The American Booksellers presented *Gone with the Wind* its annual award in the spring also.

*Pulitzer Prize and Lamar Ball, city editor of the* Atlanta Constitution. On the night of May 3, 1937, when Lamar Q. Ball learned of the selection of *Gone with the Wind* (1936) as the new Pulitzer Prize winning novel, the city editor of the *Atlanta Constitution* was unable to find the author. The novelist, her husband, Macmillan editor Harold Latham, her brother, and her sister-in-law were at Friendship Missionary Baptist Church in Atlanta; they were listening to the church choir singing (Edwards, pages 266–268).

*See also* **American Booksellers Association annual award; Friendship Baptist Church.**

## Pyron, Darden Asbury

Darden Asbury Pyron was a biographer of Margaret Mitchell. Millichap called Pyron's *Southern Daughter* (1991) the definitive biography of Mitchell. Millichap noted that there were over five hun-

dred pages that Pyron had filled with information from interviews and from various archives; Pyron includes photographs to enhance the biography, which covers Margaret Mitchell's birth until her death — and even beyond. Millichap calls the volume "readable" and "scholarly." Pyron was a full professor at Florida International University the same year as the publication of *Southern Daughter*, which has now been translated into both Czech and German.

Pyron earned his bachelor of arts from Furman University in 1964 and his master of arts (1968) and his Ph.D. (1975) from the University of Virginia. He has been on the staff of Florida International University (FIU) since 1971; his principal area of teaching has been history. He is a two-time winner of the Excellence in Teaching Award at FIU. In addition to *Southern Daughter*, Pyron has written another book relating to Margaret Mitchell: *Recasting* Gone with the Wind *in American Culture* (1983).

Pyron is working on another book that is related to the Civil War: "*I Am a Soldier*": *William Tecumseh Sherman's Civil War*. This will be an abridged, edited, annotated, illustrated edition of Sherman's two-volume memoir from 1875. His newest book is a biography: *Liberace: An American Boy* (2000). Pyron has also authored many grants, articles, reviews, essays, encyclopedia entries, and book chapters; he frequently lectures and presents at formal and scholarly meetings. His professional and academic service is valuable and frequent ("Curriculum Vita of Darden Asbury Pyron").

## "The Rabbit Hole"

John R. Marsh and Margaret Mitchell first met in late September of 1921 at the March Hare Tea Shop in downtown Atlanta. Nicknamed "the Rabbit Hole" by Mitchell and other frequent customers, the bohemian tearoom was at 2½ Auburn Avenue — only a block from Peachtree Street.

The clientele included would-be writers, flappers, students, and news reporters. Dancing and sitting around the red-checked, oilcloth-clad tables were popular pastimes in the café. The beverages of choice were corn whiskey and Coca-Cola or bootleg gin. Margaret was a popular addition to the crowd at the March Hare Tea Shop. She thought of herself as a writer, loved to be the center of attention, and entered into the dancing and conversation with gusto (Walker, pages 8–9).

Margaret captured the attention of John Marsh. He later told Henry Marsh that she was "lovely." John even remembered she was wearing a dark green dress of wool, was sitting on a table with her legs crossed daintily, and was holding her back straight (Walker, page 9). John was told that she was the most popular girl in Atlanta and that she came from a rich family, and he was intrigued. His January 22, 1922, letter to Frances Marsh about the "young revolutionary" with a "helluva lot of common sense" indicated that he was already smitten with Margaret Mitchell (Walker, pages 10–11).

## Randall, Alice

Born in Detroit, Michigan, Alice Randall grew up in Washington, D.C. A 1981 honors graduate from Harvard University, Randall majored in English and in American literature.

*Alice Randall and country music.* Alice Randall moved to Nashville with the intent of writing country songs. She became the first African American woman to write a number one country song: "XXX's and OOO's (An American Girl)"; Trisha Yearwood recorded the song in June of 1994. Randall has had over twenty songs recorded; two of these made the top ten and one made the top forty.

Randall wrote the only known song to explore the subject of lynching ("The Ballad of Sally Ann"). She broached another sensitive topic — the slaves dead and the Confederate dead in the Civil War — when she wrote "I'll Cry for Yours, Will You Cry for Mine?" Randall is also a screenwriter for a movie produced by CBS. As a writer-in-residence at Vanderbilt University, she has taught such courses as Country Lyric in American Culture, Creative Writing, and Soul Food.

*Personal life of Alice Randall.* Alice had married first Attorney Avon Williams III; he was the son of the first black state senator of Tennessee. In 1997 Randall married another lawyer: David Ewing. Caroline Randall Williams studied at Harvard as did her mother ("Gale Contemporary Black Biography: Alice Randall").

*Alice Randall as a novelist.* Randall is the author of *The Wind Done Gone, Pushkin and the Queen of Spades,* and *Rebel Yell.* She characterizes her work as a way to merge race, language, identity, and intimacy. Her particular interests are "depictions of the African American ex motherhood, reading and being southern" ("Alice Randall: Bio").

Randall often writes in her "mother tongue, the black English I learned as a child." She refers to this manner of speaking as "the vanishing language of an illiterate people." Her works often comment on other books and on other readers ("Alice Randall: Bio").

The Wind Done Gone *in litigation.* The trustees of the Margaret Mitchell estate filed suit in March 2001 against the novel *The Wind Done Gone.* As publisher Houghton Mifflin readied *The Wind Done Gone* for publication in June of 2001, trustees of Margaret Mitchell's estate moved to block publication. They called Randall's work "a blatant and wholesale theft" and described the work as a sequel to *Gone with the Wind* for which they had not given authorization. Lawyers who represented the estate of Mitchell specified that Randall had used characters, scenes, and dialogue from the original *Gone with the Wind.* Houghton Mifflin attorneys responded that *The Wind Done Gone* was a parody and as such it fell under "fair use" protection ("Alice Randall Biography from Answers.com").

The lawsuit brought national attention and much debate. Supporters of Randall included such writers as Pat Conroy, Harper Lee, Toni Morrison, Arthur Schlesinger, Jr., and Shelby Foote. Randall's attorney-husband noted that the case had both historical and racial significance. Randall herself presented 15 pages of degrading comments about African Americans taken directly from *Gone with the Wind.*

*Summary of the findings in the case involving* The Wind Done Gone. In April of 2011, U.S. District Judge Charles A. Pannell, Jr., stopped the publication of *The Wind Done Gone* (*TWDG*). Pannell ruled (1) that *The Wind Done Gone* was not a parody and (2) that *The Wind Done Gone* violated copyright of *Gone with the Wind* (*GWTW*).

An appeal ensued in the federal appeals court in Atlanta in May of 2001. Filing briefs in support of *The Wind Done Gone* were CNN, the *New York Times Company,* and four other media companies. These organizations contended that the earlier findings in April of 2011 placed free speech rights as secondary to property rights.

A three-judge panel reversed the April 2011 decision. With the reversal of the previous ruling, *The Wind Done Gone* was available for purchase within a few weeks. Houghton Mifflin had to double the print run because of the increased interest generated by the recent publicity ("Alice Randall Biography from Answers.com").

*Randall's and Houghton Mifflin's defense.* "Citations and Case Summaries page of the Copyright Registration and Renewal Information Chart and Web Site" states: "Randall's literary goal is to explode the romantic, idealized portrait of the antebellum South during and after the Civil War. In the world of *GWTW*, the white characters comprise a noble aristocracy whose idyllic existence is upset only by the intrusion of Yankee soldiers, and, eventually, by the liberation of the black slaves. Through her characters as well as through direct narration, Mitchell describes how both blacks and whites were purportedly better off in the days of slavery....

"Randall's work flips *GWTW*'s traditional race

roles, portrays powerful whites as stupid or feck-less, and generally sets out to demystify *GWTW* and strip the romanticism from Mitchell's specific account of this period of our history. Approxi-mately the last half of *TWDG* tells a completely new story that, although involving characters based on *GWTW* characters, features plot elements found nowhere within the covers of *GWTW*" ("Citations and Case Summaries page of the Copyright Reg-istration and Renewal Information Chart and Web Site").

SunTrust, which represented *Gone with the Wind* and the Margaret Mitchell Estate, argued that Randall's work went further than just commenting on *Gone with the Wind*. Randall's book — the rep-resentatives for *Gone with the Wind* noted — used superfluous details from *Gone with the Wind,* in-cluded unnecessary descriptions and presentations of characters in *Gone with the Wind*, and referenced scenes from Mitchell's novel that were not vital to the parody that Randall claimed to purport. It seemed evident to many participating that — as courts had found in the past — literary relevance was subjective.

The court also considered the effect that that *The Wind Done Gone* would have on the value of the copyright of *Gone with the Wind* and on the mar-keting of and the market for *Gone with the Wind*. The court took into account also the effect *The Wind Done Gone* and their ruling would have on other works with *Gone with the Wind* as their basis and on the resulting market for such works.

SunTrust presented the value of its copyright for *Gone with the Wind* to the court as evidence of the potential for harm to the market for derivative works that could result with certain rulings in the case. SunTrust defined such "derivative works" as including *Gone with the Wind* (the 1939 film), the book *Scarlett: The Sequel to* Gone with the Wind (1991), and *Scarlett: The Sequel* (the 1994 movie). The derivative works with *Gone with the Wind* as their basis and *Gone with the Wind* itself have brought millions of dollars to the estate and the original holders of the copyright.

At the time of the suit, SunTrust had entered into a recent contract with St. Martin's Press, which had paid a seven-figure sum to produce a derivative work with *Gone with the Wind* as its basis. Part of this agreement was that SunTrust would not au-thorize any other derivative works and that Sun-Trust would not authorize any work derivative from *Gone with the Wind* prior to the publication of the Warner book *Scarlett: The Sequel to* Gone with the Wind.

It seemed unlikely, the Appeals Court concluded, that Randall's book would displace sales of *Gone with the Wind*. The court awarded to SunTrust monetary damages for the claimed infringement of copyright ("Citations and Case Summaries page of the Copyright Registration and Renewal Infor-mation Chart and Web Site").

## Rawlings, Marjorie Kinnan (1896–1953)

A personal friend of Margaret Mitchell and a fel-low Southern woman, Marjorie Kinnan Rawlings was also a fellow Pulitzer Prize winner. Marjorie Kinnan was born to Arthur Frank Kinnan and Ida May Traphagen Kinnan in 1896 in Washington, D.C.; Arthur Frank was a patent attorney and a principle examiner in the United States Patent Office.

Marjorie attended the public schools in Wash-ington and was a 1918 Phi Beta Kappa graduate of the University of Wisconsin. Marjorie wanted to write from an early age; she even won in 1907 a prize from the *Washington Post* in the amount of $2.00.

Marjorie worked as a feature writer and reporter for the *Rochester Journal* and the *Louisville Courier-Journal* and in 1919 married Charles A. Rawlings, a college classmate. She wrote fiction at home, but she was unable to find a publisher for her articles and stories. In 1928 she left her job and moved to an orange grove in Cross Creek, Florida. Marjorie found the area around Cross Creek to be half-wild and jungle-like. She found beauty, however, in the countryside.

Marjorie made friends with her poor white neighbors, referred to as *Crackers*, in the Florida area. To Marjorie, the "Crackers" were like frontier families; they were not. Most made their living by farming, fishing, hunting — and perhaps a little "moonshining" on the side.

After Rawlings and her husband divorced in 1933, she began to focus more on her Florida en-vironment and her writing. The subject and the setting of her works began to focus on Florida.

After Rawlings submitted two stories to *Scrib-ner's* and found them successfully published, she found publishers for her books — most of which related to her new environment. Her published books with Florida as a setting include *South Moon Under* (1933); *Golden Apples* (1935); *The Yearling* (1938); *When the Whippoorwill* (1940); *Cross Creek* (1942).

*The Yearling* became her most popular work. She found it translated into thirteen languages. In 1939 it won the Pulitzer Prize.

In 1941 Rawlings married hotel manager Norton Baskin. She began to spend less time in Cross Creek. She lived more at her St. Augustine beach home and at her farmhouse in Van Hornesville,

New York. Her work began to reflect her new sur-roundings. Rawlings's last novel concerns farm life in — of all places— Michigan. Titled *The Sojourner* (1953), the work distances itself from the Florida area so prominent in her early works.

After the publication of her last novel, Rawlings began researching a biography of Ellen Glasgow. She died before she could complete the work. Her burial was in the Cross Creek area she loved: Island Grove, Florida ("Marjorie Kinnan Rawlings").

*Rawlings, Marjorie Kinnan and Margaret Mitch-ell.* Marjorie Kinnan Rawlings wrote to Margaret Mitchell after the publication of *Gone with the Wind*. Margaret described the letter as so "sweet" it gave Margaret "goosebumps" (Walker, page 304).

Rawlings won the 1939 Pulitzer Prize for *The Yearling*. She was the third Southern woman to achieve the honor. During the 1939 Atlanta pre-miere of the film *Gone with the Wind*, the three women with this distinction attended a luncheon at Rich's Department Store. The three Southern women who had won the Pulitzer were Mitchell, Julia Peterkin, and Rawlings (Walker, page 420).

John took a sabbatical from Georgia Power. With the advent of World War II, he had little to do with foreign copyrights and had some time to read. He especially enjoyed Marjorie Kinnan Rawlings's *When the Whippoorwill* and recommended it to his mother. The more he read by Rawlings, the more impressed he was.

When John and Margaret went to Florida for Christmas in 1941, he especially enjoyed meeting Rawlings. Rawlings took the couple on an all-day tour through the Florida scrub. The couple had never seen soil with such a covering of scrub oak, scrub pine, and saw palmetto. During the hours they were with Rawlings, they saw only two auto-mobiles.

For lunch, Marjorie went to a side yard and cut down a tree. From the tree she saved the heart-of-palm salad. She explained to her guests that the heart-of-palm salad was something only the very rich ate at the Waldorf-Astoria or the Ritz. After lunch, Marjorie took John and Margaret to meet the real-life people upon whom she based the char-acters in *The Yearling* (Walker, pages 447–448).

Rawlings took them also to see the cottage that she used as a basis for Jody's home. After the home had become unoccupied and had begun to deteri-orate, MGM Studios had restored the house for use in the film *The Yearling*. The restored house was faithful to Rawlings's description and did not look like a "moonlight and honeysuckle romance" or like a *Tobacco Road* residence (Walker, page 448).

*See also* Atlanta premiere of *Gone with the Wind*; Peterkin, Julia Mood; Pulitzer Prize; Rich's Department Store; *The Yearling*.

## Revenue law of 1952

Even after her death, Margaret Mitchell had an influence in public regulation. Congress passed Code Section 107-C in 1952. This law had the in-tention of providing some tax relief to a citizen who collected in one year the returns of several years of work. The law allows averaging that income over the years of work in which the citizen earned the income. The informal reference for the law is "The Margaret Mitchell Law."

Code Section 107-C recognized the tremendous taxes Margaret Mitchell owed in 1936 and 1937 from her tremendous royalties. In 1964, the In-ternal Revenue Service ruled, however, that the royalties that authors received were not "earned income." Margaret would have disagreed (Farr 232–233).

## Reynolds, Glascock (1903–1967)

Glascock Reynolds was born in Augusta, Geor-gia, and lived most of his life in Georgia. In 1916 he and his family moved to Atlanta. Reynolds stud-ied at the Art Students League in New York City.

During his lifetime Glascock Reynolds would paint more than 450 works, mainly portraits. His subjects included Georgia Governor George W. Towns and Hamilton Douglas, founder of the At-lanta Law School. His regular clients were usually from the Medical College of Georgia, especially the doctors and the deans.

Margaret Mitchell was one of his internation-ally-known subjects. Glascock knew her personally because his sister Caroline Louise ("Carrie Lou") had married Margaret's brother Stephens Mitchell in 1927, a decade before the publication of *Gone with the Wind*.

*Glascock's relationship with Margaret Mitchell.* In 1937 Glascock married Atlanta's Margueryte Scott. Shortly after their marriage, the United States en-tered World War II. Glascock served his country by instructing combat pilots.

After his discharge, he and Margueryte moved to Augusta. Glascock set up an art studio on Cot-ton Row. Later he painted at the Partridge Inn in a penthouse there. In 1950 the couple returned to Atlanta. Reynolds died in Atlanta on September 20, 1967 ("Glascock Reynolds").

Reynolds became even further intertwined with Margaret Mitchell with the location of her papers in an old house that had belonged to one of his rel-atives. These papers became a part of the book *Be-fore Scarlett*, edited by Jane Eskridge with Mary Rose Taylor (Eskridge, pages ix–xxiv).

The story of how Margaret Mitchell's papers found their ways to the old house and their discovery is complicated. The sections on Wailes Thomas, Mary Rose Taylor, and Jane Eskridge give more details on the reason that Wailes and Jane came in contact with the papers.

### Rhett Butler's People

Just after the August death of one of Margaret Mitchell's nephews, Eugene Muse Mitchell (1931–2007), *Rhett Butler's People* appeared in print in November of 2007.

*Rhett Butler's People* by Donald McCaig is the second authorized book to follow as a sequel to Margaret Mitchell's *Gone with the Wind*. The first novelized sequel to Mitchell's work approved by the Mitchell estate was Alexandra Ripley's *Scarlett: The Sequel to Gone with the Wind* (1991); Warner Books (New York) was the publisher of Ripley's successful book *Scarlett*.

The Margaret Mitchell Estate and St. Martin's Press selected McCaig to prepare the second authorized sequel to *Gone with the Wind*. McCaig was already a successful Civil War historian. Ripley's authorized sequel had been a commercial success; the hopes were that McCaig's work would be also (Stephen L. Carter).

Tess Taylor reports that the Mitchell estate and St. Martin's Publishing Company worked for twelve years to negotiate and produce *Rhett Butler's People*. McCaig had worked four years on the sequel. Taylor compares McCaig's sequel to the addition of a modern wing on an old plantation home (Tess Taylor).

*Stipulations of the Margaret Mitchell Estate about McCaig's sequel.* The commission from the Margaret Mitchell Estate made some demands of Donald McCaig. According to Taylor, the commission stipulated among other things, that McCaig not use "interracial or same-sex relationships in the text [or] the n-word" (Tess Taylor).

*Content of Rhett Butler's People.* McCaig took four years to finish his 500-page novel that completes the story left unclear in places in *Gone with the Wind*. McCaig's work covers the years 1843 until 1874; this is almost twenty years more than *Gone with the Wind* chronicles.

Stephen L. Carter indicates that Donald McCaig has one overriding purpose in *Rhett Butler's People*. His goal is to rehabilitate Rhett in the setting of the postwar struggle in the South. McCaig explains away Rhett's membership in the Klan by suggesting Butler found Kennedy suffering from wounds inflicted by a Yankee trap. Kennedy was with other KKK members who had been on a raid; but Rhett was just traveling by when he found Kennedy. The

suspicions of Butler's illegitimate child (not mentioned in the film) in New Orleans are resolved as false in the book (Carter).

*Characters added in Rhett Butler's People.* The family chronicled in detail in *Rhett Butler's People* is the Butler family—not the O'Hara family that Margaret Mitchell detailed in the original *Gone with the Wind*. McCaig features Rhett's stern father Langston, Rhett's sister Rosemary, and Rhett's best friend Tunis. Some characters—Scarlett O'Hara and Bell Watling—are part of both McCaig's novel and in the Pulitzer Prize novel by Margaret Mitchell.

McCaig presents the reader with some additional characters, including Andrew Ravanel. Ravanel is a Confederate veteran who has become a member of the Ku Klux Klan and is also romancing Rosemary, Rhett's sister (Tess Taylor).

*Characters that both Mitchell and McCaig include.* Scarlett O'Hara, Bell Watling, and other characters are present in both McCaig's novel and in the Pulitzer Prize novel by Margaret Mitchell. A frightening character present in both Mitchell's and McCaig's novels is Archie, who works for Melanie; Archie is a racist ex-con who is prone to violence.

Of course, Rhett Butler is an important character in both novels. Carter believes that McCaig seeks primarily to clear Rhett's character in *Rhett Butler's People*. Carter notes that in *Rhett Butler's People* an African American in jail asked Rhett to shoot him; he was afraid a mob would break into the jail and do worse than kill him. Rhett does as the man asks. In McCaig's novel, Rhett asks Scarlett if a Southern gentleman could have done anything else. McCaig clears, in his book, the crime of Butler (Carter).

*Race in McCaig's* Rhett Butler's People. McCaig uses the vocabulary of the time that his novel is set. He employs terms like *nigger* and *colored*. His work, then, differs in that respect from Alexandra Ripley's *Scarlett: The Sequel to Gone with the Wind* (1991). Ripley avoided those terms and called upon such culturally-accepted words of the 1990s as *black*; she has received criticism for using these "ahistorical terms" in her work. McCaig's slaves are not the happy slaves that Mitchell's work implies. His slaves leave when they have an opportunity (Carter).

**See also** McCaig, Donald; Ripley, Alexandra; **Scarlett: The Sequel to Gone with the Wind.**

### Rich's Department Store

Rich's Department Store in Atlanta dates from 1867. Its founder was the Jewish Hungarian immigrant Morris Rich. Rich grew up in Cleveland, Ohio. He borrowed $500 from his brother to open a store in Atlanta. Rich's first store was on White-

Rich's Department Store in Atlanta dates from 1924. This photograph shows the east and north sides of the 1924 store. It was here that Margaret Mitchell first met Harold Latham and here that she attended a luncheon for two Southern women Pulitzer Prize winners and herself. (Courtesy of Woodhaven Historic Photographs.)

hall Street. Rich's expanded to several locations over the next half century or so. In 1924 Rich's opened at Broad and Alabama (near the Eternal Flame of the Confederacy), its final Atlanta location. During the Great Depression, Rich's even accepted cotton in payment for its goods, offered credit to almost anyone, and accepted the scrip Georgia used to pay its teachers.

Rich's Department Store became the symbol of retail shopping in Atlanta and began expanding to shopping malls in the 1950s and 1960s. Rich's is an Atlanta and a Southern institution. After a merger with Macy's in the 1990s, the stores became known as Rich's-Macy's. Finally in 2005 Rich's-Macy's closed. Some Atlantans saw this as the end of an era (Bailey).

*Rich's and Margaret Mitchell.* Rich's Department Store figured prominently in the life of most Atlanta residents in the 1930s—as it did in Margaret Mitchell's life and profession.

Harold Latham of Macmillan was visiting Atlanta on April 11, 1935. He was scouting for new manuscripts at the time. He attended a luncheon at Rich's Department Store. It was here at Rich's that Margaret Mitchell began seriously considering submitting her manuscript to a publisher (Farr, pages 89–95).

That afternoon Margaret Mitchell had visited Latham and given him her manuscript. The place where she had given him the manuscript varies from one source to another. Edwards says the delivery was to the Georgian Terrace Hotel, 659 Peachtree, NE (corner of Peachtree and Ponce de Leon Avenue) (page 3). Lois Cole, associate editor of Macmillan Publishing Company, mentioned that Mitchell took the unorganized envelopes holding the chapters to Latham in the lobby of the Biltmore Hotel, where he was staying in Atlanta (Brown, 16). Margaret Baugh, Margaret Mitchell's personal secretary and previously a secretary in the Atlanta Office of Macmillan Publishing Company, told the story of Margaret Mitchell delivering the manuscript of *Gone with the Wind* to Latham in the lobby of the Ansley Hotel in Atlanta (Brown, page 16). In his book, Latham himself neglects to give the name of the hotel where the meeting took place.

*Rich's Department Store and the marketing of Margaret Mitchell's Gone with the Wind.* Rich's Department Store had a debatable role in the marketing of *Gone with the Wind*. Rich's role began with the book signing the first week of the release of Mitchell's novel and continued through the years.

Macmillan Publishing Company had arranged three book signings in Atlanta in advance of the release of the book. Mitchell agreed to attend all three of the signings at three local department stores the week that the book *Gone with the Wind* became available for sales. The three stores were Rich's Department Store, Davison-Paxon, and the lending library at Sears-Roebuck.

When Rich's discovered that Davison-Paxon Department Store had scheduled Mitchell's signing ahead of Rich's, the management at Rich's was upset not to be the first. Rich's cancelled Mitchell's signing. This meant that Davison-Paxon and Sears Roebuck were the first stores to host a signing for Mitchell (Brown, pages 92–93).

Rich's Department Store did carry and sell the book, but the relationship of the book buyer and the executive staff with Margaret Mitchell was strained for some time. It was at the 1939 Atlanta premiere of *Gone with the Wind* that Margaret Mitchell came to Rich's for the first event since the store had cancelled the 1936 book signing.

*Rich's as the site for an event during the 1939 Atlanta premiere of Gone with the Wind.* An important part of the Atlanta events of December 1939 was a luncheon at Rich's Department Store; this was the first event that Mitchell attended during the Atlanta premiere and the first event she attended since Rich's cancelled its 1936 book signing event.

Brown notes that the honored guests at the luncheon were Macmillan executives and Mitchell. She makes no mention of the other two Southern Pulitzer Prize winning women, Marjorie Kinnan Rawlings and Julia Mood Peterkin, or of the Atlanta Women's Press Club (205).

Walker observes that the honored guests at the December 1939 luncheon at Rich's Department Store were the Macmillan Publishing Company executives and the three Pulitzer Prize Winning Southern women, Mitchell, Peterkin, and Rawlings. The book buyer at Rich's hosted the event, according to Walker (420).

Edwards does not give the sponsor of the December 1939 luncheon. She does note that among other guests were three Southern Pulitzer Prize-winning women (page 376). Farr, on the other hand, does not mention the luncheon at Rich's Department Store as part of the events of the 1939 Atlanta premiere.

Pyron credits the Atlanta Women's Press Club as hosting the 1939 Atlanta premiere of *Gone with the Wind* luncheon. He observes that the three Southern women who had won the Pulitzer Prize were in attendance and names them (page 377).

Brown states that the book buyer at Rich's—not the Atlanta Women's Press Club—had arranged the 1939 luncheon event for Macmillan executives: "At long last, the store that had declined to hold a signing for Mitchell in June 1936 and had been finagling to make up for the gaffe ever since, managed to get the author to attend an event in celebration of *Gone with the Wind*" (page 205).

*Rich's as site for Margaret Mitchell to sell stamps and bonds for the American Red Cross.* During World War II Margaret Mitchell often sold bonds. She raised $212,000 in four hours selling bonds and stamps in Rich's Department Store in Atlanta on one occasion (Farr, page 213).

*See also* **addresses directly related to Margaret Mitchell; American Red Cross; Ansley Hotel; Atlanta premiere of *Gone with the Wind*; Baugh, Margaret Eugenia; Biltmore Hotel; Cole, Lois; Eternal Flame of the Confederacy; Georgia Terrace Hotel; Latham, Harold Strong; Macmillan Publishing Company; Peterkin, Julia Mood; Pulitzer Prize; Rawlings, Marjorie Kinnan.**

### Ripley, Alexandra (1934–2004)

Born Alexandra Braid in Charleston, South Carolina, on January 8, 1934, this historical novelist's birth came just two years before Margaret Mitchell published *Gone with the Wind*. Alexandra Ripley would write a 1991 sequel to *Gone with the Wind*. Her sequel carried the title *Scarlett: The Sequel to Gone with the Wind* (1991).

Alexandra graduated from a Charleston finishing school, Ashley Hall. On a scholarship, she attended and graduated from Vassar College in the state of New York. After her graduation she worked in the advertising department of a New York magazine and then took a job for an airline in Washington, D.C.

Alexandra married Leonard Ripley in 1958. The couple had two daughters before their marriage dissolved in 1963. They had lived in both Florence and in New York. After the divorce, Alexandra Ripley returned to Charleston. She tried several jobs in Charleston before finally returning to New York as an editor for a publisher. She finally decided that she could write better books than the ones she had been reading (Guttridge).

*Alexandra Ripley and a career in writing.* Ripley moved to Charlottesville, Virginia, where the cost of living was cheaper, to write her first book. In 1972 her first novel, *Who's That Lady in the President's Bed?*— about a female president — appeared in print. She used the pen name B.K. Ripley.

Several books of different genres followed. They did not create many ripples in the lake of books at the time. In 1981, however, she established her place as a writer of historical romances with her book *Charleston*, a Civil War epic. She used *Alexandra Ripley* as her pen name.

Alexandra married the academic John Graham, but she kept Alexandra Ripley as her pen name.

The old Virginia farmhouse into which they moved seemed conducive to writing. In 1984 her *On Leaving Charleston* appeared in print. This was a sequel to her popular 1981 novel *Charleston*.

Her time living abroad prompted Alexandra to write *The Time Returns* (1985). The novel with its Renaissance Florence setting created criticisms of historical inaccuracies. Critics complained also of her next historical romance, *New Orleans Legacy* (1987).

*Alexandra Ripley and a contract to produce a sequel to Margaret Mitchell's novel.* In 1986 the Margaret Mitchell Estate engaged Alexandra Ripley to write an authorized sequel to *Gone with the Wind*; some reviewers called it "an officially sanctioned sequel." Ripley was the author of five previous novels. Their selection of Alexandra Ripley for the work was controversial because the public was not certain that Margaret Mitchell wanted a sequel to her work. Mitchell herself had refused to write anything further after the publication of her novel (Gilpin).

Gilpin quotes from Ripley's interview in *Contemporary Authors*, in which she says: "There are two reasons why I'm doing this book. I can't resist it, and as soon as this is done I will be able to write anything I want to."

*Alexandra Ripley and* Scarlett: The Sequel to Gone with the Wind *(1991).* To prepare for the task, Alexandra re-read the novel — six times. To try to capture the fundamental nature of Mitchell's novel, Alexandra began writing the first pages— some 300 of them — in longhand. The finished, published volume totaled 884 pages (Guttridge).

Margaret Mitchell's novel and its characters were not new to Alexandra. When she was 12, she read *Gone with the Wind* for her first time in her hometown of Charleston. As an adolescent and after she read the novel, she began to sell directions to Rhett Butler's gravesite to naïve, sightseeing Charleston tourists. (Margaret Mitchell's character Rhett Butler was supposedly from Charleston.)

Alexandra admitted she was not fond of her heroine even as she wrote. "I really don't know why Scarlett has such appeal. When I began writing the sequel, I had a lot of trouble because Scarlett is not my kind of person. She's virtually illiterate, has no taste, never learns from her mistakes" (Guttridge).

Ripley even varied the setting of a large part of *Scarlett: The Sequel to Gone with the Wind* away from Atlanta. Ripley takes the reader from Atlanta to Tara to Charleston to Savannah to Ireland, which was quite a departure from Mitchell's work (Guttridge).

*Scarlett: The Sequel to Gone with the Wind* brought a reunion between the characters Rhett and Scarlett — although the reconciliation might have been for the moment only. Perhaps, some critics scoffed, Ripley tempered the characters in her work more than readers expected or wanted. Some critics even questioned if *Gone with the Wind* actually was fundamentally a love story as Ripley seemed to have assumed; they suggested that Ripley did not address certain other important parts in the sequel (Gilpin).

Ripley's *Scarlett: The Sequel to Gone with the Wind* became a commercial success. Her sequel topped the bestseller list of the *New York Times*. Ripley's novel even stimulated renewed interest in and revived sales of *Gone with the Wind*. The rights to *Scarlett* for a television mini-series sold to CBS for eight million dollars; that figure was then a record amount for a TV mini-series at that time (Guttridge). In addition, Warner Books had paid $4.94 million for the rights to publish the contracted novel (Gilpin).

Critics noted that Ripley had removed slaves from the sequel by taking much of the story to Ireland. Many negative reviewers observed that Ripley used the term *black* to refer to the African American characters in *Scarlett: The Sequel to Gone with the Wind*. Gilpin suggests that this "ahistorical term" would have been offensive at the time that *Scarlett* occurs and that Ripley should not have used that term as she did (Gilpin).

*Alexandra Ripley and her post–Scarlett writings.* Ripley's subsequent novels were *From Fields of Gold* (1994) and *Love Divine* (1997). *From Fields of Gold* had Virginia as its setting and some Virginia tobacco barons as main characters. Ripley's last novel — the 800-page *Love Divine* — takes the reader to ancient Palestine, ancient Gaul, and ancient Britain through its main character: Joseph of Arimathea. Guttridge describes the work as an "800-page blockbuster."

*Alexandra Ripley's death.* Two days after her 70th birthday, Alexandra Ripley died at her home in Richmond, Virginia. Elizabeth Lyon Ripley spoke of her mother's passing to the Associated Press; she stated that the death was a result of natural causes that she did not specify (Gilpin, Guttridge).

### Rivers, Eurith Dickinson (1895–1967)

Nicknamed "Ed" from his initials, Eurith Dickinson Rivers is best known as a Georgia politician. Rivers was the 68th governor of Georgia and was serving his second term (1938–1940) in that post during the time of the 1939 Atlanta premiere of *Gone with the Wind*.

*Eurith Dickinson Rivers: birth, education, and early life.* "Ed" Rivers was born in Center Point, Arkansas, in 1895. He was a student at Young Harris College. Rivers met his future wife, Mattie

Lucille Lashley, while they were both studying at Young Harris. They married in 1914 and had two children: Eurith Dickinson, Jr., and Geraldine. Rivers studied at the graduate level at LaSalle Extension University in Illinois. He earned his law degree in 1923 (Patton).

*The Rivers family's settlement in Georgia.* The Rivers family moved to Cairo, Georgia. Rivers established himself as the city attorney for Cairo and later as a justice of the peace. He served also as an attorney for Grady County.

The family moved next to Milltown (now called Lakeland). There Rivers became the editor of the local paper, the *Lanier County News* (Patton).

*Eurith Dickinson Rivers and state government.* Ed Rivers ran successfully for election to the Georgia House of Representatives in 1924 and for the state senate in 1926. As were many other Georgia rural county leaders, Rivers was active also in the Ku Klux Klan. Rivers, however, expressed genuine concern for the conditions on the farms of rural Georgia. He wanted to secure aid for Georgians through government programs, which his predecessor, Eugene Talmadge, opposed. Rivers openly endorsed the New Deal programs of President Franklin D. Roosevelt (Patton).

*Eurith Dickinson Rivers and the governorship (1936–1938).* Eurith Dickinson Rivers's first election to the governorship of Georgia began in the year 1936. During his first two-year term, Rivers publicized that he was bringing/had brought a "Little New Deal" to Georgia; during this term he advocated and presided over an expansion of state services, including aid to education, housing, and electrification.

Rivers was able to sway the legislature to pass legislation enabling Georgia to receive federal funds for public housing and rural electrification. The housing in some areas of Georgia — especially in parts of Atlanta — was in need of improvement. The establishment of the Georgia Housing Authority facilitated slum clearance and public housing by making acceptance of federal funds easier (Patton).

Because of the federal concern for poor housing, the first public housing in the United States was in Atlanta, Georgia. Techwood Housing in Atlanta opened during Rivers's first term as governor (Davis, *Georgia During the Great Depression*, pages 79–80).

Georgia received $17 million from the federal government for rural electrification. These grants affected Georgia Power Company, the company that employed John R. Marsh (Patton).

Rivers' first two-year term as governor saw the Georgia legislature pass the provisions necessary to bring New Deal programs into the state; Rivers received much acclaim. Under his leadership, electrical services were expanded to rural areas of the state, and Georgia moved from the lowest-ranked state to the top of the list on the number of rural electrification associations. While Rivers was in office, Georgians saw also the creation of the State Bureau of Unemployment Compensation; this office allowed Georgians to receive unemployment benefits ("Eurith D. Rivers").

Rivers also created ways to improve health and prison reform in the state. During his two consecutive terms (1936–1938; 1938–1940) the appropriations for education amounted to $49 million; this amount aided all the state's schools, textbook programs, and salaries for teachers— even though segregation remained.

*Rivers's second term (1938–1940).* Rivers ran against Talmadge for election to the position of governor of Georgia for 1938–1940. Rivers won. The 1939 premiere of *Gone with the Wind* (the film) occurred during Rivers's second term.

Rivers and his administration, however, would end the two-year term among controversy. In campaigning as an anti–Talmadge candidate, Rivers condemned Talmadge's policies, including Talmadge's use of the National Guard. Yet Rivers himself would find it necessary to call upon the National Guard to settle some political disputes before the end of his second term. Some charged the Rivers administration with corruption during his second term.

The legislature would not enact increased taxes to pay for the programs. The state was unable to pay its salaries for teachers. Rivers tried to redirect highway funds to the schools and even called in the National Guard to remove the unyielding highway commissioner from his job.

The controversy moved to the state courts. Rivers was placed under arrest for refusing to comply with a federal court order, but the arrest was overturned. The courts enabled Rivers to divert the funds, but the whole affair created much controversy. Georgia law does not allow three consecutive terms as governor so Rivers naturally had to step down— before his administration was put to the test of an election.

In 1940 a federal grand jury indicted four members of the Rivers administration on corruption charges; the grand jury convicted two. In 1942 came the arrest of Rivers and nineteen others. Although Rivers had granted fewer pardons than his predecessor, charges were that he sold pardons and one count of embezzlement. There was a jury deadlock (Patton). He was defeated by Talmadge in the 1946 governor's race. Rivers never again received election to a public position. At the time of his 1967 death, however, he was a successful businessman and owned several radio stations in Atlanta (Patton).

*Eurith D. Rivers and the Atlanta Premiere of Gone with the Wind (the film).* As governor of Georgia during the premiere of the film *Gone with the Wind*, Rivers declared Friday the 15th of December 1939 as a state holiday. He advocated statewide support of the event and encouraged the wearing of costumes for the day.

***See also** Atlanta premiere of **Gone with the Wind**.*

## Road to Tara Museum

In *Gone with the Wind* (the book), Jonesboro is the setting for the Tara Plantation. Jonesboro— in Clayton County — is just 15 miles south of midtown Atlanta. The Mitchell family designated Clayton County as the "Official Home of *Gone with the Wind*" ("Clayton County Georgia").

The Road to Tara Museum is in historic Jonesboro. The museum is not an officially sanctioned museum by the Mitchell Family. Of course, there was never a real Tara, but visitors have to be reminded of that.

An 1867 train depot holds the museum, which features memorabilia of both the book and the movie. Props, costume reproductions, doll collections, and plate collections are among the items in the gallery ("Road to Tara Museum").

The curator and owner of the Road to Tara Museum (2011) is Patsy Wiggins. She had collected memorabilia related to Margaret Mitchell and *Gone with the Wind* (the film, the book) for more than three decades.

*Lost Laysen.* One of the most publicized purchases that Peggy Wiggins made was that of *Lost Laysen*. She purchased the early novella by Margaret Mitchell from Henry Angel, Jr. This newly discovered work appeared in print in 1996 — and in several different languages (Hubbard).

Angel's grandfather had corresponded with Margaret Mitchell. It was in the elder Angel's papers that Henry Angel, Jr., found the manuscript. Henry Angel, Jr., later sold the manuscript to Wiggins (Hubbard; "Southern Draw").

***See also** Tara.*

## Roberts, Pamela

Pamela Roberts is executive producer, director and writer at Georgia Public Broadcasting in Atlanta. The documentary filmmaker is an award-winning employee of GPB. In 2010 she earned an Emmy for *The Road beyond Abuse,* which Jane Fonda narrated. She received the CINE Golden Eagle

Award and the "Best of Television" by the Society of Professional Journalists. Roberts won also an Emmy Award for *Andrew Low: A Savannah Story*; her set this historical documentary set in 19th century Savannah. Another favored documentary is *Defying the Odds*, in which she examined inner city education. Between 2008 and 2009, Roberts earned three Emmy Awards for her portrayal of Georgia artists within *State of the Arts*, a series which she produced, wrote and directed for GPB.

In considering that *Gone with the Wind* (the book) would celebrate its 75th Anniversary in 2011, she decided that the author deserved more than a segment with the arts series. The end result was *Margaret Mitchell: An American Rebel*.

Roberts has also produced programs in the *Portrait of America* series for Turner Broadcasting. She has also worked as an independent producer. During this time, she produced and directed two documentaries which PBS aired; they were *Seeds of Survival* and *The Land of Cool Sun*. She has written and directed dramatizations for such nationally-aired NBC shows as *Angels: The Mysterious Messengers* and *Ancient Prophecies* ("GPB: Behind the Scenes; Margaret Mitchell").

**Romania, sales of *Gone with the Wind*** *see* **foreign copyrights/translations and fair trade laws**

### Ropa Carmigan (sometimes listed as 'Ropa Carmigan)

*Ropa Carmigan* is a novella set in the Reconstruction era following the Civil War. Margaret Mitchell was the author of this early book. The work centers on "the life of a reclusive woman from a privileged family whose life had taken an unfortunate downward turn" (McGee).

*Margaret Mitchell writes* Ropa Carmigan. On May 3, 1926, Margaret Mitchell drew her last paycheck from her regular job with the *Atlanta Constitution*. By the fall of the same year, Margaret was bored with being in "The Dump" without a project (Edwards, page 129).

Mitchell used her sewing table and her old typewriter to write *Ropa Carmigan*. She placed the table and the typewriter between the two high, vertical windows in the sitting room of "The Dump." (The typewriter is still available for viewing at the Atlanta-Fulton County Library.)

John and Margaret hired "Lula" Tolbert to clean for them. This meant that Mitchell would have even more time to work on her novella.

Ropa Carmigan *(a summary)*. Three weeks and fifteen thousand words later (about 60 typewritten pages), Margaret Mitchell had finished *Ropa Carmigan*. Important to the novel — as it had been to Margaret Mitchell's life — was the Jonesboro Road, where Maybelle Mitchell had shown young Margaret the importance of *gumption*.

The heroine of the novel is Europa Carmigan. The precise setting is near the old Fitzgerald plantation that had been in her mother's family for years. Also included in the background are the dilapidated houses that had belonged to those without gumption. Europa's family has such a dilapidated home and farm. To compound her problems further, the neighbors force her to leave her home and land — but not before the death of her lover.

*John R. Marsh's reaction to* Ropa Carmigan. Margaret Mitchell's husband, John R. Marsh, was not overly encouraging about the novella when she showed it to him. He made some suggestions and proposed that she put it aside for a while. Mitchell put the manuscript in a manila envelope and put it away. She continued, however, to think about the book she wanted to write (Edwards, pages 129–132).

Ropa Carmigan *resurfaces*. When Mitchell presented Harold Latham with the manila envelopes containing what would be *Gone with the Wind*, she accidentally included the envelope containing her novella *Ropa Carmigan*.

Mitchell learned in early August that she had inadvertently included the envelope containing *Ropa Carmigan*. In August of 1935 the novella arrived at Margaret Mitchell's home along with the contracts for what would be her lengthy book.

Latham also included a note that he had written on August 15, 1935, about *Ropa Carmigan*. Latham was encouraging about the novella and called it a "splendid piece of work" (Edwards, page 173).

Latham noted, however, that for the time being Margaret would need to concentrate on the lengthier work. The letter is still in the archives at Macmillan Publishing Company; Edwards includes part of the letter in her *Road to Tara*. Latham wrote on August 15, 1935: "After I asked to have your manuscript returned to you [for revisions] I found I still had in my possession the novelette 'Ropa Carmigan which you gave me at the same time. I am returning this to you under separate cover. I have read this with a great deal of interest and very genuine admiration. It seems to me a splendid piece of work, expertly done. Its length is, of course, against it commercially speaking and of course it is too short for book form. I suggest that you hold it until after your novel is published. You may very easily be able to sell it to one of the better magazines after the appearance of your book. It confirms my very high opinion of you as a writer" (Edwards, pages 173–174).

John R. Marsh indicates in an interview what happened to *Ropa Carmigan*. He notes that "unfortunately" it was among the papers he destroyed at Margaret Mitchell's request after her death (McGee).

*See also* gumption; Latham, Harold Strong; Tolbert, Laura.

### Rose, Billy (1899–1966)

The lyricist and Broadway producer Billy Rose (1899–1966) was born on September 6, 1899, in New York City. He graduated from New York's High School of Commerce; after his graduation he studied Gregg shorthand; at 16, after high school graduation and after his course in shorthand, he was the winner of a dictation contest for speed in recording. During World War I Rose worked as a shorthand reporter for the War Industries Board.

After the war, he began working in New York City on scores for Broadway productions. He collaborated with Al Jolson, Mort Dixon, and other successful composers of the time. He also produced some plays and musicals, which included *Carmen Jones*, and wrote and produced for such expositions as the New York World's Fair. Rose operated and owned the Diamond Horseshoe Club in New York City and the Ziegfeld and Billy Rose Theatres.

His list of hits is vast. Some of his best-known songs included "You've Got to See Momma Every Night," "That Old Gang of Mine," "I Found a Million Dollar Baby (In a Five and Ten Cent Store)," "Me and My Shadow," "Four Walls," "Tonight You Belong to Me," "It's Only a Paper Moon," and "I Wanna Be Loved."

On February 10, 1966, Billy Rose died in Jamaica, British Virgin Islands ("Songwriters Hall of Fame: Billy Rose").

*Billy Rose and suit against him by Margaret Mitchell.* Margaret Mitchell brought a suit against Billy Rose for not securing stage rights for his use of *Gone with the Wind* in a pantomime stage production.

1. In a letter of July 22, 1937, to Mrs. Louis Davent Bolton in Mansfield, Georgia, Mitchell declined an invitation from Mrs. Bolton for the weekend. One of her explanations was the work on the suit against Rose for his use of her work (Harwell, *Letters*, page 155).

2. On September 4, 1937, Mitchell complained to Herschel Brickell about the pending case. She followed up with a letter that she was leaving at midnight to pursue the matter (Harwell, *Letters*, pages 166–167).

3. At the conclusion of the case Rose paid $3,000 in damages to Mitchell. He pledged to pay her $25,000 if he again violated her rights. Farr quotes

from his letter of apology to Mitchell after the settlement: "I realize now that I should not have used the title of your book or any of your characters, or the names of any of any of your characters, alluded to your book in any way without your consent, and I apologize to you for having done so" (page 177).

### Ross, Courtenay

Especially from the time that Eugene Muse Mitchell (1866–1944) moved his family to Peachtree Street (1149, 1401, or 1701) in 1912, Courtenay Ross and Margaret Mitchell were fast friends. Mitchell wrote a novella, *Lost Laysen*, with Courtenay Ross as the main character.

Mitchell and Ross were in a pony cart accident together when they were teenagers. Mitchell's first husband, Berrien Kinnard ("Red") Upshaw, was a suitor of Courtenay before Margaret and he became sweethearts.

Ross and Mitchell had an enduring friendship. Courtenay shared the good and the bad with Margaret. Besides living close together, they debuted together, performed in Mitchell's dramas, and double-dated. Courtenay married Bernice McFedyen in October of 1920.

When Mitchell was working on *Gone with the Wind*, she often became moody. Courtenay Ross told in an interview about one of Margaret's tantrums. "It was about this time [1926] that she had a terrible explosion with her oldest friend, Courtenay Ross McFedyen. Court had heard about Mitchell's illness and stopped by with flowers. She found the apartment door ajar, walked in, and proffered her roses. 'Peggy slammed them on the floor, stamped her foot, and shouted at me to get out and never come back.' The completely astonished friend retreated sheepishly and did not return for years" (Pyron, page 223).

*See also* accidents; Angel, Henry Love; *Lost Laysen*; Road to Tara Museum; Upshaw, Berrien Kinnard "Red"; Wiggins, Patsy.

### Russell Apartments

The second apartment building in which Margaret Mitchell and her husband, John R. Marsh, lived was the Russell Apartment Building, at 4 East 17th Street.

The Marshes lived in the Russell Apartments from 1932 until 1939. This was the third and last apartment in which the Marshes would live together. Margaret redecorated this apartment.

In 1939 John and Margaret moved to the Della-Manta Apartments at 1268 Piedmont Avenue.

*See also* addresses directly related to Margaret Mitchell.

## St. Philip's Cathedral

Established in 1846, St. Philips Episcopal Church had its first building across from the Atlanta State Capitol. As it continued to grow in membership and as the street elevation changed, still further modifications in the facilities became necessary.

In 1933, under the leadership of the Dean Raimundo de Ovies, St. Philip's Cathedral moved to its present location. The present Mikell Chapel was its main worship facility until the construction of the Cathedral proper.

In honor of Dean Raimundo De Ovies, the congregation named the De Ovies Memorial Hall for him. It was de Ovies who conducted Margaret Mitchell's funeral service at the chapel of the Spring Hill Funeral Home ("The Cathedral of St. Philips: About Us").

*See also* **de Ovies, Dean Raimundo; Spring Hill Chapel.**

## Saunders, Marion

After the publication of *Gone with the Wind*, foreign markets started showing an interest. Harold Latham began seeking an agent to help with the foreign contracts. What he did not know was that Marion Saunders was already beginning to market the novel — without a contract signed by a representative of Macmillan Publishing Company or without a contract from Margaret Mitchell. In fact, Jim Putnam, in acting for Macmillan, had written that Margaret would have to take charge of all foreign copyrights and signed those copyrights over to Margaret. Putnam recommended Marion Saunders — a British agent — who had her own small New York firm (Walker, pages 309–310). "Saunders wrote to Mitchell in early May 1936, announcing, in what appears to be a bold-face lie, that she was handling the continental European rights of *Gone with the Wind* for Macmillan" (Brown, pages 78–79). After a series of communications and after an accountant reviewed the books, Saunders wrote to tell the Marshes that she would be traveling to Atlanta to talk with them personally. The matter she wanted to discuss was a $30,000 shortfall discovered by the auditors. Saunders admitted her crime of taking more than $28,000 from the Marshes in a face-to-face meeting on October 7 — but did not accept full responsibility. She agreed to repay them, but she asked to remain with them as their agent; they declined (Brown, pages 78–80, 235).

In 1951 Marion Saunders satisfied her debt to John R. Marsh — after Margaret Mitchell's death in 1949. The public was never fully aware of Saunders's embezzlement; Saunders remained in business. Marsh wrote to her on December 7, 1951, to acknowledge receipt of the payments; he said that he would try to forget what had happened, but the estate did not retain her services (Brown, page 273).

## *Scarlett: The Sequel* (1991)

Alexandra Ripley's sequel to *Gone with the Wind* was a controversial publication of Warner Books. The Mitchell estate contracted for the book with Alexandria Ripley.

*See also* **Ripley, Alexandra.**

## Scarlett O'Hara

Scarlett O'Hara is the female protagonist of Margaret Mitchell's *Gone with the Wind*.

At the beginning of the story, Scarlett is a "vibrant, young creature with great strength of character." At the end of the novel, she has had three children, three husbands, and many trials, but she had demonstrated gumption. Scarlett allows neither men nor circumstance to control her life. She asserts herself in the face of adversity (Ludwig).

Casting the actress for the part of Scarlett O'Hara was a complicated lengthy process. At last, David O. Selznick chose Vivien Leigh for the role. Both Myron Selznick and Kay Brown were helpful in the casting.

*See also* **gumption; Brown, Katharine "Kay"; Selznick, Myron.**

## Sea Island

The smallest of the barrier islands off the coast of Georgia is Sea Island. The island remained largely uninhabited until 1924; in that year the causeway between Brunswick to St. Simons was complete and ready to use. The construction of this causeway was possible without state or federal funds. It was here on Sea Island in the Cloister Hotel that John R. Marsh suffered — and survived — a severe heart attack in 1945. (Davis, *Georgia During the Great Depression*, page 27)

*See also* **the Cloister Hotel; Marsh, John R.**

## Second premiere *see* **Atlanta premiere of *Gone with the Wind*, second premiere.**

## self-abnegation

Brown categorizes Margaret Mitchell as an example of "self-abnegation" in the literary world. Like Elmer Davis, Brown agrees that Margaret Mitchell wrote her one novel and then refused to write again — even though she received many offers of money. Brown suggests that this refusal may have been as great an achievement as writing the novel (Elmer Davis; Brown, page 256).

## Self-employed Individuals Tax Retirement Act of 1962

This legislation provided self-employed people a tax deduction for retirement plans that they had to finance from the earned income. For this bill, Margaret Mitchell received attention — even though she had died in 1949 (Farr, page 233).

## Selznick, David O. (1902–1965)

David Selznick was born in Pittsburgh, Pennsylvania, in 1902. IIe had no middle name or middle initial at birth; he added the middle initial later in life.

David was born to Lewis J. Selznick, a silent-movie producer. David studied at Columbia University until the family had financial difficulties in the 1920s. He found employment as a script reader for MGM. He moved from MGM to Paramount and then to RKO. In 1933, he married Irene Mayer, the daughter of Louis B. Mayer. David moved back to MGM Studios.

In 1936 Selznick set up Selznick International Pictures, his own production company. In 1936, he paid $50,000 to Margaret Mitchell for movie rights to *Gone with the Wind*. Selznick went through fifteen script writers and three directors before the release of the film. After the film became a hit production, he paid Mitchell another $50,000.

During David and Irene Mayer Selznick's almost nineteen years of marriage (1930–1949), the couple had two children: L. Jeffrey Selznick and Daniel Selznick. David O. Selznick remarried in 1949; his spouse Jennifer Jones and he had one child, Mary Jennifer, before David's 1965 death from a heart attack.

One day after what would have been her father's birthday in 1976, twenty-two-year-old Mary Jennifer committed suicide by jumping from the tallest building in Westwood; her psychotherapist was on vacation. After this tragedy, Jennifer Jones herself trained to be a therapist.

David placed three actresses in the movie roles that made them stars. These stars were Katharine Hepburn, Joan Fontaine, and Jennifer Jones. With his brother Myron Selznick to help him, he cast Vivien Leigh in the role of Scarlett O'Hara ("Biography for David O. Selznick").

Selznick had a reputation for writing long, detailed memos. These went to directors, writers, editors, cameramen, and others. One went to a publicist; Selznick sent him a 30-foot-long telegram. Selznick concluded that telegram by saying: "I have just received a phone call that pretty much clears up this matter. Therefore you can disregard this wire" ("Biography for David O. Selznick"). Rudy

Behlmer wrote a book called *Memos from David Selznick*. Selznick dictated enough memos to his secretaries to fill 2,000 file boxes between the years 1916 and 1965.

To date, David O. Selznick is the only producer to have won back-to-back Oscars for the Best Picture. He won the award in 1939 for *Gone with the Wind* and in 1940 for *Rebecca*.

Selznick International Pictures had changed its focus by the late 1940s. It had begun to act more as a talent agency than as a producer of movies; most of its income came from lending stars under contract to other studios.

David O. Selznick brought Ingrid Bergman to America and signed her to a contract with Selznick International Pictures. He changed the look of Hollywood by insisting that Vivien Leigh and Ingrid Bergman model a more natural brow line than the Max Factor eye brows (popular at the time) that gave the look of a doll to the stars.

In 1965, David O. Selznick — in his early 60s — died unexpectedly in Hollywood, California, from a heart attack ("Biography for David O. Selznick").

***See also*** **Academy of Motion Picture Arts and Sciences Awards; Selznick, Myron.**

## Selznick, Irene Mayer (1907–1990)

Irene Mayer married David O. Selznick in 1933. David worked on two different occasions with Irene's father, Louis B. Mayer. In 1936 her husband set up his own production company: Selznick International Pictures.

During her nineteen-year marriage (1930–1949) to David O. Selznick, the couple had two children, L. Jeffrey and Daniel Selznick. Irene Mayer Selznick began producing in her own right. In 1951 she was the presenter of the stage play *A Streetcar Named Desire*, and in 1956 she earned a nomination for Broadway's Tony Award for her production of *The Chalk Garden*. Irene Selznick produced also the New York play *Bell, Book, and Candle* (1958).

Irene Selznick lived to be eighty-three ("Biography for Irene Mayer Selznick").

## Selznick, Myron (1898–1944)

Myron Selznick was the older brother of David O. Selznick. Myron worked as a talent agent. Both Myron Selznick and Kay Brown had mentioned to David O. Selznick the possibility of using Vivien Leigh for the character of Scarlett O'Hara in the film *Gone with the Wind*. David had brushed the suggestions aside.

During the 1938 filming of the fire scene for the movie *Gone with the Wind*, Myron brought Vivien Leigh to the set and said, "I want you to meet your 'Scarlett O'Hara.'" In 1944, Myron Selznick died in California from thrombosis. Myron's words proved true (Shavin and Shartar, page 20).

*See also* fire scene filming for *Gone with the Wind.*

## "Sergeant Terry"

Margaret Mitchell's second published story was "Sergeant Terry." This short story appeared in the yearbook *Facts and Fancies* of Washington Seminary during Margaret's senior year. Eva Paisley was Margaret's English teacher that year; Paisley encouraged Margaret in her writing.

Mary Rose Taylor calls Margaret Mitchell's second published story a foreshadowing of Margaret's own life. In "Sergeant Terry" Mitchell considers the women whose men are serving in active military service. In 1918 Margaret's own sweetheart would die in France during World War I (from "Foreword" by Mary Rose Taylor in Jane Eskridge's *Before Scarlett: Childhood Writings of Margaret Mitchell*, ix–xii).

*See also* Mary Rose Taylor.

## Sims, Walter A. (1923–1931)

Walter A. Sims was mayor of Atlanta from 1923 to 1931. He was instrumental is securing the Hartsfield-Jackson Atlanta International Airport for the Atlanta area. Sims's burial site is in Atlanta's Arlington Memorial Park in the city he served ("Walter A. Sims").

*See also Before Scarlett: Childhood Writings of Margaret Mitchell*; Candler Field; Eskridge, Jane; Hartsfield-Jackson Atlanta International Airport; "Sergeant Terry"; Taylor, Mary Rose.

## Skelton, J.A. (1848–1941)

J.A. Skelton was a Confederate veteran who resided in the home for Confederate veterans near Atlanta, Georgia. Four of these veterans had special invitations to attend the 1939 Atlanta premiere of *Gone with the Wind* (the film). One of the most vocal of these veterans was J. A. Skelton. Some of his quotations at the premiere are at other places in this volume ("James A. Skelton").

During the Civil War, Skelton was a member of Company A, 7th Georgia Guards, Confederate States of America. Both he and his wife, Mary Victoria Skelton (1846–1932), are buried in Kennesaw City Cemetery, Cobb County, Georgia ("James A. Skelton").

*See also* Atlanta premiere of *Gone with the Wind*; Confederate Soldiers' Home; Hoar, Jay S.

## skits

As a teenager (1912–1917), Margaret Mitchell entertained the neighborhood children and youth with her tales of terror. Some of them ran all the way home after hearing her stories. With her success, she move to writing, directing, producing and performing in "a wide variety of plays, pageants, and skits, like *The Cow Puncher, The Fall of Ralph the Rover, In My Harem, A Darktown Tragedy, Phil Kelley, Detective Bayou Royale, The Regular Hero, The Exile, Mexico,* and *The Greaser*" (Pyron, page 55).

The Mitchell house on Peachtree was perfect for accommodating an audience to view Margaret's productions. Margaret would throw open the French doors dividing the two front rooms and the hallway. The productions allowed Margaret to "remake the world, master an environment, and adopt new identities"—like playing a female crook in *Phil Kelley* (Pyron, pages 55–56).

One of Mitchell's performances brought concern from her father and mother. They considered her adaptation of *The Traitor* by Thomas Dixon and her performance as Steve Hoyle to be plagiarism. Margaret Mitchell never forgot the lesson.

*See also* Dixon, Thomas; Hoyle, Steve; plagiarism; *The Traitor* and young Margaret Mitchell.

## Smith, Dr. Otis

Dr. Otis Smith became the first black licensed pediatrician in the state of Georgia. He was able to complete his medical education because of the anonymous financial aid he had received from Margaret Mitchell; Dr. Benjamin Mays, president of Morehouse College, helped arrange for Mitchell to provide this help. The alliance of Mitchell and May remained largely unknown until Ira Joe Johnson and William Pickens published some of the letters exchanged between the two in their book *Benjamin E. Mays and Margaret Mitchell: A Unique Legacy in Medicine.*

Dr. Smith, who served on the board of the Margaret Mitchell House, spoke out openly about the racism that surrounded Mitchell for some time. "Some blacks have never liked Margaret Mitchell.... In the '40s, black politicians jumped on her and didn't want her name spoken with respect in the black community. People felt she was a part of a racist establishment.

"Blacks didn't know her and whites didn't either. White folks would have turned against her if they had known she was trying to educate Negroes" ("Remembering Margaret Mitchell").

When Margaret Mitchell found out the full impact of her donations, she continued to make regular scholarship contributions. Margaret Mitchell's donations helped establish an emergency room at Grady Hospital to treat African Americans.

*See also* Grady Hospital; Gravitt, Hugh Dorsey;

Smith College, Northampton, Mass.

Published for Wiswell, The Druggist, by The Metropolitan News Co., Boston, Mass.

Johnson, Ira Joe; Mays, Benjamin; Morehouse College.

## Smith, Sophia (1796–1870)

The philanthropist Sophia Smith was born in 1796; she was the fourth child of Joseph and Lois White Smith in Hatfield, Massachusetts. Sophia Smith lived in the same house almost all her life. Four years before her 1870 death, Sophia had built a new home, which was beside her lifetime residence. She died inside her new home.

In 1846, Sophia Smith conceived the idea of a college for women. Her will provided instructions to found such an establishment. Smith allocated $387,468 for the first college for women in the United States. In 1875 Smith College opened its doors (S.A. Smith IV).

## Smith College

Smith College was the vision of philanthropist Sophia Smith (1796–1870). Smith's will provided for the founding of Smith College. It was chartered in 1871; the institution opened in 1875 ("The Early History of Smith College").

*Smith College and Margaret Mitchell.* In the fall of 1918 Margaret ("Peggy," as her classmates often called her) entered Smith College in Northampton, Massachusetts. She only remained there for one year because of the death of her mother, Maybelle Mitchell, in January of 1919. At the end of the school year, she returned to Atlanta to help her father run the house. She continued to write some of the friends she had made there. In 1939 Smith College presented Margaret Mitchell with an honorary degree.

When Smith held the 1942 reunion — the 20th reunion for Margaret's class had she graduated, Margaret Mitchell attended enthusiastically. The theme was Hawaii.

*See also* **Mitchell, Mary Isabel "Maybelle" Stephens; Smith, Sophia.**

## Snell, Weis C.

After the location of the painting *The Battle of Atlanta* in Grant Park, since the 1890s, Atlanta architect John Francis Downing designed a new building for the circular painting in 1921. In 1934–36, the Works Progress Administration (WPA) funded a project for Atlanta and its Cyclorama.

The WPA hired Weis Snell, Joseph Llorens, and Wilbur Kurtz to construct a diorama for the foreground of *The Battle of Atlanta*. The artists used a floor of red clay and fashioned 128 plaster figures, shrubbery, cannon, and track to give more realism to the painting. The diorama extends thirty feet toward the painting.

During the 1939 Atlanta premiere of the film *Gone with the Wind* Clark Gable and other dignitaries visited the Atlanta Cyclorama. Clark Gable made the comment to George Simmons, the Atlanta City Parks director, and Atlanta Mayor William B. Hartsfield that the diorama would be complete if it had a likeness of Rhett Butler.

Knowing that Weis Snell had worked on the diorama with Joseph Victor Llorens and Wilbur Kurtz in a Works Progress Administration project, Mayor William B. Hartsfield contacted Snell. Hartsfield asked Snell to paint a Union corpse in the diorama with the face of Clark Gable ("Cyclorama"; Davis, Stephen).

*See also* **Atlanta Cyclorama; Atlanta premiere of *Gone with the Wind*; Kurtz, Wilbur G.; Llorens, Joseph Victor, Sr.**

**Spain, sales of *Gone with the Wind*** *see* **foreign copyrights/translations and fair trade laws**

## Spring Hill Chapel

The Spring Hill Chapel is where Dean Raimundo de Ovies of the St. Philip's Episcopal Cathedral conducted the funeral service for Margaret Mitchell.

Established by Hyatt M. Patterson in 1882, Spring Hill Funeral Home began in Atlanta's Markham Block. Patterson moved his facility to Peachtree Street after his business burned in 1896. Patterson's son Fred worked with his father for eight years before they moved the business to North Forsyth Street. The new facility was the first building in the south intended for funeral direction. In 1905 Fred and his father became partners in the business, then named H. M. Patterson and Son.

Fred inherited the business at the 1923 death of his father. The new facility at the corner of Spring and Tenth Street took the name *Spring Hill*. Spring Hill Funeral Home is still in the family of Hyatt M. Patterson. Its current physical address is 1020

Spring Street, NW ("History of H.M. Patterson and Son-Spring Hill Chapel").

## Stately Oaks Tourist Site in Historical Jonesboro/Clayton County

Margaret Mitchell never lived in Clayton County. She never resided in Jonesboro, Georgia. She never modeled Tara after an existing site in Jonesboro, Clayton County, or even in the Atlanta area.

Fifteen miles south of downtown Atlanta, the tourist can find Stately Oaks, a re-creation of an antebellum plantation similar to what Tara might have been. The advertisements declare that if the tourist wondered about the source of Margaret Mitchell's ideas for *Gone with the Wind*, a visit to Stately Oaks will provide the answers. The site, according to its ads, "will take you back to the days of Scarlett, Rhett, and the time of the War Between the States. We have costumed interpreters or MP3 tours that will guide you on a personal tour of our white columned residence and share with you the history of the house, the ties with the famous book and it's [*sic*] author, and Jonesboro's role in the Atlanta campaign during the Civil War ("Welcome to Stately Oaks Plantation"). The house was not originally at the current location.

"Stately Oaks was moved from its original location off of Tara Boulevard in Jonesboro to its current location in the Margaret Mitchell Memorial Park off of Jodeco Road in Jonesboro in the 1970s. The historic campus boasts the 1839 Greek Revival antebellum home, the original log kitchen used on the property, a well house, a tenant house, Juddy's country store and the last one room school house used in Clayton County" ["Welcome to Stately Oaks Plantation"].

*See also* Historical Jonesboro; Tara.

## Stephens, Annie Fitzgerald (1844–1934)

Annie Fitzgerald Stephens was a very strong-willed woman. She had learned strength during the Civil War when she had had to negotiate with the soldiers on behalf of her family. After the war, she had helped her family survive during the Reconstruction Period.

Annie Fitzgerald married John Stephens (1833–1896), a well-to-do businessman. He was a major stockholder — among other business ventures — in the Gate City Railway Company. Even after her husband's death, she kept the city of Atlanta waiting when it pleased her. When she was not ready to leave even though her car had arrived, she would send Stephens or even her cook to hold the car until she was ready (Pyron, page 21–22).

*Relationship of Annie Fitzgerald Stephens and her granddaughter Margaret Mitchell.* The relationship of Margaret Mitchell and her grandmother Annie Stephens did not always go smoothly. Margaret Mitchell left Smith College at the end of the 1918–1919 school year and began to run the household of her father, Eugene Muse Mitchell.

Annie Fitzgerald Stephens, in her commanding way, announced that she would be moving in with Eugene Muse Mitchell and Margaret Mitchell. Grandmother Stephens brought with her Aline Fitzgerald, her younger unmarried sister. The two women overwhelmed the Mitchells with their trunks of personal possessions and with their numerous boxes of feathered hats.

Margaret's Grandmother Stephens— now in her seventies—argued loudly with Eugene Mitchell about his selfishness in "stealing Margaret's youth" by making her a household drudge. She nagged Margaret about returning to college. When she failed at that, she began her campaign to improve the appearance of Margaret. Margaret's middies and serge skirts began to disappear from the laundry. Grandmother Stephens brought in a seamstress to upgrade Margaret's wardrobe. Margaret objected furiously (Edwards, page 67).

In 1920 Grandmother Stephens criticized some of Margaret Mitchell's friends. When the discussion between granddaughter and grandmother became heated, Grandmother Stephens— with her sister Aline in tow — packed her bags and moved to the Georgian Terrace Hotel, even though it was half-past eleven at night (Farr, page 53).

*Annie Fitzgerald Stephens and Margaret Mitchell's marriage to Berrien Kinnard ("Red") Upshaw.* The family breach climaxed by Grandmother Stephens's move to the Georgian Terrace Hotel continued for years. Grandmother Stephens, however, suspended hostilities long enough to attend the trousseau tea on September 1, 1922, before Margaret Mitchell's marriage to Berrien Kinnard ("Red") Upshaw on September 3 (Farr, page 56).

During the wedding ceremony, however, Grandmother Stephens was appalled by Margaret's carrying red, long-stemmed roses and her use of an Episcopal minister, the Reverend Hiram K. Douglass (Walker, pages 86–87). Edwards reports that Margaret Mitchell changed from red long-stemmed roses to a bouquet of white roses at the insistence of Grandmother Stephens. Margaret would not, however, acquiesce to a Catholic ceremony (Grandmother Stephens was a devout Catholic).

After the ceremony, Margaret and Grandmother Stephens remained estranged. They did not attempt to repair their relationship again until Margaret's July 4th marriage to John R. Marsh. Grandmother Stephens did help with the wedding plans and to put aside her religious beliefs a second time for her granddaughter. The two, however, would remain cool to each other (Edwards, pages 85–87, 115).

*Annie Fitzgerald Stephens's death and its impact on Margaret Mitchell.* When Grandmother Stephens died on February 17, 1934, Margaret had many regrets. Margaret was deeply affected by the death of the feisty woman who had enthralled her with stories of the Civil War and Reconstruction. When Margaret's depression lasted well in the spring, John planned a trip for them to Savannah, Georgia, for the meeting of the Georgia Press Association. It was on this trip that Margaret began to notice the differences between the Gullah dialect and the Geechee dialect — both of which she would use in her novel (Walker, pages 192–193).

*See also* **Geechee; Georgian Terrace Hotel; Gullah.**

### Stephens, Mary Isabel (1872–1919)

Mary Isabel (also spelled Isabelle) Stephens (nicknamed "Maybelle") married Eugene Muse Mitchell (1866–1944). Eugene and Maybelle were the parents of Margaret Mitchell Marsh (1900–1949), Rus-

sell Stephens Mitchell (born and died 1894), and Alexander Stephens Mitchell (1896–1983).

### Stone Mountain

A prominent natural feature of the Piedmont Region of Georgia is Stone Mountain, comprised of exposed granite that extends 1,686 feet above sea level. Stone Mountain is 700 feet higher than the surrounding plain. The rock face had a carving etched on its surface in the early 20th century (Davis, *Georgia During the Great Depression*, page 16).

*Stone Mountain and the Ku Klux Klan.* Seventeen members of the revived Ku Klux Klan ascended Stone Mountain in 1915. At the top of the mountain the mob ignited a flaming cross to announce the rebirth of the Knights of the Ku Klux Klan (KKK).

The lynching of Leo Frank predicted the 1915 revival of the Ku Klux Klan. Margaret Mitchell's mother was vocal in her abhorrence of the atrocity. Maybelle Mitchell's activism may have influenced Margaret and suggested to her the inclusion of the KKK in *Gone with the Wind*.

The completed Confederate Memorial on Stone Mountain differs from the original design. There are only three figures — President Jefferson Davis, General Robert E. Lee, and General Stonewall Jackson — and incomplete horses. (Aerial Photography Services, Incorporated, Norcross, Georgia.)

The KKK gradually gained members in 1917 and 1918. Support of white supremacy, anti–Semitism, anti–Catholicism, and immigration restrictions brought many to the KKK; its professed respect support of the law, government, better schools, and family life brought more to the folds. "By 1924 the perceived power of the Klan was such that neither major political party was willing to denounce it formally" ("Ku Klux Klan in the Twentieth Century").

Georgia's Klan membership declined from 156,000 in 1925 to 1,400 in 1930. During the Great Depression the Klan still tried to make a showing; in 1939, six hundred members paraded on the streets of Atlanta. Still, the strength of the KKK seemed to be decreasing.

The original KKK had become inactive after the Civil War. This was due in part to federal legislation, including the Force Act of 1870, the Federal Election Law of 1871, and the 1871 Ku Klux Klan Act. These laws declared that secret societies were illegal. The laws also suspended the writs of habeas corpus "in disorderly areas," increased penalties for violation of the Fourteenth and Fifteenth Amendments, and gave military commanders more control over elections (Davis, *Georgia During the Great Depression*, pages 84–85).

Margaret Mitchell included the KKK in *Gone with the Wind*. The character Frank Kennedy — one of Scarlett's three husbands — was attacked and killed by a band of Ku Klux Klan members.

*See also* **Frank, Leo; Kennedy, Frank; Ku Klux Klan.**

## Stone Mountain and Margaret Mitchell's ankle injury

Margaret Mitchell was involved in a horseback riding accident possibly at Stone Mountain that injured Margaret's ankle; the ankle caused her problems the rest of her life. Her inability to move around was an influence on her writing *Gone with the Wind.*

Mitchell suffered various foot and ankle injuries. The ankle injury was one of the most bothersome. Various writers give different accounts of how she attained one of these injuries — perhaps on Stone Mountain.

Edwards states that the accident occurred on February 21, 1921. She explains that Margaret was on a date with Berrien Kinnard ("Red") Upshaw, and they were horseback riding on Stone Mountain. "Peggy drove out to a stable near Stone Mountain, where she rented a large black horse reminiscent of Bucephalus. She rode the animal off the bridal [*sic*] path to a steep, narrow hill covered with low branches. At the top of the slope was a

stone wall that separated the horse farm from the road. Instead of turning back at this point, Peggy decided to jump the wall…. Peggy was thrown and the horse came down on top of her. She lay there in pain and shock for nearly an hour before other riders happened along the same isolated path" (page 69).

Pyron states that this second, severe, horseback-related accident occurred in the fall of 1920. While she was on a weekend visit to the University of Georgia, possibly on a date with Upshaw, when "her mount went down with her, and she reinjured her foot an leg" (pages 110–111). An undated letter to Allen Edee seems to verify this (page 22–23).

Walker sets the date as in the spring of 1920 — not the fall of 1920 as Pyron suggests. Walker says the accident occurred when Upshaw invited her to a Sigma Nu house party at the University of Georgia. Walker makes no mention of where the accident occurred.

Farr mentions the accident in which Mitchell claims: "The horse sat on my stomach" (52). Although Farr gives the year as 1920, he gives no indication of exactly where the accident occurred or with whom Margaret was riding.

## Stone Mountain and the premiere of *Gone with the Wind*

A popular, undocumented legend tells of heavy tail winds that threatened to speed up the arrival of an Eastern Airline plane carrying Vivien Leigh, Olivia de Havilland, the Selznicks, and others who were attending the 1939 Atlanta premiere of *Gone with the Wind*. The welcoming committee realized that the floral arrangements were not at the airport; Atlanta Mayor William B. Hartsfield dashed to the new control tower of Candler Field to speak to the copilot in the plane.

Hartsfield pleaded for the pilot to detour over Stone Mountain. This detour would give the committee a chance to get everything ready. It would also give the passengers a view of Augustus Lukeman's carving of General Robert E. Lee and President Jefferson Davis. The third carving (Lieutenant General "Stonewall" Jackson) on Stone Mountain was not complete at this time.

*See also* **Atlanta premiere of *Gone with the Wind*; Borglum, Gutzon.**

## Stone Mountain carving

The carving on Stone Mountain required more than half a century for completion. Four hundred feet above the ground, the finished carving is 90 feet tall and 190 feet wide. The frame for the carving is three acres; the carving itself is 360 feet square. Cut into the world's largest exposed mass

Gutzon Borglum was the first person in charge of the Stone Mountain carving. Borglum's horse served as a model for the sculpture. (Aerial Photography Services, Incorporated, Norcross, Georgia.)

Augustus Lukeman wanted to depict Jefferson Davis, Robert E. Lee, and "Stonewall" Jackson without hats. Walter Kirtland Hancock later modified it slightly. Here is his vision for carving on Stone Mountain. (Aerial Photography Services, Incorporated, Norcross, Georgia.)

On May 9, 1970, Vice President Spiro Agnew dedicated the carving. He said, "Jackson's life exemplified loyalty; Davis demonstrated dignity and Lee set the highest example of honor." (Aerial Photography Services, Incorporated, Norcross, Georgia.)

of granite, it is the largest sculpture in the world (Neal, page 3 as cited by Davis, *Georgia During the Great Depression*, page 243).

*History of the carving.* In 1909, Helen C. Plane, a charter member of the United Daughters of the Confederacy (UDC), conceived the idea of a Confederate monument on the side of Stone Mountain. She suggested, as Atlanta chapter president, an image of Robert E. Lee.

*History of the carving and Gutzon Borglum.* In 1915 the UDC consulted Gutzon Borglum, who had recently finished the statue of Abraham Lincoln. He made sketches of Confederate leaders who might be included on the final carving; he thought only one such image "would be like a postage stamp stuck on a barn" (Neal, page 3 as cited by Davis, *Georgia During the Great Depression*, page 243).

Samuel Venable, the owner of the mountain, deeded in 1916 the face of Stone Mountain and ten acres adjoining the mountain to the UDC. Venable included a provision that the property must be returned if there was not a complete carving in twelve years. World War I caused a pause the activities. In 1923 Borglum announced that his designs were complete and that he was ready to begin.

In her position as newspaper reporter, Margaret Mitchell wrote an article on the carving and the swing by which the men lowered themselves over the edge of the cliff. Margaret herself tried one of the swings.

Borglum attempted to use a projector and to shine the design on the northeast face of the mountain. His men tried to outline the drawing with paint at night as they hung from a rope. After several failed attempts to sketch the image on the mountainside and after several disagreements with the committee, Borglum left Georgia shortly after completing the head of Lee (with a hat) and before his twelve-year contract in Georgia expired. Before leaving, however, he destroyed his sketches and his models.

Borglum took a position as consultant for Mt. Rushmore in South Dakota. Borglum did, however, accomplish one significant thing for Stone Mountain: the design of a Confederate half-dollar, the sales of which would benefit the carving. The coins that Borglum designed sold quickly. The income was speculated to be sufficient to pay for the rest of the monument.

*History of the carving and Augustus Lukeman.*

*Left:* Gutzon Borglum designed the Stone Mountain Commemorative Coin (half dollar) to help pay the cost of the Stone Mountain carving. The 1925 coin features General Robert E. Lee and General "Stonewall" Jackson on horseback. *Right:* The coin features an eagle on a cliff and the words "MEMORIAL TO THE VALOR OF THE SOLDIER OF THE SOUTH" on the reverse side. This metal replica of the commemorative coin is from the author's collection.

Augustus Lukeman went to work in 1925 on the Stone Mountain carving. He knew he would have to work at top speed to finish the work before the 1928 expiration of the contract between Venable and the UDC. Lukeman had the curving face of the mountain blasted away and Borglum's work removed. His sketch was of three mounted, hatless men: General Robert E. Lee, President Jefferson Davis, and Lieutenant General Stonewall Jackson.

On April 9, 1928, Lukeman unveiled his work: the faces of Lee and Davis, an outline of Lee's horse, blocked out figures of Lee and Davis. On May 20, however, the Venables reclaimed the property.

*History of the carving and Walker Kirtland Hancock.* Thirty years later (1958) Georgia would purchase the mountain and 3200 acres of surrounding land. Georgia and sponsored a competition for artists who wanted to complete the work. They chose Walker Kirtland Hancock to serve as consultant. He modified the existing carving slightly.

The dedication of the completed carving on Stone Mountain finally came on May 9, 1970. Spiro Agnew helped in the dedication ceremony. An estimated 10,000 visitors came to witness its unveiling (Neal, pages 9–45, as cited by Davis, *Georgia During the Great Depression*, pages 243–245).

## Stone Mountain, Harold Latham, and Margaret Mitchell

In April of 1935 Macmillan editor-in-chief Harold Strong Latham came to Atlanta to scout for new writers. He attended a luncheon with Medora Field Perkerson, Margaret Mitchell, and some other people at Rich's Department Store. When Latham began to push Margaret about the manuscript he heard that she had written, she avoided the issue by inviting him to visit Stone Mountain with him. Latham and Margaret Mitchell entered Margaret's 1929 green Chevrolet. The next day Mitchell delivered the manuscript for what would be *Gone with the Wind* to Harold Latham in his hotel lobby.

*See also* automobiles.

**Sweden, sales of *Gone with the Wind*** *see* **foreign copyrights/translations and fair trade laws**

**Switzerland, sales of *Gone with the Wind*** *see* **foreign copyrights/translations and fair trade laws**

### Talmadge, Betty Shingler

Betty Shingler married Herman E. Talmadge, who became a U.S. senator and Georgia governor before their divorce. Her home near Lovejoy carried the name the Crawford-Talmadge House. Mrs. Talmadge had a catering and event facility with a Southern theme. She called the grounds *Lovejoy Plantation*. Georgians suggested that Lovejoy Plantation and the Crawford-Talmadge House served as the setting for Mitchell's novel and Selznick's film. Margaret Mitchell, however, denied any real-life place as the setting for her novel.

In 1979 Betty Talmadge purchased parts of the movie set for Tara for $5,000. She planned to use some of the façade in her catering business. The front door of Tara's Hollywood set is on permanent display at the Margaret Mitchell House and Museum through her loan to them.

For business purposes, she purchased also the Fitzgerald home that had belonged to Margaret Mitchell's great-grandparents. Eventually, a temporary foundation held the antebellum portion of the Fitzgerald home in a field across the road from Lovejoy; the Fitzgerald house remained unrestored.

In May 2005 Betty died. Two months later a tornado passed through the area and damaged the Fitzgerald House. Knocked from its foundation, the house was demolished by crews. The flooring, the mantles, the woodwork and some of the lumber that had framed the house were salvaged (Tommy H. Jones).

## Tara

"Tara" was the plantation home of protagonist Scarlett O'Hara in the book and movie *Gone with the Wind*. Although tourists still come to Atlanta in their search for Tara, Margaret Mitchell insisted that there was never such an actual place in reality. She wrote: "I mixed up the Clayton County terrain to have a house on a road that could not have existed. I took much trouble to learn that there were no high hills or any hills at all in that county on the other side of the Flint River as I described the scenery to have been. And I could find no white-washed brick home set far back from the road with a long avenue of cedars…. I went to such pains because I wished to spare anybody now living in that country the embarrassment of hearing that their grandmother was Scarlett O'Hara. My trouble seems to have been all for nothing" (Frank Daniel).

Margaret Mitchell's maternal great-grandfather had been born in Ireland. After coming to America, he set up a house and plantation in Clayton County. He died (1798) before Margaret was born. Philip Fitzgerald's daughters— who had never married— still farmed the plantation when Margaret was a child. Margaret spent many happy days on the Fitzgerald plantation with them. She especially loved to listen to their tales of the Civil War and Reconstruction. Her love for the land may have suggested a setting for her *Gone with the Wind*. The Fitzgerald house, however, was certainly not the model for the film's house at Tara.

Mitchell writes in her first chapter that the structure was a "white-washed, brick plantation house"

(*Gone with the Wind*, page 4). In Chapter III, she writes: "It was built by slave labor, a clumsy sprawling building that crowned the rise of ground overlooking the green incline of pasture land running down to the river; and it pleased Gerald greatly, for, even when new, it wore a look of mellowed years (page 32).

"The house had been built according to no architectural plan whatever, with extra rooms added where and when it seemed convenient, but with Ellen's care and attention, it gained a charm that made up for its lack of design…. The wisteria tumbling over the verandas showed bright against the whitewashed brick, and it joined with the pink crepe myrtle bushes by the door and the white-blossomed magnolias in the yard to disguise some of the awkward lines of the house" (page 38).

Except for its plantation setting, the frame Fitzgerald house did not resemble the masonry Tara house of the book or movie (Frank Daniel).

### Tara, the Hollywood set

Margaret Mitchell did not approve of the Hollywood set for Tara. Selznick Studios relegated the set of Tara to the back lot. The Forty Acres back lot became a part of RKO Pictures. Desilu Productions bought the Back Lot and the former sets stored there.

Southern Attractions, Inc., bought the façade of the house in 1959. Southern Attractions had it dismantled and shipped to the Atlanta area with plans to relocate it as an attraction for tourists (*Los Angeles Times*). David O. Selznick said at the time: "Nothing in Hollywood is permanent. Once photographed, life here is ended. It is almost symbolic of Hollywood. Tara had no rooms inside. It was just a façade. So much of Hollywood is a façade" (Schumach).

When Southern Attractions appealed to the Margaret Mitchell Estate to license the attraction, however, the estate refused to grant permission for the attraction bearing the title of Margaret Mitchell's novel. The estate noted that Mitchell had remarked how little the set resembled the description in her novel.

In 1979, however, Betty Talmadge — ex-wife of former Georgia Governor Herman Talmadge — bought the papier-mâché and plyboard set for a reported $5,000 for use in her catering business. Later, she placed the front door of the set on permanent loan to the Margaret Mitchell Museum.

Also on permanent loan to the Margaret Mitchell Museum is the painting of Scarlett in the blue dress that hung in Rhett's bedroom of the set of the film *Gone with the Wind*; the painting still carries the stains from the glass of sherry that Rhett

Butler threw at the painting while enraged. Later the painting hung in Atlanta's Margaret Mitchell Elementary School. The painting is now on permanent loan to the Margaret Mitchell Museum in Atlanta.

The Culver Studios (formerly Selznick International Pictures) has other items from the film stored on their lot. These include the painting that represented the stained glass window from the top of the staircase (*"Gone with the Wind* [the film]*"*).

*See also* Margaret Mitchell Museum; Talmadge, Betty Shingler.

## Taylor, Mary Rose, and the Margaret Mitchell House

Mary Rose Taylor is a founder, former board chair, and past executive director of the Margaret Mitchell House and Museum. Beginning in 1990, she led the effort to save the historic site where Mitchell wrote *Gone with the Wind* ("Mary Rose Taylor").

*Mary Rose Taylor's experience.* Mary Rose Taylor is a veteran of broadcast journalism. She began her career with *60 Minutes* in 1968 ("Mary Rose Taylor"). For more than 20 years Taylor worked as a researcher, director, and producer of documentary films; these films aired on CBS, PBS, CBC, and BBC ("Who's Who in Hospitality"). She received the designation of Lexus Leader for her community service ("Mary Rose Taylor").

After her positions as assignment editor for Metromedia in New York City and for Post-Newsweek in Washington, D.C., she accepted a position in Atlanta in 1980 as news anchor for the NBC affiliate WXIA-TV. There she received recognition for outstanding achievement in investigative reporting ("Mary Rose Taylor").

With her retirement in 1984, she began serving her new Atlanta community in many additional ways. Her efforts included positions with the Georgia World Congress Center Authority, Atlanta–Fulton County Recreation Authority, Atlanta

History Center, Woodruff Arts Center, Atlanta Symphony Orchestra, Michael C. Carlos Museum and the Atlanta Convention and Visitors Bureau ("Who's Who in Hospitality").

*Mary Rose Taylor and the Restoration of the Margaret Mitchell House.* Although there had been some prior interest in restoring "The Dump" where Margaret Mitchell had written *Gone with the Wind*, these few circulating proposals gained little headway. By the 1980s the property values around the site housing Apartment #1 skyrocketed. The apartment building where Margaret Mitchell and John R. Marsh had lived seemed destined for demolition (Brown, "Writers Houses").

In September 1991, however, Mary Rose Taylor changed everything. She announced a "Save The Dump" campaign. The campaign raised the necessary funds to begin restoring the Margaret Mitchell House.

Brown compares Taylor's mettle to that of Scarlett O'Hara. Taylor endured adversity without flinching despite some blows that would have crushed some other people (Brown, "Writers Houses").

The first blow came when fire destroyed the top two floors of the apartment building on September

Mary Rose Taylor led the effort to save "The Dump." She is a founder of the Center for Southern Literature and past executive director of the Margaret Mitchell House and Museum. Her volunteer work is vital to Atlanta. (Courtesy of Mary Rose Taylor.)

17, 1994. Apartment #1, however, did not suffer severe damage. Arson was the cause of the fire.

Some speculated that the arsonist was a developer who wanted the property to go for a more profitable use. Others suggested that there was a racial motive in the arson and that the fire was a strike against *Gone with the Wind*. The police were not able to make any arrests.

The fire gained the attention of the public, however, and actually boosted the financial support of the project. When Daimler-Benz, a German automaker, learned of Mary Rose Taylor's campaign to restore "The Dump," the company made a $5 million donation to the fund. Daimler-Benz presented the sum as a gesture of goodwill to Atlantans. Brown wrote: "Taylor determined that the project, like Atlanta, would rise out of the ashes. It was announced that house would open in time for the 1996 Summer Olympics in Atlanta" (Brown, "Writers Houses").

Tragedy struck again on May 12, 1996, when arsonists set afire the Crescent Apartments for the second time — just days before the scheduled opening of the Margaret Mitchell House.

This time they turned most of the newly refurbished building into a pile of rubble — except for Apartment #1. Preservationists felt crushed. Some wanted to admit defeat.

They had planned to link the Margaret Mitchell House and Atlanta with the world during the Olympics in Atlanta during June of 1996. Now this would not be possible. Many of the developers wanted to stop the project. Mary Rose Taylor, however, remained undefeated (Brown, "Writers Houses").

The apartment finally opened in May 1997 as the Margaret Mitchell House, the "Birthplace of Gone with the Wind." Author Tom Wolfe delivered the keynote address, calling Mitchell's novel "one of the great tours de force in literary history" (Brown, "Writers Houses").

*Mary Rose Taylor and the description of the interior of the Margaret Mitchell House.* Margaret Mitchell's newly opened apartment contained no items belonging to her. The designer, however, recreated the apartment's interior with furnishing typical of the period. A small table which had once held her typewriter and several sheets of paper give the impression that Margaret Mitchell has just left the room. This table is the focal point of the small living room.

More than 50,000 people a year visited the 500-square-foot apartment. Taylor's staff consisted of 13 full-time and five part-time employees ("Mary Rose Taylor"; Brown, "Writers Houses"). The Atlanta History Center eventually took over the operation of the Margaret Mitchell House and Museum.

*Mary Rose Taylor and the Center for Southern Literature.* Mary Rose Taylor also set up the Center for Southern Literature at the same site as the Margaret Mitchell House. The birthplace of *Gone with the Wind* seemed a fitting location this addition.

The Center for Southern Literature produces several programs on Southern literature each month. Significant offerings are the creative writing workshops for children and adults. The center sponsors also the Townsend Awards for Literary Fiction ("Mary Rose Taylor"; Brown, "Writers Houses").

### Ten Henshaw Street

Margaret Mitchell moved into a second floor room on Ten Henshaw Street in Northampton, Massachusetts, for her first year at Smith College. Margaret immediately dubbed the residence "Ten Hen." It was here that Margaret made some lifetime friends: Ginny Morris (Nixon), Sophie Henker, Madeleine Baxter, and Helen Atkinson (Edwards, page 52).

*See also* **Atkinson, Helen; Baxter, Madeline "Red"; Henker, Sophie; Nixon, Virginia "Ginny" Morris.**

### Thomas, Elizabeth Scott

The mother of Wailes Thomas, Elizabeth Scott Thomas stored some materials for relatives in her attic over a sixty-year period. After his mother's death, Wailes found these materials included some of the very first writings of Margaret Mitchell. These early writings are now available in *Before Scarlett: Childhood Writings of Margaret Mitchell* (2000) (*Before Scarlett,* pages ix–xxiv).

*See also* **Thomas, Wailes.**

### Thomas, Wailes

Wailes Thomas was instrumental in the location and dissemination of some early writings by Margaret Mitchell. On a warm mid–August morning, he found the papers as he and his friend and fellow-teacher Jane Eskridge were cleaning and sorting the items in the attic of the Atlanta home he had inherited from his deceased mother, Elizabeth Scott Thomas. These items had accumulated over some sixty years.

Wailes's "Aunt Margueryte" had lived with Wailes's mother for a while. Aunt Margueryte had been Margueryte Scott; she had married Glascock Reynolds (1903–1967) — and later had become a Sharp.

Some of the items that Margueryte Scott Reynolds Sharp had left stored in the home of Wailes's mother were some boxes from Joseph S. Reynolds; Joseph S. Reynolds was the father of Margueryte's husband Glascock Reynolds and the father of Caroline Louise ("Carrie Lou") Reynolds Mitchell. "Carrie Lou"—Glascock's sister—was the first wife of Alexander Stephens Mitchell and, therefore, the sister-in-law of Margaret Mitchell. Glascock Reynolds was a noted portrait painter of the 1940s and 1950s; he had painted many notable people, including Margaret Mitchell ("Glascock Reynolds").

Jane Eskridge took the cardboard boxes with the papers containing the copybooks of Margaret Mitchell; the papers included 200 pages of short stories, fairy tales, essays, journal entries, and letters by her (*Before Scarlett*, xiii–xxiv). Jane compiled these papers, and—with the work of Mary Rose Taylor of the Margaret Mitchell House—edited *Before Scarlett: Childhood Writings of Margaret Mitchell* (2000). Taylor prepared the foreword (*Before Scarlett*, pages ix–xii).

*See also* Margaret Mitchell House; Taylor, Mary Rose.

## Tolbert, Laura

After John R. Marsh and Margaret Mitchell married and moved into "The Dump," the couple believed that they could afford a part-time cook-housekeeper. Margaret Mitchell's biographer explained that they could afford Laura "Lula" Tolbert because Margaret was making $30 a week through two raises of $2.50 each in recent weeks (Farr, page 71). Walker noted that John hired Lula Tolbert to cook and clean in the spring of 1926 because he had grown tired of "always coming home to find their apartment in a mess, and of having to cook their supper and shop for their groceries."

Pyron describes Loula Tolbert (not *Lula Tolbert*, as per Farr, page 71) as being a "rough and hearty" servant who cooked and cleaned (pages 220, 226). Edwards mentions that Bessie Berry (Jordan) went to work for the couple after Lula Tolbert quit (page 147).

Walker says that after the death of Lula Tolbert, Peggy's childhood nurse worked for the couple for a while. Eugene Muse Mitchell soon sent Bessie Berry Jordan, his housekeeper and cook, to help the Marshes. Bessie remained with them the rest of their lives (Walker, page 151).

## *The Traitor*

As a young girl, Margaret Mitchell loved writing plays, directing them, and performing in them. At 16, Mitchell proudly invited her father to view her production of *The*

Outside her family's 1149 Peachtree Street residence, Margaret Mitchell is dressed as "Steve Hoyle" in her production of *The Traitor*. (Courtesy of the Atlanta-Fulton Public Library System's Special Collections Department.)

*Traitor,* based upon Thomas Dixon's book by the same name.

Sixteen-year-old Margaret played the role of Steve Hoyle in her production. She posed in front of the doorway of the Mitchell house on Peachtree for a photograph of herself in costume.

Instead of praising her production, her father withheld comment until his wife arrived home. When Maybelle Mitchell returned, the two had a conference with Margaret about copyright infringement and plagiarism. For years to come, Margaret Mitchell expected to see Thomas Dixon appearing in her home demanding retribution for her stealing his work.

When Dixon wrote to her praising her novel after its June 1936 publication, Margaret replied on August 15, 1936, to confess having used *The Traitor* without permission.

*The Traitor, a summary.* In *The Traitor: A Story of the Rise and Fall of the Invisible Empire* (1907), Dixon offers his third, "true" portrait of the Ku Klux Klan. Dixon claims this organization was a desperate attempt to save a Southern way of life.

The first two books in Dixon's trilogy of the South and the KKK were *The Leopard's Spots* (1902) and *The Clansman* (1905). *The Traitor* transpires during the decline of the Klan. Dixon uses legends, gothic tales of haunted houses, and specters to tell the complex story of *The Traitor,* which covers the period from 1870 to 1872.

The lawyer John Graham serves Independence, North Carolina. Graham is the Grand Dragon of the State of North Carolina. Graham is drunk and bitter when the book opens because Judge Butler has turned him out of his home. Graham, however, meets Stella, who is Butler's daughter, and falls in love. When Judge Butler learns of Graham's threats he summons federal troops to arrest Klan members. Graham stages one last dress parade before disbanding the North Carolina unit of the KKK.

Steve Hoyle — whom Margaret Mitchell played in her rendition of *The Traitor* — organizes his own new Klan. Hoyle's group is a just a bunch of "petty marauders" that often terrorize the town. When someone dressed as a Klansman murders the judge, Graham becomes the suspect; Stella plots revenge.

The conclusion of *The Traitor* is that hope rests in human relationships. The book may have been a factor — in addition to Dixon's *The Clansman* — in the production *The Birth of a Nation.* This movie was instrumental in the rebirth of the Ku Klux Klan on Stone Mountain. The KKK was very much a part of the Reconstruction era and figures prominently in Margaret Mitchell's *Gone with the Wind.*

Thomas Dixon dedicates *The Traitor* to the Southern men who suffered for their service to the country because of their membership in the Ku Klux Klan, the Invisible Empire. The book ends with a note of hope for the blighted people of the South with their spirit and courage (Kirkpatrick).

***See also*** **Berne Convention; Dixon, Thomas; Hoyle, Steve; Ku Klux Klan; plagiarism.**

### Traver, Lewis B.

Lewis B. Traver was president of American Booksellers Association in 1929. The organization set up a White House Library on the second floor (later the first floor–basement) of the White House where members of the Roosevelt family (and later other presidents and their families) could select what they wanted to read or to place in guest rooms in the White House.

Traver, then president of the ABA, made the presentation of the 500 donated volumes in 1929. The first donation was followed by 200 more volumes in 1933. Another 200 volumes followed in 1937; among these books was Margaret Mitchell's *Gone with the Wind* ("Books: President's Books").

### Troost, Bill

Bill Troost was a great-nephew of John R. Marsh. In the family papers, Troost had found mention of Margaret Mitchell and Vimoutiers, France. He also located a corroborating letter.

In May 2008 Troost received an invitation to attend a ceremony commemorating the 65th anniversary of the bombing of Vimoutiers, France. To honor Margaret Mitchell and her work to rebuild the hospital, a plaque to her memory was unveiled in the hospital. Troost was able to attend the ceremony ("Margaret Mitchell Helped French Town after WWII").

### Truman, Harry S

Harry S Truman (1884–1972) was the 33rd president of the United States. He served from 1945 to 1953. When Margaret Mitchell died in 1949, President Truman sent his personal condolences.

### Tucker, J. G.

J. G. Tucker was Gutzon Borglum's first assistant in the carving at Stone Mountain. Tucker devised a swing for the workers who were carving the mountain to use in their work. Margaret ("Peggy") Mitchell tried out the swing and wrote of it in an article on May 5, 1923, for the *Atlanta Journal.*

***See also*** **Borglum, Gutzon; Borglum's "Swing" and Margaret Mitchell; Stone Mountain.**

### Twelve Oaks

The plantation of the Wilkes family in the novel *Gone with the Wind* was Twelve Oaks. Margaret

Mitchell deliberately did not base any of the people or places on real people or real locations. One cannot find Twelve Oaks in Atlanta or the Atlanta area.

### Tydings-Miller Bill

In August of 1937 President Franklin Delano Roosevelt signed into law the Tydings-Miller Bill. Margaret Mitchell and her *Gone with the Wind* influenced the passage of this important law.

*Gone with the Wind* had appeared in print in June of 1936. The rocketing popularity of Mitchell's novel brought about a price war. Department stores and book stores began advertising the book at reduced prices. One store would offer the book for $2.89; down the street another store might offer the book for $2.69. A third shop would perhaps advertise to sell the book for $2.29.

Runners from one store might begin running to another shop offering the low price — often below what the merchants would pay if ordered directly from the publisher. In the far West and the Middle West, outlet stores and drug stores forced the price of *Gone with the Wind* to reach a low of 89 cents. The Tydings-Miller Law is known informally as the Fair Trade Act or the Price Protection Act; it is designed to prevent such price cutting (Farr, page 233).

***See also*** fair trade laws and other laws and legislation brought about by Margaret Mitchell and *Gone with the Wind* (book).

### Ukraine, sales of *Gone with the Wind*  *see* foreign copyrights/translations and fair trade laws

### The United Daughters of the Confederacy

The United Daughters of the Confederacy (UDC) honored Margaret Mitchell with its citation "For Distinguished Service." She received a special invitation to attend the organization's national con-

On November 14, 1940, at the National Convention in Montgomery, Alabama, Mrs. William Cabell Flournoy (left) of Lexington, Virginia, the Historical General of UDC, presented Margaret Mitchell the citation "For Distinguished Service." Mrs. Charles E. Bolling (right) of Richmond, Virginia, was president general of United Daughters of the Confederacy. (Call number 818. Courtesy of the Atlanta-Fulton Public Library System's Special Collections Department.)

vention in Montgomery, Alabama, on November 14, 1940, for the presentation. Mrs. William Cabell Flournoy of Lexington, Virginia, the historical general of UDC, presented Mitchell the citation. Mrs. Charles E. Bolling of Richmond, Virginia, was president general of United Daughters of the Confederacy at the time; she attended the ceremony (The Atlanta-Fulton Public Library System's Special Collections Department).

## The United States Postal Service

The United States Postal Service has recognized Margaret Mitchell and *Gone with the Wind* (book and film) with several postage stamps.

The stamps issued by the United States Postal Service (USPS) contain a *watermark,* an application formed in the process of paper manufacture. The papers used for postage stamps of the United States are watermarked with letters "USPS."

The stamps issued by the United States Postal Service and that relate to Margaret Mitchell and *Gone with the Wind* (book and film) include

1. the Margaret Mitchell stamp, which recognizes Mitchell as a Great American in the Great American Issues. The Great Americans Issues date between 1980 and 1999. There are 63 different faces of Great Americans and 43 rate denominations from one cent through $5.00.

The Margaret Mitchell stamp of 1986 honored Mitchell as a writer and Great American and marked the 50th anniversary of the publication of her book *Gone with the Wind* (Davis and Hunt, page 289).

2. The *Gone with the Wind* (film) stamp featuring Vivien Leigh as Scarlett O'Hara and Clark Gable as Rhett Butler; in the background the Hollywood version of Tara is evident. The postage stamp is part of the Classic Films series of United States postage stamps issued on March 23, 1990, in Hollywood, California. The issue date approached the 50th anniversary of the Atlanta premiere of *Gone with the Wind* that occurred in December of 1939 (Davis and Hunt, page 288).

3. The 1998 stamp showing the cover of the book *Gone with the Wind* (1936). The stamp shows a photo of a magnolia on the left and a photo of a Confederate sword on the right. The stamp showing the book cover was a part of the Celebrate the Century Series—1930s (Davis and Hunt, page 74).

4. The stamp honoring Hattie McDaniel. The United States Postal Service in 2006 issued a stamp bearing the image of Hattie McDaniel, the first African American to receive an Oscar. McDaniel won the award for her role in *Gone with the Wind* (the film).

The stamp honoring McDaniel is part of the Black Heritage Series, which the U.S. Postal Service began in 1978, issuing a new image annually — usually at the start of the year (Davis and Hunt, pages 126–127).

McDaniel joined the ranks of Sojourner Truth (1986) and Harriet Tubman (1978) who had worked for the freedom of the slaves. She has since been joined by Ella Scott Fitzgerald (2007) and Marian Anderson (2005) (Davis and Hunt, page 286).

## The Universal Copyright Convention

Margaret Mitchell helped to establish two laws. One began as the Tydings-Miller Bill. Commonly known as the fair trade or private protection act, President Franklin Delano Roosevelt signed it into law in August of 1937. It regulated the selling price of jewelry, cosmetics, and books.

The other law that she worked to establish was one which would make the government of the United States a member of the Universal Copyright Convention. She had been working with the State Department and with legislators for years to encourage the United States to enter into this pact. She had tried to demonstrate the need for membership after her experiences with *Gone with the Wind.*

In 1954, Stephens Mitchell submitted a statement of the problems with *Gone with the Wind* as evidence in favor of the United States entering into the convention. Finally, the United States entered into the Universal Copyright Convention in 1954 — after the death of Margaret Mitchell and John R. Marsh.

## Upshaw, Berrien ("Red") Kinnard (1901–1949)

Berrien Kinnard Upshaw was the first husband of Margaret Mitchell and the oldest son of William and Annie Berrien Upshaw of Madison, Georgia. He was born in March of 1901, four months after Margaret Mitchell was born. When Berrien was four, the family moved to Raleigh, North Carolina, and he grew up there (Pyron, page 132–133).

Berrien did not get along well with his father, a successful insurance man who ran his own business. Berrien soon found himself in prep school.

Like Maybelle Mitchell, Annie Berrien Upshaw died in the Spanish influenza epidemic of 1918–1919. Her death left William Upshaw with four sons to rear. William soon remarried. Berrien Kinnard ("Red") Upshaw's step-mother was generous and kind, but Berrien did not reciprocate her kindness or affection. His parents tried to provide the best college education for him, but he did not prove himself a scholar (Pyron, page 133).

Berrien was fair complexioned. As his nickname

suggests, his hair was a dark red. He had high cheekbones and a high forehead. His eyes were deep-set and he was very tall. Berrien was very thin — almost sepulchral (Pyron, page 133).

"Red" spent an unsuccessful year at the University of Georgia. He dropped out of the program there. Berrien's father, William, helped secure Berrien admittance to the United States Naval Academy, but he soon failed academically and could not return. Berrien returned to the University of Georgia for one semester, but he failed again. Young Berrien somehow gained re-admittance to Annapolis, where he promptly failed again after one term. The University of Georgia permitted him to re-enroll, but he never completed the work there and left with "incompletes."

Margaret Mitchell had her first date with "Red" Upshaw at a University of Georgia Sigma Nu house party. Walker dates this event as the spring of 1920.

*Berrien Kinnard "Red" Upshaw's early girlfriend Courtenay Ross.* When Margaret Mitchell first met Red Upshaw, he was dating Courtenay Ross, a friend of Margaret's. Courtenay remembered him as "a peculiar fellow." She recalled that it was always someone else's fault that he could not stay in any school. She often laughed and said that she dated him out of her Christian duty (Pyron, page 132).

*Berrien Kinnard ("Red") Upshaw and Margaret Mitchell marry.* Margaret Mitchell and "Red" Upshaw wed on September 2, 1922, in the home of Eugene Muse Mitchell (1866–1944). Pyron and Farr both see the ceremony as symbolic of Margaret's break with the Catholic religion because she had a pastor from St. Luke's Episcopal Church to conduct the ceremony (Pyron, page 1137; Farr, page 57).

John R. Marsh served as best man for Berrien Upshaw. Augusta Dearborn was Margaret's maid of honor. Mitchell's friend Courtenay Ross had married Bernice McFedyen in October of 1920. He was serving in the Philippines; she was with him and unable to attend (Pyron, page 104).

*Upshaw and Mitchell's marriage.* The couple spent their first night at the apartment that Upshaw and John R. Marsh shared (Edwards, page 87). Walker, however, notes that the first night of their married life was in an Atlanta hotel (Walker, page 87).

Early the next morning the two drove to the Grove Park Inn in Asheville. The couple also took a trip to Raleigh to visit Upshaw's father and his step-mother (Edwards, page 87; Pyron, pages 137–139). Only Walker suggests that the Upshaws spent part of their honeymoon elsewhere. Walker names Wrightsville Beach in North Carolina (page 87).

Margaret Mitchell suffered maltreatment at the hands of Upshaw. Perhaps this abuse started on

their honeymoon — as implied by friends; they noted that the couple returned from their honeymoon with an "edge." Margaret commented that she should not have talked about Clifford Henry on their honeymoon or sent his parents a postcard (Edwards, page 87).

Red was often drunk in public and openly abusive to Margaret. She wrote to Marsh in Washington, D.C., and asked him to come home to talk with Red about his problems with alcohol.

In December, Margaret and "Red" notified John that they were going to seek a divorce. Red left Margaret without emotion and told her he was going to North Carolina.

On July 10, 1923, Red returned unexpectedly and put Margaret in the hospital for two weeks. Margaret tried to keep the details of the hospitalization secret. She was out of work for six weeks from the ordeal (Edwards, page 101–103).

Margaret kept a pistol beside her every night from then until the death of Berrien Kinnard ("Red") Upshaw on January 13, 1949 — just months before her own death. Edwards notes that John brought her the pistol to her hospital room in July of 1923 (page 103). Pyron maintains that Margaret herself bought the pistol. Farr acknowledges the pistol (Farr, page 57; Pyron, page 194).

*Upshaw after Margaret Mitchell.* Mitchell and Upshaw were officially divorced in October of 1924. This was about two years after their September 22, 1922, wedding, and a little over a year after her two-week hospitalization in July of 1923 after his beating her.

Red Upshaw was married two times after his first marriage to Margaret Mitchell. His next marriage was to Billie Hitt of Savannah, Tennessee. Billie and he had one son, named after Berrien's father: William Francis Upshaw III.

His third marriage was to Virginia Nolan; Virginia Nolan Upshaw was— like Margaret Mitchell — a newspaper woman. She worked with a San Francisco newspaper ("Historic Oakwood Cemetery: Our Stories: Berrien Kinnard ("Red") Upshaw").

*Upshaw's death.* Berrien Kinnard ("Red") Upshaw's death, according to his family, occurred in Galveston, Texas, on January 12, 1949. Berrien was 47 at the time and was a ship's fireman ("Historic Oakwood Cemetery: Our Stories: Berrien Kinnard ("Red") Upshaw").

Upshaw's step-mother wrote to Margaret Mitchell Marsh about the death of Red. She told Margaret that the police suspected suicide. She also told Margaret that Red had left behind a nineteen-year-old son.

The newspapers give the report that he plunged

from a fifth-floor fire escape of the Alvin Hotel at 20th and Market streets downtown. On his fall, he broke two telephone lines. Dr. J. C. Wright pronounced Upshaw dead at the United States Marine Hospital. After a subsequent inquest, the ruling was that the death was a suicide. The family requested Berrien's body for burial in a Raleigh, the city in which the family still lived. His interment was in Oakwood Cemetery on January 15, 1949.

Other versions of Berrien's death exist. One legend reports that losers in a card game in Galveston killed him to get his winnings (their losings). Another legend reports that Berrien had cheated in the game and his fellow players killed him for punishment. Another legend suggests that someone pushed Berrien from the window; others suggest that Berrien accidentally fell to his death ("Historic Oakwood Cemetery: Our Stories: Berrien Kinnard ["Red"] Upshaw").

*Berrien Kinnard ("Red") Upshaw's death and Margaret Mitchell's reaction.* Margaret Mitchell responded to the letter that Berrien's step-mother wrote to her about Berrien's death. Margaret indicated that she had not heard from Red in several years and did not know of his death. Margaret asked about Berrien's past health and about his marital status. Seven months later Margaret herself would die from injuries sustained when a car

Margaret Mitchell before the launch of the USS *Atlanta* after a long training session as a Red Cross launchee. (Library of Congress)

struck her as she crossed the street ("Historic Oakwood Cemetery: Our Stories: Berrien Kinnard ["Red"] Upshaw").

## The USS *Atlanta*: preparations for its christening

On June 23, 1941, Margaret Mitchell received the invitation of Lieutenant Colonel E. John Long to christen a new cruiser: the USS *Atlanta*. Margaret eagerly accepted the invitation to perform the ceremony at the U.S. Navy Shipyards in Kearny, New Jersey.

Margaret wrote an eight-page, single-spaced letter on June 23, 1941. The letter was filled with questions and reflected her enthusiasm. She began by explaining that she had lived her entire life in Atlanta — an inland city; she had never attended a christening. She needed some information and wrote that she hoped he would keep her questions secret.

She asked what she should wear and asked how many changes of clothes she should bring. She explained that she was small and requested no large bouquet of flowers; she also asked what she should do with the bouquet when she smashed the bottle into the ship.

She asked for a good technique for smashing the champagne. She asked that the construction of the platform accommodate her small size and ensure her being able to reach the ship easily (Walker, pages 451–452).

Margaret wanted to know if she should expect a spray of the liquid on her clothes. Would she "christen a dress as well as the USS *Atlanta*?" (June 23, 1941, letter to Lieutenant Colonel E. John Long from Margaret Mitchell, as cited by Edwards, page 452). She wanted to know if the bottle had a covering on it, or should she expect flying glass with the impact.

Margaret asked for directions to the shipyard. She inquired if someone would escort her. If she would have no escort, she asked how she should present herself in Kearny.

Margaret wanted to know what kind of gift she should bring to give to the USS *Atlanta*. She described in three paragraphs some after-dinner coffee cups made in England by Wedgewood; the Atlanta Historical Society had had the cups made. Margaret wanted to donate them to the USS *Atlanta* — if they were not too dainty. She asked Lieutenant Colonel E. John Long if he thought the cups appropriate.

No one knows Lieutenant Colonel E. John Long's true reaction to the letter. He evidently kept his feelings and her content private, as she had requested.

Margaret left on September 4, 1941, for the Waldorf-Astoria. She arrived in New York on the morning of September 5.

Macmillan publicity officials and members of

Margaret Mitchell christens the USS *Atlanta* (CL-51) on September 6, 1941. This photograph shows the moment of impact when the bottle hits the ship. (Call No. 968. Courtesy of the Atlanta-Fulton Public Library System's Special Collections Department.)

the New York press club met her at her suite later in the day. The press recorded her christening the USS *Atlanta* (Walker, pages 451–452).

*The USS* Atlanta *and its commissioning.* Margaret received an invitation to return to the navy shipyard on December 24, 1941, to attend the commissioning of the USS *Atlanta*. John urged her not to attend at Christmas, but she told him that she did not want the ship to go without someone from Atlanta present to wish the vessel luck. She promised to be home by 4:00 P.M. on Christmas Day.

For this occasion, she wore her Red Cross uniform. She laughingly told the officers that both her dresses were at the cleaners. Samuel Power Jenkins, the ship's captain, had all 400 sailors to line up on deck to shake hands with her (Walker, pages 452–453).

*The USS* Atlanta *and its specifications.* The length of the USS *Atlanta* was 541 feet with a beam of 52 feet, 10 inches. Its draft was 20 feet and 6 inches.

The USS *Atlanta* had 16 of the 5-inch, .38-caliber guns. It had 9 of the 1.1 inch, .75-caliber anti-aircraft cannons and 8 of the 21-inch torpedo tubes. The ship was capable of reaching a speed of 32.5 knots and could house a crew of 650. Its displacement was 6,000 tons. The light cruiser USS *Atlanta* (CL-51) was first of a class of cruisers built at Kearny, New Jersey (Yarnall).

*The USS* Atlanta *(CL-51) and its service record.* After its Christmas Eve commissioning in 1941, the USS *Atlanta* spent the next four months in work along the Atlantic coast. In early April of 1942, the *Atlanta* left for the Pacific coast.

The *Atlanta* participated in an escort voyage in the Pacific in May 1942. She became part of a task force with the *Enterprise* and *Hornet,* two aircraft carriers. In early June 1942, the *Atlanta, Enterprise,* and *Hornet* participated in the Battle of Midway.

This scene is before the launching of the USS *Atlanta*, February 6, 1944. Left to right are Brigadier General Clark Howell; Margaret Mitchell, sponsor of the ship; and George Biggers, vice president and general manager of the *Atlanta Journal*. (Call no. 784. Courtesy of the Atlanta-Fulton Public Library System's Special Collections Department.)

In mid–July 1942, *Atlanta* left Pearl Harbor for operations in the South Pacific. The Guadalcanal campaign began in early August. It assisted with screening the carriers that supported both the Guadalcanal and the Tulagi landings. It participated in the Battle of the Eastern Solomons by escorting the *Enterprise*. It also protected the USS *Saratoga*, which was damaged by a Japanese submarine torpedo.

The USS *Atlanta* remained busy with the vital tasks of escorting both auxiliary and combat ships involved in the struggle to hold Guadalcanal. In late October the *Atlanta* provided support during the Battle of the Santa Cruz Islands.

The USS *Atlanta* used its five-inch guns on October 30. It bombarded the Japanese positions on Guadalcanal. During November 11–12, it helped in the fight against enemy planes that were attacking the supply ships and U.S. transports.

Then the fateful night of November 12–13, 1942,

arrived. As part of a cruiser-destroyer force, the USS *Atlanta* received orders to stop the Japanese bombardment of the airfield on Guadalcanal that the United States held. The Naval Battle of Guadalcanal ensued. History defines this engagement as "one of World War II's most brutally chaotic surface actions." As a result of the battle, the Japanese left the area. The cost that the USS *Atlanta* paid for the victory, however, was high.

Both enemy and friendly gunfire riddled the cruiser. A Japanese torpedo found the *Atlanta*. The crew suffered a heavy toll, and the cruiser was almost inoperative. The able crew worked throughout the day of November 13, but it became apparent by the late afternoon that it was going down. The men left the USS *Atlanta* by the orders of the captain. The captain then ordered a demolition charge to completely sink the vessel.

The wreck of the USS *Atlanta* has been examined several times over the years. It lies off Lunga

Point at Iron Bottom Sound, off the coast of Guadalcanal. The cruiser is five-hundred feet below the surface.

The U.S. Navy removed the USS *Atlanta* from its rolls of active vessels on January 13, 1943. The removal, however, was not without accompanying orders. The *Atlanta* earned five battle stars for service in World War II and received the Presidential Unit Citation; the citation noted the "heroic example of invincible fighting spirit" in the Battle of Guadalcanal on November 13, 1942 (Yarnall).

In November of 1942 Margaret learned of the sinking of the USS *Atlanta* off the coast of Guadalcanal and of the loss of many of its men. She recalled christening the cruiser and shaking hands with the crew. She admitted that the news made her stomach feel sick. She grieved to find out what had happened.

*The USS* Atlanta *bond-raising events.* The saddened Margaret went to work thereafter. She gathered the Red Cross women around her. Together, they began a campaign to raise $35 million in bonds to replace the *Atlanta.*

Margaret Mitchell even accepted an invitation to speak at a large event — a task she normally would have declined. The fact that a father of a wounded crewman on the USS *Atlanta* made the request influenced her acceptance. She boarded a train for Blue Ridge, Georgia, to deliver her presentation despite the fact that she was suffering with back problems; in fact she would have spine surgery at Johns Hopkins in late March after the war-bond campaign had ended. She found herself making many public appearances and public speeches to achieve her goal of replacing the USS *Atlanta.*

In February 1943 Margaret Mitchell and the other women of the local Red Cross held an outdoor bond sales event at Five Points. It just happened that the event was on the coldest day that Atlanta had ever seen. Guards from the Atlanta Marines were present; they made sure that the currency, bonds, and certificates did not blow off the table. They fired cannon each time they received a donation of $1,000 (Walker, pages 455–456). Margaret Mitchell summed up the day in a letter: "We were deafened and frozen but we had a wonderful time and raised $500,000" (Harwell, *Letters,* page 308).

In a matter of six weeks, Margaret Mitchell and her friends had raised $65 million. This was enough to replace the USS *Atlanta* and to purchase two destroyers also (Edwards, page 308).

*The USS* Atlanta *(CL-104) specifications.* The New York Shipbuilding Corporation laid the hull of the USS *Atlanta* (CL-104) on January 25, 1943,

at Camden, New Jersey. Its launch and christening date was February 5, 1944.

The new vessel had a displacement of 10,000 tons, as compared to the 6,000-ton displacement of the old *Atlanta* (CL-51). Whereas the earlier *Atlanta* could house slightly more than 600 crew members, the *Atlanta* (CL-104) could have a complement of 1,426 officers and enlisted crew. The newer *Atlanta* was 610' 1" in length with a beam of 66' 4". The older *Atlanta* was 541 feet in length with a beam of 52' 10".

The draft of the newer *Atlanta* was 24 feet 10 inches. By comparison, the older *Atlanta* had a draft of 20 feet 6 inches. The *Atlanta* (CL-104) had a flank speed of 31 knots, as compared to the somewhat faster speed of 32.5 knots on the earlier vessel ("USS *Atlanta* [CL-104]"). The armament of the USS *Atlanta* (CL-104) included 28 of the 40mm guns and 22 of the 20mm guns ("WW II Archives: Preserving Their Sacrifice").

*The USS* Atlanta *(CL-104): Its launching and commissioning.* The sponsor of the USS *Atlanta* (CL-104) was Margaret Mitchell. She — with the women of the Red Cross — had raised the money for the newer *Atlanta.*

The christening and launching was on February 6, 1944. Mitchell attended and again christened a USS *Atlanta*; this cruiser, however, was the CL-104. John R. Marsh was able to accompany her this time. She was more comfortable this time — even in a conversation with Brigadier General Clark Howell and George Biggers, vice president and general manager of the *Atlanta Journal.*

Mitchell also helped with the commissioning of the new *Atlanta* on December 3, 1944. Captain B. H. Colyear was in command ("USS *Atlanta* [CL-104]").

***See also*** **American Red Cross; Waldorf-Astoria Hotel.**

## Valentino, Rudolph

In her work with the *Atlanta Journal,* Margaret wrote on a variety of subjects. Her investigations included going behind the scenes at a circus, being lifted by an elephant, holding a monkey, talking with convicts and bootleggers, interviewing politicians, researching Confederate generals, and hanging from one of the swings that the workers used for carving on Stone Mountain.

Farr describes Margaret Mitchell's interview with the star Rudolph Valentino as one of the most perceptive of her articles (Farr, page 63). Valentino was one of the symbols of romance after his role as a chieftain in *The Sheik,* but Mitchell said that Valentino seemed not to understand why women reacted to him as a lover.

Edwards observed that Mitchell's "most famous interview was the one with Rudolph Valentino" (page 111). In the article, Margaret described him as "[d]ressed in a fuzzy tan golf suit with tan sox to match and well-worn brogues." She observed that Valentino "seemed shorter and stockier than when on the screen as the Sheik. He seemed older — and just a bit tired" ("Valentine Declares He Isn't a Sheik," by Mitchell in Allen, page 152).

Mitchell's interview with Valentino was on the graveled roof of the Georgian Terrace, which had figured prominently in Mitchell's life. It was the hotel at which many stars resided during the Atlanta premiere of *Gone with the Wind* (the film), and it might have been the hotel lobby where Margaret had delivered the manuscript for what would become the book *Gone with the Wind.*

"Margaret had dropped through a window to meet Rudolph Valentino on the roof.

"And then—*then*—came the thrill of a lifetime — the great event which the 10,000 flappers referred to before would have parted their hair to have experienced.

"'Allow me,' breathed a husky voice in my ear and as masterfully as ever he sheiked Agnes Ayres, he picked me up in his arms and lifted me through the window!

"As he stood there, with me in his arms, one girl gasped, 'Oh, the lucky little devil!'" ("Valentine Declares He Isn't a Sheik," by Mitchell in Allen, page 154).

Margaret concluded her article: "I ended by registering a world-beating blush, dropping my vanity case, pulling the hem out of the back of my dress with my heel as I bent to retrieve it, and bumping heads with Valentino" ("Valentine Declares He Isn't a Sheik," by Mitchell in Allen, page 154).

**See also Atlanta Journal/Atlanta Sunday Magazine; Borglum's "Swing" and Margaret Mitchell; elephant; Georgian Terrace Hotel; monkey.**

### Venable, Samuel Hoyt (1856–1939)

Samuel Hoyt Venable was the owner of Stone Mountain in Georgia. Stone Mountain had figured prominently into the life of Margaret Mitchell.

*Samuel Hoyt Venable's Stone Mountain, Margaret Mitchell, and the Ku Klux Klan.* Stone Mountain was the site for the rebirth of the Ku Klux Klan, which had figured prominently in *Gone with the Wind.* Perhaps her visits to Stone Mountain, her reading *The Traitor,* the movie *The Birth of a Nation,* and the newspaper accounts of the KKK influenced Margaret Mitchell's including the KKK in her novel.

*Samuel Hoyt Venable's Stone Mountain, Margaret Mitchell, and Margaret Mitchell's accident.* Stone Mountain was possibly the site where Margaret Mitchell had a horseback riding accident and injured her ankle. This ankle would cause her difficulty for much of her life, took her off her feet, and was an impetus to her writing *Gone with the Wind.*

*The Stone Mountain carving and Margaret Mitchell's newspaper article.* While Mitchell was working as a newspaper reporter, she wrote an article on the process of carving the figures on Stone Mountain. She actually tried out one of the swings that Gutzon Borglum's workers were using on the side of Stone Mountain. She earned the respect of the photographer and her fellow workers when she allowed them to lower her from the side of a building.

*Samuel Hoyt Venable's Stone Mountain, Margaret Mitchell, and the premiere of the film Gone with the Wind.* Stone Mountain was the site around which the pilot of the plane carrying the stars to the Atlanta Premiere of *Gone with the Wind* detoured when tailwinds pushed their arrival time to the place that they were arriving before the local Atlanta dignitaries were able to meet them, according to an unverified story.

*Samuel Hoyt Venable's biography (1856–1939).* Samuel Hoyt Venable and his brother William brought Stone Mountain in 1887 from several owners. Samuel was a young man, about 21 years old, at the time. The Venable family was the first to own the entire mountain.

Samuel and William founded Venable Brothers. The pair opened and operated the marble quarries at Stone Mountain. Their able management made granite one of the major industries of Georgia and helped rebuild Atlanta during Reconstruction.

The Venables imported skilled workers from Scotland and Wales to quarry the mineral. Granite was used as paving blocks for streets prior to the use of other materials. Stone Mountain granite was in use in many places. Hundreds of post office buildings and other public buildings in the United States have Stone Mountain granite in their construction.

In Atlanta the Fulton County Court House, the Carnegie Library that Eugene Muse Mitchell (1866–1944) helped to establish, the Federal Prison where Margaret Mitchell held writing competitions and raised money for war bonds, the United States Post Office, and Sam Venable's residence (1410 Ponce de Leon Ave.) all incorporated granite into their structure.

In Washington, D.C., the foundation of the Lincoln Memorial used Stone Mountain granite. The chair on which Lincoln is sitting inside the memorial is one of granite from Stone Mountain ("Samuel Hoyt Venable").

*Samuel Hoyt Venable, the United Daughters of*

the Confederacy, and Stone Mountain. In 1916, Samuel Hoyt Venable, his sister Elizabeth Venable Mason, and their relatives Coribel V. Kellogg and Robert V. Roper deeded the steep side of Stone Mountain and the adjacent land to the United Daughters of the Confederacy (UDC). The UDC wanted to carve a Confederate memorial on the side of the mountain. The deed stipulated that the land would revert to the Venables if the memorial were not completed in twelve years.

Gutzon Borglum advised the UDC that placing merely the head of Robert E. Lee on the mountain as they had intended would be like a postage stamp on the giant surface. He altered the design and began work before they discharged him and hired Augustus Lukeman. Meanwhile, Samuel Hoyt Venable had deeded his half of the mountain to his sister, Elizabeth Venable Mason, in 1925 (Davis, Georgia During the Great Depression, pages 243–244).

On April 9, 1928, Lukeman unveiled his work: the faces of Lee and Davis, an outline of Lee's horse, blocked out figures of Lee and Jefferson Davis. On May 20, 1928, however, the Venables reclaimed the property because the work was not complete.

Thirty years later (1958) the State of Georgia purchased the mountain and 3200 acres of surrounding land. The state hired Walker Kirtland Hancock as consultant for completing the carving. The dedication of the completed carving finally came on May 9, 1970 (Davis, Georgia During the Great Depression, pages 243–244).

Samuel Hoyt Venable did not live to see the sale of the land to the state or the finished memorial. After his 1939 death, his final resting place was in 243 of the Ellis/Venable/Mason Mausoleum in Oakland Cemetery, Atlanta ("Samuel Hoyt Venable").

Samuel Hoyt Venable and the Ku Klux Klan. Samuel Hoyt Venable was a member of the Ku Klux Klan. He was very active in the Klan's revival, which officially began on Stone Mountain on November 25, 1915. In 1923, Venable granted permission to the Ku Klux Klan to use his property and Stone Mountain for celebrations. Gutzon Borglum, the original designer of the Confederate Memorial on Stone Mountain, was a fellow member of the Klan ("Samuel Hoyt Venable").

See also accidents; Atlanta premiere of Gone with the Wind; Borglum, Gutzon; Ku Klux Klan; Stone Mountain.

## Vimoutiers, France

Vimoutiers is in northwestern France. In July of 1949, the town made Margaret Mitchell an honorary citizen due to her aid to Vimoutiers.

Details of Mitchell's efforts to aid Vimoutiers are obscure. Of her four primary biographers—Edwards, Farr, Pyron, and Walker—only Edwards mentions her aiding the old Normandy village, which had been leveled mistakenly by Allied bombers in 1944. Even Edwards does not elaborate on what the "help" really was (page 330).

Mitchell received her honorary citizenship in July of 1949—just before the August accident that would take her life. The people of Vimoutiers were grateful to Margaret for helping the city to obtain American aid after World War II ("Margaret Mitchell Helped French Town after WWII").

A more recent event renewed acknowledgment in Margaret Mitchell's efforts on behalf of Vimoutiers. French pilot Denis Barois was at his home in Mexico City, Mexico, Monday, on June 15, 2009, when he spoke of Margaret Mitchell and her unselfishness.

The story of Barois and Mitchell began in mid–1944. Margaret received a letter from Denis, a French Air Force pilot. Barois was stationed in southwest Georgia, and he wrote Mitchell to tell her that he related to Scarlett's flight. He said that Scarlett's escape reminded him of the roads he traveled when he left France in 1942, crossed the Pyrenees, and continued to North Africa to join General Charles de Gaulle's resistance forces.

In Morocco, Barois joined the French Air Force. His training was in the United States. After Barois completed his advanced training in November 1944, he and his friend came to Atlanta. Mitchell invited them into her home. She signed a copy of Gone with the Wind and gave it and a monogrammed handkerchief to Barois. He still treasured those items in 2009.

Barois—on his return to France—married a resident of Vimoutiers. It was only then that he discovered the devastation in the town that the Allied forces had mistakenly bombed.

Barois and Mitchell continued to correspond. Mitchell even sent the couple things that they could obtain easily after the war. These items included color film and toothpaste. The couple sent her perfume, French lace, and other gifts over the years ("Margaret Mitchell Helped French Town after WWII").

When Vimoutiers began trying to raise funds for reconstruction, Barois thought of his friend Margaret Mitchell. True to her form, Mitchell sent a check to aid in rebuilding the hospital. She obtained some other American aid for the town and the additional help of a service organization—the Pilot Club—to assist with the rebuilding. As always, she kept the size of her donations private ("Margaret Mitchell Helped French Town after WWII").

The grateful town made Margaret Mitchell an honorary citizen in July 1949. Mitchell treasured the honor and wrote to the director of the hospital on July 27 to voice her gratitude: "Nothing that has happened to me before has ever pleased and touched me as much as this honor which you and the Municipal Court of Vimoutiers have paid me" ("Margaret Mitchell Helped French Town after WWII"). Mitchell's letter indicated that she hoped to be able to visit the rebuilt city of Vimoutiers. Her wish was not to be. She died in August 1949 after being struck by an automobile.

Mitchell's volunteer work for Vimoutiers was largely unpublicized in the United States. The Hargrett Rare Book and Manuscript Library at the University of Georgia holds a large collection of Margaret Mitchell and Mitchell family papers, including some of her personal correspondence, photographs, and legal papers. Still, in 2008, Mary Ellen Brooks—the curator of rare books and director emeritus of the Hargrett Rare Book and Manuscript Library at the University of Georgia—was unaware of Mitchell's work with Vimoutiers. Then Bill Troost contacted her. She helped him conduct research about Margaret Mitchell's role in rebuilding Vimoutiers ("Margaret Mitchell Helped French Town after WWII").

Bill Troost had a connection with Margaret Mitchell. Troost's great-uncle was John R. Marsh. In the family papers, Troost had found mention of Mitchell and Vimoutiers. He also located a corroborating letter.

In May 2008 Troost received an invitation to attend a ceremony to unveil a plaque in the hospital in Vimoutiers. The plaque honored Margaret Mitchell and the work she had done to help rebuild the hospital after the 1943 bombing. Troost found that Mitchell was still a beloved figure in Vimoutiers. Troost was able to attend the ceremony ("Margaret Mitchell Helped French Town after WWII").

*See also* Barois, Denis; Boullard, Marie-Christiane.

### Waldorf-Astoria Hotel (New York)

On her trips to christen both cruisers the USS *Atlanta*, CL-51 and CL-104 in New Jersey, Margaret Mitchell stayed at the Waldorf-Astoria Hotel in New York City ("Waldorf-Astoria").

*Waldorf-Astoria's Famous Facts.* As a proponent of women's rights, Mitchell's mother, Maybelle Mitchell, would have liked the fact that her daughter was staying at the Waldorf-Astoria. The hotel was the first to eradicate the "ladies' entrance."

The Waldorf-Astoria prided itself on some other firsts that it initiated. It was the first hotel to provide room service for its guests and the first to have its assistant managers moving about the lobbies and offering help to the guests. The Waldorf-Astoria offered permanent living spaces; it was the first hotel to do so. Three American five-star generals and several celebrities made their home there.

It received the status as an official New York City landmark in 1993. Since 1931 the current Waldorf-Astoria Hotel on Park Avenue between 49th and 50th streets has received its New York guests. This, however, was not the first hotel to carry the name Waldorf-Astoria ("Waldorf-Astoria").

### Walker, Marianne

Marianne Walker, a native of Monroe, Louisiana, is a retired professor of English and philosophy at Henderson Community College in Kentucky. Walker is the author of *Margaret Mitchell and John Marsh: The Love Story Behind* Gone with the Wind (1993). It is one of four main biographies of Margaret Mitchell written before 1995 ("Marianne Walker: Author Biography").

*Margaret Mitchell and John Marsh: The Love Story Behind* Gone with the Wind is not the only publication of Marianne Walker. She has also written *When Cuba Conquered Kentucky: The Triumphant Basketball Story of a Tiny High School that Achieved the American Dream* (1999).

*Marianne Walker and her interest in Kentucky.* Walker was born and reared in Monroe, Louisiana, but she has lived much of her life in Kentucky. She married Ulvester Walker from Henderson, Kentucky, and they returned to Henderson after college graduation.

The couple met and married while they were in college in New Orleans. Ulvester Walker went to Tulane for both his undergraduate and his law degrees. Marianne graduated from St. Mary's Dominican College and earned her Masters from the University of Evansville in Indiana.

Ulvester started a law practice there in Henderson, Kentucky. He later served as city attorney and county attorney. For sixteen years he was commonwealth attorney ("Host Bill Goodman interviewed *When Cuba Conquered Kentucky* author Marianne Walker").

*Marianne Walker's career.* In addition to serving as a professor of English and philosophy in the University of Kentucky Community College System, Walker developed courses in bioethics and in hospice care for the University of Kentucky Community College system. She was honored as the 1993 recipient of the University of Kentucky Alumni Award for Teacher of the Year; she also earned the Henderson Community College Outstanding Faculty Achievement Award. The Henderson Business and Professional Woman's Organization named her the Woman of the Year in 1982 ("Marianne Walker: Author Biography").

*Writings and media contacts by Marianne Walker.* Walker has written for *The New York Times* and *The Louisville Courier-Journal Sunday Magazine.* PBS, NPR, GPB (Georgia Public Broadcasting), and KET (Kentucky Education Television) have featured Walker and her work.

**See also Edwards, Anne; Farr, Finis; Pyron, Darden Asbury.**

## Walker Terrace house

Just before Christmas of 1949, Margaret Baugh helped widower John R. Marsh move into the Atlanta house that she had located for him. The one-floor house at 26 Walker Terrace would eliminate the necessity of his having to climb stairs (Edwards, page 337).

Walker notes that John purchased the house in the summer of 1950 — not before Christmas of 1949. She, too, notes that a main attraction of the Walker Terrace home was that it would enable Marsh to carry on his life and his business from one floor. For his bedroom, he chose a large room that enabled him to look out over a wooded backyard with squirrels, chipmunks, and birds.

John had the house repainted and cleaned. He liked the high ceilings and the tall windows. The house had floors of longleaf pine. It also had an apartment attached. Marsh had the terrace apartment remodeled for Bessie Berry Jordan. This would enable Bessie and her husband Charlie Jordan to move in with him (Edwards, 337–338).

The house was just a few doors down from the Della Manta Apartment at 1258 Piedmont Avenue. It seemed just what Marsh wanted (Farr, page 234).

John had one room set up as an office. Margaret Baugh and her assistant organized the papers and worked from that room. John still managed the foreign market and translations of *Gone with the Wind.* He continued to decline offers from those who wanted to write plays, produce musical dramas, and prepare sequences.

John still tried to stamp out any rumors about Margaret Mitchell, about him, and about *Gone with the Wind.* He sponsored the writing contest for prisoners in the federal prison in Atlanta and contributed to the charities in Margaret's name. John lived and worked in the Walker Terrace house until his death in May of 1952 (Walker, pages 516–517).

## Washington Seminary

Washington Seminary was a private school for young women in Atlanta, Georgia. Three sisters from the Washington family established Washing-

ton Seminary in 1878; they were descendants of the family of the first president of the United States.

Miss Lola Washington was the first principal of Washington Seminary. She was highly intelligent. Mrs. Katie Washington Bond was the first matron. She was a conscientious woman who exerted a lasting influence on the students. Washington Seminary's best-known founder, Miss Anita Washington, was always ready with a smile. She belonged to many social clubs and was a devoted member of St. Philip's Episcopal Church. In August of 1949 Dean Raimundo De Ovies, pastor of St. Philip's Cathedral, would conduct the services for Margaret Mitchell.

The 1878 Misses Washington's School for Girls was on West Peachtree Street near Baker Street. The school moved to Church Street — now Carnegie Way — in 1881. The senior class of 1882 changed the name of the school to Washington Seminary.

The school has undergone several changes in location. It has moved to Cain Street and to the corner of Walton and Fairlie streets. From 1912 until the 1950s Washington Seminary was housed in the estate called La Colina (The Hill). Colonel Clifford L. Anderson, an attorney, legislator, and the founder of Trust Company of Georgia, had established the estate in 1895 (Student Body of Washington Seminary).

In 1951, Washington Seminary joined with Westminster School, a reorganization of Atlanta's North Avenue Presbyterian School. Westminster School became co-educational. It has continued to prosper and moved into new facilities after the turn of the century ("Westminster Schools: History").

## wedding of Berrien Kinnard "Red" Upshaw and Margaret Mitchell

On Thursday, August 31, 1922, John R. Marsh arrived for the wedding of Berrien Kinnard ("Red") Upshaw and Margaret Mitchell. The wedding would be at the home of her father, Eugene Muse Mitchell.

John found Margaret Mitchell in overalls trying to get the house ready for the wedding. Three of the workers had not arrived. John wrote to his mother after the wedding. He told her that he buffed floors, moved furniture, wrote some articles for the paper, and arranged presents in the display room (Walker, page 86).

*Decorations.* An altar constructed in the large front hall was the site for the wedding. The altar faced the stairs. Guests could watch the ceremony from the parlor and from the library on either side of the hall.

Palms, ferns, and lilies filled the hall. The entire house had pink and white roses, gladioli, and garlands of smilax. Walker reports that there were so many white candles in candelabra that Eugene Mitchell feared a fire might burn down the house (pages 86–87).

*The wedding party.* The wedding party included Augusta Dearborn as maid of honor. She wore an orchid gown of brocaded satin. Her bouquet was orchids and pink roses (Edwards, pages 86–87).

Stephens Mitchell and Winston Withers were the groomsmen. John R. Marsh was the best man. Two of Margaret Mitchell's cousins in the wedding party wore lavender dresses.

Courtenay Ross had married Lt. Bernice M. McFedyen a year earlier. McFedyen was in the Philippines, and Courtenay was with him. She was, therefore, unable to attend. Margaret Mitchell had two bridesmaids. They were Dorothy Bates Kelly and Martha Bratton Stevens (Walker, pages 86–87).

*Margaret Mitchell's attire.* Margaret Mitchell — "always a show-stopper"—appeared at the top of the stairs with a dozen long-stemmed red roses. Francesca Marsh, John Marsh's sister-in-law, quotes Eugene Muse Mitchell as saying, "What the hell are those doing here?" Margaret quieted him and took his arm (Walker, page 87).

Walker and Pyron also see Margaret's use of red roses for the bride's bouquet as symbolizing a break with the Catholic religion (Walker, page 87; Pyron, page 137). Edwards, however, notes that Margaret Mitchell used a white bouquet — not a red one (page 87).

Margaret wore a white, long satin gown. The traditional gown had tiny pearls sprinkling it (Walker, pages 86–87).

Edwards describes the gown differently. She indicates that the dress had a low waist and ended at her knees. It had a long train that was narrow and trimmed with pearls; it was bordered with orange blossoms of silk with seeded centers. A flapper-style band on her forehead held her lace-and-tulle veil. Edwards remarks that Margaret Mitchell's "flapper bridal gown, with its long grafted train and the oversized coronet and veil, was disastrous … she looked like nothing so much as a child playing dress-up" (page 87).

*Honeymoon of Berrien Kinnard ("Red") Upshaw and Margaret Mitchell.* The couple spent their first night at the apartment that Upshaw and John R. Marsh shared (Edwards, page 87). Walker counters that the first night of the married life of the Upshaws was in an unidentified Atlanta hotel (Walker, page 87).

Early the next morning the two drove to Asheville, where they spent some time at the Grove Park Inn. The couple then drove to Raleigh to visit Upshaw's father and step-mother.

Indications are that the honeymoon had not been entirely idyllic. The couple returned from their honeymoon with an "edge" in their attitude toward each other. Friends gathered that it had not been the happiest of times. Margaret took some blame for the abuse, as abused women often do. She told friends that she should not have discussed her feelings about Clifford Henry or sent a postcard to his parents during their time together (Edwards, page 87).

The abuse continued. Their divorce was final on October 16, 1924.

### Wehner, William

William Wehner was a painter and entrepreneur from Munich, Germany. In 1883, Wehner established the American Panorama Company in Milwaukee, Wisconsin. Its main purpose was to paint historical events on such a large scale that the viewer would feel involved in the scene.

To create the huge panoramas and to produce an illusion of involvement, Wehner realized that ideally each painting would use more than one artist. He hired ten German artists and brought them to the United States.

The *Battle of Missionary Ridge* was the first of the paintings. In 1885 *The Battle of Atlanta* became the second of their works. After their research, the artists painted the battle scenes in five large sections. The Hollywood studios studied *The Battle of Atlanta* in the Atlanta Cyclorama as inspiration to their filming *Gone with the Wind* ("The Munich Style").

***See also*** Atlanta Cyclorama; *Battle of Atlanta* **painting.**

### Weil, A. S.

A. S. (Albert Sigmund) Weil was a student at the Georgia Institute of Technology. At the Junior League Debutante Ball in Atlanta, A. S. and Margaret performed a daring dance: the Apache dance. After their March 13, 1921, performance, both the *Atlanta Journal* and the *Atlanta Constitution* reported their dance was a striking feature of the Mi-carême Ball. Some of the members were shocked by the performance (Walker, page 76).

***See also*** **Apache dance; Atlanta premiere of** *Gone with the Wind*; **Junior League Ball.**

### Wiggins, Patsy

Patsy Wiggins is the proprietor of the Road to Tara Museum. Her museum and gift shop is in the old Jonesboro Train Depot, which houses the Jonesboro Welcome Center in Jonesboro, Georgia. For over thirty years Wiggins, the owner and curator, has been collecting scripts, posts, photographs, programs, dolls, costumes, and other memorabilia related both to the movie and book *Gone with the Wind*. The Road to Tara Museum contains much of her collection ("Southern Draw: Atlanta's Sweet-Talkin' Suburbs").

*Patsy Wiggins and Henry Love Angel's Materials.* In 1952 Henry Love Angel's step-grandson, Henry Love Angel, Jr., sold his step-grandfather's materials to Wiggins for $60,000. Henry, Jr., hoped to use the money for a Florida retirement home. Debra Freer had pronounced the collection authentic.

Henry, Jr., was dismayed at a later date to find that Scribner Publishing Company had paid the Margaret Mitchell Estate and Patsy Wiggins some $1 million for the publishing rights to the materials. Among the materials was the manuscript for Mitchell's *Lost Laysen*, which Scribner's would publish in 1996 in English; the same year volumes in Dutch, Czechoslovakian, Chinese, and Romanian were also available.

In hindsight Henry Angel, Jr., said that if he had known what was going to happen with the materials, he would have gone to New York to auction the materials himself. There were, however, provisions that Wiggins, Freer, and Henry, Jr., would receive royalties from *Lost Laysen* and any other published materials (Kim Hubbard, "Buried Treasure").

Jonesboro is just 15 miles south of Atlanta and in Clayton County. In *Gone with the Wind,* the Tara plantation was in Jonesboro, but — of course — there was no actual Tara ("Clayton County Georgia").

*See also* Angel, Henry Love.

## Wiley, John, Jr.

John Wiley, Jr., is a collector over 10,000 items of Margaret Mitchell and *Gone with the Wind*. He is the author of and the subject of articles about Margaret Mitchell and her novel. Wiley has worked on his collection and his own knowledge for over 40 years.

John Wiley's collection is a feature of Pauline Bartel's *Complete Gone with the Wind Sourcebook*. He is an expert on the life of Margaret Mitchell and her novel. His library consists of more than 700 foreign editions and every American edition of *Gone with the Wind* (Ellen F. Brown, "Writers Houses").

Wiley was the subject of interviews in *Entertainment Weekly* and *USA Today*. The United States Postal Service consulted Wiley as an artistic adviser for its postage stamp appearing in 1998; the 32-cent *Gone with the Wind* stamp was a part of the 1930s Celebrate the Century series (Ellen F. Brown, "Writers Houses").

*John Wiley, Jr., and The Scarlett Letter.* John Wiley, Jr., has published the quarterly newsletter *The Scarlett Letter* for more than 20 years. His newsletter is the only periodical devoted to Margaret Mitchell, her book *Gone with the Wind*, and the Selznick film by the same name.

*John Wiley, Jr., and Ellen F. Brown decide to work together.* In 2007, *Fine Books and Collections* magazine commissioned Ellen F. Brown to write a profile of John Wiley, Jr.; as a collector of memorabilia related to Margaret Mitchell, *Gone with the Wind* (the book), and *Gone with the Wind* (the film), Wiley seemed like a perfect topic for the magazine.

When Ellen F. Brown accepted the commission, she had never read Mitchell's novel. The information that she gleaned from Wiley piqued her desire to find out more about Mitchell and about her Pulitzer Prize winning novel.

Brown read the thousand-page work of Mitchell and described it as "beautifully written, historically rich, and compulsively readable." She called Wiley to find out more about the history of the novel *Gone with the Wind*. When he told her that no such history of *Gone with the Wind* was in print, a seed of an idea was born.

After more discussion, Brown and Wiley decided to co-author the "biography"— literary history — of *Gone with the Wind*. The book would cover the entire story of *Gone with the Wind* from its inception through 2011, the 75th anniversary of the novel.

*John Wiley, Jr., Ellen F. Brown, and the steps in writing.* The co-authors visited Atlanta's Margaret Mitchell House to begin research on what would be *Margaret Mitchell's Gone with the Wind: A Bestseller's Odyssey from Atlanta to Hollywood*. Brown had never visited the Atlanta residence and museum until the two went together. Brown found out about the history of the apartment and about the efforts of Mary Rose Taylor to preserve Margaret Mitchell and John R. Marsh's residence.

The second trip of Wiley and Brown to the Margaret Mitchell House was in 2011. The occasion of this February visit was the release of their *Margaret Mitchell's Gone with the Wind: A Bestseller's Odyssey from Atlanta to Hollywood*. Brown wrote (with the support of John Wiley, Jr.,) that she felt somewhat "uncomfortable dissecting Mitchell's life and work on her home turf — she disliked being written or talked about. I like to think though that she would approve of our project. *Gone with the Wind* was her pride and joy, and I suspect she'd be happy for its story to be told" (Brown, "Writers Houses").

*See also* addresses directly related to Margaret Mitchell; Margaret Mitchell House; Taylor, Mary Rose.

## Wilkes, Ashley

In Margaret Mitchell's book *Gone with the Wind* (1936) and in Selznick's film (1939), Ashley Wilkes is the object of Scarlett O'Hara's affection much of the time. Leslie Howard portrayed Margaret Mitchell's Southern gentleman in the film. *SparkNotes* describes Wilkes: "[A] passive, blond, handsome man, Ashley is so caught up in visions of the world as he feels it should be that he never does anything to affect the world as it is…. Unlike Rhett with his daughter, Bonnie, Ashley is rarely shown having contact with his son, Beau" ("Ashley Wilkes").

Howard did not attend the Atlanta premiere of *Gone with the Wind*. He had enlisted in the military by that time.

***See also*** Academy of Motion Picture Arts and Sciences; Atlanta premiere of *Gone with the Wind*; Howard, Leslie.

## Wilkes, Melanie Hamilton

The character Ashley Wilkes marries Melanie Hamilton, who is always eager to help anyone in need. Even the local madam and the community leaders think highly of Melanie.

After Scarlett O'Hara marries Melanie's brother Charles Hamilton, Melanie sees Scarlett as a supportive friend and sister-in-law. Melanie defends Scarlett if a negative comment arises from anyone. Melanie is also a practical person, who does whatever she can to save those she loves from fire, enemy raiders, or economic pressures.

In Selznick's film *Gone with the Wind*, Olivia de Havilland plays Melanie Hamilton Wilkes. She received a nomination — without a concomitant award — as Best Actress in a Supporting Role ("*SparkNotes:* Melanie Hamilton Wilkes").

***See also*** Academy of Motion Picture Arts and Sciences; Atlanta premiere of the film *Gone with the Wind*; de Havilland, Olivia.

## Will of John Marsh

John R. Marsh's will, dated July 26, 1951, was a typewritten document signed by Margaret Eugenia Baugh, Ruth Connelly, and Nell Simmons. The document, photocopied in 2011 by Jim Carruthers of Mount Dora, Florida, and sold to Anita Price Davis, is a four-page document with a five-page codicil. The will — which is a document of public record — reads:

I, John R. Marsh of said State and County [Fulton County, State of Georgia] do make this my last will and testament.

Item first: I give and bequeath to Bessie Jordan and Deon Ward, who have been the faithful servants of myself and my late wife, $1000.00 each in fee simple.

Item second: I give and bequeath to Eugene Carr, who has been our friend and helper as well as janitor at 1268 Piedmont Avenue, N.E., Atlanta $500.00 in fee simple.

Item third: I give and bequeath to Margaret Eugenia Baugh, secretary of my late wife and myself, $2500, in fee simple.

Item fourth: I give and bequeath to each of my nieces, nephews, great nephews $100.00 in fee simple.

Item fifth: I give and bequeath to Eugene M. Mitchell and Joseph R. Mitchell of Fulton County, Georgia, the nephews of my late wife, $100.00 each in fee simple.

Item sixth: I give and bequeath to the Fulton-DeKalb Hospital Authority for the use of the Margaret Mitchell Memorial at Henry Grady Memorial Hospital, Atlanta, Georgia, $10,000 in fee simple.

Item seventh: I give and bequeath to the Margaret Mitchell Library, at Fayetteville, Georgia, $1,000 in fee simple.

Item eighth: I give and bequeath to the Good Samaritan Clinic, Atlanta, Georgia, $1000.00 in fee simple.

Item ninth: I give and bequeath to Saint Joseph's Infirmary, Atlanta, Georgia, $1000.00 in fee simple.

Item tenth: I give and bequeath to Georgia Baptist Hospital, Atlanta, Georgia, $1,000 in fee simple.

Item eleventh: I give and bequeath to the Atlanta Historical Society $1000.00 in fee simple.

Item twelfth: I give and bequeath to my brother-in-law, Stephens Mitchell of Fulton County, Georgia, if he be then in life, or if he be dead to his heirs at law, all rights in the novel known as "Gone with the Wind," which was written by my late wife. This included royalties from publication rights, copyrights, radio rights, television rights, dramatic and opera rights and any other rights which I now have or which may later come into being. It was my wife's desire that these rights stay in her family, and this bequest is in fulfillment of that wish. I also bequeath to Stephens Mitchell all contracts, business records, and papers dealing with rights in "Gone with the Wind" and all essential business correspondence in relation thereto, together with the file cases, office furniture and equipment used in connection with "Gone with the Wind" business affairs.

Item thirteenth: I have inherited from my wife Margaret Mitchell Marsh her collection of souvenirs and mementoes of her library career (including specifically but not by limitation newspaper and magazine clippings, the certificate presented to her by the Pulitzer Prize committee, the bronze paperweight presented her by the American Booksellers Association and other certificates, awards and tokens presented to her in recognition of the excellence of her literary work, the six framed originals of the illustrations published in the Danish edition of "Gone with the Wind" which were presented to her by the artist Axel Mathiesen, press photographs, her collection of copies of the various editions of her novel and the dust cases which she had made for them, her collection of historical and other reference works, her collection of mementos, given her by literary and other public figures including books autographed by their authors, some of which books are inscribed to me as well as to her). I believe that these items, and any other not specifically mentioned which make up the record of my wife's literary career, should not be split up among my various heirs but should be held together in one collection. I give and bequeath said items above described (remaining in my possession at the time of my death) to the City of Atlanta for the use of the Atlanta Public Library.

Item fourteenth: I give and bequeath to my mother, Mrs. Mary D. Marsh, 2101 Gilles Street, Wilmington, Delaware, all items of personal effects, furniture and house furnishings not otherwise disposed of. This includes my collection of editions of my wife's novel, which were given to me by her, and my personal collection of pictures of her.

Item fifteenth: I give, devise and bequeath one-half of the residue of my estate to

(a) My mother, Mrs. Mary D. Marsh, 2101 Gilles Street, Wilmington, Delaware,

(b) My sister, Mrs. Katharine Marsh Bowden, 4815 Angeles Vista Blvd., Los Angeles, California,

(c) My brother, Henry N. Marsh, Ramsey Road, Route 2, Wilmington, Delaware [sic]

(d) My brother, Ben Gordon Marsh, Richmond Road, R. D. 7, Cedar Hills, Lexington, Kentucky,

(e) My sister, Mrs. C. R. Zane, 48½ Union Street, Rockville, Connecticut, equally, share and share alike, absolutely and in fee simple.

Item sixteenth: If for any reason the bequest set forth in Item fifteenth does not amount to $100,000 net to the legatees, after payment of all taxes and expenses of all kind, then all of the other legacies herein set forth, specific, general and residuary, shall abate pro rata until such sum is realized or until the other legacies are exhausted. In calculating the value of the residue,

the amounts payable under my policies of life insurance shall not be taken into account.

Item seventeenth: After the above bequest set forth in Items fifteenth and sixteenth has been satisfied [sic] I give and bequeath to Stephens Mitchell, if he be then in life, or if he be dead, to his heirs at law, the other one-half of the residue of my net estate.

Item eighteenth: I nominate, constitute and appoint the Citizens & Southern National Bank of Atlanta, Georgia, and Stephens Mitchell as Executors of this my last will and testament and direct that they shall not be required to give any bond or security, file any inventory or cause any appraisement to be made of my estate or make any returns or reports, either annual or final, to any court or authority. They shall have power to sell, exchange or otherwise dispose of any part or all of my property and estate either at public sale or private contract at such time and place, in such manner, for such price and on such terms, for cash or on time or for part cash and part on time as they may see fit, to borrow money for any purpose and secure the same in such way as they may see fit and to settle, compromise or compose any claims either in favor of or against my estate for such sums as they may see fit, all of which powers they may exercise without obtaining any order of court.

W. J. Yahannan, Julian F. Harris, Basil E. Gray signed to the will on August 24, 1949. John R. Marsh had set his hand and sealed the will on August 24, 1949.

CODICIL TO THE WILL OF JOHN R. MARSH
Concerning the Manuscript
of "Gone with the Wind"
File in the office of
V. J. Yarbrough
S. F.
Book V, Page 108

My wife, Margaret Mitchell Marsh, wanted her private papers destroyed. She did not wish them to fall into the hands of strangers. This meant a great deal to her. She believed that an author should stand or fall before the public on the basis of the author's *published* work. She believed that little was ever gained from studying an author's manuscript and private papers, and that, more often than not, this led to false and misleading conclusions.

Knowing the uncertainties of life, she placed upon me the duty of destroying her papers if she should die without having done it. She did so die, and I have tried to fulfill the obligation. As a part of the painful job, I have destroyed the original manuscript of her novel "Gone with the Wind" and all related papers, proof sheets, notebooks, notes, et cetera, except as described below.

Peggy [Margaret Mitchell Marsh] left me discretion as to the disposal of the papers. I have decided that some of the "Gone with the Wind" papers should be saved, as a means of authenticating her authorship of her novel. If some schemer were to rise up with the claim that her novel was written by another person, it would be tragic if we had no documentary evidence and therefore were unable to beat down the false claim. So I am saving these original "Gone with the Wind" papers for use in proving, if the need arises, that Peggy and no one else was the author of her novel.

I have placed these papers in a sealed envelope, in my safety box in the vault of the Citizens & Southern National Bank, Marietta Street, Atlanta. They are to remain sealed unless a real and actual need for them arises for the purpose stated. If such a need never arises, the envelope and contents are eventually to be destroyed unopened. I desire the legatees and trustees to whom I have bequeathed these papers to preserve this envelope, sealed, for the stated purpose. I also authorize them to break the envelope, and I place upon them the duty to use the said papers in defending the good name and literary reputation of my wife as the one and only authentic author of "Gone with the Wind," if her authorship of the novel should be seriously challenged.

The material in the envelope includes the following "Gone with the Wind" papers:

(1) The original manuscript of certain chapters, typewritten by my wife, and with many corrections and changes in her writing. Also two or three drafts of some chapters, showing their development and changes as she wrote and rewrote.

(2) Several proof sheets carrying her handwriting and mine.

(3) Several chronologies prepared by my wife while the book was being written, giving events in the book and historical events side by side, to keep these in step; age of various characters with relation to the progress of events in the story and with relation to other characters; pregnancies and other time-important situations. These were one of the means by which Peggy achieved her remarkable success in avoiding errors in her book.

(4) A few samples of the mass of notes she made in collecting data and information for her book. She kept these notes in large manilla [sic] envelopes labeled in her handwriting "Notes on Reconstruction," "Miscellaneous References," et

cetera. In saving some of this material I also noted down the total amount of material in the envelopes from which it was taken. For example, one of the tables on the retained material in the sealed envelope reads, "From Envelope labeled 'Miscellaneous References'— which contained 37 sheets, handwritten, mostly on both sides. Also various letters. Amount saved — 6 sheets and 4 letters."

(5) Lists she made up of items to be checked for accuracy, and material she dug up in answer to her questions.

(6) She was especially diligent about accuracy in the sections of her book about the Atlanta Campaign. The story of the fighting is told simply in the book, but she did a large amount of research in order to get it simple, and accurate. Included are some of her research notes, chronologies, her notes on items to be checked further. Also notes made by her father and brother, who were asked by her to read the manuscript and let her know of any errors they found.

(7) A few of the large manilla [sic] envelopes in which she kept the chapters of her book during the years she was writing it. Each envelope contained all of her materials related to a certain chapter, her various rewrites of it, reference notes, et cetera. The envelopes are labeled in her handwriting and have notes scribbled on the outsides of them, as ideas came to her of changes and corrections.

With this material, I am confident it can be proved not only that my wife, Margaret Mitchell Marsh, wrote "Gone with the Wind," but that she alone could have written it.

Upon my death, I give to my wife's brother, Stephens Mitchell, the sealed envelope and its contents herein referred in, during his lifetime, and upon his death to the Citizens and Southern National Bank, Atlanta, Georgia, as permanent trustee. The said sealed envelope shall be kept in the vault of said bank and its successors after my death.

The trustees herein named shall have the following title and duties:

(1) The title to said papers shall vest in Stephens Mitchell, during his life, and at his death shall vest in Citizens and Southern National Bank, Atlanta, in fee simple.

(2) Stephens Mitchell and Citizens and Southern National Bank shall hold its title, as trustees for the purposes herein expressed, and for no other purpose.

(3) In order to effectuate the carrying out of said trust, I direct my executors to pay over to Citizens and Southern National Bank, a sum

which, when invested, will pay the rental on the safety vault in which the papers are stored, and the charges made by Citizens and Southern National Bank as trustee.

(4) If there is never a need to open the envelope to make the proof set forth above, this trust shall not ever end. In case the purposes of the trust might fail for lack of a trustee, the Superior Court of Fulton County, Georgia, or its successor, holding equitable jurisdiction, shall appoint a new trustee, and shall oversee the investment of the fund and the carrying out of the purposes of this trust.

(5) In case that beneficial title to the papers contained in said envelope ever becomes a point at issue, I hereby vest said title in Stephens Mitchell and his descendants, but this title does not carry with it any right to possession of the papers or of the trust fund, and shall last only until the need for opening of the envelope containing said papers shall occur.

(6) In case the need for opening the envelope and disclosing the papers in said envelope does arise, the trustees shall use them as directed above, and shall use the trust fund for the purpose of establishing and authenticating the authorship of *Gone with the Wind* by Margaret Mitchell Marsh. The trust shall thereupon terminate, and title to said papers shall vest in Atlanta Historical Society or its successors, or if there be no such Society or successor, in such Public Library of the City of Atlanta as is then in existence.

(7) In case this trust should be ended in any manner by any governmental authority or court, the said envelope and the papers therein shall be destroyed unopened, and the Trust Fund shall be paid to and shall vest in the Atlanta Historical Society or its successors.

I have therefore executed this as a Codicil to my Will, and have hereunto set my hand and seal this 26th day of July, 1951.

John R. Marsh SEAL

Signed, sealed, declared and published by JOHN R. MARSH as a Codicil to his last Will and Testament in the presence of us, the subscribers, who sign our names hereto as witnesses, in the presence of the testator, at his special instance and request an in the presence of each other, this 26 day of July, 1951.

*Margaret Baugh*
118 Lafayette Drive, N.E.
*Ruth Connelly*
1410 Peachtree Street, N. E., Apt. 804
*Nell W. Simmons*
224 East Virginia Avenue,
College Park, Georgia

## Will of Margaret Mitchell

The will of Margaret Mitchell Marsh was filed August 23, 1949.
    V. G. Yarbrough.
    C. F. August 23, 1949.
    S. F. September 6, 1949.
    Book S, Page 480
Estate of Margaret Mitchell Marsh (Mrs. John R. Marsh)

I want John, Steve Mitchell, and the Trust of Georgia to be the Executors of my Will.

I want Bessie Jordan and her daughter, Deon Berry Ward, to have the house and lot on 446 Ripley Street, NE — which they now occupy. They are buying it from me at so much a week. What ever they owe on the house, I don't want them to pay it. I want the property to be theirs with no further payment to me, my heirs, or my Estate. I want Bessie Jordan to be given $500 (five hundred dollars) in addition to the house. I want Deon Ward to be given $200 (two hundred dollars).

The first call on my Estate shall be the payment to Margaret Eugenia Baugh, my secretary, of the sum to pay up the annuity I am buying for her. If she prefers to have the annuity paid up at once I want this done. If she prefers that my Executors pay it up, so much a year, as I am now doing, and as she prefers at present, then pay it up by the year. I want her wishes followed in this matter. In addition to the annuity, I want Margaret Baugh to receive $5000 (five thousand dollars) from my Estate in cash, stocks, bonds, or government Bonds, as she prefers.

I want my two nephews Eugene Muse Mitchell II and Joseph Reynolds Mitchell, to receive my share of the farm on the Chattahoochee River (formerly known as the Nesbit farm) which is now in the joint possession of my brother Stephens Mitchell, Mrs. Gertrude ... Wright and me. I want each of my nephews (Eugene and Joseph) to be given $500 (five hundred dollars).

To my god children Mitchell Gibson, Taumay Taylor, and Josephine Guidici, I want one thousand dollars ($1000) to be given.

To the Margaret Mitchell Library of Fayetteville, Ga. $1000 (one thousand dollars)

To the Atlanta Historical Society $1000 (one thousand dollars)

To my husband's and my nephews or nieces on the Marsh side, I want to give $100 each. [She specifies each by name.]

I want $100 (one hundred dollars) to be given to Lee Edwards, son of Joseph Lee and Augusta Dearborn Edwards.

Of the rest of my Estate, I want one quarter (¼)

to go to my only brother, Stephens Mitchell. The remaining three quarters (¾) to go to my husband, John Robert Marsh.

I have made a list of furniture and silver belonging to my family. If my brother Stephens Mitchell wants them, let him have them.

I want all right to *Gone with the Wind*, domestic and foreign, of all kinds to go to my husband, John R. Marsh.

I give all my papers and writer matter of all kinds and all my household furnishings and personal belongings and effects to my husband John R. Marsh in fee simple.

If my Executors find that the proportion of the residue of my Estate will be received by my husband, John R. Marsh, amounts to less than $200,000 (two hundred thousand dollars) they shall abate all legacies equally until such specific legacies are abated. However, I except the legacy of the notes that Bessie Jordan owes me on 446 Ripley Street, NE. I want this cancelled. I also except the bequest of an annuity to Margaret Eugenia Baugh. I want this paid [Will of Margaret Mitchell in the author's collection].

## Williams, Annie Laurie (1894–1977)

Two agents who were concerned with *Gone with the Wind* were Marion Saunders and Annie Laurie Williams. Saunders was attempting to sell *Gone with the Wind* abroad; Williams was attempting to market *Gone with the Wind* with Hollywood.

*Annie Laurie Williams and Macmillan Publishing Company.* Pyron suggests that Williams— whom he does not describe in glowing terms—had worked with Macmillan before her work with *Gone with the Wind*: "A Texas country girl who made good in Hollywood and New York, Annie Laurie Williams had marketed all the Macmillan Company's cinematic rights to the West Coast studios before 1936. Well before she secured an actual copy of the manuscript in the late spring, this wheeler-dealer Texas hustler presumed to do the same with this hottest of all hot Macmillan properties" (page 352).

Walker was not overly complimentary about Williams. Walker quotes Lois Cole as saying that Williams had caused everyone at Macmillan to be "sick by going around saying that she was their official movie representative when she was not" (page 253).

Williams, however, also felt hurt at times. She wrote to Harold Latham to be sure that he knew she obtained the highest price for the film *Gone with the Wind* that any agent had ever gotten. She also wanted him to know that she worked for Macmillan Publishing Company — not for Margaret Mitchell (Walker, pages 308–309).

*Annie Laurie Williams, film rights for* Gone with the Wind, *and Margaret Mitchell.* In early July of 1937, Margaret Mitchell learned from Lois Cole, a former employee of Macmillan Publishing Company, that Annie Laurie Williams had closed a contract with David O. Selznick. Williams had told Cole that the closing amount for film rights to *Gone with the Wind* with Selznick International Pictures was $50,000 (Stanfill, Laura).

Mitchell and John R. Marsh were concerned about Williams's negotiations. The couple had believed that Macmillan Publishing Company — not Annie Laurie Williams— would be the agent for negotiating filming contracts. They believed that according to Mitchell's 1935 contract for *Gone with the Wind*, the author was to retain all "dramatic rights" to the book (Walker, page 289).

The relationship between Williams and Mitchell was sometimes troubled. Even her grand-niece Kristin Bailey Murphy admits that her great-aunt Laurie "didn't always have the gift of tact" (Laura Stanfill). The two women, however, were honest with each other about their feelings and beliefs; their relationship endured (Laura Stanfill).

*Kristin Bailey Murphy's Research for* Affectionately, Devotedly, As Ever. Although Kristin Bailey Murphy was only about six years old when Annie Laurie Williams died, she remembered her great-aunt. Murphy's mother also could remember Aunt Annie Laurie. Both of them and Kristin's sister considered writing about Williams's career.

Murphy's mother and her sister found that Annie Laurie Williams's correspondence is archived at Columbia University. Materials were plentiful. Murphy was living in California and raising small children; her researching the material was out of the question.

In 2009, things changed. Two nieces had graduated from college and were without jobs. Kristin was having a third child and would be unable to return to work for a while. Kerry, Kristin's oldest sister, "came into a large sum of money." She was able to rent an apartment for the nieces and pay them to reproduce the correspondence. The research took six months.

Murphy assumed the rest of the project when her nieces had finished their task. She found that she grew to know her family better with the research. Because Williams was a "Packrat," according to Murphy, she had from her mother many boxes of personal artifacts of the agent — who had also been a feature writer for the *New York Morning Telegraph* (Laura Stanfill).

*Annie Laurie Williams and her husband Maurice Crain.* Kristin Bailey Murphy describes Annie Laurie Williams and her husband, Maurice Crain, as "formidable agents who represented some very famous American authors" (Laura Stanfill).

Until his service in World War II, Annie Laurie's husband worked for a newspaper. For two years Maurice was in Stalag 17, a German prison camp. After his liberation and discharge, he, too, worked as a literary agent. He did collaborate with his wife, but he did not work directly for her. His first sale was *Cheaper by the Dozen* (Laura Stanfill).

*See also* **Alderman, Grace; contract for *Gone with the Wind* (film).**

## Williams, Rhoda

Rhoda Williams worked at Georgia Power as John Marsh's secretary. Few people knew of Margaret Mitchell's signed contract with Macmillan Publishing Company. It was Rhoda Williams who suggested the Georgia Power stenographer Grace Alderman to help with typing the manuscript. Rhoda Williams married Joe Kling. The Klings were particularly kind to John R. Marsh after the death of Margaret (Walker, page 516).

*See also* **Grace Alderman.**

## *Wind Done Gone*

In 2001 Houghton Mifflin began to release advance copies of a new novel by Alice Randall. The book carried the title *The Wind Done Gone*. Houghton Mifflin characterized the book as a "rejoinder" to *Gone with the Wind* (Brown and Wiley, page 314).

Written by a Nashville, Tennessee, songwriter, *The Wind Done Gone* is meant to be, according to its author, "an antidote" to *Gone with the Wind*, a novel that has wounded African Americans for years. *The Wind Done Gone* attempts "to provide a mirror world to the one in 'Gone with the Wind.' Unfortunately, it ends up inadvertently diminishing the horrors and deprivations of slavery, while undermining sympathy for some of the very characters it wants to promote" (Kakutani). Kakutani suggests that Randall's "contrarian aspects of 'The Wind Done Gone' played a considerable role in the desire of the Mitchell trusts to squash its publication."

The Associated Press reported on May 10, 2002, that a settlement had been reached in the battle to prevent the publication of *The Wind Done Gone*. The protectors of the copyright of *Gone with the Wind* finally agreed with the publishers of Randall's novel to an out-of-court settlement. For almost a year, the Margaret Mitchell Estate had been trying to stop publication of *The Wind Done Gone* on the grounds of copyright infringement.

Under the settlement terms, Houghton Mifflin — Randall's publisher — agreed to make an unspeci-

fied contribution to Morehouse College; Randall retains rights to any movie adaptations of *The Wind Done Gone*. The lawyers for the estate of Margaret Mitchell agreed, in return, to stop trying to block sales of Randall's book.

Morehouse College had long been a part of the life of the Mitchell family. In the 1940s Margaret Mitchell paid for scholarships for dozens of Morehouse College students through secret arrangements with the President Benjamin Mays. In 2002, Mitchell's nephew Eugene Muse Mitchell (1931–2007) gave Morehouse College $1.5 million. The money was to endow a humanities chair in her name at Morehouse College (Associated Press).

David Ewing, the husband of Randall, remarked that he and his wife were glad when the settlement was complete. He said the book was in the hands of the librarians, the bookstores, and the readers.

The attorney who worked for the Mitchell Estate on the suit against the publisher of *The Wind Done Gone* was Martin Garbus. He was not permitted to talk about the specific details of the settlement (Associated Press).

*See also* **King, Martin Luther, Jr.; Margaret Mitchell Chair in the Humanities at Morehouse College; Mays, Benjamin; Mitchell, Eugene Muse (1931–2007); Morehouse College.**

## *The Yearling*

Marjorie Kinnan Rawlings won the Pulitzer Prize in 1938 for her novel *The Yearling*. She became the third Southern woman to become a Pulitzer Prize–winning author. She followed Julia Peterkin (1928) for *Scarlet Sister Mary* and Margaret Mitchell (1936) for *Gone with the Wind*.

During the 1939 Atlanta premiere of *Gone with the Wind* (the film), the three women attended a luncheon in their honor. The luncheon was at Rich's Department store.

*See also* **American Academy of Motion Picture Arts and Sciences; Atlanta premiere of *Gone with the Wind*; Rich's Department Store.**

## Yugoslavia, sales of *Gone with the Wind* see foreign copyrights/translations and fair trade laws

## Zane, Frances Marsh

In 1928 John's sister Frances Marsh (Zane) included an essay in her memoirs about her childhood in Maysville, Kentucky. She described the town and the family relationships fondly. Like John, she appreciated her mother and her siblings (Pyron, page 191, 231).

Frances was well-educated, as were the rest of

her siblings. She had taken a degree in sociology and social work from the University of Pennsylvania. She married a professor of sociology (Edwards, page 263).

Frances had shared with John in a 1922 letter her decision to go to New York for a career. John rejoiced with her on her decision (Pyron, page 191, 231).

Zane and Marsh sometimes lived far apart. John still often confided in his sister. He also felt protective about his young sister, whom his mother had asked him to help take care of after the death of Millard Fillmore Marsh. Frances was only three years old at the time; John was eight.

He shared with her in the winter of 1921–1922 that he was courting — and serious about — Margaret Munnerlyn Mitchell. He sent Frances photographs of them together, some with Berrien Kinnard ("Red") Upshaw included. Both Red and John were vying for her affection (Pyron, page 135).

*Frances Marsh (Zane), John R. Marsh, and Margaret Mitchell: a lasting friendship.* When Frances came to Atlanta to visit John in April of 1922, Frances stayed with the Mitchells. Margaret and Frances would soon become fast friends.

Frances, however, was frankly alarmed about the trio. Some years later Frances would recount in her memoirs that she saw Red Upshaw and John in the act of tossing a coin to see who would have Margaret for the last half of the evening and who would have her for the first half. On one occasion Frances remembered, John had bent over and kissed Margaret's hand; he placed her hand in Berrien's and said, "'Red, I now surrender to you the woman we both love'" (Pyron, page 135). This statement seems to foreshadow later developments. John shared much with Frances — as did Margaret. He even wrote to her of the breakup of Red and Margaret (Pyron, page 192).

Frances realized the financial hardships that John and Margaret were going through during the first years of their marriage. In 1928 after Frances's marriage to Rollin Zane and the impending birth of their child, she sent Margaret a blue velvet dress from her own wardrobe.

Margaret was most appreciative and wrote to tell Frances so. Margaret noted that the flare of the skirt made her look taller and that she had wept with joy when the dress arrived. Because of Frances, she would have a new dress for the Christmas parties. She had planned to try to add a new collar on an old dress, but that now she would not have to do so. She could wear the dress that Frances had sent (Edwards, page 148).

John's will provided for Frances Marsh Zane. Her part was to be equal to that of John's other siblings, Henry, Katharine, and Ben Gordon.

*See also* will of John R. Marsh.

### Zanuck, Darryl (1902–1979)

Darryl F. Zanuck was a successful Hollywood producer and movie executive for about 40 years. He tried unsuccessfully to get the film rights to the novel *Gone with the Wind.*

His early years had been difficult ones. Abandoned by his parents at age 13, Zanuck was a barely literate adult. Zanuck joined the United States Army and fought in Belgium in World War I. While pursuing a career as a writer, he worked as a steelworker, as a foreman at a garment factory, and as a professional boxer.

In 1923 Zanuck sold a film scenario to Irving Thalberg. He began serving apprenticeships with Charlie Chaplin and others. In 1924 he joined Warner Bros. Studio and contributed scripts for the *Rin Tin Tin* series.

By 1927 Zanuck had advanced to executive producer. He produced in 1927 the first sound film: *The Jazz Singer.* Zanuck initiated the popular series of gangster films; these included *Little Caesar* (1930) and *The Public Enemy* (1931).

He was a cofounder (1933) of Twentieth Century Pictures; the company merged (1935) with the Fox Film Corporation. The result was 20th Century–Fox ("Darryl F. Zanuck"). As the controlling executive of 20th Century–Fox, Zanuck received an advance copy of *Gone with the Wind.* He began to try to get the film rights to the novel. He offered $40,000. Selznick International Pictures, however, obtained the film rights for $50,000 (Edwards, pages 315, 93).

Some of the Zanuck productions were *The Grapes of Wrath* (1940), *How Green Was My Valley* (1941), and *The Razor's Edge* (1946). His *All About Eve* (1950) earned Zanuck the Best Picture Award.

Zanuck left 20th Century–Fox in 1956. He returned in 1962 and helped the company to recover financially. Two box-office hits helped get 20th Century–Fox on its feet; these were *The Longest Day* (1962) and *The Sound of Music* (1965). *The Sound of Music* earned ten Academy Award nominations and received five awards.

Zanuck retired in 1971. He won the Irving G. Thalberg Memorial Award of the Academy of Motion Picture Arts and Sciences three times and produced more than 165 films during his career ("Darryl F. Zanuck").

# Bibliography

"About Morehouse College." http://www.morehouse. edu/about/legacy.html.

"About the Junior League of Atlanta, Inc." http://www. jlatlanta.org/?nd=who_we_are.

"About the United Daughters of the Confederacy." http://www.hqudc.org/.

"Airport History: Hartsfield-Jackson Atlanta International Airport." http://www.atlanta-airport.com/Air port/ATL/Airport_History.aspx.

"Album: Atlanta History Center." http://album.atlanta historycenter.com/store/Advanced_Search.aspx?c=43 3&t=home.

"Alexander Stephens Mitchell." http://www.findagrave. com/cgi-bin/fg.cgi?page=gr&GRid=53271325.

"Alexander-the-Great.co.uk." http://www.alexander-the-great.co.uk/bucephalus.htm.

"Alice Randall: Bio." http://www.alicerandall.com/ bio.

Allen, James, Hilton Als, Congressman John Lewis, and Leon F. Litwack. *Without Sanctuary: Lynching Photography in America.* Santa Fe, New Mexico: Twin Palms, 2000.

Allen, Patrick. *Margaret Mitchell, Reporter: Journalism by the Author of* Gone with the Wind. Athens, Georgia: Hill Street Press, 2000.

Ament, Phil. "John Pemberton." http://www.ideafin-der.com/history/inventors/pemberton.htm.

"Anita Benteen Mitchell." http://www.findagrave.com/ cgi-bin/fg.cgi?page=gr&GRid=68188892.

Applebome, Peter. "Scarlett O'Hara Is Back, and City Is Again Taken." *Atlanta Journal,* September 29, 1991. http://www.nytimes.com/1991/09/29/us/atlanta-journal-scarlett-o-hara-is-back-and-city-is-again-taken.html.

"Art Deco." Hiller, Kanne, and Bayer, as cited by http:// en.wikipedia.org/wiki/Art_Deco.

Associated Press. "Settlement Reached over *Wind Done Gone*" (May 10, 2002). http://www.freedomforum. org/templates/document.asp?documentID=16230.

*The Atlanta City Directories: 1885–1960* and *The City of Atlanta Building Permits.* http://www.atlantaga.gov/ government/urbandesign_windsorhouse.aspx.

"Atlanta Cyclorama and Civil War Museum." http:// www.atlantacyclorama.org/history.php.

"Atlanta Cyclorama: The Story of the Painting." http: //www.atlantacyclorama.org/history.php.

"Atlanta-Fulton Public Library." http://www.archi

planet.org/wiki/Atlanta_Public_Library_(central_lo cation),_Atlanta,Georgia.

Atlanta-Fulton Public Library Foundation. *Margaret Mitchell: The Book, the Film, the Woman.* Baton Rouge: Louisiana State University Press, 1981.

The Atlanta-Fulton Public Library System's Special Collections Department.

Atlanta Historical Society. *Margaret Mitchell Memorial Issue of the Atlanta Historical Bulletin.* Atlanta: Atlanta Historical Society, 1950.

*Atlanta Journal/Atlanta Constitution. Her Byline Was Peggy Mitchell: Anniversary Celebration.* Atlanta, Georgia: Atlanta Journal/Atlanta Constitution, 1986.

Atlanta Public Library. *Margaret Mitchell Memorial of the Atlanta Public Library: Dedicated December 15, 1954.* Atlanta, Georgia: Atlanta Public Library, 1954.

"The Atlanta Speedway." http://www.sunshineskies. net/atlanta010.html.

"Atlanta Terminal Station." http://railga.com/Depots/ atlterminal.html.

"Awards for *Gone with the Wind* [the film]. http://www. imdb.com/title/tt0031381/awards.

Bailey, Matthew. "Rich's Department Store" for *New Georgia Encyclopedia.* http://www.georgiaencyclope-dia.org/nge/Article.jsp?id=h-1888.

Baldwin, Faith. *Margaret Mitchell: The Woman Who Wrote* Gone with the Wind: *An Inclusive and Authentic Interview.* New York: Pictorial Review, 1937.

Bartel, Pauline C. *The Complete* Gone with the Wind *Sourcebook.* Dallas, Texas: Taylor, 1993.

Baumgardt, Kenneth. *Scarlett's Buried Secret: The Sad but True Story Behind Margaret Mitchell's* Gone with the Wind. Pittsburgh, Pennsylvania: Red Lead Press, 2009.

Beck, Robert. *The Edward G. Robinson Encyclopedia.* Jefferson, North Carolina: McFarland, 2002.

Behlmer, Rudy. *Memo from David O. Selznick.* New York: Viking Press, 1972.

Bellis, Mary. "The History of Coca Cola." http://inven-tors.about.com/od/cstartinventions/a/coca_cola_2. htm.

Bertagnoli, Lisa. *Scarlett Rules: When Life Gives You Green Velvet Curtains, Make a Green Velvet Dress.* New York: Villard, 2006.

Biles, Roger. *The South and the New Deal.* Lexington: University of Kentucky Press, 1994.

"Biography: Carole Lombard." http://www.murphs place.com/lombard/bio.html.

"Biography for David O. Selznick." http://www.imdb.com/name/nm0006388/bio.

"Biography for Irene Mayer Selznick." http://www.imdb.com/name/nm1245243/bio.

"Biography for Victor Fleming." http://www.imdb.com/name/nm0281808/bio.

"*The Birth of a Nation*." http://www.imdb.com/title/tt0004972/trivia.

Blickman, Tom. "Coca Leaf: Myths and Reality." *Transnational Institute*, February, 2011. http://www.tni.org/primer/coca-leaf-myths-and-reality.

"Boll Weevil." http://insects.tamu.edu/fieldguide/bimg198.html.

"The Boll Weevil Song." http://www.uic.edu/educ/bctpi/historyGIS/greatmigration/gmdocs/boll_weevil_song.html.

Bond, Jenny, and Chris Sheedy. *Who the Hell Is Pansy O'Hara? The Fascinating Stories behind 50 of the World's Best-Loved Books.* New York: Penguin, 2008.

Bonner, Peter. *Lost in Yesterday.* Marietta, Georgia: FirstWorks, 2006.

Bookman, Julie. "Longtime Buckhead Resident's Play Captures Margaret Mitchell: Melita Easters' Revised Work Premieres Tonight [June 2, 2011] in Celebration of *Gone with the Wind*'s 75th Anniversary." http://buckhead.patch.com/articles/longtime-buckhead-residents-play-about-margaret-mitchell-marks-gone-with-the-wind-anniversary#.

"Books: President's Books." *Time*, Monday, December 20, 1937. http://www.time.com/time/magazine/article/0,9171,758717,00.html.

Bridges, Herb. Gone with the Wind: *The Three-Day Premiere in Atlanta.* Macon, Georgia: Mercer University Press, 1979–1999.

Bridges, Herb, and Terryl C. Boodman. Gone with the Wind: *The Definitive Illustrated History of the Book, the Movie, and the Legend.* New York: Simon & Schuster, 1967.

Brown, Ellen F., with John Wiley, Jr. "The House that Lived." June 30, 2011. http://writershouses.com/guest/the-house-that-lived.

Brown, Ellen F., and John Wiley, Jr. *Margaret Mitchell's Gone with the Wind: A Bestseller's Odyssey from Atlanta to Hollywood.* Lanham, Maryland: Taylor Trade, 2011.

*A Burning Passion.* A made-for-television drama/biography of Margaret Mitchell. http://www.imdb.com/title/tt0109350/.

Cadwalader, Wickersham and Taft, LLP. http://www.martindale.com/Cadwalader-Wickersham-Taft-LLP/law-firm-296452.htm.

Calhoon, Margaret Obear. "Georgia Power Company." http://www.georgiaencyclopedia.org/nge/Article.jsp?id=h-1879.

Cameron, Judy, and Paul J. Christman. *The Art of Gone with the Wind.* New York: Prentice Hall Editions, 1989.

"Candler Field Race Track." http://www.atlantatimemachine.com/misc/airport01.htm.

"Captain William F. Plane." http://www.findagrave.com/cgi-bin/fg.cgi?page=gr&GSln=plane&GSfn=william&GSmn=f&GSbyrel=all&GSdyrel=all&GSob=n&GRid=8276397&df=all&.

Capua, Michelangelo. *Vivien Leigh: A Biography.* Jefferson, North Carolina: McFarland, 2003.

Carlson, Trudy. *Scarlett, Rhett and You.* Duluth, Minnesota: Benline Press, 2001.

"Caroline Louise Reynolds Mitchell." http://www.findagrave.com/cgi-bin/fg.cgi?page=gsr&GSfn=caroline&GSmn=&GSln=mitchell&GSbyrel=all&GSby=&GSdyrel=all&GSdy=&GScntry=4&GSst=12&GScnty=0&GSgrid=&df=all&GSob=n.

"Carrie Chapman Catt." http://womenshistory.about.com/od/cattcarriec/p/carrie_catt.htm.

Carter, Stephen L. "Almost a Gentleman." *New York Times Sunday Book Review* (November 4, 2007). http://www.nytimes.com/2007/11/04/books/review/Carter-t.html?pagewanted=all.

"The Cathedral of St. Philips: About Us." http://www.stphilipscathedral.org/Content/About_Us.asp.

"Chamblee54: Google Goose Chase." http://chamblee54.wordpress.com/2011/05/30/google-goose-chase/.

Chitwood, Oliver Perry, Frank Lawrence Owsley, and H.C. Nixon. *The United States from Colony to World Power.* New York: D. Van Nostrand, 1953.

"Cinema Treasures: Astor Theatre." http://cinematreasures.org/theaters/518.

"Cinema Treasures: Loew's Grand Theatre, Atlanta, Georgia." http://cinematreasures.org/theater/2468/.

"Cinema Treasures: Loew's Grand Theatre, Atlanta, Georgia." http://cinematreasures.org/theaters/1158.

"Cinema Treasures: The Capitol Theatre (New York)." http://cinematreasures.org/theaters/522.

"Citations and Case Summaries page of the Copyright Registration and Renewal Information Chart and Web Site." http://chart.copyrightdata.com/c13A.html.

"City of Jonesboro, Historic Figures." http://www.jonesboroga.com/history_tourism/history/historic_figures.htm.

"Clayton County Georgia." http://www.visitscarlett.com/.

"Clifford Dowdey." http://en.wikipedia.org/wiki/Clifford_Dowdey.

"Clifford Dowdey." http://www.findagrave.com/cgi-bin/fg.cgi?page=gr&GRid=15416182.

"Clifford (Shirley) Dowdey (Jr.)." *Contemporary Authors Online.* Detroit: Gale, 2001. *Gale Biography in Context.* Web. 9 August 2011. Document URL, http://0-ic.galegroup.com.marie.converse.edu/ic/bic1/ReferenceDetailsPage/ReferenceDetailsWindow?displayGroupName=Reference&disableHighlighting=false&prodId=BIC1&action=e&windowstate=normal&catId=&documentId=GALE%7CH1000026626&mode=view&userGroupName=mickel_lcc&jsid=ad92597d334075a1db2bbb0ea4d047f6, Gale Document Number: GALE|H1000026626.

Coleman, Kenneth, editor; Numan V. Bartley, William F. Holmes, F.N. Boney, Phinizy Spalding, and Charles E. Wynes. *A History of Georgia.* Second Edition. Athens: University of Georgia, 1977.

"Confederate General John B. Hood." http://americancivilwar.com/south/hood.html.

"Confederate General 'Stonewall' Thomas Jonathan Jackson, 1824–1863." http://americancivilwar.com/south/stonewall_jackson.html.

Conroy, Pat. "About Pat Conroy." http://www.patconroy.com/about.php.

Conroy, Pat. "I Was Raised by Scarlett O'Hara." *CNN*

*Entertainment*, February 04, 2000. http://articles. cnn.com/2000-02-04/entertainment/pat.conroy_1_ pat-conroy-mitchell-book-margaret-mitchell-estate?_s=PM:books.

"Controversial History: Thomas Dixon and the Klan Trilogy." http://docsouth.unc.edu/highlights/dixon. html.

Coulter, E. Merton. *Georgia: A Short History*. Chapel Hill: University of North Carolina Press, 1933, 1947, 1960.

Crenshaw, Wayne. "Twiggs Native Who Met King Headed to Memorial Dedication." August 26, 2011. http://www.macon.com/2011/08/26/1678360/twiggs-native-who-met-king-headed.html#ixzz1WYwRU zvf.

Crimmins, C.E., Thomas Maeder, and Margaret Mitchell. *Private Diary of Scarlett O'Hara*. West Hollywood, California: Dove Books, 1996.

Crutchfield, James Andrew. *It Happened in Georgia*. Guilford, Connecticut: TwoDot Press, 2007.

"Curriculum Vita of Darden Asbury Pyron." http://cas-group.fiu.edu/faculty/587/1267716225_Full_CV.RTF.

"Cyclorama." *Georgia's Encyclopedia.* http://www.georgiaencyclopedia.org/nge/Article.jsp?id=h-825.

Daniel, Frank. "Mr. Kurtz at Least Achieved This One Note of Authenticity." *Atlanta Journal*, June 1, 1959.

"Darryl F. Zanuck" in Encyclopædia Britannica. http:// www.biography.com/people/darryl-f-zanuck-9540 319.

Davis, Anita Price. *Georgia During the Great Depression*. Jefferson, North Carolina: McFarland, 2008.

Davis, Anita P. *Margaret Mitchell: A Link to Atlanta and the World; Teacher's Guide to the Author of* Gone with the Wind. Atlanta, Georgia: Atlanta Historical Society, 2006.

Davis, Anita Price. *North Carolina During the Great Depression*. Jefferson, North Carolina: McFarland, 2003.

Davis, Anita P., and Louise Hunt. *Women on U.S. Postage Stamps*. Jefferson, North Carolina: McFarland, 2008.

Davis, Elmer. "The Economics of Authorship." *The Saturday Review of Literature*. November 23, 1940, as cited by Brown, page 256.

Davis, Stephen. "Cyclorama." *New Georgia Encyclopedia.* http://www.georgiaencyclopedia.org/nge/Article.jsp?id=h-825.

Davis, Susan Lawrence. *The Authentic History of the Ku Klux Klan, 1865–1877*. Birmingham, Alabama: W.G. Mori, 1924.

"Dean Raimundo de Ovies." http://en.wikipedia.org/ wiki/Raimundo_de_Ovies.

"Deborah Margaret Sweet Mitchell." http://www.finda-grave.com/cgi-bin/fg.cgi?page=gr&GRid=53267793.

"Dixon's *The Leopard's Spots*." http://utc.iath.virginia. edu/proslav/dixonhp.html.

Dodd, Donald B., and Wynelle S. Dodd. *Historical Statistics of the South, 1790–1979.* University of Alabama Press, 1973.

Donovan, Frank Robert. *Wheels for a Nation*. New York: Crowell, 1965.

"Don't Miss This Event: May 24, 2011." http://gawin-list.com/?p=2183#comments.

"Douglas Fairbanks, Sr." http://www.biography.com/ articles/Douglas-Fairbanks-Sr.-9290911.

Drake, James and Rebecca. "Portraits: Generals and Commanders." http://battleofraymond.org/command 6.htm.

Drew, Bernard. *Literary Afterlife: The Posthumous Continuations of 325 Authors' Fictional Characters*. Jefferson, North Carolina: McFarland, 2010.

Ducla, Sophie. *Women in Margaret Mitchell's* Gone with the Wind *and Gail Godwin's* A Mother and Two Daughters. Bordeaux, 2000.

Dunn, Mark. "Fort Gordon." http://www.georgiaency-clopedia.org/nge/Article.jsp?id=h-1321.

"Early Commemorative Coins: 1925 Stone Mountain Memorial Commemorative Half Dollar." http://ear-lycommemorativecoins.com/1925-stone-mountain-half-dollar/.

"The Early History of Smith College." http://sophia. smith.edu/blog/smithipedia/founders/the-early-his-tory-of-smith-college/.

"Ebenezer Baptist Church: Church History." http:// www.historicebenezer.org/History.html.

Eberly, Tim, and Paul Shea. "Friday Tornado Pummels Downtown; Saturday Storm Kills 2." *The Atlanta Journal-Constitution*, March 14, 2008.

Edwards, Anne. *Road to Tara: The Life of Margaret Mitchell*. New York: Dell, 1983.

"Edwin Granberry." http://asp3.rollins.edu/olin/old-site/archives/golden/Granberry.htm.

"Ellen F. Brown." http://www.ellenfbrown.com/.

"Ellen Glasgow." http://www.bookrags.com/biogra-phy/ellen-glasgow/.

Engel, Elliot. *Scarlett Fever: The Greatness of* Gone with the Wind. Sound recording. Raleigh, North Carolina: Authors Ink, 1994.

Entzminger, Betina. *The Belle Gone Bad: White Southern Women Writers and the Dark Seductress*. Baton Rouge: Louisiana State University Press, 2002.

Erickson, Hal (Rovi). "Claudette Colbert." http://mov ies.nytimes.com/person/14003/Claudette-Colbert/ biography.

Eskridge, Jane (editor). *Before Scarlett: Childhood Writings of Margaret Mitchell*. Athens, Georgia: Hill Street Press, 2000.

"The Eternal Flame of the Confederacy." http://www. hmdb.org/Marker.asp?Marker=18622.

"Eurith D. Rivers." http://wn.com/Eurith_D_Rivers.

"Facebook: Anne Edwards" https://www.facebook. com/pages/Anne-Edwards/113131208700371.

Farr, Finis. *Margaret Mitchell of Atlanta: The Author of* Gone with the Wind. New York: William Morrow, 1965.

"Federal Writers' Project." http://www.loc.gov/rr/pro-gram/bib/newdeal/fwp.html.

Federal Writers' Project. *Georgia: A Guide to Its Towns and Countryside*. Augusta: University of Georgia Press, 1940.

"Federal Writers' Project: New Deal Programs: Selected Library of Congress Resources." Go to http://mem-ory.loc.gov/ammem/index.html and enter the search term "Federal Writers' Project."

"Federal Writers' Project: New Deal Programs: Selected Library of Congress Resources." http://www.loc.gov/ rr/program/bib/newdeal/fwp.html.

Federal Writers' Project. *Savannah*. Savannah, Georgia: Review Print, 1937.

Federal Writers' Project. *These Are Our Lives, as Told*

*by the People and Written by Members of the Federal Writers' Project on the Works Progress Administration in North Carolina, Tennessee, and Georgia.* Chapel Hill: University of North Carolina, 1939.

Fedo, Michael. "A Visit with Donald McCaig." *American Magazine* (October 15, 2007). http://www.america-magazine.org/content/article.cfm?article_id=10 282.

Felder, Deborah G. *100 American Women Who Shaped American History.* San Mateo, California: Bluewood Books, 2005.

"Final Days Margaret Mitchell, U.S. Author." http://www.trivia-library.com/c/final-days-of-united-states-author-margaret-mitchell.htm.

"Find a Death: Margaret Mitchell." http://www.findadeath.com/Deceased/m/Margaret%20Mitchell/margaret_mitchell.htm.

"Finis Farr." http://www.worldcat.org/search?qt=worldcat_org_all&q=farr%2C+finis).

Finletter, Gretchen. "Parents and Parades," *Atlantic Monthly,* 176 (1945), pages 80–84.

*Fire Over England.* http://www.imdb.com/title/tt0028872/.

Fisher, Jerilyn, and Ellen S. Silber. *Women in Literature: Reading through the Lens of Gender.* Westport, Connecticut: Greenwood Press, 2003.

Florida State Parks. "Marjorie Kinnan Rawlings State Historic Site." http://funandsun.com/parks/MarjorieKinnanRawlings/marjoriekinnanrawlings.html.

Forbes, Malcolm S., and Jeff Bloch. *They Went That-away.* New York: Ballantine Books, 1988.

"Fort Gordon." http://www.globalsecurity.org/military/facility/fort-gordon.htm.

"Frank Mason Robinson." *Encyclopedia Britannica,* 1992. http://en.wikipedia.org/wiki/Frank_Mason_Robinson.

Freemasonry. "Susan Lawrence Davis and Albert Pike." http://freemasonry.bcy.ca/anti-masonry/davis_sl.html.

The Friends of Marjorie Kinnan Rawlings Farm, Inc. "MKR Commemorative Stamp." http://www.marjoriekinnanrawlings.org/events.php?evt=8.

"Friendship Baptist Church." http://www.fbcatlanta.org/about.htm.

Frommer's. "Searching for Margaret Mitchell." http://travel.nytimes.com/frommers/travel/guides/north-america/united-states/georgia/atlanta/frm_atlanta_0002038060.html.

"Gable and Miss Mitchell Talk Alone After He Begs Audience with Author." *The Atlanta Constitution,* 72, December 16, 1939, No. 187, p. 1.

"Gale Contemporary Black Biography: Alice Randall." http://www.answers.com/topic/alice-randall#ixzz1Zd9l5LUa.

"Gale Notable Literature and Its History: *Gone with the Wind.*" http://www.answers.com/topic/gone-with-the-wind-events-in-history-at-the-time-the-novel-was-written#ixzz1MzjG0igf.

Gale, Steven H. "Joel Chandler Harris." *American National Biography.* Edited by John A. Garraty and Mark C. Carnes, Vol. 10. New York: Oxford University Press, 1999, pages 169–172.

Galloway, Tammy H. "Grant Park." http://www.georgiaencyclopedia.org/nge/Article.jsp?id=h-2897.

Galloway, Tammy H. "Lemur P. Grant." http://www.georgiaencyclopedia.org/nge/Article.jsp?id=h-2888.

Gardner, Gerald, and Harriet Modell Gardner. *A Pictorial History of* Gone with the Wind. New York: Bonanza Books, 1980.

Gemme, Leila B. *Margaret Mitchell's* Gone with the Wind*: A Critical Commentary.* New York: Monarch Press, 1974.

"Georgia Hall: Original Grady Hospital." http://www.atlantaga.gov/government/urbandesign_georgia-hall.aspx.

"Georgia History Timeline: 1924." http://ourgeorgiahistory.com/year/1924.

"Georgia: Memories of Peachtree Street." *Time,* Monday, Nov. 28, 1949. http://www.time.com/time/magazine/article/0,9171,856375,00.html#ixzz1VQxOxp9L.

"Georgia Pacific Tower." http://en.wikipedia.org/wiki/Georgia-Pacific_Tower.

"Georgia Population." http://ngeorgia.com/facts/population.html.

"Georgia Power: Charitable Giving." http://www.georgiapower.com/community/charitable_home.asp).

"Georgia Women of Achievement Website." http://www.georgiawomen.org/.

"Georgia Writer's Hall of Fame." http://www.libs.uga.edu/gawriters/.

Georgia Writers' Project. *Augusta.* Augusta, Georgia: Tidwell Print, 1938.

"Georgia's Aviation History." http://aerospace.georgiainnovation.org/100years/aviation_history

Gilpin, Kenneth N. "Alexandra Ripley, *Scarlett* Author Dies at 70." *New York Times,* January 27, 2004. http://www.nytimes.com/2004/01/27/arts/alexandra-ripley-scarlett-author-dies-at-70.html.

"Glascock Reynolds." Morris Museum of Art, Augusta, Georgia. http://www.themorris.org/library/reynoldspaperguide.html.

"*Gone with the Wind*/Awards." http://www.fandango.com/gonewiththewind_v20278/awards.

"*Gone with the Wind* by Margaret Mitchell with a Preface by Pat Conroy." http://www.amazon.com/s/ref=nb_sb_noss?url=search-alias%3Daps&field-keywords=gone+with+the+wind+conroy&x=0&y=0 Amazon.com.

"GPB: Behind the Scenes; Margaret Mitchell." http://www.gpb.org/margaret-mitchell/behind-the-scenes.

"Grady Memorial Hospital: The New Georgia Encyclopedia." http://www.georgiaencyclopedia.org/nge/Article.jsp?id=h-1216.

Granberry, Edwin. *The Private Life of Margaret Mitchell.* Springfield, Ohio: Crowell-Collier, 1937.

Granberry, Julian. *Letters from Margaret.* Copyright by Edwin Granberry, Jr., and Julian Granberry. No place of publication: 1st Books, 2001.

"Gravitt, Hugh Dorsey: Find-a-Grave." http://www.findagrave.com/cgi-bin/fg.cgi?page=gr&GSln=gravitt&GSfn=hugh&GSmn=d.&GSbyrel=all&GSdyrel=all&GSob=n&GRid=13547648&df=all&.

"Green Park Inn." http://www.greenparkinn.com/.

"Grove, Edwin Wiley: Find-a-Grave." http://www.findagrave.com/cgi-bin/fg.cgi?page=gr&GSln=grove&GSfn=edwin&GSmn=w&GSbyrel=all&GSdyrel=all&GSob=n&GRid=14089462&df=all&.

Guttridge, Peter. "Alexandra Ripley: Author of *Scarlett,*

the Best-selling Sequel to Margaret Mitchell's *Gone with the Wind*." *The Independent*: "Obituaries." January 31, 2004. http://www.independent.co.uk/news/obituaries/alexandra-ripley-549361.html.

"Gutzon Borglum," from *Encyclopedia Britannica* (online). http://www.britannica.com/EBchecked/topic/74150/Gutzon-Borglum.

Gwin, Yolande. *I Remember Margaret Mitchell*. Lakemont, Georgia: Copple House, 1987.

Hacht, Anne Marie. *Literary Themes For Students: Examining Diverse Literature to Understand and Compare Universal Themes*. Detroit: Thomson Gale, 2006.

Hancock and Harwell Rare Coins, 3155 Roswell Road, Suite 310, Atlanta, Georgia, 30305. "1925 Stone Mountain Commemorative Half Dollars." http://www.raregold.com/r-stone.htm.

Hanson, Elizabeth I. *Margaret Mitchell*. Boston: Twayne Publishers, 1991.

"Hardeman Fine Art Glass." http://www.llorensstainedglass.com/history.html.

Harding, Anneliese. "The Munich Style." http://www.germanheritage.com/Publications/germanpainters/paintchapter8.html.

Hardman, Sammy J. *Margaret Mitchell's Literary and Real-life Models and* Gone with the Wind. Commerce, Georgia: Samuel J. Hardman, 2006.

Hardman, Sammy, and Ella M. Powell. *Margaret Mitchell's Models*. Commerce, Georgia: S.J. Hardman, 1994.

"Hartsfield Atlanta Airport in the Early 1970s." http://www.sunshineskies.net/atlanta280.html.

Harvey, Henry S. *Atlanta Campaign: As Seen in* Gone with the Wind *and the Official Documents*. Amherst, Massachusetts: s.n., 1937.

Harwell, Richard Barksdale, Madison-Morgan Cultural Center. *The Big Book: Fifty Years of* Gone with the Wind: *An Exhibit at the Madison-Morgan Cultural Center: From the Collection of Richard Harwell, April 4–May 25, 1986*. Madison, Georgia: Madison-Morgan Cultural Center, 1986.

Harwell, Richard Barksdale (compiler and editor). Gone with the Wind *as Book and Film*. Columbia: University of South Carolina Press, 1983.

Harwell, Richard Barksdale (editor). *Margaret Mitchell's* Gone with the Wind *Letters, 1936–1949*. New York: Macmillan, 1976.

Haskell, Molly. *Frankly My Dear:* Gone with the Wind *Revisited*. New Haven, Connecticut: Yale University Press, 2009.

"Hattie McDaniel." *Dictionary of American Biography*. New York: Scribner's, 1977. *Gale Biography in Context*. Web. 22 Sep. 2011. Document URL, http://0ic.galegroup.com.marie.converse.edu/ic/bic1/ReferenceDetailsPage/ReferenceDetailsWindow?displayGroupName=Reference&disableHighlighting=false&prodId=BIC1&action=e&windowstate=normal&catId=&documentId=GALE%7CBT2310007924&mode=view&userGroupName=mickel_lcc&jsid=d2378dd3db649b2a5b5eb367c622300d, Gale Document Number: GALE|BT2310007924.

"Hattie McDaniel." *Encyclopedia of World Biography*. http://www.notablebiographies.com/Ma-Mo/McDaniel-Hattie.html.

"Hattie McDaniel." NNDB. http://www.nndb.com/people/077/000063885/.

"Helen Plane." http://xroads.virginia.edu/~ug97/stone/plane.html.

"Henry Augustus Lukeman." *Dictionary of American Biography*. New York: Scribner's, 1944. *Gale Biography in Context*. Web. 6 Sep. 2011. Document URL, http://0-ic.galegroup.com.marie.converse.edu/ic/bic1/ReferenceDetailsPage/ReferenceDetailsWindow?displayGroupName=Reference&disableHighlighting=false&prodId=BIC1&action=e&windowstate=normal&catId=&documentId=GALE%7CBT2310008647&mode=view&userGroupName=mickel_lcc&jsid=cd821d5e2f2358b50efec461dea3a4dd, Gale Document Number: GALE|BT2310008647.

"Henry Grady, A Georgia Biography." http://www.gpb.org/georgiastories/story/henry_grady.

"Henry Herschel Brickell." *Dictionary of American Biography*. New York: Scribner's, 1977. *Gale Biography In Context*. Web. 9 Aug. 2011. http://0-ic.galegroup.com.marie.converse.edu/ic/bic1/ReferenceDetailsPage/ReferenceDetailsWindow?displayGroupName=Reference&disableHighlighting=false&prodId=BIC1&action=e&windowstate=normal&catId=&documentId=GALE%7CBT2310017161&mode=view&userGroupName=mickel_lcc&jsid=d6faafdb16ea7a619cbd8cc5292c1411, Gale Document Number: GALE|BT2310017161.

"Henry W. Grady Statue." http://www.atlantatimemachine.com/downtown/gradystatue1.htm.

Hepburn, Lawrence R. *Contemporary Georgia*. Athens: University of Georgia Press, 1987.

"Herb Bridges Collection of *Gone with the Wind* Items Goes for $334,588." http://www.liveauctiontalk.com/free_article_detail.php?article=365.

Herring, Hubert B. "Featured Artist: Walter Kirtland Hancock." http://www.portraitsculptors.org/FeatureImg/Hancock/Feature_WalterHancock.html.

"Historic Oakland Cemetery." http://www.oakland-cemetery.com/history.html.

"Historic Oakwood Cemetery: Our Stories: Berrien Kinnard ("Red") Upshaw." http://www.historicoakwoodcemetery.com/stories_berrien_upshaw.aspLorrimer Publications, 1979.

"History and Archaeology: World War I in Georgia." http://www.georgiaencyclopedia.org/nge/Article.jsp?id=h-3223.

"The History of Atlanta Airport." http://www.sunshineskies.net/atlanta010.html.

"History of H.M. Patterson and Son — Spring Hill Chapel." http://www.hmpattersonspringhill.com/dm20/en_US/locations/49/4944/history.page?.

"History of the Fayette County Library." http://www.fayettecountyga.gov/public_library/history.htm.

"Host Bill Goodman interviewed *When Cuba Conquered Kentucky* author Marianne Walker." http://www.ket.org/bookclub/books/2000_mar/interview.htm.

"Howard Earle Coffin." *Dictionary of American Biography*. New York: Scribner's, 1944. *Gale Biography in Context*. Web. 14 Sep. 2011. Document URL, http://0-ic.galegroup.com.marie.converse.edu/ic/bic1/ReferenceDetailsPage/ReferenceDetailsWindow?displayGroupName=Reference&disableHighlighting=false&prodId=BIC1&action=e&windowstate=normal&catId=&documentId=GALE%7CBT2310015851&mode=view&userGroupName=mickel_lcc&jsid=2644557e

bde065e5e2f23c526e54fa88, Gale Document Number: GALE|BT2310015851.

Howard, Hugh, and Roger Straus. *Writers of the American South: Their Literary Landscapes*. New York: Rizzoli, 2005.

Howard, Sidney, Andrew Sinclair, and Margaret Mitchell. *GWTW, the Screenplay: Based on the Novel by Margaret Mitchell*. London: Lorrimer, 1979.

Hubbard, Kim. "Buried Treasure." *People*, May 13, 1996, Vol. 45, No. 19. http://www.people.com/people/archive/article/0,20141282,00.html.

"Hugh Gravitt, Driver Who Killed Margaret Mitchell." http://articles.orlandosentinel.com/1994-04-22/news/9404220538_1_margaret-mitchell-gravitt-wind-author-margaret.

Hunt, Mary Louise. Interview on October 7, 2011.

"International Copyright Law — The Berne Convention." http://www.copyrightservice.co.uk/copyright/p08_berne_convention.

"James A. Skelton." http://www.findagrave.com/cgi-bin/fg.cgi?page=gr&GSln=skelton&GSfn=j&GSbyrel=all&GSdyrel=all&GSst=12&GScntry=4&GSob=n&GRid=17732222&df=all&.

"James Birdseye McPherson." http://www.findagrave.com/cgi-bin/fg.cgi?page=gr&GRid=4423.

"James Branch Cabell." *Dictionary of Virginia Biography*. http://www.EncyclopediaVirginia.org/Cabell_James_Branch_1879-1958.

Jennings, Peter, and Todd Brewster. *The Century*. New York: Doubleday, 1998.

"Jim Crow Laws" (referenced). http://en.wikipedia.org/wiki/Jim_Crow_laws.

Johnson, Ira Joe, and William G. Pickens. *Benjamin E. Mays and Margaret Mitchell: A Unique Legacy in Medicine*. Winter Park, Florida: Four-G, 1996.

Jones, Anne Goodwyn. *Tomorrow Is Another Day: The Woman Writer in the South, 1859–1936*. Baton Rouge: Louisiana State University Press, 1981.

Jones, Tommy H. "Razing *Gone with the Wind*." http://tomitronics.com/old_buildings/gwtwindex.html.

Jordan, Bessie. "My Dear Employer." *Atlanta Journal Magazine*, August 16, 1951.

"Julia Mood Peterkin." *Dictionary of American Biography*. New York: Scribner's, 1981. *Gale Biography in Context*. Web. 27 Sep. 2011. Document URL, http://0-ic.galegroup.com.marie.converse.edu/ic/bic1/ReferenceDetailsPage/ReferenceDetailsWindow?displayGroupName=Reference&disableHighlighting=false&prodId=BIC1&action=e&windowstate=normal&catId.

Kakutani, Michiko. "*The Wind Done Gone*." http://www.racematters.org/thewinddonegone.htm.

Kemp, Kathryn. "Asa Candler." http://www.georgiaencyclopedia.org/ngc/Article.jsp?id=h-633).

King, Monroe Martin. "John Stith Pemberton," *New Georgia Encyclopedia*. http://www.georgiaencyclopedia.org/nge/Article.jsp?id=h-2747.

Kirkpatrick, Mary Alice. "Thomas Dixon, 1864–1946: *The Traitor: A Story of the Fall of the Invisible Empire*. http://docsouth.unc.edu/southlit/dixon/summary.html.

Knight, Marion A., and Mertice M. James. *The Book Review Digest*. New York: H.W. Wilson, 1925.

Kolb, Richard K. "Thin Gray Line: Confederate Veterans in the New South." http://vaudc.org/confed_vets.html.

"Ku Klux Klan in the Twentieth Century." *Georgia Encyclopedia*. http://www.newgeorgiaencyclopedia.org/nge/Article.jsp?id=h-2730).

Kurian, George Thomas. *Datapedia of the United States: 1790–2000*. Lanham, Maryland: Bernan Press, 1994.

Lambert, Gavin. *The Making of* Gone with the Wind. Boston: Little, Brown, 1973.

Latham, Harold S. *My Life in Publishing*. New York: E.P. Dutton, 1965.

"Laura Hope Crews." http://www.findagrave.com/cgi-bin/fg.cgi?page=gr&GRid=5304.

Lefler, Hugh Talmage, and Albert Ray Newsome. *North Carolina: The History of a Southern State*. Chapel Hill: University of North Carolina Press, 1963.

"Letter, Eleanor Roosevelt to Walter White Detailing the First Lady's Lobbying Efforts for Federal Action Against Lynchings, 19 March 1936." http://memory.loc.gov/ammem/ndlpedu/features/timeline/depwwii/race/letter.html.

LeVasseur, Andrea. "Shannen Doherty Biography." http://www.starpulse.com/Actresses/Doherty,_Shannen/Biography/.

"Local Minister to Kick Off Trip to MLK Memorial Event." Saturday, August 20, 2011. http://www.macon.com/2011/08/20/1671695/local-minister-to-kick-off-trip.html#ixzz1WtQGiVc7.

Lopez, Toni. Gone with the Wind: *Historical Fiction as Popular Culture*, Gainesville: University of Florida, 1979.

*Los Angeles Times*, May 17, 1959, p. G10, as cited by "*Gone with the Wind* (the film)," http://en.wikipedia.org/wiki/Gone_with_the_Wind_(film)#cite_ref-40.

"*Lost Laysen*: Book Review," in *Life Is a Patchwork Quilt*. http://lifeisapatchworkquilt.com/blog/?p=324.

Love, Lucille Thompson, Mary Ellen DeBarbieri Kozuch, Linda Bourgeois Davidson, Margaret Mitchell, and Lucille Alladio Busey. *Remembering Margaret Mitchell, Author of* Gone with the Wind. Huntsville, Alabama: Ellen Ross, 1992.

Ludwig, Linda. "Mitchell, Margaret." http://www.jiffynotes.com/a_study_guides/book_notes/aww_03/aww_03_00833.html.

Macmillan Company. *Margaret Mitchell and Her Novel*, Gone with the Wind. New York: Macmillan, 1936.

"Macmillan, Inc." *International Directory of Company Histories*, Vol. 7. St. James Press, 1993. http://www.fundinguniverse.com/company-histories/Macmillan-Inc-Company-History.html.

"Maj. Gen. John Alexander Logan Camp # 4, Sons of Union Veterans of the Civil War, Raleigh, NC." http://suvcwcamplogan.org/index_files/Page888.htm.

"The Making of *Gone with the Wind*, Part II." *The Atlantic Monthly*. March 1973, Vol. 265, No. 6, pages 56–72. http://www.theatlantic.com/past/docs/issues/73mar/wind3.htm.

"Margaret Mitchell and Clifford West Henry." http://www.whosdatedwho.com/tpx_4723327/margaret-mitchell-and-clifford-west-henry/.

"Margaret Mitchell Biography." http://www.angelfire.com/movies/LindysGWTWPage/mitchell1.html.

"Margaret Mitchell Helped French Town After WW II." *Deseret News* archives. Sunday, July 5, 2009. http://www.deseretnews.com/article/705315019/Margaret-Mitchell-helped-French-town-after-WWII.html.

"Margaret Mitchell House and Museum of Atlanta: Travel Guide." http://www.123atlanta.net/attractions/margaret-mitchell-house-&-museum.html.

"Marianne Walker: Author Biography." http://www.filedby.com/author/marianne_walker/2198128/.

"Marjorie Kinnan Rawlings." *Dictionary of American Biography*. New York: Scribner's, 1977. *Gale Biography in Context*. Web. 30 Sep. 2011. Document URL, http://0ic.galegroup.com.marie.converse.edu/ic/bic1/ReferenceDetailsPage/ReferenceDetailsWindow?displayGroupName=Reference&disableHighlighting=false&prodId=BIC1&action=e&windowstate=normal&catId=&documentId=GALE%7CBT2310005022&mode=view&userGroupName=mickel_lcc&jsid=3c61b5013742dda0b22f5d5ce81457b4, Gale Document Number: GALE|BT2310005022.

Marsh, John R. "Will of John R. Marsh." July 26, 1951 (a document of public record).

"Marsh, John Robert: Find-a-Grave." http://www.findagrave.com/cgi-bin/fg.cgi?page=gr&GSln=marsh&GSfn=john&GSmn=r&GSbyrel=all&GSdyrel=all&GSst=12&GScntry=4&GSob=n&GRid=9562352&df=all&.

Martin, Harold. "Atlanta's Most Brilliant Event," in Harwell, Richard, Gone with the Wind *as Book and Film*. New York: Paragon House Books, 1983, p. 148–153.

"Martin Luther King: Biography." Nobelprize.org. 30 August 2011. http://www.nobelprize.org/nobel_prizes/peace/laureates/1964/king-bio.html.

"Martin Luther King, Jr., Biography and Quick Facts." http://www.mlkonline.net/bio.html.

Martin, Sarah Hines. *More Than Petticoats: Remarkable Georgia Women*. Guilford, Connecticut: TwoDot Press, 2003.

"Mary Rose Taylor." http://www.pba.org/programming/programs/lexusleader/531/.

"Master Craftsmen of Stained Glass Windows: Joseph Victor Llorens, Sr." http://www.llorensleadedartglass.com/history.html.

McCaig, Donald. *Rhett Butler's People*. New York: St. Martin's Press, 2007.

McElvaine, Robert S. *Down and Out in the Great Depression*. Chapel Hill: University of North Carolina Press, 1983.

McElvaine, Robert S. *The Great Depression: America, 1929–1941*. New York: Times Books, 1984.

McGee, David. "The Rich Life of Margaret Mitchell's *Gone with the Wind*." Bluegrass Special.com, May 2011. http://thebluegrassspecial.com/archive/2011/may2011/gone-with-wind-mitchell-75-anniversary.html.

McInerney, Rita. "DeGive Family Colorful in City, Catholic History," *The Georgia Bulletin* (May 20, 1993). http://www.georgiabulletin.org/local/1993/05/20/a/.

"Memorial Day History." http://www.usmemorialday.org/backgrnd.html.

Michener, James A. *Literary Reflections*. New York: Forge, 1994.

Millichap, Joseph. "Margaret Mitchell." Beacham Publishing Company online at http://beachampublishing.com/articles/samples/mitchell.pdf.

Mims, Jocelyn, Melanie Pearson, and Margaret Mitchell. *My Beloved Tara*. Spindale, North Carolina: Kaleidoscope, 1996.

"Mitchell, Alexander Stephens: Find-a-Grave." http://www.findagrave.com/cgi-bin/fg.cgi?page=gsr&GSfn=alexander&GSmn=stephens&GSln=mitchell&GSbyrel=all&GSby=&GSdyrel=all&GSdy=&GScntry=0&GSst=0&GSgrid=&df=all&GSob=n.

"Mitchell, Anita Benteen: Find-a-Grave." http://www.findagrave.com/cgi-bin/fg.cgi?page=gr&GRid=68188892.

"Mitchell, Carolyn Louise Reynolds: Find-a-Grave." http://www.findagrave.com/cgi-bin/fg.cgi?page=gr&GSln=mitchell&GSfn=caroline+&GSmn=louise&GSbyrel=all&GSdyrel=all&GSob=n&GRid=53271333&df=all&.

"Mitchell, Clara Belle Neal Robinson: Find-a-Grave." http://www.findagrave.com/cgi-bin/fg.cgi?page=gr&GSln=mitchell&GSfn=clara&GSmn=bell&GSbyrel=all&GSdyrel=all&GSst=12&GScntry=4&GSob=n&GRid=41178527&df=all&.

"Mitchell, Deborah Sweet: Find-a-Grave." http://www.findagrave.com/cgi-bin/fg.cgi?page=gr&GRid=53267793.

"Mitchell, Eugene Muse [1866–1944]." http://www.findagrave.com/cgi-bin/fg.cgi?page=gr&GSln=mitchell&GSfn=EUGENE&GSmn=MUSE&GSbyrel=all&GSdyrel=all&GSob=n&GRid=9562356&df=all&.

"Mitchell, Eugene Muse [1931–2007]: Find-a-Grave." http://www.findagrave.com/cgi-bin/fg.cgi?page=gr&GSln=mitchell&GSfn=eugene&GSmn=muse&GSbyrel=all&GSdyrel=all&GSst=12&GScntry=4&GSob=n&GRid=20937946&df=all&.

"Mitchell, Eugene Muse: Find-a-Grave." http://www.findagrave.com/cgi-bin/fg.cgi?page=gr&GSln=mitchell&GSfn=eugene+&GSmn=muse+&GSbyrel=all&GSdyrel=all&GSob=n&GRid=9562356&df=all&.

Mitchell, Margaret. *The Film Story of* Gone with the Wind. London: Hollywood Publications, 1948.

Mitchell, Margaret. *Gone with the Wind*. New York: Macmillan, 1936.

Mitchell, Margaret. *Her Byline Was Peggy Mitchell: A Collection of* Gone with the Wind *Author Margaret Mitchell's Stories Published in the Atlanta Journal Magazine, 1922–1926*. Natchitiches: Southern Studies Institute, 1980.

Mitchell, Margaret. *"I Want to Be Famous": The Writings of Young Margaret Mitchell*. Athens: Hill Street Press, 2001.

Mitchell, Margaret. *Peggy: Childhood Writings of Margaret Mitchell*. Athens, Georgia: Hill Street Press, 2000.

Mitchell, Margaret. Radio script prepared for Medora Field Perkerson by Margaret Mitchell, as quoted by Finis Farr in *Margaret Mitchell of Atlanta: The Author of* Gone with the Wind. New York: William Morrow, 1965.

Mitchell, Margaret. "Will of Margaret Mitchell," August 22, 1949 (a matter of public record).

Mitchell, Margaret, Allen Barnett Edee, and Jane Bonner Peacock. *A Dynamo Going to Waste: Letters to Allen Edee*. Atlanta: Peachtree Publishers, 1985.

Mitchell, Margaret, and Allen Patrick. *Margaret Mitchell: Reporter*. Athens, Georgia: Hill Street Press, 2000.

Mitchell, Margaret, and Debra Freer. *Lost Laysen*. New York: Scribner's, 1996.

Mitchell, Margaret, and Jane Eskridge, editor. *Before Scarlett: Girlhood Writings of Margaret Mitchell*. Athens, Georgia: Hill Street Press, 2000.

Mitchell, Margaret, and Julian Granberry. *Letters from Margaret: Letters from Margaret Mitchell, Author of* Gone with the Wind *to Edwin and Mabel Granberry, 1936–1947.* Bloomington, Indiana: 1st Books Library, 2001.

Mitchell, Margaret, Rudy Behlmer, and Stacey Behlmer. *David O. Selznick's Production of Margaret Mitchell's* Gone with the Wind. Atlanta, Georgia: Turner Entertainment, 2009.

"Mitchell, Maybelle Isabelle Stephens: Find-a-Grave." http://www.findagrave.com/cgi-bin/fg.cgi?page=gr&GSln=Mitchell&GSfn=+&GSmn=isabel&GSbyrel=all&GSdy=1919&GSdyrel=in&GSst=12&GScntry=4&GSob=n&GRid=9562358&df=all&.

"Mitchell, Russell Crawford: Find-a-Grave." http://www.findagrave.com/cgi-bin/fg.cgi?page=gsr&GSfn=russell&GSmn=crawford&GSln=mitchell&GSbyrel=all&GSby=&GSdyrel=all&GSdy=&GScntry=0&GSst=0&GSgrid=&df=all&GSob=n.

"Mitchell, Russell Stephens: Find-a-Grave." http://www.findagrave.com/cgi-bin/fg.cgi?page=gr&GRid=38986567.

"Morehouse College Receives $1.5 Million from Nephew of Late *Gone with the Wind* Author Margaret Mitchell." *Jet*, April 22, 2002.

"Munson, Oma." http://www.findagrave.com/cgi-bin/fg.cgi?page=gr&GRid=4749.

"Myrick, Susan." http://www.findagrave.com/cgi-bin/fg.cgi?page=gr&GSln=myrick&GSfn=susan&GSbyrel=all&GSdy=1978&GSdyrel=in&GSob=n&GRid=7968343&df=all&.

"The Nation: Where Atlanta's 'Big Mules' Relax." http://www.time.com/time/magaine/article/0,9171,712335,00.html#ixzz1NY49WFhm.

Natoli, Jane Louise. *Growing Up with Scarlett.* New Britain: Central Connecticut State University, 2008.

Neal, Willard. *Georgia's Stone Mountain.* 46-page booklet, n.d., n.p.

"New Deal Programs: Selected Library of Congress Resources." http://www.loc.gov/rr/program/bib/newdeal/fwp.html.

"1920s Film History: Foundations of the Prolific Film Industry." *Free Movie Encyclopedia.* http://numberonestars.com/freemovieencyclopedia/1920sfilmhistory.htm.

"1925 Stone Mountain Commemorative Half Dollars." http://www.raregold.com/r-stone.htm.

"The 19th Academy Awards (1947) Nominees and Winners." http://www.oscars.org/awards/academyawards/legacy/ceremony/19th-winners.html.

"Non Non Sum Qualis Eram Bonae Sub Regno Cynarae." http://poetry.elcore.net/CatholicPoets/Dowson/Dowson16.html.

"Obituary of Mary Isabel Mitchell," *Atlanta Constitution*, January 26, 1919, page 5. http://www.findagrave.com/cgi-bin/fg.cgi?page=gr&GSln=Mitchell&GSfn=+&GSmn=isabel&GSbyrel=all&GSdy=1919&GSdyrel=in&GSst=12&GScntry=4&GSob=n&GRid=9562358&df=all&.

O'Briant, Don, and Kay O'Briant. *Looking for Tara: The* Gone with the Wind *Guide to Margaret Mitchell's Atlanta.* Atlanta, Georgia: Longstreet Press, 1994.

O'Connell, David. *The Irish Roots of Margaret Mitchell's* Gone with the Wind. Decatur, Georgia: Claves and Petry, 1996.

"Oscar Awards: Irving Thalberg Memorial Award." http://www.oscar-awards.deepthi.com/irving-h-thalberg-award.html.

Ossman, Laurie, and Steven Brooke. *Great Houses of the South.* New York: Rizzoli, 2010.

"Ozzie Nelson." http://www.parabrisas.com/d_nelsono.php.

Patton, Randall L. "Eurith D. Rivers." http://www.georgiaencyclopedia.org/nge/Article.jsp?id=h-1390.

Peachtree, Polly. Social Section of *Atlanta Journal*, March 13, 1921, as cited by Farr, Finis, in *Margaret Mitchell of Atlanta: The Author of* Gone with the Wind. New York: William Morrow, 1965, pages 53–54.

Penguin Readers Factsheet. "The Yearling." Written by Yvonne Harmer and Louise James, published by Pearson Education. http://plrcatalogue.pearson.com/Samples/PRFS_0582344395.pdf.

"Perkerson, Angus Millard, Jr." http://www.findagrave.com/cgi-bin/fg.cgi?page=gr&GSln=perkerson&GSfn=angus&GSbyrel=all&GSdyrel=all&GSob=n&GRid=53369446&df=all&.

"Perkerson, Medora Field." http://www.findagrave.com/cgi-bin/fg.cgi?page=gr&GSln=perkerson&GSfn=medora&GSbyrel=all&GSdyrel=all&GSob=n&GRid=53369471&df=all&.

Petreti, Allan. *Warman's Coca-Cola Field Guide.* Iola, Wisconsin: KP Books, 2005.

Pierpont, Claudia Roth. *Passionate Minds: Women Rewriting the World.* New York: Knopf, 2000.

"Plagiarism." http://dictionary.reference.com/browse/plagiarism.

"Plane, Caroline Helen Jemison." http://www.findagrave.com/cgi-bin/fg.cgi?page=gr&GSln=plane&GSmn=helen&GSbyrel=all&GSdyrel=all&GSob=n&GRid=8276392&df=all&.

Pratt, William. *Scarlett Fever: The Ultimate Pictorial Treasury of* Gone with the Wind: *Featuring the Collection of Herb Bridges.* New York: Macmillan, 1977.

Project for Public Spaces. *Atlanta: Margaret Mitchell Square; Central City Park.* New York: The Project, 1980.

"Public Art around the World: Henry W. Grady Monument." http://www.publicartaroundtheworld.com/Henry_W_Grady_Monument.html.

"Pulitzer Prize." *Encyclopædia Britannica Online Library Edition.* Encyclopædia Britannica, 2011. Web. 30 Sept. 2011. http://0-www.library.eb.com.marie.converse.edu/eb/article-298603.

Pyron, Darden-Asbury. *Recasting* Gone with the Wind *in American Culture.* Miami: University Press of Florida, 1983.

Pyron, Darden-Asbury. *Southern Daughter: The Life of Margaret Mitchell.* New York: Oxford University Press, 1991.

Rains, Sally Tippett, and Margaret Mitchell. *The Making of a Masterpiece: The True Story of Margaret Mitchell's Classic Novel* Gone with the Wind. Beverly Hills, California: Global Books, 2009.

Randall, Alice. *The Wind Done Gone.* Boston: Houghton Mifflin, 2001.

"Remembering Margaret Mitchell." http://atlantahis

torycenter.tumblr.com/post/8994720823/remember
ing-margaret-mitchell.

"Remembering Margaret Mitchell, Author of *Gone with
the Wind.*" http://www.worldcat.org/search?q=ti%3
Aremembering+margaret+mitchell+au%3Alove&qt
=advanced&dblist=638 (by Lucille Thompson Love
and others)."Richard Barksdale Harwell." *Contemporary Authors Online.* Detroit: Gale, 2002. *Gale Biography in Context.* Web. 22 Aug. 2011. http://0-
ic.galegroup.com.marie.converse.edu/ic/bic1/Refere
nceDetailsPage/ReferenceDetailsWindow?display-
GroupName=Reference&disableHighlighting=false
&prodId=BIC1&action=e&windowstate=normal&ca
tId=&documentId=GALE%7CH1000043173&mode
=view&userGroupName=mickel_lcc&jsid=b0888b8
bc4ca529b7e61f76c29b4da69, Gale Document Num-
ber: GALE |H1000043173.

Richardson, Nigel. "Civil War and Civil Rights." *The
Telegraph,* March 27, 2008. http://www.telegraph.co.
uk/travel/destinations/northamerica/usa/943274/Ma
rtin-Luther-King-and-Gone-With-the-Wind-Civil-
war-and-civil-rights.html.

Ripley, Alexandra, and Margaret Mitchell. *Scarlett: The
Sequel to Margaret Mitchell's* Gone with the Wind.
New York: Warner Books, 1991.

"Road to Tara Museum." http://travel.yahoo.com/p-tra
velguide-2822624-road_to_tara_museum_atlanta-i.

"Robert E. Lee." http://xroads.virginia.edu/~ug97/mon
ument/leebio.html.

Rosenburg, R.B. *Living Monuments: Confederate Soldiers' Homes in the New South.* Chapel Hill: University of North Carolina Press, 1995.

Ruppersburg, Harold M. *Georgia Voices.* Athens: University of Georgia, 1992.

"Samuel Hoyt Venable." http://www.findagrave.com/
cgi-bin/fg.cgi?page=gr&GSln=venable&GSfn=sam
uel&GSmn=hoyt&GSbyrel=all&GSdyrel=all&GSob
=n&GRid=31351280&df=all&.

"Samuel Hoyt Venable." http://xroads.virginia.edu/~
ug97/stone/venable.html.

Sandburg, Carl. "We Don't Cotton to Boll Weevil
'Round Here Anymore." http://www.ars.usda.gov/
is/AR/archive/feb03/boll0203.htm.

Schefski, Harold Klassel. *Margaret Mitchell:* Gone with
the Wind *and* War and Peace. Natchitoches: Southern
Studies Institute, 1980.

Schumach, Murray. "Hollywood Gives Tara to Atlanta."
*New York Times,* May 25, 1959, p. 33.

"Screen Online: Howard, Leslie (1893–1943)." http://
www.screenonline.org.uk/people/id/476673/.

Selznick, David O. *Memo from David O. Selznick.* New
York: Viking, 1974.

"Shannen Doherty Biography." http://www.starpulse.
com/Actresses/Doherty,_Shannen/Biography/.

Shavin, Norman, and Martin Shatar. *The Million Dollar
Legends: Margaret Mitchell and* Gone with the Wind.
Atlanta: Capricorn, 1974.

Shaw, Francis. Gone with the Wind: *The Book and the
Film: A Commentary.* Dublin: IrishMessenger, 1942.

Sheehy, Helen, Leslie Stainton, and William Inge. *On
Writers and Writing.* East Hartford, Connecticut:
Tide-Mark, 1991.

"A Short History of Atlanta." http://www.city-direc-
tory.com/Overview/history/history6.htm.

Skelton, Kathryn. "2,000 Pages and 40 Years Later."
Book completed in http://www.jayshoar.com/Re-
cent_Articles.php.

"Skidmore, Owings, and Merrill." http://en.wikipedia.
org/wiki/Skidmore,_Owings_and_Merrill.

Smith, S.A., IV. "Sophia Smith." http://www.finda
grave.com/cgi-bin/fg.cgi?page=gr&GSln=smith&
GSfn=sophia+&GSbyrel=all&GSdy=1870&GS
dyrel=in&GSob=n&GRid=7082051&df=all&.

Snyder, Karen K. "Searching for Margaret Mitchell."
http://www.frommers.com/destinations/atlanta/000
2020255.html.

"Songwriters Hall of Fame: Billy Rose." http://www.
songwritershalloffame.org/exhibits/C307.

"Southern Draw: Atlanta's Sweet-Talkin' Suburbs."
http://www.greatestescapes.com/index.php?article
id=3.

"*SparkNotes:* Ashley Wilkes." http://www.sparknotes.
com/film/gonewiththewind/characters.html.

"*SparkNotes:* Melanie Hamilton Wilkes." http://www.
sparknotes.com/film/gonewiththewind/characters.
html.

Stanfill, Laura. "Kristin Bailey Murphy Offers Insights
about Famous American Authors in a Book about
Her Great-aunt's Career." http://laurastanfill.word
press.com/2011/07/27/interview-kristin-bailey-mur
phy-2/.

"Stately Oaks Plantation." http://www.historicaljones-
boro.org/aboutus.htm.

"Stephens, Annie Fitzgerald: Find-a-Grave." http://
www.findagrave.com/cgi-bin/fg.cgi?page=gr&GRid
=15840287.

"Stephens, John: Find-a-Grave." http://www.finda-
grave.com/cgi-bin/fg.cgi?page=gr&GRid=53221436.

"Stone Mountain." Online at http://www.stonemoun
tainpark.com/outdoors-recreation/outdoor-detail.
aspx?AttractionID=1277.

Stout, Dorian. "*Gone with the Wind* Suit Dismissed."
*Atlanta Constitution,* July 31, 1937.

Student Body of Washington Seminary. *Facts and Fancies: 50th Anniversary of Washington Seminary* (1928).
http://www.biblio.com/books/261453188.html.

"Sunshine Skies. Special Section: The History of the
Hartsfield-Jackson Airport." http://www.sunshine
skies.net/atlanta010.html.

Sutherland, Sidney. "The Mystery of the Pencil Factory." http://gaslight.mtroyal.ca/penclfct.htm.

Taylor, Helen. *Scarlett's Women:* Gone with the Wind
*and Its Female Fans.* New Brunswick, New Jersey:
Rutgers University Press, 1989.

Taylor, Mary Rose. "Foreword," "Preface," and "Intro-
duction" in *Before Scarlett: Childhood Writings of
Margaret Mitchell,* edited by Jane Eskridge. Athens,
Georgia: Hill Street Press, 2000.

Taylor, Tess. "*Rhett Butler's People* Review," December
7, 2007. Barnesandnoblereview.com.

Thomas, Bob. *The Story of* Gone with the Wind. New
York: National Publishers, 1967.

"Thomas Dixon." http://freemasonry.bcy.ca/anti-ma-
sonry/discredited.html.

"Thomas Gregory Mitchell." *Dictionary of American
Biography.* New York: Scribner's, 1981. *Gale Biography in Context.* Web. 29 Sep. 2011. Document URL,
http://0-ic.galegroup.com.marie.converse.edu/ic/

bic1/ReferenceDetailsPage/ReferenceDetailsWindow ?displayGroupName=Reference&disableHighlighting =false&prodId=BIC1&action=e&windowstate=nor mal&catId=&documentId=GALE%7CBT231000733 9&mode=view&userGroupName=mickel_lcc&jsid= 9421b3f42989bb182c44d3e3ca17990c, Gale Document Number: GALE|BT2310007339.

Thomas, Jane. "Margaret Mitchell: 1900–1949," *New Georgia Encyclopedia*. http://www.georgiaencyclope dia.org/nge/ArticlePrintable.jsp?id=h-2566.

"Tickets to Go: The Tabernacle." http://www.ticketsto go.com/the_tabernacle_tickets.html.

Time-Life Editors. *This Fabulous Century: 1930–1940*. New York: Time-Life Books, 1969.

Tindall, George Brown. *The Emergence of the New South, 1913–1945*. N.p. Louisiana State University Press and the Littlefield Fund for Southern History of the University of Texas, 1967.

Trust Company of Georgia. *A Tribute to Margaret Mitchell*. Atlanta: Trust Company of Georgia, 1950.

Tucker, Elizabeth, and Fred A. Parrish. *On the Set of* Gone with the Wind: *Photographs by Fred A. Parris; Homes of Margaret Mitchell*. Compiled by Elizabeth Tucker.

Turner, Adrian. *A Celebration of* Gone with the Wind: *Margaret Mitchell's Story of the Old South*. Athens: Hill Street Press, 2001.

"The 25 Most Controversial Movies of All Time." *Entertainment Weekly*. Issue 882, June 16, 2006, pages 35–39.

*2004 Scott Specialized Catalogue of United States Stamps and Covers*. 82nd edition.

"The USGenWeb Project: Alexander Doyle." http:// www.rootsweb.ancestry.com/~ohjeffer/doylebioin dex/adoyle.html.

"USS *Atlanta* (CL-104)." http://www.hullnumber.com/ CL-104.

Vejnoska, Jill. "Eugene Mitchell, 76, Nephew of *Gone with the Wind* Author." *Atlanta Journal-Constitution* (August 10, 2007). http://www.gwtwmemories.com/ forums/bbdaily/messages/715.html.

Vezjak, Anita, Victor Kennedy, and Michelle Gadpaille. *In Search of Identity: Transition of Traditional Southern Women's Roles in 19th Century America as Seen in Margaret Mitchell's* Gone with the Wind *and Charles Frazier's* Cold Mountain. Maribor: A. Vezjak, 2005.

"Victor Fleming Biography." http://www.biography. com/articles/Victor-Fleming-9297044.

"Vivien Leigh." http://www.biography.com/articles/ Vivien-Leigh-9378241?part=1.

"Waldorf=Astoria." http://www.aviewoncities.com/ nyc/waldorfastoria.htm.

Walker, Alexander. *Vivien: The Life of Vivien Leigh*. New York: Weidenfeld and Nicholson, 1987.

Walker, Marianne. *Margaret Mitchell and John Marsh: The Love Story Behind* Gone with the Wind. Atlanta: Peachtree Publishers, 1993.

"Walter A. Sims." http://www.findagrave.com/cgi-bin/ fg.cgi?page=gr&GSln=sims&GSfn=walter&GSmn=a &GSbyrel=all&GSdyrel=all&GSob=n&GRid=84787 79&df=all&.

"Walter Hancock." http://xroads.virginia.edu/~ug97/ stone/hancock.html.

"Water Resources of Georgia." http://ga.water.usgs. gov/publications/ofr00-380.pdf.

Wecter, Dixon. *The Age of the Great Depression: 1929– 1941*. New York: Macmillan, 1948.

"Welcome to Stately Oaks Plantation." http://www.his toricaljonesboro.org/.

"Westminster Schools: History." http://www.westmin ster.net/about_us/history/index.aspx.

Wexler, Bruce. *The Authentic South of* Gone with the Wind: *The Illustrated Guide to the Grandeur of a Lost Era*. Philadelphia: Courage, 2007.

"Who's Who in Hospitality." *Atlanta Business Chronicle*, July 14, 2003. http://www.bizjournals.com/at lanta/stories/2003/07/14/focus7.html?page=all.

"Wilbur Kurtz." http://generalthomas.com/kurtz.htm.

Wiley, John, Jr. "70 Years Later, 'Scarlett Fever' Still Raging around the World." http://www.go-star.com/ antiquing/gone_with_the_wind.htm.

Wiley, John, Jr. *The Scarlett Letter: A Quarterly Newsletter*. http://www.thescarlettletter.com/.

"William Berry Hartsfield." *Dictionary of American Biography*. New York: Scribner's, 1994.

"William Berry Hartsfield." *Gale Biography in Context*. Web. 11 August 2011. Document URL, http://0-ic.gale group.com.marie.converse.edu/ic/bic1/ReferenceDe tailsPage/ ReferenceDetailsWindow?displayGroup Name=Reference&disableHighlighting=false&pro dId=BIC1&action=e&windowstate=normal&catId= &documentId=GALE%7CBT2310011738&mode=view &userGroupName=mickel_lcc&jsid=3c09b99d016aa 0de39266dd955bfd749, Gale Document Number: GALE|BT2310011738.

"(William) Clark Gable." *Dictionary of American Biography*. New York: Scribner's, 1980. *Gale Biography in Context*. Web. 18 September 2011. Document URL, http://0-ic.galegroup.com.marie.converse.edu/ic/ bic1/ReferenceDetailsPage/ReferenceDetailsWindow ?displayGroupName=Reference&disableHighlight ing=false&prodId=BIC1&action=e&windowstate=n ormal&catId=&documentId=GALE%7CBT23100131 23&mode=view&userGroupName=mickel_lcc&jsid =5d78442e3b62351978a334cbedf92897, Gale Document Number: GALE|BT2310013123.

Winterthur Library. "The Gustav Berger Papers." http: //findingaid.winterthur.org/html/HTML_Finding_ Aids/COL0723.htm.

Womack, Ted. "World War I in Georgia." http://www. georgiaencyclopedia.org/nge/Article.jsp?id=h-3223.

Woodhaven Historic Photographs. Chandler, Arizona 85248.

"World War I Statistics" from Georgia Department of Veteran Services and U.S. Department of Veteran Affairs, as cited by Davis, *Georgia During the Great Depression*, page 5.

Worthy, Larry, editor-in-chief. "Atlanta Premiere of *Gone with the Wind*," *About North Georgia*, Winter 2002–2003. http://ngeorgia.com/ang/Atlanta_Pre miere_of_Gone_With_The_Wind.

"WW II Archives: Preserving Their Sacrifice." http:// wwiiarchives.net/servlet/shipClass/54/0.

Yarnall, Paul R. "NavSource Online: Cruiser Photo Archive: USS *Atlanta* (CL 51)." http://www.nav source.org/archives/04/051/04051.htm.

Zainaldin, Jamil S., Georgia Humanities Council. "Coca-Cola Philanthropy." http://www.georgiaencyclope dia.org/nge/Article.jsp?id=h-1952&hl=y.

Zegarac, Nick. "Real *Gone with the Wind*: Part I." February 25, 2006. http://thehollywoodart.blogspot.com/2006_02_01_archive.html.

Zerfas, Bridgette. "Barrett, Kate Harwood Waller." http://learningtogive.org/papers/paper216.html.

"Zoo Atlanta." http://www.zooatlanta.org/home/history/the_early_days.

## Related Websites

http://roadsidegeorgia.com/site/cyclorama.html
http://www.bcaatlanta.com/index.php?pid=81
http://www.enotes.com/gone-Wind/13709/print
http://www.georgiaencyclopedia.org/nge/Article.jsp?id+h-815
http://www.ipl.org.ar/ref/QUE/FARQ/bestsellerFARQ.html
http://www.jsonline.com/onwisconsin/arts/mar03/122788.asp

## Theses and Dissertations

Alexander, Grayce. "Mitchell's Scarlett O'Hara and Thackeray's Rebecca Sharp Compared," 1965.

Anderson, Jeffrey Scott. "*Gone with the Wind* as Guest and Host: A Study in Literary Symbiosis," 2004.

Barber, Bobbie Lou. "*Gone with the Wind*: Scarlett O'Hara the New Southern Woman," 2007.

Bearden, Ethel Mae. "Margaret Mitchell and Her Place in Atlanta," 1957.

Born, Stephen M. "Carnegie Plaza: Margaret Mitchell Square on Peachtree, Atlanta, Georgia," 1984.

Broaddus, Virginia Blanton. "Sowing Barren Ground: Constructions of Motherhood, the Body, and Subjectivity in American Women's Writing, 1928–1948," 2002.

Brock, Karen L. "*Gone with the Wind*: A Critical Introduction," 1986.

Cheney, Merlin Gene. "*Vanity Fair* and *Gone with the Wind*: A Critical Comparison." 1966.

Corsetti, Michael. "'You Are Very Irish, You Know': How Scarlett O'Hara's Irish Identity Dismantles Her Status as Southern Belle," 2008. http://www.docstoc.com/docs/46811159/You-are-very-Irish-you-know-How-Scarlett-OHaras-Irish-identity-dismantles-her-status-as-Southern-belle.

Demarco, Kathleen Ann. "Medora Field Perkerson: A Study of Her Literary Career and Especially of Her Friendship with Margaret Mitchell," 2002. Thesis, University of Georgia.

Dickey, Jennifer W. "'A Tough Little Patch of History': Atlanta's Marketplace for *Gone with the Wind* Memory," 2007.

Dorminey, Marjorie Loy. "The Theme of Southern Agrarianism in Margaret Mitchell's *Gone with the Wind*: A Thesis Presented to the Faculty of the Graduate School, Tennessee Technological University," 1980.

Hitchcock, C. Staley. "Tomorrow Is Another Day: *Gone with the Wind* and the American Mind," 1970.

Hollander-Blumhoff, Rebecca. "Visions of 'Another Day': Women's Roles of the 1920s in Margaret Mitchell's *Gone with the Wind*." Thesis, 1992.

Homer, Patricia, and Howard Keeley. "Kinship: Margaret Mitchell's *Gone with the Wind* and the Irish Big House Genre." Thesis. Statesboro: Georgia Southern University, 2010.

Howe, Darcy E. "Scarlett and Sethe: Ruled by Race, Ruled by Gender: An Examination of the 'Unredeemable Woman' in Twentieth-century American Literature," 1994.

Latino, Bradley A. "'To Isolate Her from the Loud World': Rhett Butler, the Compsons, and the Unprotected Southern Woman," 2005.

Lê, Thi Thanh. "*Gone with the Wind* and the Vietnamese Mind," 2003.

Lee, Susan M. "Scarlett as a Character Shaped by Her Community of Women in Margaret Mitchell's *Gone with the Wind*," 1991.

Maday, Melissa H. "Repositioning Tara: A Critical Assessment of *Gone with the Wind* by Margaret Mitchell," 2001.

Minton, Alice. "Long Row to Hoe: Domesticity and the Community of Women in Margaret Mitchell's *Gone with the Wind*, Margaret Walker's *Jubilee*, and Kaye Gibbons's *On the Occasion of My Last Afternoon*." Thesis, 2002.

Mulligan, Erin M. "Chivalry, Carnival, and 'Knights and Their Ladies Fair': Locating the Medieval in Margaret Mitchell's *Gone with the Wind*," 2007.

Peery, Angela Bushnell. "Explorations of Individualism in the Works of Five Southern Women Writers," 1992.

Pendleton, Eva M. "Layers of Meaning: The Multitexual *Gone with the Wind*," 1991.

Pollard, William Carter. "*Gone with the Wind*: Story of a Best Seller." Thesis. Rochester, New York: University of Rochester, 1954.

Propst, Susan Earle. "Stereotypes and Tradition in *Gone with the Wind*," 1973.

Quinn, Laura Ann. "Home to Tara." Thesis, 1992.

Shen, Yan. "A Comparative Study of *Gone with the Wind* and *Jubilee*," 1990.

Smith, Teresa L. "The Search for Scarlett O'Hara: Newspaper Coverage of *Gone with the Wind*," 2000.

Tarell, Whitnery M. "Kinship: Margaret Mitchell's *Gone with the Wind* and the Irish Big House Genre." Honors thesis. Loudonville, New York: Siena College, 2007. http://www.worldcat.org/title/kinship-margaret-mitchells-gone-with-the-wind-and-the-irish-big-housegenre/oclc/666478833?title=&detail=&page=frame&url=http%3A%2F%2Fwww.georgiasouthern.edu%2Fetd%2Farchive%2Fspring2010%2Fpatricia_n_homer%2Fhomer_patricia_n_201001_ma.pdf%26checksum%3D6bfbea2d28be9dcc0fde2ead46d1e965&linktype=digital.

Walker, Andrea Lynne. "The Newspaper Woman Behind the Novelist: An Exploration of the Relationship between Margaret Mitchell's Journalism and *Gone with the Wind*." Master's thesis. University of Georgia, 1988.

Wesley, Sarah Devon. "Tomorrow Is Another Day: Scarlett O'Hara as the Symbolic Rise of the New South in Margaret Mitchell's *Gone with the Wind*." 2002.

# Index